Advances in African Economic, Social and Political Development

Series Editors
Diery Seck, CREPOL – Center for Research on Political Economy, Dakar, Senegal

Juliet U. Elu, Morehouse College, Atlanta, GA, USA

Yaw Nyarko, New York University, New York, NY, USA

Africa is emerging as a rapidly growing region, still facing major challenges, but with a potential for significant progress – a transformation that necessitates vigorous efforts in research and policy thinking. This book series focuses on three intricately related key aspects of modern-day Africa: economic, social and political development. Making use of recent theoretical and empirical advances, the series aims to provide fresh answers to Africa's development challenges. All the socio-political dimensions of today's Africa are incorporated as they unfold and new policy options are presented. The series aims to provide a broad and interactive forum of science at work for policymaking and to bring together African and international researchers and experts. The series welcomes monographs and contributed volumes for an academic and professional audience, as well as tightly edited conference proceedings. Relevant topics include, but are not limited to, economic policy and trade, regional integration, labor market policies, demographic development, social issues, political economy and political systems, and environmental and energy issues.

All titles in the series are peer-reviewed. The book series is indexed in SCOPUS.

Kempe Ronald Hope, Sr.

Corruption, Sustainable Development and Security Challenges in Africa

Prospects and Policy Implications for Peace and Stability

Kempe Ronald Hope, Sr. ⓘ
Development Practice International
Oakville, ON, Canada

ISSN 2198-7262   ISSN 2198-7270   (electronic)
Advances in African Economic, Social and Political Development
ISBN 978-3-031-32228-0   ISBN 978-3-031-32229-7   (eBook)
https://doi.org/10.1007/978-3-031-32229-7

© The Editor(s) (if applicable) and The Author(s), under exclusive license to Springer Nature Switzerland AG 2023

This work is subject to copyright. All rights are solely and exclusively licensed by the Publisher, whether the whole or part of the material is concerned, specifically the rights of translation, reprinting, reuse of illustrations, recitation, broadcasting, reproduction on microfilms or in any other physical way, and transmission or information storage and retrieval, electronic adaptation, computer software, or by similar or dissimilar methodology now known or hereafter developed.

The use of general descriptive names, registered names, trademarks, service marks, etc. in this publication does not imply, even in the absence of a specific statement, that such names are exempt from the relevant protective laws and regulations and therefore free for general use.

The publisher, the authors, and the editors are safe to assume that the advice and information in this book are believed to be true and accurate at the date of publication. Neither the publisher nor the authors or the editors give a warranty, expressed or implied, with respect to the material contained herein or for any errors or omissions that may have been made. The publisher remains neutral with regard to jurisdictional claims in published maps and institutional affiliations.

This Springer imprint is published by the registered company Springer Nature Switzerland AG
The registered company address is: Gewerbestrasse 11, 6330 Cham, Switzerland

Preface

This book brings together a logically presented and sequenced set of essays on my current thinking and analyses about Africa's development performance and dynamics arising from the interface between corruption and sustainable development on the one hand, the challenges that poses for security on the continent on the other, and the resultant prospects and policy implications for peace and stability. My overall thinking on Africa's development performance and dynamics has been considerably influenced by my tours of duty in several countries, and my mission visits to many others, across the continent. That field experience further illuminated for me the significant difference between on the ground actual practices and performance on the one hand, and academic thinking and theorizing on the other.

As the chapters show, Africa is not only the poorest region in the world but one of the most corrupt regions also as measured by various indices. Despite having abundant resources and even periodic episodes of improvements in governance performance, large-scale plunder, kleptocratic behavior, and everyday bribery remain the norm on most of the continent. In such an environment, sustainable development will remain elusive, and that has indeed been the case, with concomitant impacts on peace, security, and stability.

The past few years have been a period of social and economic transformation in Africa and beyond. On the continent, steady democratic gains began to erode and promising economic growth and development took a downturn as the COVID-19 disease wreaked havoc across the globe and coups returned on the continent. Interestingly enough, while many of the Western nations experienced much death and despair, Africa's death toll from this COVID disease was considerably lower and much less socially and psychologically devastating. Most African countries have been able to escape the worst health impacts of the COVID-19 pandemic. Nonetheless, due to Africa's dependence on trade with partners outside of the region (particularly the European Union, China, United States, India), there has been much disruption to the movement and receipt of goods as well as the flow of people across borders. Primary, secondary, and positive externality businesses and economic interests that depended on tourists, for example, have been hard hit and some have had to permanently shutter their doors and others have announced plans to do so in the near future. This state of affairs further supports the need for greater diversification of African economies and their trade markets (especially for exports) as a significant means of attempts to counteract economic shocks and stabilize development performance.

However, all is not doom and gloom, nor should it be, and this book is certainly not about that although it may read like that in parts as the facts and analyses are being presented. Apart from coups becoming a sport in West Africa, and if kleptomania can be somehow controlled, it may be a good bet that we will see some semblance of economic and governance progress over the long-term post-COVID era and that will have to be spearheaded by African leaders themselves. In fact, despite estimating that there will be an economic downturn in Africa due to both some lingering impacts of COVID and the Russia invasion of Ukraine that has triggered a global economic shock, including rising inflation, the Bretton Woods institutions and the African Development Bank have also forecasted that economic activity on the continent should expand by 3–4% during the immediate medium to longer-term. Anyway, the real and much more important question is what would such an expansion in economic activity look like in per capita terms.

Several colleagues (they know who they are) were consulted for their views and comments on the theme and contents of this book and I am most grateful to them for taking time out of their busy schedules to engage with me in that regard. Their frank advice, not only on the contents of the chapters, but also on their sequencing in the book, has considerably improved the presentation of the ideas and analyses contained in the book's pages.

Some of the chapters in this book borrow heavily from some of my work previously published in a different form elsewhere. They have been significantly revamped, restructured, reworked, reshaped, revised, updated, and re-titled in some cases for this book and are being drawn upon in the context of author retained rights and license. The customary acknowledgements are as follows: chapter 3 in *Journal of Financial Crime* 27(1), 2020 (Emerald Publishing); chapter 5 in *African Security* 11(1), 2018 (Routledge/Taylor and Francis Group); chapter 6 in *Global Change, Peace and Security* 32(1), 2020 (Routledge/Taylor and Francis Group); chapter 7 in *Journal of Money Laundering Control* 25(2), 2022 (Emerald Publishing); chapter 8 in *Journal of Applied Security Research* 16(4), 2021 (Routledge/Taylor and Francis Group).

Oakville, ON, Canada   Kempe Ronald Hope, Sr.

Contents

1 **Introduction**... 1
   1.1 Focus of the Book 1
   1.2 Definition of Terms 4
         1.2.1   Corruption 4
         1.2.2   Sustainable Development............................ 5
         1.2.3   Security 5
   1.3 Organization of the Book................................... 6
   References.. 9

2 **Africa at the Crossroads: Moonwalking in Slow Motion** 11
   2.1 Introduction 11
   2.2 Africa at the Crossroads..................................... 13
   2.3 Moonwalking in Slow Motion............................... 19
   2.4 Concluding Reflections 26
   References.. 28

3 **Channels of Corruption in Africa: An Analytical Review and Assessment of Trends in Economic and Financial Crimes** 35
   3.1 Introduction 35
   3.2 Corruption Channels in Africa: Trends and Extent of Economic and Financial Crimes... 37
         3.2.1   Embezzlement and Theft 37
         3.2.2   Bribes and Kickbacks 39
         3.2.3   Money Laundering and Other Illicit Financial Flows 43
         3.2.4   State Capture 45
   3.3 Summary Analysis.. 47
   3.4 Conclusion 49
   References.. 51

4	**Revisiting the Corruption and Sustainable Development Nexus in Africa**		57
	4.1	Introduction	57
	4.2	Corruption and Sustainable Development: Literature Review and Analysis	58
	4.3	The Corruption and Sustainable Development Nexus in Africa	60
		4.3.1 The Corruption Indicators	61
		4.3.2 The Development Indicators	62
		4.3.3 The Contemporary Evidence	64
	4.4	Policy Implications and Conclusion	71
		4.4.1 Leadership and Anti-Corruption Institutions	71
		4.4.2 Enhancing Asset Recovery	73
		4.4.3 Emphasizing E-Government Implementation	74
	References		76
5	**Police Corruption and Its Security Challenges in Africa: Kenya As a Country Case Study**		85
	5.1	Introduction	85
	5.2	What Is Police Corruption?	86
	5.3	The Nature and Extent of Police Corruption in Kenya and Across Africa	87
		5.3.1 Perceptions of Police Corruption	88
		5.3.2 The Bribery Menace	91
		5.3.3 Criminality and Other Misconduct Abuses of Power	94
		5.3.4 Recruitment for Sale	100
		5.3.5 The Retention Vetting Realities	103
		5.3.6 Super Cops: The Dirty Harry Syndrome	106
	5.4	The Security Challenges of Police Corruption in Kenya and Across Africa	107
		5.4.1 Contributor to Crime	107
		5.4.2 Safe Haven for Terrorists and Radicalization Influences	108
		5.4.3 Tourism Impact	114
	5.5	Concluding Comments	115
		5.5.1 Further Readings and Information on Police Corruption and Security Challenges in Africa	118
	References		118
6	**Peace, Justice, and Inclusive Institutions: Overcoming Challenges to the Implementation of Sustainable Development Goal 16 in Africa and Beyond**		131
	6.1	Introduction	131
	6.2	SDG 16: Peace, Justice, and Inclusive Institutions	132
		6.2.1 Why SDG 16 Matters to Sustainable Development and the Overall SDGs	133
	6.3	Progress on SDG 16 and Its Impact Relationship to Other SDGs	135
	6.4	Challenges to SDG 16 Progress and Implementation	145

		6.4.1	Inadequate Capacity	145
		6.4.2	Poor Data and Information	146
		6.4.3	Inadequate Delivery Systems	146
		6.4.4	Insufficient Financing	147
		6.4.5	Lack of Political Will and Leadership	148
	6.5	Overcoming the Challenges to SDG 16 Progress and Implementation		149
		6.5.1	Capacity Development	150
		6.5.2	Data and Information Sharing	151
		6.5.3	Improved Delivery Systems	152
		6.5.4	Meeting the Financing Requirements	153
		6.5.5	Enhancing Political Will and Good Leadership	154
	6.6	Concluding Comments		155
	References			156
7	**Reducing Corruption and Bribery in Africa As a Target of the Sustainable Development Goals: Applying Indicators for Assessing Performance**			**161**
	7.1	Introduction		161
	7.2	Assessing Corruption and Bribery Reduction in Africa As a Target of the SDGs		163
		7.2.1	Applying the Official Bribery/Corruption Indicators	163
		7.2.2	Proposed Other Indicators	165
	7.3	Concluding Remarks		172
	References			174
8	**Civilian Oversight for Democratic Policing and Its Challenges: Overcoming Obstacles for Improved Police Accountability and Better Security in Africa and Beyond**			**177**
	8.1	Introduction		177
	8.2	What Is Civilian Oversight for Democratic Policing?		179
		8.2.1	Extant Model Types of Civilian Oversight of the Police	181
		8.2.2	Benefits of Civilian Oversight of the Police: Accountability/Transparency/Independence	186
	8.3	Key Challenges to Effective Civilian Oversight of the Police		193
		8.3.1	Insufficient Political and Influential Leadership Support	193
		8.3.2	Lack of Disciplining Authority	193
		8.3.3	Inadequate Access to Documents and Information	194
		8.3.4	Limited Budgetary Resources	195
	8.4	Overcoming the Challenges to Civilian Oversight of the Police		196
		8.4.1	Nestled in an Appropriate and Transparent Legal Framework	196
		8.4.2	Sufficiently Funded	198
		8.4.3	Fully Supported by the Political Leadership and Other National Governance Structures	199

		8.4.4	Bestowed with the Necessary Investigative Powers to Coerce Police Cooperation	199
		8.4.5	Adequately Staffed with the Requisite Personnel and Expertise to Fulfill Their Mandate.....................	200
		8.4.6	Operations Conducted Based on a Sound Strategic Plan...	200
		8.4.7	Robust Outreach Exercises Embraced and Implemented...	201
	8.5	Improved Police Accountability and Better Security Through Civilian Oversight for Democratic Policing: Final Summary Thoughts		202
References..				207
Index				217

About the Author

Kempe Ronald Hope, Sr. is a Director at Development Practice International (DPI), Ontario, Canada. He was formerly a senior official with the United Nations and a Program Manager at the Agency for International Development (USAID) of the US Department of State. He has also been a Professor of Economics, Development Management, and/or African Studies at the University of North Carolina (Charlotte); the Atlanta University Center; the University of Botswana, where he was also the Founding Director of the Center of Specialization in Public Administration and Management (CESPAM); and a Fulbright Professor of Economics at the University of the West Indies (Jamaica campus). He has also advised several governments on anti-corruption and development policy and management reforms. The views he expresses here are private and do not necessarily represent the views of DPI or any other organization to which he is currently or was formerly affiliated. Dr. Hope is the author of more than 20 books and monographs on development policy and management and more than 150 articles and numerous chapters published in refereed journals and edited works, respectively. His most recent books are *Corruption and Governance in Africa: Swaziland [Eswatini], Kenya, Nigeria* (Palgrave Macmillan/Springer, 2017, https://doi.org/10.1007/978-3-319-50191-8); *Police Corruption and Police Reforms in Developing Societies* (CRC Press/Taylor and Francis, 2016, https://www.routledge.com/Police-Corruption-and-Police-Reforms-in-Developing-Societies/Sr/p/book/9780367598136); and *The Political Economy of Development in Kenya* (Bloomsbury Publishing, 2013, https://www.bloomsbury.com/us/political-economy-of-development-in-kenya-9781441191212/).

Abbreviations, Terms and Acronyms

AAAA	Addis Ababa Action Agenda
AAAJD	Afro-Asian Association for Justice Development
AACC	All Africa Conference of Churches
ACAs	Anti-Corruption Agencies
ACB	Anti-Corruption Bureau
ACBF	African Capacity Building Foundation
ACDEG	African Charter on Democracy, Elections and Governance
ACGC	Anti-Corruption and Governance Center
ACHPR	African Charter on Human and Peoples' Rights
ACSS	Africa Center for Strategic Studies
ACTA	Anti-Corruption, Transparency, and Accountability
ADB	Asian Development Bank
AfCFTA	African Continental Free Trade Area
AfDB	African Development Bank
AFMs	Anti-Fraud Measures
AFP	Agence France Presse
AGA	African Governance Architecture
AGR	Africa Governance Report
AML/CFT	Anti-Money Laundering and Countering the Financing of Terrorism
ANC	African National Congress
APCOF	African Policing Civilian Oversight Forum
APRM	African Peer Review Mechanism
APSA	African Peace and Security Architecture
ARDL	Autoregressive Distributed Lag
ARV	Antiretroviral
ASC	American Society of Criminology
ASCCC	Anti-State Capture and Corruption Commission
ASF	African Standby Force
ASIs	Ad-Hoc Security Initiatives
ATMs	Automatic Teller Machines

ATPU	Anti-Terrorism Police Unit
AU	African Union
AUC	African Union Commission
AUCPCC	African Union Convention on Preventing and Combating Corruption
AUDA	African Union Development Agency
CACBs	Commonwealth Anti-Corruption Benchmarks
CACOLE	Canadian Association for Civilian Oversight of Law Enforcement
CAPG	Canadian Association of Police Governance
CAPO	Complaints Against Police Office
CCC	Crime and Corruption Commission
CDD-Ghana	Ghana Center for Democratic Development
C/E	Corruption/Extortion
CEWS	Continental Early Warning System
CFAs	Child-Focused Agencies
CHRI	Commonwealth Human Rights Initiative
CIP	Centro de Integridade Pública
CIPE	Center for International Private Enterprise
CMI	Chr. Michelsen Institute
COB	Citizen Oversight Board
CoC	Control of Corruption
COVID-19	Coronavirus Disease 2019
CPI	Corruption Perceptions Index
CPRB	Civilian Police Review Board
CPRC	Community Police Review Commission
CRBPP	Community Review Board on Police Practices
CRCC	Civilian Review and Complaints Commission
CRF	Corruption Risk Forecast
CSOs	Civil Society Organizations
CTGAP	Cape Town Global Action Plan for Sustainable Development Data
Data 4Now	Data For Now
DCAF	Geneva Center for Security Sector Governance
DCI	Directorate of Criminal Investigations
DCP	Deputy Commissioner of Police
DFID	Department for International Development
DKNs	Diaspora Knowledge Networks
DOJ	Department of Justice
DPA	Department of Police Accountability
DPP	Director of Public Prosecutions
DRC	Democratic Republic of the Congo
DRM	Domestic Resource Mobilization
EABI	East African Bribery Index
EACC	Ethics and Anti-Corruption Commission

EC	European Commission
ECOWAS	Economic Community of West African States
EFCC	Economic and Financial Crimes Commission
EGDI	E-Government Development Index
EOSs	Executive Opinion Surveys
EPAC	European Partners Against Corruption
EPC	Edmonton Police Commission
ERCAS	European Research Center for Anti-Corruption and State-Building
ESAAMLG	Eastern and Southern Africa Anti-Money Laundering Group
EU	European Union
FATF	Financial Action Task Force
FCDO	Foreign, Commonwealth & Development Office
FCN	Financial Crime News
FDI	Foreign Direct Investment
FIC	Financial Intelligence Center
FJP	Fair and Just Prosecution
GANHRI	Global Alliance of National Human Rights Institutions
G7	Informal grouping of seven of the world's advanced economies: Canada, France, Germany, Italy, Japan, the United Kingdom, and the United States
G8	Group of Eight (formerly the G7 plus Russia)
GCB	Global Corruption Barometer
GDP	Gross Domestic Product
GFI	Global Financial Integrity
GIABA	Inter-Governmental Action Group against Money Laundering in West Africa
GI-TOC	Global Initiative Against Transnational Organized Crime
HCI	Human Capital Index
HICs	High-Income Countries
HLPFs	High Level Political Forums
HRW	Human Rights Watch
IACP	International Association of Chiefs of Police
IAEG-SDGs	Inter-Agency and Expert Group on SDGs
IBP	International Budget Partnership
ICC	Independent Complaints Commission
ICD	Independent Complaints Directorate
ICG	International Crisis Group
ICJ-Kenya	International Commission of Jurists (Kenyan Section)
ICPC	Independent Corrupt Practices and other Related Offences Commission
ICTJ	International Center for Transitional Justice
ICTs	Information and Communication Technologies
IDC-India	Institute for Development and Communication (India)
IDS-UON	Institute of Development Studies (University of Nairobi)

IEP	Institute for Economics and Peace
IFFs	Illicit Financial Flows
IIAG	Ibrahim Index of African Governance
IIDEA	International Institute for Democracy and Electoral Assistance
IIO	Independent Investigations Office
IMF	International Monetary Fund
IMLU	Independent Medico-Legal Unit
INDECOM	Independent Commission of Investigations
INTERPOL	International Criminal Police Organization
IOG	Inspectorate of Government
IOPC	Independent Office for Police Conduct
IPCA-Denmark	Independent Police Complaints Authority (Denmark)
IPCA-New Zealand	Independent Police Conduct Authority (New Zealand)
IPCC-for Ghana	Independent Police Complaints Council (for Ghana)
IPCC-Hong Kong	Independent Police Complaints Council (Hong-Kong)
IPI	Index of Public Integrity
IPID	Independent Police Investigative Directorate
IPOA	Independent Policing Oversight Authority
IPUSA	Independent Policing Union of South Africa
ISI	International Spillover Index
KEMSA	Kenya Medical Supplies Authority
KES	Kenya Shillings
KHRC	Kenya Human Rights Commission
KIIS	Kellogg Institute for International Studies
KNCHR	Kenya National Commission for Human Rights
LECC	Law Enforcement Conduct Commission
LERB	Law Enforcement Review Board
LMPS	Lesotho Mounted Police Service
MACB	Malawi Anti-Corruption Bureau
MENA	Middle East and North Africa
MIF	Mo Ibrahim Foundation
MPI	Multidimensional Poverty Index
MPS	Metro Police Services
MALAWI-PS	Malawi Police Service
NACIWA	National Anti-Corruption Institutions of West Africa
NACOLE	National Association for Civilian Oversight of Law Enforcement
NACS	National Anti-Corruption Strategy
NBS	National Bureau of Statistics
NDLEA	National Drug Law Enforcement Agency
NEPAD	New Partnership for Africa's Development
NGOs	Non-Governmental Organizations
NPS	National Police Service
NPSC	National Police Service Commission

NSC	National Security Council
NSOs	National Statistical Offices
NSW	New South Wales
OBG	Oxford Business Group
OBI	Open Budget Initiative
OBS	Open Budget Survey
OCC	Office of Citizen Complaints
ODA	Overseas Development Assistance
OECD	Organization for Economic Cooperation and Development
OIPA	Office of the Independent Police Auditor
OIPRD	Office of the Independent Police Review Director
OPCC	Office of the Police Complaint Commissioner
OPHI	Oxford Poverty and Human Development Initiative
OSF	Open Society Foundation
OSCE	Organization for Security and Cooperation in Europe
OSI	Online Services Index
OUTA	Organization Undoing Tax Abuse
PA	Prudential Authority
PAC	Protocol Against Corruption
PCA	Police Complaints Authority
PCI	Political Corruption Index
PEGSD	Principles of Effective Governance for Sustainable Development
PETS	Public Expenditure Tracking Surveys
PF	Peace Fund
PIRC	Police Investigations and Review Commissioner
PMG	Parliamentary Monitoring Group
PMLs	Professional Money Launderers
PoW	Panel of the Wise
PPACA	Public Procurement Anti-Corruption Agency
PPSA	Public Protector South Africa
PRECCA	Prevention and Combatting of Corrupt Activities Act
PSC	Peace and Security Council
PwC	PricewaterhouseCoopers
QSDS	Quantitative Service Delivery Surveys
RMCP	Risk Management and Compliance Program
RSF	Reporters Sans Frontières
RWB	Reporters Without Borders
SAA	South African Airways
SABC	South African Broadcasting Corporation
SADC	Southern African Development Community
SAPs	Structural Adjustment Programs
SAPS	South African Police Service
SARB	South African Reserve Bank
SCSPS	Standing Committee of Supervision of Police Services

SDC	Sustainable Development Commission
SDGCA	Sustainable Development Goals Centre for Africa
SDGs	Sustainable Development Goals
SLACC	Sierra Leone Anti-Corruption Commission
SOEs	State-Owned Enterprises
SSG	Security Sector Governance
SSR	Security Sector Reform
SSR/G	Security Sector Reform/Governance
SSU	Special Service Unit
START	National Consortium for the Study of Terrorism and Responses to Terrorism
TAI	Transparency and Accountability Initiative
TI	Transparency International
TII	Telecommunications Infrastructure Index
TJRC	Truth, Justice, and Reconciliation Commission
UBDF	Ulaanbaatar Democracy Forum
UCLG	United Cities and Local Governments
UK	United Kingdom
UN	United Nations
UNCAC	United Nations Convention Against Corruption
UNCAT	United Nations Committee Against Torture
UN-CEPA	United Nations Committee of Experts on Public Administration
UNCTAD	United Nations Conference on Trade and Development
UNDESA	United Nations Department of Economic and Social Affairs
UNDP	United Nations Development Program
UNECA	United Nations Economic Commission for Africa
UNECOSOC	United Nations Economic and Social Council
UN-HRC	United Nations Human Rights Committee
UNHRC	United Nations Human Rights Council
UNICEF	United Nations Children's Fund
UNICRI	United Nations Interregional Crime and Justice Research Institute
UN-ITFFD	United Nations Inter-Agency Task Force on Financing for Development
UNODC	United Nations Office on Drugs and Crime
UNSC	United Nations Statistical Commission
UP/AO	Unethical Practices/Abuse of Office
US	United States
USAID	United States Agency for International Development
VAT	Value-Added Tax
V-DEM	Varieties of Democracy
VICPD	Victoria (British Columbia) Police Department
VNRs	Voluntary National Reviews
VVI	Van Vollenhoven Institute for Law, Governance and Society

WAEMU	West African Economic and Monetary Union
WEF	World Economic Forum
WGI	Worldwide Governance Indicators
WHO	World Health Organization
WIN	Water Integrity Network
WMO	World Meteorological Organization
WPFI	World Press Freedom Index
ZAMCO	Zimbabwe Asset Management Company
ZHRC	Zimbabwe Human Rights Commission

List of Figures

Fig. 3.1	Averages of proportion of people in sub-Saharan Africa who, in the previous 12 months, paid a bribe (bribery rates) for public services, 2013–2021	41
Fig. 4.1	Comparative relationship between the corruption perceptions index score and poverty rates (%), at the US$1.90-a-day poverty line and the multidimensional poverty index incidence (%), for sub-Saharan Africa, 2010–2020	65
Fig. 4.2	Control of Corruption Indicator by Region (Percentile Rank), 2010–2020	65
Fig. 4.3	Comparison relationship between corruption and GDP per capita growth for sub-Saharan Africa, 2010–2020	66
Fig. 4.4	Sub-Saharan Africa real GDP growth (%), 2010–2020	68
Fig. 4.5	Comparison relationship between the control of corruption percentile ranking and the gross debt-to-GDP ratio for sub-Saharan Africa, 2010–2020	69
Fig. 5.1	Police corruption indicator—bribery rates: averages of the proportion of people in sub-Saharan Africa who, during the previous 12 months, paid a bribe to the police for police assistance, 2013–2021 (%)	93
Fig. 5.2	Complaints to the IPOA about police corruption/extortion and unethical practices/abuse of office as a proportion of total complaints, 2019–2020 (%)	98
Fig. 5.3	Terrorist attacks, fatalities and injuries in Kenya, 2010–2020	110
Fig. 6.1	SDG 16 index performance score by regional/income classification, 2022	137
Fig. 6.2	SDG 16 index performance score and overall SDG index performance score for the ten lowest scoring African countries, 2022	138

Fig. 6.3	Continental and sub-regional performance of Agenda 2063 Aspiration 3 against its targets, 2019–2021 (%)	141
Fig. 6.4	Continental and sub-regional performance of Agenda 2063 Aspiration 4 against its targets, 2019–2021 (%)	142

List of Tables

Table 3.1	Statistics on businesses paying bribes: sub-Saharan Africa and all countries, 2010–2020 (averages)	42
Table 3.2	Statistics on private sector financial crime in sub-Saharan Africa, 2018 (%)	48
Table 5.1	Police corruption indicator—perceptions: proportion of citizens in sub-Saharan Africa countries who perceive their police to be corrupt, 2015–21 (%)	90
Table 6.1	The 17 Sustainable development goals	132
Table 7.1	Summary list of proposed other indicators for assessing progress in reducing corruption and bribery in Africa and their sources	165
Table 8.1	Typology of models of civilian oversight of police by features and characteristics	182

Chapter 1
Introduction

This chapter provides a summary of the book. It outlines the argument and provides a more detailed chapter-by-chapter description of the book's contents than available in the respective chapter abstracts. It is structured into three sections: (1) Focus of the book; (2) Definition of terms; and (3) Organization of the book.

1.1 Focus of the Book

The focus of the chapters and, hence, the book, is primarily on sub-Saharan Africa. The volume empirically and critically analyzes the issues related to the corruption and sustainable development nexus, the challenges that poses for security, and the resultant prospects and policy implications for peace and stability in the region. Consequently, the point of convergence is related to some key internal factors closely related to the promotion of sustainable development and the creation of capacities for long-term security, peace, and stability. The central theme running throughout is that corruption has been increasingly shown and acknowledged as a major threat to security, stability, and peace. Corruption helps create the conditions for conflict to thrive by, among other things, undermining the effective functioning of governance institutions, which in turn leads to poor service delivery, increased marginalization, and grievances. Poor or bad governance that deliberately ignores the development needs of citizens, is associated with an increased probability of violent conflict and protracted insecurity (African Development Bank [AfDB], 2022). Research conducted by the Institute for Economics and Peace (IEP), for example, shows that there is an empirical link between corruption and peace with corruption being a key explanatory variable in assessing low levels of peace. Countries with the strongest democratic institutions tend to be both the most peaceful and the least corrupt (IEP, 2015). At the same time, there can be no sustainable development without peace and no peace without sustainable development. As argued by the AfDB (2022, p. 8), "security is a public good that cannot be disentangled from sustainable development. Conflict and violence are major drivers of intractable fragility in many areas in Africa, undermining good governance, economic development, and social cohesion, and resulting in long-term negative impacts on human and physical assets."

Tackling corruption is therefore vital to achieving the Sustainable Development Goals (SDGs), particularly SDG 16 (Peace, Justice, and Strong Institutions) which is discussed in Chap. 6. Consequently, the rampant corruption that is found in Africa is a significant factor that needs to be permanently constrained to sustain development and allow for such development to occur in an environment of security, peace, and stability. As the world has been warned by United Nations (UN) Secretary-General António Guterres:

> Corruption is not only immoral, but is a serious crime.... It steals trillions of dollars from people all over the world—usually from those most in need, as it siphons off resources for sustainable development. When powerful people get away with corruption, people lose trust in their governing institutions. Democracies are weakened by cynicism and hopelessness.... Turning the tide against corruption is essential if we are to achieve the Sustainable Development Goals, promote peace, and protect human rights (UN, 2021a, p. 1).

Drawing on the author's extensive field experience in Africa, this book also offers practical policy options that are nuanced enough for country ownership implementation and require no significant external assistance beyond the usual cooperating donor country programming contributions. In addition to current national approaches for sustaining development and democratic reforms, the proposed policy solutions can best be implemented through the African Union Development Agency–New Partnership for Africa's Development (AUDA–NEPAD) and the African Peer Review Mechanism (APRM) processes and principles, as well as also adhering to the Commonwealth Anti-Corruption Benchmarks (CACBs) of good anti-corruption practice for national governments and public sector bodies, especially for the Commonwealth members, as discussed in Chap. 2, thereby being easily adapted to become African solutions to African problems.

A fundamental message that therefore emerges is that the majority of African states still need to find the kind of political leadership willing to pursue the types of democratic reforms that can reduce corruption, strengthen institutions, decentralize power, and create the type of environment where peace, security, and sustainable development can thrive. If poverty and inequality persist while the political elite are blindly looting their respective countries, for example, then societies in Africa will eventually become aggrieved and instability will inevitably percolate leading to internal political conflicts where violence may even follow, including unconstitutional means to remove not only the government but all of the national political leadership as well as those bureaucrats in the other branches of government that participated and benefitted from such looting.

As also observed by the UN (2021b, p. 3):

1.1 Focus of the Book

Corruption and the looting of staggering amounts of assets undermine the achievement of the SDGs and has a negative impact on peace, stability, security, the rule of law, gender equality, the environment and human rights. Corruption also contributes to the spread of terrorism and violent extremism. Pervasive corruption networks often include politicians, civil servants working at all levels of state institutions, representatives of the private sector and members of crime syndicates. The consequences of corruption are detrimental in many aspects, such as undermining governments' ability to serve public interests and eroding public trust in political processes.

Similarly, the then Permanent Representative of France to the UN, Ambassador François Delattre, in a statement to the Security Council, expounded that:

Corruption is both a consequence of instability and conflict and an important factor in exacerbating them …. In addition to significantly weakening institutions that safeguard the rule of law, corruption leads to drastic economic disparity and promotes organized crime and the financing of terrorism. It thereby undermines the security and the political, economic and social development of affected states. In that regard, it can be an obstacle to international peace and security, particularly in countries in conflict or post-conflict situations, which often suffer a lack of institutions or weak institutions. Those countries, already vulnerable, are often the first victims of the ravages of corruption, which affects the stability of the state, the security of its citizens and the future of the country …. Beyond the threat it poses to peace, corruption is a major obstacle to development (Delattre, 2018, p. 1).

More than two decades ago, Hope (1999, p. 291) had concluded, with respect to Africa, that "widespread corruption is a symptom that the state is functioning poorly. It is therefore not only a failure of ethical leadership but of governance as well." Ethical leadership is positively related to commitment to behave ethically and can also reduce corruption in public organizations in Africa and beyond (see, for example, Asencio, 2022; Bashir & Hassan, 2020; Hope, 2017a, 2017b; Naidoo, 2012). Moreover, establishing sustainable security and peace cannot be possible without ethical leadership (Mayanja, 2013). In fact, to a large extent, efforts to ensure sustainable development, peace, security, transformation, and ethics and good governance in Africa have always been undermined by, among other things, the continent's poor leadership and overall leadership deficit (see also Alidu, 2023; Jones et al., 2022; Ogunyemi et al., 2022; Tettey, 2012; Wenyah, 2022). Consequently, and as also agreed with Jones et al. (2022, pp. 3–4), "the notion of the overall objective that leadership plays an overarching role in rooting out corruption in Africa" needs to be reinforced as "what is clear, is that [Africa] needs to develop a generation of new African leaders to tackle corruption and make Africa's indelible mark on the world stage."

So, leadership looms large here. Leadership with the capacity to lead, to change mindsets, to act in the best interests of their respective nations by demonstrating a fidelity to democratic traditions and the promotion and implementation of policies that can sustain development and help to reduce societal inequality and its attendant negative consequences such as corruption, conflict, and instability, for instance. As argued by the African Capacity Building Foundation (ACBF), Botswana, for example, exhibits the type of development-oriented leadership centered around a long-term development vision through democratic means (ACBF, 2019). Sackey (2021) has also conducted an empirical analysis comprising 44 sub-Saharan Africa countries covering the period from 1970 to 2010 and found that Africa's pursuit of sustainable development and growth depends largely on the quality of its leaders as well as its political regimes. Democratically-oriented leaders were considered to be capable of attracting private investments that contribute to gross domestic product (GDP) growth relatively more than an autocratic leader, while a transition from a democratic leader to an autocratic leader negatively impacts GDP growth and sustainable development (see Sackey, 2021). Consequently, and as also concluded by Ekpo (2020), for example, African nations need to move toward improving their democratic leadership to provide for better governance to mobilize domestic resources such as savings, tax revenues and private–public partnership arrangements to finance development that can be sustainable. Such sustainable development can, in turn, contain the continent's escalating security challenges (see, for example, Ojakorotu & Onwughalu, 2023).

1.2 Definition of Terms

The three key areas and concepts (corruption, sustainable development, and security) on which the book is focused, and as applied in the book, are defined as outlined below.

1.2.1 Corruption

Corruption involves behavior on the part of officeholders or employees in the public and private sectors, in which they improperly and unlawfully advance their private interests of any kind and/or those of others contrary to the interests of the office or position they occupy, or otherwise enrich themselves and/or others, or induce others to do so, by misusing the position in which they are placed. There are basically two classifications of corruption—petty (low level, small scale, administrative, or bureaucratic) or grand (high level, elite, or usually political)—and these may be exhibited through many channels with the principal ones being: (1) Bribery, kickbacks, and facilitation payments; (2) Embezzlement, theft, and fraud; (3) Offering or receiving of an unlawful gratuity, favor, or illegal commission; (4) Favoritism, nepotism, patronage, and clientelism; (5) Money laundering and illicit financial flows; and (6) State capture, conflict of interest/influence peddling (see, for example, Bussell, 2015; Graycar, 2015; Hope, 2017a; Nichols, 2017).

1.2.2 Sustainable Development

Sustainable development relates to an economy's ability to maintain living standards through time beyond just economic growth. The concept was coined in the 1980s and essentially emerged from the awareness that the solution to the poverty of developing countries did not lie in economic growth only. Other factors, such as the conservation of the environment and social equality needed to be taken into consideration and this led to the promotion of three dimensions or pillars of sustainable development. Accordingly, the overall goal of sustainable development is the long-term stability of the economy and environment in a socially-inclusive way. Moreover, it is also about ensuring a strong, healthy, and just society. This means, meeting the diverse needs of all people in existing and future communities, promoting economic growth, environmental protection, social cohesion and inclusion, personal wellbeing, and creating equal opportunity (see, for example, Mensah, 2019; Sustainable Development Commission [SDC], n.d.). This embraces the three pillars of sustainable development (economic sustainability, social sustainability, and environmental sustainability). As a framework, in both theory and practice, sustainable development thrives best in a climate of good governance, peace and security.

1.2.3 Security

Security has to do with the presence of peace, safety, and stability. It is therefore taken to represent a situation where there is (1) an absence of violence or crisis; (2) the avoidance of, or non-exposure to, danger; (3) the absence of threat to the protection of human and physical resources; and (4) the management of future risks to human and physical resources. In that context, and as advocated by Jore (2019, p. 169), security is regarded as "the perceived or actual ability to [prevent], prepare for, adapt to, withstand, and recover from, dangers and crises caused by people's deliberate, intentional, and malicious acts such as [coups, political violence], terrorism, sabotage, organized crime, or hacking." As demonstrated by Luckham (2015), this can be further broken down from the perspective of the demand side where security is seen as an entitlement of citizens—or more generally human beings—to protection from violence, abuses of rights and social injustice, along with other existential risks such as famine or disease and facilitated on the supply side by the state as a process of political and social ordering. However, that ordering ought to be accomplished within basic democratic norms. As applied in this book, security is therefore primarily people-centered—sometimes referred to as human security—as opposed to being state-centered. It puts people at the center of the conventional state-security framework, and is grounded with, and linked to, SDG 16 which is the centerpiece of the approach of *Agenda 2030* that formally links sustainable development with peace and security.

1.3 Organization of the Book

One of the major features of this book is the amount of data it provides in support of its arguments and analyses. Despite the lack, or insufficiency, of some time series data in a few areas—as also discussed in the book—a considerable quantity of statistics has been painstakingly assembled from the scouring of credible databases and other reliable data sources, as well as from sound survey and research outputs.

The book is comprised of a total of eight chapters including this introduction chapter. Chapter 2, essentially, sets the stage with a contextual analysis of the key trends and current issues facing Africa vis-à-vis the corruption and sustainable development environment, the challenges that poses for security, and the resultant policy implications for peace and stability. Africa is deemed to be at a crossroads currently, slowly moonwalking its way to nowhere as corruption rages, development stagnates, and peace and security become elusive. Some combination of predatory behavior, lack of growth and development, insecurity and instability, bad governance, the ignoring of term limits by the political leaders, and the seemingly lack of capability to deal with threats from violent extremist groups have all been identified as reasons for coups to remove some governments in the quest for a better, more equal society. However, it is also vehemently stressed that coups are anti-democratic, anti-development, and most often lead to greater insecurity and instability.

Coups, where successful, simply unseat existing governments by unconstitutional means and, therefore, by definition and practice, setback the current democratic order if it exists or entrenches the anti-democratic norms that were already in place. Some coup leaders may eventually allow democratic elections or promise to hold such elections. Nonetheless, whatever the outcome of such elections, these coup leaders are always either lurking in the forefront or in the background of their nations' politics. Moreover, there has never been a successful coup in Africa that thereafter contributed to a lessening of corruption or to improved economic performance. In fact, coups lead to further political instability and insecurity which are not conducive to the promotion or achievement of sustainable development.

Chapter 3 outlines the trends in economic and financial crimes corruption in Africa through a compilation of statistics derived from a scan of the credible publicly available survey and other published data related thereto. It identifies and analytically reviews and assesses the trends of the principal economic and financial crimes as channels of corruption which impact the development process and economic progress in Africa. It therefore provides an analysis of the nature and extent of the trends in economic and financial crimes, as channels of corruption in Africa, and the resultant negative impact on sustainable development in the region.

The economic and financial crimes of embezzlement and theft, bribes and kickbacks, money laundering and illicit financial flows, and state capture are all identified as channels of corruption that are prevalent in Africa with significant negative effects on the continent's sustainable development progress. The magnitude of these crimes has been trending upward with the resultant effect that corruption continues

1.3 Organization of the Book

to have significant negative impacts on Africa's current and future development prospects. To develop policies to minimize these negative effects, it is necessary to quantify and continuously monitor the magnitude of these various corruption channels.

Chapter 4 follows-up logically from the previous chapter on the channels of corruption by examining how corruption and development actually interact from a nexus perspective in Africa. It offers a contemporary analysis of that relationship in the region along with a resulting set of policy implications for controlling corruption to mitigate its impact on sustainable development. Drawing on the available and accessible relevant data from credible sources, the chapter quantifies, outlines, and analyzes the nexus between corruption and sustainable development as it applies primarily to sub-Saharan Africa. It employs the relevant disaggregated data and complements that with the results of reliable empirical studies to further cross-reference and demonstrate the corruption and sustainable development nexus.

The chapter shows that corruption in Africa continues to be negatively associated with development objectives and that, in turn, will continue to affect the continent's progress in achieving sustainable development. Undoubtedly, corruption is very damaging to economies across all nations and regions. However, in Africa, this impact on development has been particularly severe and ongoing. Consequently, the views expressed several decades ago of corruption being able to grease the wheels and potentially contribute to economic development is not valid and, in fact, has been severally discredited over the years. The main value of the chapter, in the context of this book, is the insights it provides, and with cross-reference to the empirical literature and time series data, on the corruption and sustainable development nexus in Africa.

Chapter 5 further demonstrates the corruption problem in Africa and through a Kenya country case study of the key internal security organ—the police—and the challenges that poses for security and stability. Undoubtedly, police corruption has emerged as a serious security challenge in Africa. This chapter discusses and provides an analytical survey of the nature and extent of police corruption in Kenya, serving as an illustration of the police corruption problem in sub-Saharan Africa with cross-country comparisons. It draws on the available data and other research information and synthesizes them to provide a coherent picture and understanding of the police corruption problem and environment in Kenya and across Africa, and its linkage to, influence on, and implications for national security.

Where police corruption is persistent, it represents a systemic failure of governance where the principal institutions responsible for ensuring police governance, the observance of ethics and integrity standards, and enforcing the rule of law are compromised and are themselves infested with corrupt individuals and syndicates. The result is that a chain environment of personal and collective impunity prevails and police corruption is therefore both perceived and real as running rampant. That, in turn, has considerable negative impacts on justice or security sector development and performance and is a challenge to nation-building, the maintenance of public order and the rule of law, and to supporting the legitimacy of the state.

Chapter 6 is the first of the final three chapters that provide analytical content for drilling down on policy prescriptions to deal with overcoming the challenges corruption and its monitoring poses to sustainable development in Africa and beyond, and for improving police reform and accountability for better police performance to enhance national security and stability. The chapter is concerned with Goal 16 of the *2030 Agenda for Sustainable Development* which is officially titled: "*Promote peaceful and inclusive societies for sustainable development, provide access to justice for all and build effective, accountable and inclusive institutions at all levels.*" SDG 16 is one of the more innovative aspects of the sustainable development framework, focusing on advancing government accountability, building trust, and sustaining peace. It offers an insight into how we might actually hold leaders to account, and achieve all the SDGs by 2030. There are 12 targets of SDG 16 along with 24 associated official indicators.

The chapter provides an analysis of the importance of SDG 16 to achieving all the SDGs, the progress on implementation of SDG 16 to date, the principal challenges that countries in Africa and beyond are encountering in the implementation of SDG 16, and proposes a set of policy solutions to overcome those challenges. It argues that progress on SDG 16 is critical to progress on the other SDGs and, therefore, it is imperative that countries vigorously attempt to overcome those SDG 16 challenges to meet the targets indicated for all goals.

Chapter 7 follows-on from Chap. 6 with an assessment of African performance for substantially reducing all forms of corruption and bribery on the continent by 2030, through the indicators for achieving Target 16.5 of the SDGs. The chapter draws on the data from Chaps. 3 and 4 to assess the trends in the region through the official indicators for achieving Target 16.5 of the SDGs; and recommends other indicators for assessing ethical behavior in African political, administrative, and business leadership and institutions for achieving sustainable development and improved ethical performance toward significant reductions in all manifestations of bribery and corruption on the continent by 2030.

The chapter demonstrates and reiterates that corruption and bribery affect all SDG-related sectors, undermining sustainable development outcomes and severely compromising efforts to achieve the SDGs in Africa. Consequently, prioritizing corruption reduction—including from money laundering, bribery, and other illegal activities—is a necessary requirement for achieving sustainable development, good governance, the building of effective and inclusive institutions as required by SDG 16, and funding the achievement of the SDGs. The main value of the chapter is the insights it provides on the types of alternative and additional indicators that African nations can access and apply for assessing performance with respect to Target 16.5 of SDG 16.

Chapter 8, the final chapter, provides an analytical review of formal civilian oversight for democratic policing, outlining the benefits as well as the key challenges such oversight encounters. It extends the comparative analysis about formal civilian oversight for democratic policing by providing a much more international perspective, beyond Africa, including examples of the use of the various classifications and approaches to such oversight. Currently, only Kenya and South Africa have mechanisms of independent civilian oversight of police accountability.

Drawing on the author's field experience, it then offers some insights on the required framework and environment for overcoming the civilian oversight challenges in pursuit of much more improved police accountability and better internal security. Civilian oversight has emerged as the preferred approach for policing the police in support of more democratic societies in the pursuit of better police governance and improved prospects for national stability and enhanced national security in Africa and beyond. African nations need to establish independent institutions of civilian oversight in the pursuit of democratic policing and the general deepening of democracy.

References

ACBF. (2019). *Africa capacity report 2019: Fostering transformative leadership for Africa's development*. ACBF.
AfDB. (2022). *Security, investment and development: A diagnostic assessment*. Retrieved from https://www.afdb.org/en/documents/security-investment-and-development-diagnostic-assessment
Alidu, S. (2023). Leadership, governance and public policy in Africa. In E. R. Aiyede & B. Muganda (Eds.), *Public policy and research in Africa* (pp. 213–234). Palgrave Macmillan/Springer Nature.
Asencio, H. D. (2022). Ethical leadership and commitment to behave ethically in government agencies. *International Journal of Public Administration, 45*(12), 907–916. https://doi.org/10.1080/01900692.2021.1928186
Bashir, M., & Hassan, S. (2020). The need for ethical leadership in combating corruption. *International Review of Administrative Sciences, 86*(4), 673–690. https://doi.org/10.1177/2F0020852318825386
Bussell, J. (2015). Typologies of corruption: A pragmatic approach. In S. Rose-Ackerman & P. Lagunes (Eds.), *Greed, corruption, and the modern state: Essays in political economy* (pp. 21–45). Edward Elgar.
Delattre, F. (2018, September 10). Corruption is a threat to peace and development, corruption and security statement to the UN Security Council. Retrieved from https://onu.delegfrance.org/Corruption-is-a-threat-to-peace-and-development
Ekpo, A. H. (2020). Financing development without tears: An empirical investigation on sub-Saharan Africa. In D. Seck (Ed.), *Financing Africa's development: Paths to sustainable economic growth* (pp. 15–31). Springer Nature.
Graycar, A. (2015). Corruption: Classification and analysis. *Policy and Society, 34*(2), 87–96. https://doi.org/10.1016/j.polsoc.2015.04.001
Hope, K. R. (1999). Corruption in Africa: A crisis in ethical leadership. *Public Integrity, 1*(3), 289–308.
Hope, K. R. (2017a). *Corruption and governance in Africa: Swaziland [Eswatini], Kenya, Nigeria*. Palgrave Macmillan/Springer Nature.
Hope, K. R. (2017b). Fighting corruption in developing countries: Some aspects of policy from lessons from the field. *Journal of Public Affairs, 17*(4), e1683. https://doi.org/10.1002/pa.1683
IEP. (2015). *Peace and corruption: Lowering corruption—A transformative factor for peace*. IEP.
Jones, C., Pillay, P., Reddy, P. S., & Zondi, S. I. (Eds.). (2022). *Lessons from political leadership in Africa: Towards inspirational and transformational leaders*. Cambridge Scholars Publishing.

Jore, S. H. (2019). The conceptual and scientific demarcation of security in contrast to safety. *European Journal for Security Research, 4*(1), 157–174. https://doi.org/10.1007/s41125-017-0021-9

Luckham, R. (2015). Whose security? Building inclusive and secure societies in an unequal and insecure world. [Evidence report no 151]. Institute of Development Studies. Retrieved from https://www.ids.ac.uk/publications/whose-security-building-inclusiveand-secure-societies-in-an-unequal-and-insecure-world/

Mayanja, E. (2013). Strengthening ethical political leadership for sustainable peace and social justice in Africa: Uganda as a case study. *African Journal of Conflict Resolution, 13*(2), 113–146.

Mensah, J. (2019). Sustainable development: Meaning, history, principles, pillars, and implications for human action: Literature review. *Cogent Social Sciences, 5*(1), 1653531. https://doi.org/10.1080/23311886.2019.1653531

Naidoo, G. (2012). A critical need for ethical leadership to curb corruption and promote good governance in the public sector of South Africa. *African Journal of Public Affairs, 5*(2), 25–35.

Nichols, P. M. (2017). Organizational corruption. In M. S. Aßländer & S. Hudson (Eds.), *The handbook of business and corruption: Cross-sectoral experiences* (pp. 3–24). Emerald Publishing.

Ogunyemi, K., Adisa, I., & Hinson, R. E. (2022). Leadership and policy implementation for good governance in Africa. In K. Ogunyemi, I. Adisa, & R. E. Hinson (Eds.), *Ethics and accountable governance in Africa's public sector* (*Mapping a path for the future*) (Vol. II, pp. 1–14). Palgrave Macmillan/Springer Nature.

Ojakorotu, V., & Onwughalu, V. C. (2023). The dialectics of insecurity and development in Africa: The role of development partners. *African Security Review, 32*(1), 115–129. https://doi.org/10.1080/10246029.2022.2141580

Sackey, F. G. (2021). Impact of African leaders' characteristics and regime transitions on economic growth in Africa: A dynamic model approach. *Social Sciences & Humanities Open, 4*(1), 1–10. https://doi.org/10.1016/j.ssaho.2021.100147

SDC. (n.d.). What is sustainable development. Retrieved from https://www.sd-commission.org.uk/pages/what-is-sustainabledevelopment.html

Tettey, W. J. (2012). Africa's leadership deficit: Exploring pathways to good governance and transformative politics. In K. T. Hanson, G. Kararach, & T. M. Shaw (Eds.), *Rethinking development challenges for public policy* (pp. 18–53). Palgrave Macmillan.

UN. (2021a, June 3). Turning tide against corruption essential to achieving Sustainable Development Goals, promoting peace, Secretary-General says at Globe Network launch. [Press Release]. Retrieved from https://press.un.org/en/2021/sgsm20759.doc.htm

UN. (2021b). *The UN common position to address global corruption–towards UNGASS 2021*. UN.

Wenyah, S. (2022). Anti-corruption initiatives in Africa's public sector. In K. Ogunyemi, I. Adisa, & R. E. Hinson (Eds.), *Ethics and accountable governance in Africa's public sector, Volume I: Ethical compliance and institutional performance* (pp. 131–152). Palgrave Macmillan/Springer Nature.

Chapter 2
Africa at the Crossroads: Moonwalking in Slow Motion

This chapter provides a contextual analysis of the key issues and current trends in Africa vis-à-vis corruption and sustainable development, the resultant challenges for security, and the implications for peace, security, and stability on the continent. Africa is deemed to be at a crossroads currently, slowly moonwalking its way to nowhere as corruption rages, development stagnates, and peace and security therefore become elusive. It is shown why some combination of predatory behavior, insecurity and instability, and bad governance have all been identified and proven to be the reasons for the lack of sustainable development on the continent.

2.1 Introduction

Africa is a unique and, therefore, a very fascinating developing region in the world. It is the second largest, second most populous, and the most centrally located continent on earth. It is much more youthful, mobile, and educated than ever before. And, it also has vibrant and distinct cultures and a rich natural history. No other continent, or group of countries within the developing world, receives as much attention as Africa, and/or its constituent countries, from both within and outside of Africa's geographic area. It is the most researched, analyzed, or casually written about region of the world. Of course, a primary reason for this concern with Africa is its lack of post-colonial sustainable development and the consequences stemming therefrom that, in turn, hinder security, peace, and stability and vice versa. Emerson and Solomon (2018, p. 1), for example, have observed that "the African security environment of today is a dynamic one, characterized by a volatile mix of conflict, instability, and state weakness." That state of affairs tends to give the impression of a continent lacking in transformation, in frequent turmoil, and in need of external interventions and assistance which, in turn gives rise to further considerable internal and external scrutiny, debate, and contemplation about its (the continent's) fate and future prospects.

To be clear, and from the point of view of this book's author, colonialism was not beneficial for former colonies. In fact, among other things, it was morally unjust, dehumanizing, exploitative, repressive, and denied human rights; created economic dependence on the colonizers; led to land displacement and land degradation; and has had other disastrous consequences and devastating negative effects on the indigenous populations and society. Indeed, colonialism remains a bad deal for currently existing colonies (see also, for example, Acemoglu & Robinson, 2017; Elkins, 2022; Renzo, 2019; Robinson, 2017; Ypi, 2013). Nonetheless, unlike almost all other developing nations that have also long exited from the shackles of colonialism, and made strides (some big, some small) toward sustainable development in environments of security and peace, most African countries continue to be left behind. Each time much of the continent seems to be making some headway in terms of socio-economic progress and good governance, mostly homegrown or homemade setbacks emerge in the form of internal conflicts, coups, even more rampant corruption, unconstitutional governance, and generally poor leadership, for example. Consequently, colonialism is not to blame for all of Africa's problems. As noted by, and agreed with, Adekoya (2022, pp. 1–2):

> It is fanciful, for example, to suggest that the US$600 billion stolen from the Nigerian people by Nigerian rulers since independence is down to colonialism. If that had been used to fund roads, schools, hospitals, universities and power systems, Nigeria would be in a very different place today. We would definitely not be in a situation whereby three-quarters of Nigerians aged 18–24 want to emigrate to richer pastures, including often to the land of their former conquerors, Britain.

However, it must also be acknowledged that, like all other developing regions, Africa has also fallen victim to externally driven shocks such as, for instance, pandemics, whose initial outbreaks originated from outside of the continent; dysfunctional global markets due to wars initiated and/or fronted by a super power nation (one of the permanent members of the UN Security Council); inflation and recession in regions beyond the continent's borders; inward-looking developed country policies; and donor policy frameworks like that of the eventually discredited structural adjustment programs (SAPs) that were imposed in the 1980s and 1990s. Nonetheless, the historical record shows that Africa has been experiencing, and continues to experience, development, security, and governance problems prior to the inception of most external shocks and long after the effects of those external shocks have subsided.

As this book shows, despite its vast natural and human resources, Africa is consistently behind all other developing regions in the key indicators or measurements of sustainable development performance. Yet, as this book's author firmly believes, and as this book also demonstrates, Africa still has the potential to move to a state of renewal and fulfill its development promise. It is therefore concurred here with Signé and Gurib-Fakim (2019) that the continent represents an opportunity where governments, citizens, and organizations—both within and outside the continent—are better positioned to confront sustainable development challenges and further boost all existing positive trends within a necessary framework of country/continental ownership. As also acknowledged by The White House (2022, p. 43), "the continent's booming population, vital natural resources, and vibrant entrepreneurship, coupled with the African Continental Free Trade Area (AfCFTA), have the potential to drive transformative economic growth." In that regard, and with that perspective in mind, below we set the stage pertaining to the key issues and theme of this book.

2.2 Africa at the Crossroads

A little more than two decades ago, an Oxfam Briefing Paper observed that Africa was standing at a crossroads facing a crisis because of failures at all levels, both within the continent and outside of it (see Van Woudenberg, 2002). Among the factors prominently featured as contributing to that state of affairs were corruption/bribery and a lack of respect for human rights and the rule of law, all of which are essential to durable peace and long-term development (Van Woudenberg, 2002). Today, Africa is again facing a crossroads as the problem of corruption in the region continues to be a focus not only of the continent's citizens but now also of many other parties beyond Africa, including Western governments, development institutions, and think tanks. The majority of the nation states of then Africa region, although rich in human and natural resources, still seem unable and/or unwilling to individually and collectively move toward a path of a solid commitment to anti-corruption reforms to sustain development and the implementation of democratic reforms to maintain peace, security, and stability.

This situation plays out despite the fact that a majority of the countries have anti-corruption legislation and institutions in place and are also signatories to anti-corruption conventions and governance and democracy charters, principles, and all sorts of architectures and protocols such as the United Nations Convention Against Corruption (UNCAC); the African Union Convention on Preventing and Combating Corruption (AUCPCC); the African Charter on Democracy, Elections and Governance (ACDEG); the African Charter on Human and Peoples' Rights (ACHPR); the African Governance Architecture (AGA); the African Peace and Security Architecture (APSA); and the Protocol Relating to the Establishment of the Peace and Security Council (PSC) of the African Union, for example. There are also some sub-regional frameworks agreed to by those respective member states such as the Protocol Against Corruption (PAC) of the Southern African Development Community (SADC), and the Policy Framework for Security Sector Reform and Governance of the Economic Community of West African States (ECOWAS) which also includes a Code of Conduct for the Armed Forces and Security Services. By 2021, 85% of the 55 AU member states had signed the ACDEG, and 60% had gone further to ratify it (African Union [AU], 2022a).

At this stage, it is relevant and therefore useful, in the context of this book, to highlight the APSA of the AU. The APSA, launched in 2002, is the AU's blueprint for the promotion of peace, security and stability in Africa and is built around structures, objectives, principles and values, as well as decision-making processes relating to the prevention, management and resolution of crises and conflicts and post-conflict reconstruction and development in the continent (AU, n.d.-a.; see also, Kuwali, 2022a; Vlavonou, 2019). The main pillar of the APSA is the PSC and its (the PSC's) objectives as outlined in Article 3 of its establishment protocol are the following:

- Promote peace, security, and stability in Africa to guarantee the protection and preservation of life and property, the well-being of the African people and their environment, as well as the creation of conditions conducive to sustainable development.
- Anticipate and prevent conflicts. In circumstances where conflicts have occurred, the PSC shall have the responsibility to undertake peace-making and peacebuilding functions for the resolution of these conflicts.
- Promote and implement peace-building and post-conflict reconstruction activities to consolidate peace and prevent the resurgence of violence.
- Co-ordinate and harmonize continental efforts in the prevention and combating of international terrorism in all its aspects.
- Develop a common defense policy for the Union under Article 4(d) of the Constitutive Act.
- Promote and encourage democratic practices, good governance and the rule of law, protect human rights and fundamental freedoms, respect for the sanctity of human life and international humanitarian law, as part of efforts for preventing conflicts (AU, 2002; see also, Kuwali, 2022a).

The PSC is supported in the discharge of its mandate by various structures, including:

- The Continental Early Warning System (CEWS) which is designed to predict and prevent crises and conflicts on the continent. It aims to provide timely and reliable data to warn the PSC and the AU Commission of potential conflicts and outbreaks of violence (AU, 2018a).
- The African Standby Force (ASF) that was created to provide support in managing conflicts and to avoid their escalation or proliferation. It is composed of multidimensional capabilities, including military, police and civilian, on standby in their countries of origin and ready for rapid deployment. Its range of functions assigned includes: The range of functions assigned to the ASF includes: (1) observation and monitoring missions; (2) other types of peace support operations; (3) intervention in a member state in respect of grave circumstances or at the request of a member state to restore peace and security, in accordance with the AU Constitutive Act; (4) preventive deployment to prevent a dispute or a conflict from escalating, an ongoing violent conflict from spreading to neighboring areas or states and the resurgence of violence after parties to conflict have reached an agreement; (5) peace building, including post conflict disarmament and demobilization; (6) humanitarian assistance to alleviate the suffering of civilian population in conflict areas and support efforts to address major natural

disasters; and (7) any further functions as may be mandated by the PSC or the Assembly of Heads of State (AU, 2019; see also, Apuuli, 2018; Nagar, 2018).
- The Peace Fund (PF) which provides the financial support for the peace and security activities undertaken by the AU. The overall legal basis for the PF is set out in the Protocol Relating to the Establishment of the PSC (AU, n.d.-b; see also, Lumina, 2022).
- The Panel of the Wise (PoW), which includes five prominent African leaders from each subregion, with a diverse experience of peace and security on the continent, is an advisory body based on the African tradition of mediation entrusted to elders. It acts on its own initiative or on behalf of the PSC, or the Chairperson of the African Union Commission. Its mandate is to (1) support and advise the effort of the chairperson of the AU Commission and the PSC, in the area of conflict prevention; (2) advise both the Commission and the PSC on issues that are necessarily considered by the policy organs of the AU such as the issues of impunity, justice and reconciliation as well as, women and children in armed conflicts and its impact on the most vulnerable ones; (3) use its good offices to carry out conflict mediation and broker peace agreements between warring parties; and (4) assist the AU Commission in mapping out threats to peace and security by providing regular advice and analysis and requesting the Commission to deploy fact-finding or mediation teams to specific countries (see AU, 2018b; Ngandu, 2017).
- Ad-Hoc Security Initiatives (ASIs) which, according to de Coning et al. (2022), have emerged to serve as a stopgap for the AU and the wider international security framework to diffuse new and emerging crises. ASIs put national states in the center of finding their own security solutions to respond to threats with transregional collaboration. Their use can result in swift action and are not held back by cumbersome decision-making processes in the face of immediate threats (de Coning et al., 2022).

Governance gains that had been accomplished in Africa in the 1990s and in the early years of the 21st century have begun to erode and primarily through the behavior and facilitation of the political leadership and their cronies in the bureaucracy as well as in the private sector. Among other things, term limits are being ignored and, in some cases, being changed through unconstitutional means and in violation of the ACDEG and other democratic norms and principles; government accountability mechanisms and citizen freedoms are being eroded; opposition candidates and parties are being prevented from participating in elections, through intimidation and violence, judicial harassment or legal restrictions; application of the rule of law and recourse to an independent judiciary through the courts are being impeded; corrupt deals are being made with unethical local and international business firms for personal private gains at the expense of society; and huge sums are being siphoned off and illicitly sent across borders (see, for example, Chisadza, 2020; Fomunyoh, 2020; Gyimah-Boadi, 2021, 2022; Rakner, 2018; Wiebusch & Murray, 2019; Zamfir, 2021). In addition, street-level bureaucrats, such as the police, are abusing their powers (including through extra-judicial killings) and shaking down and scaring their fellow citizens into compliance with their (the police) corrupt activities. This they (the police) do with impunity as their police bosses tend also to be their syndicate leaders who positively sanction and benefit themselves from these corrupt activities (Hope, 2016).

Moreover, military coups (also referred to as coup d'états or putsches) have also returned. In the decade prior to 2020, successful coups in Africa averaged less than one per year (Duzor & Williamson, 2022). Since 2017, multiple countries have been marred by growing insecurity with a sharp increase of coups and armed conflicts There have been 23 successful and attempted coups on the African continent since 2012 with eight of these being successful between 2019 and 2022 (Mo Ibrahim Foundation [MIF], 2023a, 2023b). Since 2020, there have been successful coups in Burkina Faso (September 2022 and January 2022 prior to that), Chad (April 2021), Guinea (September 2021), Mali (May 2021 and August 2020 prior to that), and Sudan (October 2021 and April 2019 prior to that). In addition, there were failed coups in Ethiopia (June 2019), Guinea Bissau (February 2022), and Niger (March 2021). The Economist (2021) has noted, that more coups have occurred in Africa in 2021 than in the previous 5 years combined. In his expert contribution to the *Global Terrorism Index 2022* report of the IEP, Kfir (2022, p. 80) has adamantly proclaimed that "coups are products of systemic failures relating to corruption, mismanagement, and poverty." Indeed, the coup leaders have blamed corruption, lack of development, insecurity and instability, and the ignoring of term limits by the political leaders as their primary reasons for ousting their governments.

The evidence also shows that recent coups in Africa now tend to occur in the poorest of the continent's countries and that is also used as reasoning for the undertaking of some of these military coups. For example, Colonel Mamady Doumbouya, the leader of the September 2021 coup in Guinea, said in a televised address that "poverty and endemic corruption" had obliged him and his troops to act against the former government. He also expressed concerns about the fact that his country's now deposed President, Alpha Condé, had changed the constitution to serve a third term. In Mali and Burkina Faso, the coup leaders claimed that insecurity, instability and the lack of capability to deal with threats from violent extremist groups had precipitated the coups (see, for example, Aina & Nyei, 2022a; Duzor & Williamson, 2022; Engels, 2022; Ioanes, 2022; Powell et al., 2022; Zeigler, 2021). This line of argument has also been eloquently captured by Ford and Versi (2022, pp. 4–5) thusly:

> Given an already febrile atmosphere, with various terrorist groups seemingly running amok, and carrying out brazen attacks with impunity, allied to rising prices of essentials, the poor-to-non-existent social services, and a political elite that cocooned itself behind brutal security forces while filling in their private coffers, is it any wonder that the hard-pressed populace came out in protests and demonstrations? … Is it also any wonder that when the military stepped in and removed these people, the public rejoiced? Where they had failed through their demonstrations and protests, the military had succeeded.

However, these justifications by the coup leaders are not surprising as they are somewhat logical, notwithstanding the fact that coups represent an undemocratic and unconstitutional seizure of power. With respect to Burkina Faso, Engels (2022, p. 318) has noted that "frustration and anger within the state security forces and

2.2 Africa at the Crossroads

within organized civil society and the population in general have steadily increased ...." More generally, Carbone and Pellegata (2020, p. 144), for example, have eloquently observed that:

> Soldiers who seize power hardly ever fail to claim that they are doing so to redress a country's development trajectory: overcome economic stagnation, fight corruption, improve citizens' welfare, or restore stability in the face of mounting social tensions. These justifications thus typically refer to the record of the governments that are being overthrown, allegedly responsible for development failures.

Undoubtedly, and as also argued by Joly et al. (2020) with respect to West Africa, given the significant threat that corruption presents to peace and stability in that sub-region, a greater focus should be placed on anti-corruption programming within the security sector reform-governance (SSR/G) framework. According to the Geneva Center for Security Sector Governance (DCAF), security sector governance (SSG) is described as the rules, structures and processes of state security provision, management, and oversight in a national setting (DCAF, 2015). Good SSG refers to the application of the general principles of good governance to a state's security sector and is based on the notion that the security sector must be held to the same high standards of public service delivery as other public sector service providers (DCAF, 2015).

In recent years, security sector experts, academics, and the international community have all come to accept the view that security and development are mutually reinforcing areas and, as such, there is a necessary requirement to pursue development and security concurrently (see, for example, Hope, 2019; Dursun-Özkanca, 2021; Ojakorotu & Onwughalu, 2023). However, in even more recent times, there has been a further recognition that without sustained peace and security, development will not be sustained and, mutually, without sustainable development there will likely be insecurity and instability as some of the rationale and outcomes of the recent coups in West Africa have demonstrated. Of course, and as also discussed in Chap. 6, foresight was shown by UN member states by including peace as one of the five pillars of *Agenda 2030*. In its preamble, the *Agenda* states: "There can be no sustainable development without peace and no peace without sustainable development" (UN, 2015, p. 6).

So, we can see the logical interlinkages among the factors of corruption, development, peace, security, and stability. Corruption has been increasingly acknowledged as a major threat to security, stability, and peace (see, for example, Chayes, 2016; Kuwali, 2022b; Pyman et al., 2014). It is now therefore widely established that "the nexus between security and development is mutually reinforcing, and that peace and prosperity are needed for sustainable economic, social and political advancement" (AfDB, 2022, p. 29). Insecurity retards development and conflict reverses development gains. Through the illegal siphoning and pocketing of state resources, corruption weakens the ability of the state to provide key public services, including security (Pyman et al., 2014). And, this leads to disgruntlement among the leaders and cadre of the armed forces who then feel empowered to topple their country's government. Hunter et al. (2020, p. 1093), employing a case-study analysis with six states in Africa, Asia, and Latin America, and covering the period 1970–2010, found that "three common factors contributed to the likelihood of successful military coups. These factors were the military feeling threatened by the ruling administration, the perception of corruption within the regime, and low levels of support among the citizenry and key factions within society," and "the simultaneous combination of these three factors appeared to significantly increase the likelihood that successful military coups would take place." In many instances, these coup leaders are celebrated and welcomed with open arms by their fellow citizens as they are seen and regarded as the saviors of their respective countries.

In any case, the very nature of coups renders them as undemocratic, unconstitutional, and sometimes bloody affairs. There has never been a successful coup in Africa that has been followed by a reduction of corruption or by economic progress. In fact, coups lead to further political instability and insecurity which are not conducive to promoting or achieving sustainable development. Instead, when coups overthrow governments, especially democratically-elected ones, they (coups) tend to be overwhelmingly detrimental with generally no prospects for sustainable growth and development or any particular concern for maintaining or re-establishing democratic institutions (Meyersson, 2016). For example, by the end of 2022, there were four of the longest-serving African heads of state whom came into power through military coups—Teodoro Obiang Nguema Mbasogo of Equatorial Guinea, with 43 years in office; Paul Biya of Cameroon, with 40 years in office; Denis Sassou of the Republic of the Congo with 36 years in office; and Uganda's Yoweri Museveni, also with 36 years in office (Cook & Siegle, 2021; Klobucista, 2021; Ndebele, 2022). It is not surprising that these four countries are ranked among the lowest in terms of their corruption and other governance scores, as greater democratization, development, and security are impeded (Siegle & Cook, 2021) and, in that regard, there is good survey and research data showing that most Africans want to see presidential term limits reinstated where they have been removed and age limits also imposed (see, for example, Kakumba, 2021; Ngwang, 2021). Nonetheless, it is also recognized that in fragile states with weak democracy, such as Mali, for example, corruption, insecurity, and socio-economic challenges function as the breeding grounds that have led to the various coups that have been experienced in such states with some of these coups, emerging from anti-government mass protests by the citizenry (see, for example, Adetuyi, 2021; Majiga, 2022).

However, coups are also usually the final manifestation of violent conflict to overthrow governments. But, such conflicts, or the legacy of such conflicts, are not good or useful for enhancing democracy or democratic norms and institutions (see also, Carbone & Pellegata, 2020; Cheeseman et al., 2018; Derpanopoulos et al., 2016; Iroanya, 2018). Also, conflicts retard sustainable development. Empirical research by the IMF (2019) found that conflicts impose large social and economic costs in sub-Saharan Africa with active conflicts tending to depress annual growth by 2.5 percentage points per year in directly affected countries. In the last three decades, this has translated into an annual regionwide loss of about 0.75% of GDP. However, the recent increase in the incidence of conflicts, has led to the estimated loss of GDP increasing to almost 1.5% annually (IMF, 2022). Similarly, Fang et al. (2020) conducted an empirical analysis based on a sample of 45 sub-Saharan Africa countries, covering the period 1989–2019, and found the economic impact of conflict in sub-Saharan Africa to be large and persistent with annual growth in countries in conflict being about 2.5 percentage points lower, and the cumulative impact on per capita GDP increasing over time. Some other empirical work by Akinlo and Okunlola (2022), for example, has also shown that reduced conflict levels can improve Africans' quality of life measured to include, among other things, longer life expectancy, higher literacy rates, higher levels of economic growth and prosperity, economic well-being conditioned on the country's level of democracy, and per capita consumption expenditure. There is therefore a strong association between violent conflict and development.

2.3 Moonwalking in Slow Motion

As this book shows, corruption is an enduring problem in Africa. Most African nations have been moonwalking in slow motion, casually sliding backward while giving the impression of forward progress on the creation of an environment conducive to good governance, sustainable development, peace, security, and stability. In that regard, even the prominent anti-corruption advocacy organization, Transparency International (TI), has confirmed that "some leaders invoke a sham fight against corruption as a means for furthering their own interests, while sabotaging democracy" (TI, 2021, p. 3). As also astutely observed by Balogun (2022, p. 196), "corruption seems to be the bane of the existence of democracy in Africa, as many African countries run defective democratic systems, steal from their people, manipulate electoral processes and results and continue to hide their acts under the umbrella of democracy," leading to "the thinking … that the problem with Africa is not with the system or democratic model in operation, but with the handlers of the system."

Whatever the corruption channel, it results in a leakage of resources of an order of magnitude that significantly affects development in a negative way and that, in turn, also negatively impacts peace, security, and stability. "Corruption and the related grievances resulting from lack of rule of law, elite rent-seeking, perceived injustice, unfair treatment and marginalization in society are considered central push factors for contestation, unrest and violent conflict" (Hopp-Nishanka, 2021, p. 3). Recent empirical research by Gillanders and van der Werff (2022), using several rounds of representative household survey data for sub-Saharan Africa countries, has also shown that men and women that have experienced petty corruption are much more likely to view violence as justifiable. However, it is the view of this book's author that anti-corruption efforts and other measures to strengthen democracy and sustain development in Africa must also be ongoing and enduring. Anything less would suggest that no one (in the domestic or international realm) particularly cares anymore about the fate of the region and that will certainly have all kinds of spillover effects in the region and beyond as it is certain to encourage even more worse kinds of behavior to acquire and/or maintain power and pillage national treasuries resulting in greater poverty, inequality, insecurity, and instability.

As also recognized by the AU, undoubtedly, "a democratic and politically stable Africa is imperative to bring about lasting peace and create the conducive ecosystem for the realization of the aspirations of *Agenda 2063: The Africa we Want* [Africa's blueprint and master plan for transforming Africa into the global powerhouse of the future]" (AU, 2022b, p. 5), as a shared framework for inclusive growth and sustainable development for Africa. The same is true with respect to achieving the global SDGs of *Agenda 2030*. Indeed, recent empirical work by Veri and Sass (2022) has reconfirmed the fact that the most effective way to constrain political violence, including coups, and maintain domestic peace is with more democracy. That means that the formal democratic institutions need to be governed by committed democrats and state elites who are inclined and motivated to engage with the grievances and political claims of all interest groups (see Veri & Sass, 2022). That would most certainly also include the leadership of the military forces and would definitely provide the environment for improvements in both negative and positive peace. Moreover, such an approach would also potentially change the way security is perceived, planned, and delivered to citizens by African nations and is necessary to foster good governance and civilian democratic control of the security sector (Kuol & Amegboh, 2021).

Negative peace is regarded as the absence of violence or the fear of violence (IEP, 2022). Positive peace is defined as the attitudes, institutions and structures that create and sustain peaceful societies and is comprised of the following eight pillars: (1) a well-functioning government; (2) a sound business environment; (3) the acceptance of the rights of others; (4) good relations with neighbors; (5) a free-flow of information; (6) an equitable distribution of resources; (7) high levels of human capital; and (8) low levels of corruption (see IEP, 2022 for greater details). The indicators of positive peace tend to focus on prevention and the drivers of negative peace and may include measures or indicators such as the incidence of corruption or government capacities to deliver basic services in an equitable and inclusive way. Ultimately, it is the progress in both negative and positive peace which contributes to stability and progress in peace and development (see IEP, 2014).

A key observation here pertains to two lessons learned or to be learned from the West Africa coups. First, is the fact that the AU and other sub-regional bodies, such as the ECOWAS, for instance, are rather impotent in terms of their ability to get timely results through their sanctions regime framework pertaining to unconstitutional changes of government. Apart from suspending the coup affected countries from membership in these two bodies, the coup leaders can simply ignore all other sanctions for any period of time that suits them, prolonging negotiations and transition dialogues, before finally agreeing to restoring some semblance of constitutional order. In fact, support for the coup leaders have led to anti-sanctions demonstrations by growing numbers of the citizenry in some of these successful coup states and, as observed by Elischer and Lawrance (2022, p. 4), "the military juntas currently display little willingness to return power to democratically elected leaders." According to Warah (2022, p. 1), for example, "civilians were seen kissing the hands of soldiers loyal to [the then Burkina Faso] coup leader Lieutenant Colonel Paul-Henry Damiba, [whom] they [believed would have been] more effective than the ousted president in dealing with violent Islamic insurgents in the country." Similar public support was exhibited for Captain Ibrahim Traoré who deposed Damiba in September 2022. In that regard, Aina and Nyei (2022b, pp. 4–5) have expressed that:

> Widespread civilian support for these coups reinforces the notion that the armed forces are the guardians of states. Convinced that existing constitutional processes are not adequate to support good governance in their countries, citizens in Mali, Burkina Faso and Guinea appear to believe that the military may be a credible alternative to the band of corrupt and unrepentant political elites that have betrayed their confidence.

Further, Ford and Versi (2022, p. 5) have observed that:

> What the coups showed in most of these cases, was that the outward manifestations of democracy—the ritual electioneering, the voting (in most cases rigged) and the loud claims of victory at the end of the exercise—had been exposed for what they were: shameful distortions of what real democracy should be; horrible fakes that no longer fooled anybody, least of all the electorate.

Nonetheless, post-coup interventions by the AU through its PSC, which is mandated to exercise responsibilities to maintain the constitutional order in response to situations where the democratic political institutional arrangements or the legitimate exercise of power are affected, and other sub-regional bodies such as ECOWAS or the SADC, for example, are necessary not only from a legal regional perspective but as a representation of the necessity to demonstrate "African solutions to African problems" as the extant architecture with that responsibility (see, for instance, Ani, 2021; Badmus, 2015; Degila & Amegan, 2019; Momodu & Owonikoko, 2021; Stocker & Quirk, 2022; Wiebusch, 2016; Witt, 2020). Fofack (2022) in his exposition on promoting security in Africa has also noted that the region's development depends solely on its own regional ownership of its security. In that regard, he correctly argues, in the view of this book's author, that:

> Reversing the trend of rising insecurity in Africa is key not only for putting the region on the road towards long-run growth, but also for optimizing the allocation of scarce resources towards productive investments that will boost industrial output and eventually lift supply-side constraints to support the AfCFTA's implementation (Fofack, 2022, p. 15).

Secondly, the recent overthrow of governments and the rapid deterioration in peace, security, and stability that plagues West Africa must be a lesson for political leaders, in some of the countries in other sub-regions such as Southern Africa, for example, that have been slowly backpedaling on fundamental governance reforms and thereby creating an environment of dissent and ongoing explosive civil unrest. Any environment where there is frequent civil unrest because of calls for democratic reforms will not only result in increased violence, but sooner or later will likely result in alliances being formed, including with the security services, to remove the government and allied others who would have come to be fully regarded as the root cause of the civil upheaval that is not only interfering with everyday life but with overall peace, security, and stability as well.

This governance and sustainable development backsliding that has recently been occurring in Africa is disappointing given that at the beginning of the 21st century, specifically in 2001, a new generation of enlightened leaders—primarily led at that time by President Thabo Mbeki of South Africa, President Olusegun Obasanjo of Nigeria, and President Abdoulaye Wade of Senegal—decided to stake Africa's claim to the 21st century and successfully advanced the NEPAD, that was subsequently ratified by the AU in 2002, to address Africa's development problems within a new paradigm. NEPAD's main objectives were to reduce poverty, promote sustainable growth and development, integrate Africa into the world economy, and accelerate the empowerment of women. As originally conceived, it was couched within five core principles — (1) good governance; (2) entrenchment of democracy, peace and security; (3) sound economic policy-making and execution; (4) productive partnerships; and (5) domestic ownership and leadership—which were deemed as the preconditions for Africa's renewal (see Hope, 2002, 2005). The NEPAD was seen and regarded as perhaps the most innovative and forward-looking framework for pulling Africa back from the brink of totally bad governance and economic disaster. From the point of view of Hope (2002, p. 401), writing at the time, "the NEPAD present[ed] a home-grown initiative for development based on a set of core principles that have been embraced by national, regional, and international public opinion as being preconditions for the renewal of the African continent," and "potentially, it constitute[d] the most important advance in African development policy during the past four decades."

The NEPAD was a direct response not only to what was being observed by the political leaders but to the unrelenting domestic and international criticisms of Africa as a continent betrayed, in chaos, hopeless, in self-destruction, in crisis, in plight, in self-destruction, shackled, deprived, existing in name only, being predatory or kleptocratic, being governed by tropical gangsters, or collapsed into anarchy and viciousness (Hope, 2002, 2008). These were but a few of the colorful negative images painted about a region that seemed to have lacked the capacity and willingness to come to grips with the need to develop, own, and implement a sustained policy and an institutional environment conducive to, among other things, good governance, entrenchment of democracy, peace and security, growth and development, and poverty reduction (Hope, 2002, 2008).

Of course, NEPAD has had its critics. Not unexpectedly, some African social movements and some academics criticized NEPAD as a system that predicated Africa's development on foreign aid; a system that encouraged African leaders to expect to be "paid" by rich donors to govern better. It was dubbed "the proverbial begging bowl" and, as such, was regarded as having the potential to increase Africa's dependency on aid, as opposed to using the continent's own resources effectively to maximize production. This notion seemed to undermine one of its (NEPAD's) own key objectives "to reduce aid dependency." Some even questioned the concept of a "partnership" between the industrialized world and a continent steeped in abject poverty, underdevelopment, poor governance, poor human rights record, lack of regional integration, and so on, and feared that this unequal partnership would create an uneven playing field that would advance the interests of richer nations (see, for example, Akokpari, 2004; Ngwane, 2002; Taylor, 2005).

Nonetheless, among others, Kingsley Y. Amoako, a former Executive Secretary of the United Nations Economic Commission for Africa (UNECA), who is more known and referred to as KY, also proclaimed that "NEPAD was the biggest attempt yet by African countries to unite behind a single development framework that aimed to reduce aid dependency, promote debt relief, and rebalance trade while acknowledging the need for political reform through accountability, transparency, and good governance" (Amoako, 2020, p. 8; see also, Banda, 2020; Hope, 2006; Maloka, 2004; Republic of South Africa, 2004). For full disclosure here, the UNECA, under the executive management of KY, played the lead policy and advisory roles to African Heads of State and/or Government in the crafting, development, and promotion of the NEPAD framework, and he (KY) was ably assisted in that regard by his senior policy and technical team that included this book's author as the focal point and the Chief Policy Advisor. For some historical perspective on the UNECA's role in the processes and negotiations that culminated in the formalization and approval of the NEPAD and the APRM (discussed below), and the historical antecedents that gave rise to these two initiatives, see, for example, Amoako (2020); Hope (2002, 2005); and UNECA (2011, 2021).

To accomplish the objectives and the outcomes of the NEPAD, African leaders also agreed, among other things, to subject their countries to peer review using a unique and innovative peer review process—the APRM that came into practice in 2003. The APRM framework was originally devised and crafted by the UNECA. It was created and intended for use to assess the performance of African countries in terms of their compliance with a number of agreed codes, standards, and commitments that underpin the good governance and sustainable development framework (Hope, 2005; UNECA, 2002). The primary purpose of the APRM is still to foster the adoption of policies, standards, and practices that lead to political stability, high economic growth, sustainable development, and accelerated integration through the sharing of experiences and the reinforcement of successful and best practice, including identifying deficiencies and assessing the needs for capacity building. This was to be accomplished by using the relevant indicators contained in the APRM to measure and determine the progress of peer-reviewed countries in meeting the goals of achieving good governance and sustainable development (for greater details, see Hope, 2005; UNECA, 2002). After a flying start, the APRM had started to lose much of its steam.

However, as of 2016, the APRM was given an expanded dual mandate of monitoring and evaluating both *Agenda 2063* and *Agenda 2030* with a "particular focus on SDG 16—effective, strong, and efficient institutions and peaceful societies which [interlinks] Aspirations three and four of *Agenda* 2063: Aspiration three—An Africa of Good Governance, Democracy, Respect for Human Rights, Justice and the Rule of Law and Aspiration four—A Peaceful and Secure Africa" (APRM Secretariat, 2021, p. 7). Commendably, the intention is to accelerate the attainment of the two Agendas by implementation, reporting, and realization of both agendas through the application of the Principles of Effective Governance for Sustainable

Development (PEGSD) developed by the United Nations Committee of Experts on Public Administration (UN-CEPA) and approved by the United Nations Economic and Social Council (UNECOSOC) in July 2018. The UN-CEPA is an expert body of the UN that studies and makes recommendations to improve governance and public administration structures and processes for development, particularly in relationship to A*genda 2030* and in support of the implementation and progress reviews of the SDGs (see UN-CEPA, n.d.).

There are 11 principles in the PEGSD couched within three categories and linked to 62 commonly used strategies for operationalizing responsive and effective governance. The categories and the associated principles are the following: (1) *Effectiveness*, associated with three principles—competence, sound policy-making, and collaboration; (2) *Accountability*, associated with three principles also—integrity, transparency, and independent oversight; and (3) *Inclusiveness*, associated with five principles—leaving no one behind, non-discrimination, participation, subsidiarity, and intergenerational equity (for greater details see, UN-CEPA, n.d.).

The expanded mandate of the APRM was provided with a further synergy boost in 2018 when the APRM was assigned the function as an additional early warning system for conflict prevention on the continent in harmony with the APSA and AGA. Also, in 2018, the AU Assembly decided that the APRM would collaborate with the AGA to regularly develop and present to member states a report—the Africa Governance Report (AGR)—on the state of governance in Africa, and to assist AU member states in their development of their own national governance reports (APRM Secretariat and AGA, 2021). The AGR was previously produced and published by the UNECA. Despite these attempts to reinvigorate, renew, and restore the APRM, and through the appropriate channels, other recommendations have been offered to further resuscitate the APRM and propel it to bridge some gaps and make even more important strides in support of sustainable governance, peace and development on the continent (see, for example, Semela, 2021; UNECA, 2021).

Undoubtedly, the NEPAD framework, and particularly the APRM, now need to be more positively promoted and implemented with greater intensity. As a comprehensive integrated sustainable development initiative for the economic and social revival of Africa, the NEPAD is still recognized, both on the continent and beyond, as offering the best opportunity through which steady progress toward sustainable development can be achieved. The NEPAD, at inception, did put Africa on the global agenda and galvanized international support for the region with both technical and financial assistance from the UN system, the Organization for Economic Cooperation and Development (OECD), the European Union (EU), the World Bank, the International Monetary Fund (IMF), the United States (US) Agency for International Development (USAID), the then Group of Eight (G8) countries, and others, for example. As of July 2018, the NEPAD was officially renamed the AUDA-NEPAD as the leading development agency of the AU. The mandate of the AUDA-NEPAD is to: (1) coordinate and execute priority regional and continental projects to promote regional integration towards the accelerated realization of the aspirations of *Agenda 2063* and the SDGs of *Agenda 2030*; and (2) strengthen the capacity of AU member states and regional bodies, advance knowledge-based advisory support, undertake the full range of resource mobilization, and serve as the continent's technical interface with all of Africa's development stakeholders and development partners (see AUDA-NEPAD, n.d.).

The APRM with its current focus on the aspirations and goals of *Agenda 2063* and *Agenda 2030*, respectively, and through the application of the PEGSD of the UN-CEPA, certainly provides the best practice opportunity to the implementation of fundamental strategies that can inform, create, build, and/or yield the governance outcomes that can sustain development in an environment where peace, security, and stability are not only present but prevail generally (see also, UN, 2022a). In addition, to national approaches for sustaining development and democratic reforms, the AUDA-NEPAD and the APRM must now be seen by African leaders and policymakers as strategies that can allow for development projects to be implemented and democratic reforms to become sufficiently entrenched to result in economic progress and good governance that can be satisfying enough to suppress and prevent political uprisings, political violence, and potential coups, as opposed to the non-occurrence of any of that and then reaching the stage where the APSA/PSC processes have to be activated.

Furthermore, and complementarily, African countries (particularly those that are members of the Commonwealth) should also adhere to the CACBs of good anti-corruption practice for national governments and public sector bodies that were published in 2021. The CACBs were developed in consultation with regional and international organizations (the AU, the IMF, the United Nations Office on Drugs and Crime [UNODC]), and Commonwealth law ministries, anti-corruption agencies (ACAs), as well as partner organizations (Stansbury et al., 2021). The CACBs are "recommended as good practice anti-corruption measures that are intended primarily to help governments and public sector organizations assess their anti-corruption laws, regulations, policies and procedures against international good practice, and consider implementing appropriate improvements" (Stansbury et al., 2021, p. 4). The CACBs "address corruption across key areas of the public and private sectors which are either important for combating corruption or are vulnerable to significant corruption" (Stansbury et al., 2021, p. 4).

From the point of view of this book's author, the CACBs represent the most comprehensive anti-corruption benchmark framework that has ever been put forward. There are 25 benchmarks that, among others, include the following: corruption offences, sanctions and remedies; the authority responsible for preventing corruption; investigation, prosecution, asset recovery and policing; the court system; parliament; regulatory authorities; regulation of financial institutions and the financial system; transparency of asset ownership; political lobbying, financing, spending and elections; public sector organizations; public officials; issuing of permits; procurement; anti-corruption training; reporting of corruption; and transparency to the public (see Stansbury et al., 2021 for greater details on the benchmarks and the principles underlying them).

As an important informational note here, as of July 2022, the Commonwealth is comprised of 56 independent countries located in Africa, Asia, the Americas,

Europe, and the Pacific. The majority of the countries (more than one-third and numbering 21) are located in Africa.

2.4 Concluding Reflections

Africa is at a crossroads and the continent is slowly moonwalking its way out of the range of credible and plausible solutions to its problems related to rampant corruption, lack of sustainable development, and inaction to create an environment of peace and security. Lest it be misunderstood, it must be made clear that there are indeed some African states where the governance and development indicators consistently show good performance. Simard and Viseth (2022, p. 47) have demonstrated, for example, that "Botswana, Rwanda, and Seychelles have established a relatively sound foundation for governance through strong political will, commitment, and societal consensus." These nations are stable states that have emerged as the top governance performers in sub-Saharan Africa, while also achieving relatively strong economic growth (Simard & Viseth, 2022). However, for most of the other states a considerable sea change is required in both leadership thinking and policies, as this book discusses, to accomplish some tolerable sense of reductions in corruption, accelerated development progress, and an environment of peace and security.

Clearly, the lack of good governance in many African countries has severely affected the ability of their respective governments to intervene, particularly for the maintenance of peace and security, as well as for the promotion of sustainable development (see also Hope, 2017; Matlosa, 2017; Mbaku, 2020; Munyai, 2020). Corruption can lead to dissatisfaction and distrust in leaders, public institutions, and the rule of law, and can eventually spiral into anger and unrest. According to Lewis (2021), corruption produces adverse outcomes that generate and mobilize further grievances. Therefore, "for many Africans, corruption is not simply abstract government dysfunction; it is an intrusive and often coercive presence in their lives" (Lewis, 2021, p. 230). Consequently, corruption, especially elite corruption, motivates contention by generating grievances about poverty and inequality, service delivery, and sustainable development, and this has been empirically found to positively correlate with an increase in general anti-government contention, protests, and conflict (Lewis, 2021).

This, unfortunately, continues to mean, as further lamented by Mbaku (2020, p. 23) that "too many countries have not yet achieved the type of reforms that can prevent dictatorship, corruption, and economic decline." Such a state of affairs breeds disenchantment and may eventually lead to political violence, including potential or actual coups, as we have seen in recent times in West Africa. Indeed, as reported by Sanni (2022, p. 1), even the Chairperson of Nigeria's Independent Corrupt Practices and other Related Offences Commission (ICPC), Professor Bolaji Owasanoye, in his address to the fifth General Assembly of the Network of National Anti-Corruption Institutions of West Africa (NACIWA) in March 2022,

2.4 Concluding Reflections

acknowledged that "the menace of corruption is fueling several military takeovers of existing democratic governments in many African countries." Also, in a well-researched report on the current Islamic state-linked insurgency in Cabo Delgado, Mozambique, it was similarly determined that the factors which helped to create the insurgency included rampant corruption, elite capture of resources, a breakdown in governance and delivery of government services, socio-economic exclusion, organized crime, and ethnic and religious divides (see Stanyard et al., 2022). And, in the South African government's current National Anti-Corruption Strategy (NACS), among other things, it was also recognized that "corruption, having permeated key institutions in both the public and private sector, poses a threat to national security, undermines the rule of law and institutions vital to ensuring the centrality of the state as a protector and promoter of the rights of its citizens" (Republic of South Africa, 2020, p. 8). Similarly, in Sierra Leone's current NACS, it states that one of the three outcomes in the country's overarching vision to combat corruption, is "to reduce the threat to our national security, by promoting zero tolerance for corruption" (Sierra Leone Anti-Corruption Commission [SLACC, 2019, p. 33).

Recent work by Stefan Dercon has also laid out a persuasive argument, based partially on his own field experience, about why some countries win and others lose in development outcomes (Dercon, 2022). Using several African nations, among others, as examples, his argument advocates that development success rests on the foundation of a bargain among elites, who commit to gambling on national development rather than simply protecting their own interests, and in that development bargain, the role, importance, and necessity of providing the basis for peace and stability are also recognized. In fact, in that regard, Dercon (2022, p. 46) has been categorical that "peace and stability are also preconditions for development. They definitely mattered for those countries that have taken off in recent decades or have failed to do so." As an example, "ending violence and distributing the gains from economic assets during peacetime tend to be intrinsically linked" (Dercon, 2022, p. 46). The elites—economic and political—are those with power and influence across society and are generally comprised of the political establishment, business leaders, and the military officials, but may often also include union leaders, journalists, and prominent academics as well as public intellectuals (Dercon, 2022).

Others, such as Omeje (2021), for example, in his excellent book on dysfunctional capitalism in Africa, have similarly concurred with the peace and development nexus thesis with the observation that violent conflicts do not only hurt positive peace in contemporary Africa, but it gives pause to development actors, such as investors and entrepreneurs, and impedes the drivers of markets and other economic activities. The fundamental, and now even more obvious, truth is that there must be a peaceful environment for development to first take hold and then be sustained. Similarly, Erdogan and Acaravci (2022), in their empirical study of 17 sub-Saharan Africa countries, and based on data covering 1990–2016, found that democracy and peace have a positive and statistically significant effect on economic development. Therefore, an increase in the peace and democracy levels will increase the economic development levels in the sub-Saharan Africa countries (see also UN, 2022b). This is an important finding and narrative given the imperative, and as also observed by

Koper (2018), that most Africans, although frequently disappointed with the outcome, maintain confidence in multiparty democracy as the best political system for securing a better future. In other words, "the ideal of democracy, good governance, or at least less corruption exert, just like in other parts of the world, a real attraction for the population in Africa" (Koper, 2018, p. 202).

The bottom line here is that corruption undermines development efforts and the ability of governments to protect people as well as erodes public trust, provoking more and much harder to control security threats. On the other hand, conflict creates opportunities for corruption and subverts the efforts of governments to control or reduce it. In that regard, recent data show that Africa is now less safe and less secure than it was 10 years ago, hampering continental progress toward sustainable development and peace and stability. Almost 70% of Africa's population live in a country where the security and rule of law environment was worse in 2021 than in 2012, mostly driven by a worsening security situation due largely to increased armed conflicts and violence against civilians (MIF, 2023b). Decades of governance progress have now been put at risk by resurgent conflict and democratic backsliding. It is therefore concurred with the MIF (2023b, p. 9) that "with 2023 being the halfway point to meeting the global SDGs, action is urgently needed to address the democratic backsliding and growing insecurity [on the continent]."

Other empirical evidence of this democratic backsliding, attributed to corruption and insecurity, can also be found in the democracy index that is compiled by The Economist Intelligence Unit (EIU). The democracy index is based on a scoring scale of 0–10 which translates into a classification of four regime types: (1) Full democracy (score > 8); (2) Flawed democracy (score > 6 but ≤ 8); (3) Hybrid regime (score > 4 but ≤ 6); and (4) Authoritarian regime (score ≤ 4) (for greater details on these classifications see EIU, 2023). The average score for sub-Saharan Africa has scarcely changed, rising slightly from 4.12 in 2021 to 4.14 in 2022, with the region failing to reverse a decline in its average score since its peak of 4.38 in 2015, and resulting in the region being the second-lowest ranked in the world, above only the Middle East and North Africa, which has an average score of 3.34 (EIU, 2023). Of the 44 African nations for which data are available, 23 were classified as authoritarian regimes, 14 as hybrid regimes, and six as flawed democracies (EIU, 2023). Of the top five scoring African countries, four were classified as somewhat flawed democracies (Botswana, Cabo Verde, Republic of South Africa, and Tunisia), and only one (Mauritius) was deemed as a full democracy (see EIU, 2023).

References

Acemoglu, D., & Robinson, J. A. (2017). The economic impact of colonialism. In S. Michalopoulos & E. Papaioannou (Eds.), *The long economic and political shadow of history–Volume I: A global view* (pp. 81–87). Centre for Economic Policy Research Press.

Adekoya, R. (2022, September 13). The truth about Elizabeth's empire: Colonialism isn't to blame for all Africa's ills. *The Post-UnHerd*. Retrieved from https://unherd.com/2022/09/we-need-to-talk-about-empire/

References

Adetuyi, A. (2021). Military coup and its effect on the democratization process in Mali and in the region. [IPSS Policy Brief]. Institute for Peace and Security Studies, Addis Ababa University.

AfDB. (2022). *Security, investment and development: A diagnostic assessment*. Retrieved from https://www.afdb.org/en/documents/security-investment-and-development-diagnostic-assessment

Aina, F., & Nyei, I. A. (2022a, March 18). Why Africa should expect more coups, *The Africa Report*. Retrieved from https://www.theafricareport.com/185024/why-africa-should-expect-more-coups/

Aina, F., & Nyei, I. A. (2022b, February 11). Why have civilians welcomed the recent coups in West Africa? Citizens in Mali, Burkina Faso and Guinea are punishing corrupt political elites who have long ruled their countries by ascribing legitimacy to military juntas. *Aljazeera Opinions*. Retrieved from https://www.aljazeera.com/opinions/2022/2/11/why-have-civilians-welcomed-the-recent-coups-in-west-africa

Akinlo, A. E., & Okunlola, C. O. (2022). The effect of economic freedom on quality of life: Exploring the role of political risk factors in Africa. *Journal of Interdisciplinary Economics*. [Advance online publication]. https://doi.org/10.1177/02601079221121894

Akokpari, J. (2004). The AU, NEPAD and the promotion of good governance in Africa. *Nordic Journal of African Studies, 13*(3), 243–263.

Amoako, K. Y. (2020). *Know the beginning well: An inside journey through five decades of African development*. Africa World Press.

Ani, N. C. (2021). Coup or not coup: The African union and the dilemma of "popular uprisings" in Africa. *Democracy and Security, 17*(3), 257–277. https://doi.org/10.1080/17419166.2021.1899915

APRM Secretariat. (2021). *APRM baseline survey: Implementation of the UN-CEPA principles of effective governance for sustainable development in Africa*. APRM Secretariat.

APRM Secretariat, & AGA. (2021). *The Africa governance report 2021: Africa's governance futures for the Africa we want*. APRM Secretariat.

Apuuli, K. P. (2018). The AU's peace and security architecture: The African standby force. In T. Karbo & T. Murithi (Eds.), *The African union: Autocracy, diplomacy and peacebuilding in Africa* (pp. 172–208). I. B. Tauris & Co. Ltd.

AU. (n.d.-a). African peace and security architecture. Retrieved from https://www.peaceau.org/uploads/african-peace-and-security-architecture-apsa-final.pdf

AU. (n.d.-b). Peace fund. Retrieved from https://au.int/en/aureforms/peacefund

AU. (2002). *Protocol relating to the establishment of the peace and security council of the African Union*. Retrieved from https://au.int/en/treaties/protocol-relating-establishment-peace-and-security-council-african-union

AU. (2018a). The continental early warning system. Retrieved from https://www.peaceau.org/en/article/the-continental-early-warning-system

AU. (2018b). Panel of the wise. Retrieved from https://www.peaceau.org/en/article/panel-of-the-wise

AU. (2019). The African standby force. Retrieved from https://www.peaceau.org/en/page/82-african-standby-force-asf-amani-africa-1

AU. (2022a). *Second continental report on the implementation of agenda 2063*. AUDA–NEPAD.

AU. (2022b, February 6). Presentation of the report of the state of peace and security on the continent by the Commissioner for Political Affairs Peace and Security (CPAPS) Amb. Bankole Adeoye to the 35th ordinary session of the AU assembly, Addis Ababa. Retrieved from https://www.peaceau.org/uploads/cpaps-statemtment-on-spesar.pdf

AUDA–NEPAD. (n.d.). About us. Retrieved from https://www.nepad.org/microsite/who-we-are-0

Badmus, I. A. (2015). *The African Union's role in peacekeeping: Building on lessons learned from security operations*. Palgrave Macmillan/Springer.

Balogun, O. A. (2022). Decolonizing power: A critique of majoritarian democracy in Africa. *South African Journal of Philosophy, 41*(2), 195–204. https://doi.org/10.1080/02580136.2022.2073068

Banda, P. C. (2020). NEPAD: A brief history and its significance for Africa. Retrieved from https://diplomatist.com/2020/11/30/nepad-a-brief-history-and-its-significance-for-africa/

Carbone, G., & Pellegata, A. (2020). *Political leadership in Africa: Leaders and development south of the Sahara*. Cambridge University Press.

Chayes, S. (2016). *Corruption: Violent extremism, kleptocracy, and the dangers of failing governance. [Testimony before the senate foreign relations committee]*. Carnegie Endowment for International Peace.

Cheeseman, N., Collord, M., & Reyntjens, F. (2018). War and democracy: The legacy of conflict in East Africa. *Journal of Modern African Studies, 56*(1), 31–61. https://doi.org/10.1017/S0022278X17000623

Chisadza, C. (2020). Leaders and tenures in sub-Saharan Africa. *South African Journal of Economics, 88*(3), 323–340. https://doi.org/10.1111/saje.12255

Cook, C., & Siegle, J. (2021). Circumvention of term limits weakens governance in Africa. [Infographic]. Retrieved from https://africacenter.org/spotlight/circumvention-of-term-limits-weakens-governance-in-africa/

DCAF. (2015). Security sector governance. [SSR Backgrounder Series]. DCAF.

de Coning, C., Yaw Tchie, A. E., & Grand, A. O. (2022). Ad-hoc security initiatives, an African response to insecurity. *African Security Review, 31*(4), 383–398. https://doi.org/10.1080/10246029.2022.2134810

Degila, D. E., & Amegan, C. K. (2019). The African peace and security architecture: An African response to regional peace and security challenges. In A. Kulnazarova & V. Popovski (Eds.), *The Palgrave handbook of global approaches to peace* (pp. 393–409). Palgrave Macmillan/Springer Nature.

Dercon, S. (2022). *Gambling on development: Why some countries win and others lose*. Hurst Publishers.

Derpanopoulos, G., Frantz, E., Geddes, B., & Wright, J. (2016). Are coups good for democracy? *Research & Politics, 3*(1), 1–7. https://doi.org/10.1177/2F2053168016630837

Dursun-Özkanca, O. (2021). *The nexus between security sector governance/reform and sustainable development Goal-16: An examination of conceptual linkages and policy recommendations*. Ubiquity Press.

Duzor, M., & Williamson, B. (2022). By the numbers: Coups in Africa. Retrieved from https://projects.voanews.com/african-coups/

EIU. (2023). *Democracy index 2022*. Retrieved from https://www.eiu.com/n/campaigns/democracy-index-2022/

Elischer, S., & Lawrance, B. N. (2022). Reassessing Africa's new post-coup landscape. *African Studies Review, 65*(1), 1–7. https://doi.org/10.1017/asr.2022.33

Elkins, C. (2022). *Legacy of violence: A history of the British empire*. Alfred A. Knopf.

Emerson, S., & Solomon, H. (2018). *African security in the twenty-first century: Challenges and opportunities*. Manchester University Press.

Engels, B. (2022). Transition now? Another *coup d'état* in Burkina Faso. *Review of African Political Economy, 49*(172), 315–326. https://doi.org/10.1080/03056244.2022.2075127

Erdogan, S., & Acaravci, A. (2022). On the nexus between institutions and economic development: An empirical analysis for sub-Saharan African countries. *The European Journal of Development Research, 34*(4), 1857–1892. https://doi.org/10.1057/s41287-021-00445-6

Fang, X., Kothari, S., McLoughlin, C., & Yenice, M. (2020). The economic consequences of conflict in sub-Saharan Africa. [IMF Working Paper WP/20/221]. IMF.

Fofack, H. (2022). Dawn of a second cold war and the "scramble for Africa": adopting a united approach to security promotion is crucial if the continent is to achieve its economic aims. [Africa Growth Initiative at Brookings]. Retrieved from https://www.brookings.edu/wp-content/uploads/2022/05/Dawn-of-a-Second-Cold-War.pdf

Fomunyoh, C. (2020, September 30). Facing democratic backsliding in Africa & reversing the trend. [Presented at democratic backsliding in sub-Saharan Africa, house foreign affairs committee, subcommittee on Africa, Global Health, global human rights, and international organizations]. Retrieved from https://www.ndi.org/publications/christopher-fomunyoh-facing-democratic-backsliding-africa-reversing-trend

Ford, N., & Versi, A. (2022, April 27). What is behind the spate of coups in West Africa? *New African*. https://newafricanmagazine.com/28086/

References

Gillanders, R., & van der Werff, L. (2022). Corruption experiences and attitudes to political, interpersonal, and domestic violence. *Governance, 35*(1), 167–185. https://doi.org/10.1111/gove.12570

Gyimah-Boadi, E. (2021). *Democratic backsliding in West Africa: nature, causes, remedies.* Retrieved from https://www.kofiannanfoundation.org/app/uploads/2021/11/Democratic-backsliding-in-West-Africa-Nature-causes-remedies-Nov-2021.pdf

Gyimah-Boadi, E. (2022, July 11). West Africa's authoritarian turn: Democratic backsliding, youth resistance, and the case for American help, *Foreign Affairs.* https://www.foreignaffairs.com/articles/west-africa/2022-07-11/west-africas-authoritarian-turn

Hope, K. R. (2002). From crisis to renewal: Towards a successful implementation of the new Partnership for Africa's development. *African Affairs, 101*(404), 387–402. https://doi.org/10.1093/afraf/101.404.387

Hope, K. R. (2005). Toward good governance and sustainable development: The African peer review mechanism. *Governance, 18*(2), 283–311. https://doi.org/10.1111/j.1468-0491.2005.00276.x

Hope, K. R. (2006). Prospects and challenges for the new partnership for Africa's development: Addressing capacity deficits. *Journal of Contemporary African Studies, 24*(2), 203–228. https://doi.org/10.1080/02589000600769967

Hope, K. R. (2008). *Poverty, livelihoods and governance in Africa: Fulfilling the development promise.* Palgrave Macmillan/Springer Nature.

Hope, K. R. (2016). An analytical perspective on police corruption and police reforms in developing societies. In K. R. Hope (Ed.), *Police corruption and police reforms in developing societies* (pp. 3–31). CRC Press/Taylor and Francis.

Hope, K. R. (2017). *Corruption and governance in Africa: Swaziland [Eswatini], Kenya, Nigeria.* Palgrave Macmillan/Springer Nature.

Hope, K. R. (2019). *Realizing SDG 16 interlinkages: A background paper.* [Commissioned by the United Nations Development Program (UNDP) Oslo Governance Centre].

Hopp-Nishanka, U. (2021). Corruption and conflict: Breaking the vicious circle from a peacebuilding perspective. [Briefing]. Retrieved from https://www.frient.de/en/publikationen/corruption-and-conflict

Hunter, L. Y., Rutland, J., & King, Z. (2020). Leaving the barracks: Military coups in developing democracies. *Politics & Policy, 48*(6), 1062–1103. https://doi.org/10.1111/polp.12383

IEP. (2014). *Measuring goal 16: Identifying priority indicators based on key statistical and normative criteria.* IEP.

IEP. (2022). *Positive peace report 2022: Analyzing the factors that build, predict and sustain peace.* IEP.

IMF. (2019). *Regional economic outlook: Sub-Saharan Africa: Recovery amid elevated uncertainty.* IMF.

IMF. (2022). *Regional economic outlook: Sub-Saharan Africa: A new shock and little room to maneuver.* IMF.

Ioanes, E. (2022). How to understand the recent coups in Africa. Retrieved from https://www.vox.com/2022/2/5/22919160/coup-guinea-bissau-africa-burkina-faso-sudan-why

Iroanya, R. O. (2018). Coups and countercoups in Africa. In S. O. Oloruntoba & T. Falola (Eds.), *The Palgrave handbook of African politics, governance and development* (pp. 243–258). Palgrave Macmillan/Springer Nature.

Joly, J., Steadman, M., Stevens, F., Tisseron, A., & Zuliani, C. (2020). *The missing element: Addressing corruption through security sector reform in West Africa.* Transparency International UK.

Kakumba, R. M. (2021). Gone but not forgotten: Most Ugandans want presidential term and age limits reinstated. [Afrobarometer dispatch no. 464]. Retrieved from https://www.afrobarometer.org/publication/ad464-gone-not-forgotten-most-ugandans-want-presidential-term-and-age-limits-reinstated/

Kfir, I. (2022). Sub-Saharan Africa at a crossroad. Expert contribution. In *Global terrorism index 2022: Measuring the impact of terrorism* (pp. 79–82). IEP.

Klobucista, C. (2021, June 30). Africa's "leaders for life." [Council on Foreign Relations backgrounder]. Retrieved from https://www.cfr.org/backgrounder/africas-leaders-life

Koper, M. (2018). *Does democracy help Africa? An inquiry into multiparty democracy, political settlement, and economic development in Africa*. African Studies Center, Leiden University.

Kuol, L., & Amegboh, J. (2021). Rethinking national security strategies in Africa. *International Relations and Diplomacy, 9*(1), 1–17. https://doi.org/10.17265/2328-2134/2021.01.001

Kuwali, D. (2022a). The African union agenda for sustainable peace and security. In D. Kuwali (Ed.), *The Palgrave handbook of sustainable peace and security in Africa* (pp. 47–77). Palgrave Macmillan/Springer Nature.

Kuwali, D. (2022b). Commend and condemn: Combating corruption in Africa. In D. Kuwali (Ed.), *The Palgrave handbook of sustainable peace and security in Africa* (pp. 581–595). Palgrave Macmillan/Springer Nature.

Lewis, J. S. (2021). Corruption perceptions and contentious politics in Africa: How different types of corruption have shaped Africa's third wave of protest. *Political Studies Review, 19*(2), 227–244. https://doi.org/10.1177/1478929920903657

Lumina, C. (2022). Financing the African peace and security agenda. In D. Kuwali (Ed.), *The palgrave handbook of sustainable peace and security in Africa* (pp. 561–580). Palgrave Macmillan/Springer Nature.

Majiga, P. B. (2022). The proliferation of popular protests and coups d'états in Africa. In D. Kuwali (Ed.), *The Palgrave handbook of sustainable peace and security in Africa* (pp. 181–195). Palgrave Macmillan/Springer Nature.

Maloka, E. (2004). NEPAD and its critics. *Africa Insight, 34*(4), 3–11. https://hdl.handle.net/10520/EJC17409

Matlosa, K. (2017). The state of democratization in southern Africa: Blocked transitions, reversals, stagnation, progress and prospects. *Politikon, 44*(1), 5–26. https://doi.org/10.1080/02589346.2017.1278640

Mbaku, J. M. (2020). Good and inclusive governance is imperative for Africa's future. In *Foresight Africa: Top priorities for the continent 2020-2030* (pp. 23–27). Retrieved from https://www.brookings.edu/research/good-and-inclusive-governance-is-imperative-for-africas-future/

Meyersson, E. (2016). Political man on horseback: Coups and development. [SITE Research]. Stockholm Institute for Transition Economics.

MIF. (2023a). *2022 Ibrahim index of African governance: Index report*. MIF.

MIF. (2023b). *2022 Ibrahim index of African governance: Key findings*. MIF.

Momodu, J. A., & Owonikoko, S. B. (2021). Security challenges and African peace and security architecture. In E. T. Aniche, I. M. Alumona, & I. Moyo (Eds.), *Regionalism, security and development in Africa* (pp. 145–157). Routledge/Taylor and Francis.

Munyai, A. (2020). *Overcoming the corruption conundrum in Africa: A socio-legal perspective*. Cambridge Scholars Publishing.

Nagar, D. (2018). Pillars of Africa's peace and security architecture: The African standby force. In T. Karbo & K. Virk (Eds.), *The Palgrave handbook of peacebuilding in Africa* (pp. 65–79). Palgrave Macmillan/Springer Nature.

Ndebele, L. (2022, October 24). Decline of democracy: African leaders who have grabbed power through coups, *News24*. Retrieved from https://www.news24.com/news24/africa/news/decline-of-democracy-african-leaders-who-have-grabbed-power-through-coups-20221024

Ngandu, K. Y. (2017). The panel of the wise: Its role in preventing violent conflicts in Africa. *UN Chronicle, 54*(3), 16–20. https://doi.org/10.18356/85fd280c-en

Ngwane, T. (2002, February 2). Should African social movements be part of the new Partnership for Africa's development (NEPAD)? [Notes from a speech given to the African social Forum's African seminar at the world social forum, Porto Alegre, Brazil]. Retrieved from https://halifaxinitiative.org/content/african-ngos-critique-nepad

Ngwang, R. (2021, 2 July). A tug of war over presidential term limits in Africa: A wake-up call for the African union, *On Policy Magazine*. Retrieved from https://onpolicy.org/a-tug-of-war-over-presidential-term-limits-in-africa-a-wake-up-call-for-the-african-union/

References

Ojakorotu, V., & Onwughalu, V. C. (2023). The dialectics of insecurity and development in Africa: The role of development partners. *African Security Review, 32*(1), 115–129. https://doi.org/10.1080/10246029.2022.2141580

Omeje, K. (2021). *The failure and feasibility of capitalism in Africa*. Palgrave Macmillan/Springer Nature.

Powell, J., Reynolds, A., & Chacha, M. (2022). A new coup era for Africa? Retrieved from https://www.accord.org.za/conflict-trends/a-new-coup-era-for-africa/

Pyman, M., Bock, T., Vidal de la Blache, E., Mustafa, S., & Zaum, D. (2014). *Corruption as a threat to stability and peace*. Transparency International Germany.

Rakner, L. (2018). Breaking bad: Understanding backlash against democracy in Africa. [CMI insight 3]. Retrieved from https://www.cmi.no/publications/6518-breaking-bad-understanding-backlash-against

Renzo, M. (2019). Why colonialism is wrong. *Current Legal Problems, 72*(1), 347–373. https://doi.org/10.1093/clp/cuz011

Republic of South Africa. (2004). NEPAD: historical overview. Retrieved from http://www.dirco.gov.za/au.nepad/historical_overview.htm

Republic of South Africa. (2020). *National Anti-Corruption Strategy: 2020–2030*. Department of Planning, Monitoring and Evaluation, Republic of South Africa.

Robinson, N. J. (2017, September 14). A quick reminder of why colonialism was bad, *Current Affairs*. Retrieved from https://www.currentaffairs.org/2017/09/a-quick-reminder-of-why-colonialism-was-bad

Sanni, K. (2022, March 22), How corruption fuels coup d'état in African countries–ICPC Chairperson Owasanoye, *Premium Times*. Retrieved from https://www.premiumtimesng.com/news/top-news/518857-how-corruption-fuels-coup-detat-in-african-countries-icpc-chairperson-owasanoye.html

Semela, K. (2021). Assessing the implications of the APRM's expanded mandate. [Occasional paper 328, Institute for Security Studies]. Retrieved from https://saiia.org.za/research/assessing-the-implications-of-the-aprms-expanded-mandate/

Siegle, J., & Cook, C. (2021). Presidential term limits key to democratic progress and security in Africa. *Orbis, 65*(3), 467–482. https://doi.org/10.1016/j.orbis.2021.06.009

Signé, L., & Gurib-Fakim, A. (2019, January 25). Africa is an opportunity for the world: Overlooked progress in governance and human development. [Brookings Africa in Focus]. Retrieved from https://www.brookings.edu/blog/africa-in-focus/2019/01/25/africa-is-an-opportunity-for-the-world-overlooked-progress-in-governance-and-human-development/

Simard, D., & Viseth, A. (2022). Three strong governance performers in sub-Saharan Africa: Achievements and way forward. In M. Newiak, A. Segura-Ubiergo, & A. A. Wane (Eds.), *Good governance in sub-Saharan Africa: Opportunities and lessons* (pp. 47–73). IMF.

SLACC. (2019). *Sierra Leone National Anti-Corruption Strategy (2019–2023): A public-private initiative against corruption*. SLACC.

Stansbury, C., Stansbury, N., Alder, C., & Moorhead, M. (2021). *Commonwealth anti-corruption benchmarks*. Commonwealth Secretariat.

Stanyard, J., Nelson, A., Ardé, G., & Rademeyer, J. (2022). *Insurgency, illicit markets and corruption: The Cabo Delgado conflict and its regional implications*. Global Initiative Against Transnational Organized Crime.

Stocker, S., & Quirk, P. (2022, July 8). The false tradeoff: revisiting the democracy vs security paradigm in Africa. [Democracy in Africa Blog]. Retrieved from http://democracyinafrica.org/the-false-tradeoff-revisiting-the-democracy-vs-security-paradigm-in-africa/

Taylor, I. (2005). *NEPAD: Toward Africa's development or another false start*. Lynne Rienner Publishers.

The Economist. (2021, October 25). As Sudan's government wobbles, coups are making a comeback. https://www.economist.com/graphic-detail/2021/10/25/as-sudans-government-wobbles-coups-are-making-a-comeback

The White House. (2022). *National security strategy*. The White House.

TI. (2021). *Addressing corruption as a driver of democratic decline*. TI.

UN. (2015). *Transforming our world: The 2030 agenda for sustainable development*. UN.

UN. (2022a). *Implementation of the recommendations contained in the report of the secretary-general on the causes of conflict and the promotion of durable peace and sustainable development in Africa*. UN.

UN. (2022b). *Promotion of durable peace and sustainable development in Africa: Report of the secretary-general*. UN.

UN-CEPA. (n.d.). *Principles of effective governance for sustainable development*. Retrieved from https://publicadministration.un.org/en/Intergovernmental-Support/CEPA/Principles-of-Effective-Governance

UNECA. (2002). The African peer review mechanism: Process and procedures. *African Security Review, 11*(4), 6–13. https://doi.org/10.1080/10246029.2002.9628140

UNECA. (2011). *Capturing the 21st century: African peer review (APRM) best practices and lessons learned*. UNECA.

UNECA. (2021). *Rethinking the idea and original vision of the African peer review mechanism (APRM)*. UNECA.

Van Woudenberg, A. (2002). Africa at the crossroads: Time to deliver. [Oxfam briefing paper]. Retrieved from https://oxfamilibrary.openrepository.com/bitstream/handle/10546/114078/bp19-africa-crossroads-010302-en.pdf?sequence=1&isAllowed=y

Veri, F., & Sass, J. (2022). The domestic democratic peace: How democracy constrains political violence. *International Political Science Review*. [Advance online publication]. https://doi.org/10.1177/2F01925121221092391.

Vlavonou, G. (2019). The APSA and (complex) international security regime theory: A critique. *African Security, 12*(1), 87–110. https://doi.org/10.1080/19392206.2019.1587143

Warah, R. (2022). African military coups on the rise amidst increased economic hardship and insecurity. Retrieved from https://www.one.org/africa/blog/african-military-coups-increase/

Wiebusch, M. (2016). The role of regional organizations in the protection of constitutionalism. [IIDEA Discussion Paper 17]. IIDEA.

Wiebusch, M., & Murray, C. (2019). Presidential term limits and the African union. *Journal of African Law, 63*(S1), 131–160. https://doi.org/10.1017/S0021855319000056

Witt, A. (2020). *Undoing coups: The African union and post-coup intervention in Madagascar*. Zed Books.

Ypi, L. (2013). What's wrong with colonialism. *Philosophy & Public Affairs, 41*(2), 158–191. https://doi.org/10.1111/papa.12014

Zamfir, I. (2021). State of democracy in sub-Saharan Africa: Democratic progress at risk. [European Parliament Research Service]. Retrieved from https://www.europarl.europa.eu/RegData/etudes/BRIE/2021/690647/EPRS_BRI(2021)690647_EN.pdf

Zeigler, S. M. (2021). Are military coups back in style in Africa? Retrieved from https://www.rand.org/blog/2021/12/are-military-coups-back-in-style-in-africa.html

Chapter 3
Channels of Corruption in Africa: An Analytical Review and Assessment of Trends in Economic and Financial Crimes

The economic and financial crimes of embezzlement and theft, bribes and kickbacks, money laundering and illicit financial flows, and through state capture, are all channels of corruption that are prevalent in Africa with significant negative effects on the continent's sustainable development outcomes. This chapter identifies and analytically reviews and assesses the trends of these principal economic and financial crimes as channels of corruption that impact the development process and economic progress in Africa. It therefore provides an analysis of the nature and extent of the trends in economic and financial crimes, as channels of corruption in Africa, and the resultant negative impact on sustainable development in the region.

3.1 Introduction

Corruption is a pervasive problem in African countries where bad governance tends to proliferate and institutions are weak. As the research of Kleinfeld (2019, p. 117) has found, and most applicable to Africa, "while often compared to cancer, corruption is much more like an epidemic," as "it is infectious," and "this 'culture of corruption' is real." However, "it is not born from any national, religious, or ethnic predilection" since "it is caused by a particular configuration of power in which those who follow the rules look like fools, while success comes through connections and taking what you can get when you are in a position to get it." Among, other things, this systemic corruption drains economic and financial resources away from expenditures on, and access to, public goods and services that are necessary and required for development to be sustainable. According to Songwe (2018) as well as UN (2019), and based on a recycled estimate attributed to the AU, about US$148 billion was being drained out of the continent through various corrupt activities representing about 25% of Africa's average GDP (see also Blunt, 2002; Kimenyi &

Mbaku, 2011; Olaniyan, 2004; Vanguard, 2018). The staff economists at the AfDB also estimate that corruption costs Africa up to 50% in lost tax revenues and over US$30 billion in aid annually (AfDB., 2013).

In Madagascar, it is estimated that as much as 40% of the country's budget is lost to corruption (Pring, 2015). In Malawi, there is an estimate of 13%–17% of GDP being lost to corruption and tax fraud (Yikona et al., 2011). In Tanzania, according to recent research, corruption is annually responsible for 20% of national budget leakage in the country and when combined with tax revenue losses from illicit financial flows (IFFs), approximately US$1.8 billion is lost each year from corrupt activities in the country (see Curtis & Ngowi, 2017). In Kenya, 8% of total government revenue, equivalent to US$0.9 billion, is lost annually to trade mis-invoicing as an IFF activity, while for Nigeria it is 4% of total government revenue equivalent to US$2.2 billion that is similarly lost (Global Financial Integrity [GFI], 2018a, 2018b). In South Africa, although the Minister of Economic Development, has claimed that corruption in the public sector annually costs the country approximately US$2 billion and the loss of creation of 76,000 jobs (see BusinessTech, 2017; Leoka, 2017), it was credibly estimated that the country loses US$7.4 billion just from trade mis-invoicing alone as an IFF activity (see GFI, 2018c). More recently, the OECD (2022) found that between US$3.5 and US$5 billion in IFFs are leaving South Africa each year, representing approximately 1%–1.5% of the country's GDP.

Consequently, there is significant economic/financial leakage from corruption as further discussed below. Yikona et al. (2011, p. 12), in their study of Malawi and Namibia, for example, observed that:

> Corruption brings about a diversion ("leakages") of financial resources from the national budget to private spending purposes, and even more so in the case of the embezzlement of state funds. In general, these private expenses or expenditures have much lower "multiplier effects" than expenditures on, for example, agricultural fertilizers, education, health, and infrastructure. Money derived from crime (including corruption) will mostly be spent on direct consumption (small volumes) or invested in valuable assets (in the case of large volumes) such as art, gold and diamonds, luxury vehicles, real estate, and so forth.

Corruption therefore presents a major obstacle to achieving and sustaining development in Africa. The magnitude of corruption, through economic and financial crimes across the continent, hampers economic growth and increases poverty, depriving the most marginalized groups of equitable access to vital services such as healthcare, education, and water and sanitation, for example (TI, 2017). In fact, where corruption is persistent, there will be no sustainable development. Indeed, there is now a substantial body of international evidence which suggests that corruption threatens the health, prosperity and happiness of many residents of the world and especially those in the developing world which includes all African countries.

Accordingly, there is need to understand the trends and extent of economic and financial crimes as the channels through which corruption is primarily perpetrated in Africa with the resultant negative effects on the development process and development progress. In that regard, by way of definition, it is recognized that the terms economic crime and financial crime tend to be used interchangeably. They refer to illegal acts committed by an individual or a group of individuals to obtain an economic, financial or professional advantage. These crimes are perpetrated primarily through theft, embezzlement, any form of fraud, bribes and kickbacks, forgery, state capture, counterfeiting, money laundering and IFFs, drug trafficking, human trafficking and child labor exploitation, illegal mining, foreign exchange malpractices, theft of intellectual property and piracy, illegal arms dealing, and tax evasion (see, for example, Achim & Borlea, 2020; Economic and Financial Crimes Commission [EFCC], 2021; UN, 2005). This chapter identifies, examines, and analytically reviews and assesses the trends of these economic and financial crimes.

3.2 Corruption Channels in Africa: Trends and Extent of Economic and Financial Crimes

Within the various categorizations and types of corruption, the principal channels of corruption in Africa tend to be the economic and financial crimes which cover four specific areas as discussed below.

3.2.1 Embezzlement and Theft

First, corruption through kleptocratic behavior considerably reduces the resources available for public investment in sustainable development projects. Embezzlement—which refers to the crime of misappropriating, for personal use, property, securities, and resources belonging to an institution/organization and/or entrusted to a person's care—has a particularly significant effect. When embezzlement occurs in public institutions in Africa, and other developing countries as well, it siphons off already scarce funds that could otherwise be used for planning and implementing sustainable development projects.

The use of Public Expenditure Tracking Surveys (PETS) and Quantitative Service Delivery Surveys (QSDS) to track the flow of resources through the government bureaucracy, have found, for example, that the rate of leakage of funds through embezzlement and theft to be between 30 and 76% of non-wage funds designated for primary schools in African countries (Kenny, 2017). In Tanzania, the leakage, in flows of teacher salaries, school grants, supplies, textbooks, and food, is 10% of rule-based funds (Poisson, 2016). Other cases of the nature and extent of such embezzlement across a variety of other African countries can be found in several studies (see, for example, Epstein, 2014; Hope, 2017). Other good sources are the Auditor General and Public Prosecutor reports of the countries.

For Malawi, for example, Chingaipe (2022) has shown the extent of embezzlement and theft of public finances as outlined in the Auditor General's and other reports over the period 2010–2020. These reports reveal persistent patterns of mismanagement and theft of public funds through multiple schemes and, as a result of its findings, the Auditor General has referred dozens of case files to the Anti-Corruption Bureau (ACB) for prosecution. Chingaipe (2022, pp. 52–53) has coined the term "roving banditry" to describe this corruption channel in Malawi which he defines as:

> a phenomenon of competitive theft of public resources (money and assets) involving state elites (politicians and bureaucrats) and many of their supporters and beneficiaries who deployed multiple ruses to siphon and privatize public resources in the short periods they had control of the levers of power of the state, punctuated by pre-determined dates of presidential and parliamentary elections.

Development aid or overseas development assistance (ODA) is also one of the areas that has historically been plagued by theft and embezzlement in African countries and the extent of such theft has been well documented as ODA has been found to fuel this channel of corruption (see, for example, Asongu & Nwachukwu, 2016; Burgis, 2015; Hope, 2014, 2017; Moyo, 2009; Okonjo-Iweala, 2018). The consequences of the theft of ODA have been severe. In many cases, conditional repayment of development funding is attached to its receipt, making the strategic investment of said funds critical to justifying its receipt. Indeed, it is found that the impact of embezzlement, theft and misappropriation of state resources has been significant particularly with respect to aid disbursements to the most aid-dependent countries and this has been coinciding with significant increases in deposits held in offshore financial centers known for bank secrecy and private wealth management, resulting in a general leakage rate of 7.5%–15% of aid disbursements from the World Bank, for instance, during the period 1990–2010 (Andersen et al., 2020). Country example estimates for the period 1990–2010 indicate that ODA captured/diverted from Kenya to offshore bank accounts was some US$3.1 billion and for Côte d'Ivoire and the Democratic Republic of the Congo (DRC) it was US$ 1.2 billion and US$ 1 billion, respectively (Andersen et al., 2020).

Notwithstanding the foregoing, there is also much emerging evidence that corrupt governments receive no less ODA than if they were not corrupt, and there is no significant relation between aid and corruption running in both directions. These findings support the view that aid does not influence corruption in its current design, while the level of corruption does not influence incentives of donor countries to allocate aid (see, for example, de la Croix & Delavallade, 2014; Menard & Weill, 2016). In fact, some research has found that the most corrupt countries receive the highest amounts of foreign aid as this may be explained by their poverty status, as the most corrupt countries are also the poorest, and this is why they may receive more aid (de la Croix & Delavallade, 2014). However, there is other research that indicates that foreign aid has a significant negative impact on the level of corruption. This infers that ODA decreases the level of the corruption perception index, hence more corruption in any given country (see, for example, Ali et al., 2019).

3.2.2 Bribes and Kickbacks

In the second channel, we have bribes and kickbacks. Bribery is defined as giving someone a financial or other advantage to encourage that person to perform their functions or activities improperly or to reward that person for having already done so or their willingness to do so. More technically, it is the offering, giving, receiving, or soliciting of something of value for the purpose of influencing the action of an official in the discharge of his or her public or legal duties. Every country in the world criminalizes the bribery of its own officials. Bribes result in a negative influence on labor productivity and service delivery, and on private investment. Labor productivity and service delivery are affected as bribes impede the efficiency of work flow and deny services to those who are entitled to get them without having to be victims of rent-seeking.

Where corruption is prevalent, too many people, especially the poor, are forced to bear the added burden of having to pay bribes to gain access to essential services (Hope, 2017; Labelle, 2009). Pring and Vrushi (2019) have estimated that 67% of the poorest and moderately poor people in Africa paid bribes for public services compared to only 44% of the wealthiest and moderately well off who paid these bribes. Disaggregated, 36% of the poorest paid the bribes, while only 19% of the wealthiest paid. As a practical matter, that means that the poorest are twice as likely to pay a bribe as the richest people in Africa. Of course, for the very poor, whom are unable to afford these bribes, they will have no choice but to forego the services and put their welfare and that of their respective families in jeopardy. Foregoing the services can result in lack of access to necessary health care or quality education, for example. Moreover, empirical studies have consistently found that lower-income households pay a higher proportion of their income in bribes than do middle- or upper-income households and, as such, bribes are like a regressive tax on the poor since they (the poor) must allocate a greater amount of their income than the rich to paying bribes (see, for example, Justesen & Bjørnskov, 2014; Mbate, 2018; Menocal & Others., 2015; Peiffer & Rose, 2018).

The AfDB had estimated that lower income households in Africa spend on average 2%–3% of their income on bribes, while high income households spend an average of 0.9% (AfDB., 2013). In many individual countries it can be much more. For example, in Sierra Leone the poor pay 13% of their income to bribes while the higher income households pay 3.8% (World Bank, 2017). Also, when the poor in Africa forego services, in some instances they may even suffer harassment, or even risk getting arrested in the case of police bribe demands (Hope, 2017). Most of a nation's citizens' perceptions about corruption, as well as the actual corruption, are derived from the extent of bribery in that nation.

Based on the most recent publicly available and credible surveys and other data on bribery in African countries, it is shown that the share of the total population that paid a bribe, in the previous 12 months, to obtain any public service was greatest in Liberia at 60% during 2019–2021 and lowest in Cabo Verde at 3% (Afrobarometer n.d.; Keulder, 2021). In Nigeria, it was estimated that bribes paid to public officials exceeded US$2 billion annually (UNODC and National Bureau of Statistics [NBS], 2019). In Ghana, the average size of bribe paid was found to be "Cedi 348 in 2021 or roughly US$44 based on the 2021 spot exchange rate" (UNODC, 2022, p. 43), and amounting to a national total of bribes paid of Cedi 5 billion (equivalent to US$847 million)—based on the annual average exchange rate for 2021—and corresponding to about one-third of the budget of the country's Ministry of Education in the same year (UNODC, 2022). In East Africa, a national average size of bribe exceeding US$60 was recorded in Kenya in 2019 with the judiciary being paid an average bribe of US$239 and land administration services US$100 (TI-Kenya, 2020). Other public services that have attracted high bribe amounts include the police services in Rwanda at US$95, motor vehicle licensing services in Kenya at US$74, and the judiciary in Uganda at US$81 (TI-Kenya, 2017, 2020). In Zimbabwe, 89% of the people who sought services from the public sector were found to have paid a bribe in the range of US$1–$100 with the majority (70%) paying up to US$50 (TI-Zimbabwe, 2022). All these bribes when aggregated in each country amount to enormous national sums given that, of the population that encountered a bribery incident (demanded, expected or offered), a considerable proportion of them acceded to the bribery transaction. The 2020 *Financial Crime Threat Assessment* for sub-Saharan Africa, published through Financial Crime News (FCN), for example, estimated that bribery and corruption facilitated and protected criminal activity in 2018 amounting to US$79–$92 billion or 4.9%–5.7% of sub-Saharan Africa GDP, with higher levels expected in countries with higher levels of corruption (Cusack, 2020).

Figure 3.1 depicts averages of the proportion of people who, in the previous 12 months, paid a bribe (bribery rates) for public services across sub-Saharan Africa. The figure indicates that the bribery rate trended downward from 53% in 2013 to 22% in 2015 and ever so slightly increasing to 23% by 2017 before increasing again to 28% by the beginning of 2019 and remaining the same in 2021. However, as one would expect from these averages, there is considerable variation across countries from single digit lows in countries recognized as generally having good governance (Cabo Verde (3%), Mauritius (8%), and Botswana (9%) to highs in the range of 50%–60% in Guinea, Cameroon, Uganda, and the afore-mentioned Liberia (Afrobarometer n.d.; Keulder, 2021; Pring, 2017; Pring & Vrushi, 2019). In Table 3.1, we also have data pertaining to businesses paying bribes which show that sub-Saharan Africa leads (with a larger proportion) in a comparison with all economies in the entire set of the indices related to bribe paying by businesses for the period 2010–2020. Target 16.5 of the SDGs is also the requirement to substantially reduce corruption and bribery in all their forms and this is discussed in Chaps. 6 and 7.

Another disturbing, and now all too brazenly prevalent, use of bribery—with significant negative impacts on both sustainable development and democracy in Africa—is that of vote buying in elections. It is acknowledged that this book is not the place for any extensive discussion or analysis of electoral bribery. Excellent works in that regard can be found elsewhere (see, for example, Cheeseman & Klaas, 2018; Erasmus, 2020; the essays by Gyimah-Boadi (2021) and others in Ghana

3.2 Corruption Channels in Africa: Trends and Extent of Economic and Financial... 41

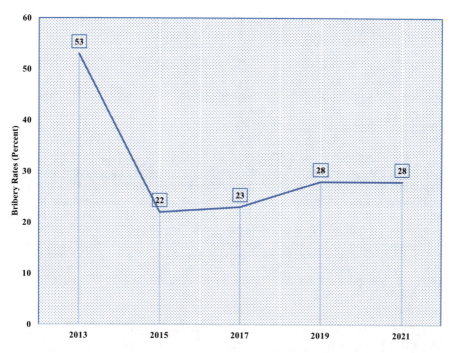

Fig. 3.1 Averages of proportion of people in sub-Saharan Africa who, in the previous 12 months, paid a bribe (bribery rates) for public services, 2013–2021. *Source:* Author, based on data derived from Afrobarometer (n.d.); Hardoon and Heinrich (2013); Keulder (2021); Pring (2015, 2017); and Pring and Vrushi (2019)

Center for Democratic Development [CDD-Ghana], 2021; Hoffmann & Patel, 2022; Nwagwu et al., 2022; Yoon, 2020). Nonetheless, however considered, whether from an academic or real-world perspective, vote buying is an illegal act. By statute, in almost all countries, it is a crime as usually set out in an Election Offences Act or other related laws. It distorts the democratic process and is therefore anti-democratic. Consequently, it cannot in any way, shape, or form be considered as anything else but bad for democratic governance and therefore also inconsistent with pathways for sustainable development or the achievement of SDG 16 as discussed in Chap. 6. Among other things, vote buying, like fake news or propaganda, undermines political legitimacy, results in election rigging or election fraud, interferes with the independence and rights of voters to fairly assess candidates for electoral offices, can suppress voter turnout, and can lead to electoral outcomes that are rejected by one or more segments of society and thereby influence, or naturally result, in political violence. Such post-election violence has, unfortunately, occurred much too often in Africa and with devastating human and economic consequences while jeopardizing lasting domestic peace, security, and stability.

Data from Afrobarometer surveys, covering the period 2019–2021, indicate that an average of at least 19% of voters across sub-Saharan Africa countries have been offered money, food, or gifts in return for their vote during their last national

Table 3.1 Statistics on businesses paying bribes: sub-Saharan Africa and all countries, 2010–2020 (averages)

Economy[1]	Bribery incidence[2]	Bribery depth[3]	Gifts to tax officials[4]	Gifts to secure government contracts[5]	Value of gift to secure a government contract[6]	Gifts to get an operating license[7]	Gifts to get an import license[8]	Gifts to get a construction permit[9]
All countries	15.8	12.5	12.3	29.2	1.2	12.7	12.0	20.4
Sub-Saharan Africa	22.3	17.0	16.9	35.5	2.4	16.5	14.6	26.1

Notes: [1]sub-Saharan Africa and "All Countries" averages of indicators posted during the years 2010–2020 and computed based on the Enterprise Surveys Global Methodology; [2]Percent of firms experiencing at least one bribe payment request; [3]Percent of public transactions where a gift or informal payment was requested; [4]Percent of firms expected to give gifts or informal payments in meetings with tax officials; [5]Percent of firms expected to give gifts or informal payments to secure a government contract; [6]Percent of contract value; [7]Percent of firms expected to give gifts or informal payments to get an operating license; [8]Percent of firms expected to give gifts or informal payments to get an import license; and [9]Percent of firms expected to give gifts or informal payments to get a construction permit. *Source:* Author, based on data derived from World Bank (n.d.)

election, with Nigeria having the largest number of respondents (44%) whom were so offered followed by Kenya and Gabon both at 38% (Afrobarometer, n.d.). For Nigeria, this practice of vote buying has led to the country being characterized as a moneyocracy or "cash-and-carry" democracy (Onuoha & Okafor, 2020). And, during Kenya's 2022 general election campaign, banks and government officials had complained and sounded the alarm that there was a shortage of small denomination banknotes due to demand for and resultant very large withdrawals comprising those types of banknotes to be used for voter bribery (see, for instance, Agence France Presse [AFP], 2022; Jöst & Lust, 2022; Kimeria & Ngila, 2022).

Vote buying, accompanied with the reciprocated act of vote selling (creating a vote market), has been regarded or categorized by some as an aspect of clientelism or electoral clientelism (see, for instance, Erasmus, 2020; Jensen & Justesen, 2014; Kramon, 2018; Nichter, 2014). However, vote buying is electoral bribery and is best defined as the act or acts of paying particular individual potential voters or groups of potential voters in cash, goods, food, drinks, gifts, or services either for their direct vote or for their vote abstention (not to turnout). It is solely intended to influence the outcome of an election or elections in favor of a particular candidate or candidates. In other words, to increase the probability of winning by the candidate or candidates on whose behalf the bribes were negotiated and paid. Although some segments of society, especially the poor, may derive some short-term benefit or gain from having their votes bought, in the longer-term they may be worse off as they would have contributed to the election of corrupt politicians whom, among other potentially corrupt acts, will be seeking to recoup the bribes they paid to get elected or re-elected and at the detriment of society as a whole (see, for instance, the case of Nigeria in Hoffmann & Patel, 2022; and the case of Tanzania in Yoon, 2020).

One final comment that must necessarily be made here on this issue is the fact that elections are not designed to effect regime change. They are intended for citizens to freely, fairly, and democratically express their choice of whom they desire to represent and/or govern them. The buying of votes (bribery of voters) to influence that choice does not allow for a free, fair, and democratic election process. In fact, it simply contributes to and/or reinforces corruption, including through state capture, which, in turn, negatively impacts sustainable development and can result in an environment where peace and security are challenged.

Kickbacks and facilitation payments—which may be solicited, extorted, or offered—are another form of bribery (negotiated or commission) payments. Such payments are usually derived through the process of procurement contracting for goods, services and works (especially high value areas such as the construction, extractive, transportation, information and communication, and defense sectors) or in development projects. Those paying the kickbacks tend to seek to recover their money by inflating prices, billing for work not performed, failing to meet contract standards, reducing quality of work, or using inferior materials (OECD, 2016, 2018a). As a result, it is estimated that project costs are increased by some 10%–25%. The World Bank, for example, has estimated that 20%–40% of water sector finances are lost annually to dishonest and corrupt practices according to the Water Integrity Network (WIN) (2016). In some countries, corrupt public officials may even engage in fake procurements complete with official-looking but fake suppliers and fake receipts (Vashisht, 2017). All these corruption practices, in turn, have an influence on households' access to quality water services in Africa. As empirically shown, for example, by Breen and Gillanders (2022), based on data covering 2016–2018, those living in areas with more corruption in utilities are less likely to have access to enough clean water. In other words, while a household that has paid a bribe is more likely to have a water access point, the area incidence of utilities corruption predicts that the household will not have enough clean water.

3.2.3 Money Laundering and Other Illicit Financial Flows

The third channel is money laundering and other IFFs. Money laundering is the act or process of disguising the source, ownership, control, or the true nature of money obtained through illegal/unlawful means. In essence, it is a series of financial transactions that are intended to transform ill-gotten gains into legitimate money or other assets by disguising those proceeds and integrating them into the legitimate financial system. IFFs—which facilitate cross-border money laundering—are illegal movements of money or capital from one country to another. Flows are illicit when the funds are illegally earned, transferred, and/or utilized. This may include funds from illicit activities, such as drug-trafficking; trade mis-invoicing; tax evasion and tax avoidance, through the transfer of funds abroad in violation of national tax regulations; and funds used for illegal purposes, such as the financing of terrorism. However, for clarity, not all IFFs stem from illegal activity. There can be illicit transactions to transfer funds that have a licit origin, and there can be illicit flows stemming from licit activity being used in an illicit way such as aggressive tax avoidance as opposed to tax evasion, for example (United Nations Conference on Trade and Development [UNCTAD] and UNODC, 2020).

Target 16.4 of the SDGs also includes the requirement to significantly reducing illicit financial flows and strengthen the recovery and return of stolen assets and combat all forms of organized crime. As Hendriyetty and Grewal (2017, p. 65) have shown, money laundering is of major global concern, because it is a pivotal link in tracking funds from organized crime, as "criminals try to conceal their proceeds of crime by laundering money in financial systems, international trade or through other efforts."

Based on the most comprehensively complete data available, the calculated estimates of IFFs remain persistently high in Africa. The UNECA (2018, 2021a) had issued estimates indicating that between 2000 and 2016 Africa lost, on average, US$73–$83 billion annually in net IFFs through trade mis-invoicing by itself. On aggregate, over the period 2000–2016, this loss amounted to US$1.4 trillion, equivalent to 5.3% of the continent's GDP, or 11.4% of the value of its trade (UNECA, 2021a). In 2020, the UNCTAD issued its *Economic Development in Africa Report* that showed IFFs had contributed to a total illicit capital flight of some US$89 billion annually by 2020 (UNCTAD, 2020), and this has now become the data point often touted and quoted by most UN and development-oriented international organizations. Ndikumana and Boyce (2021, 2022a) have also shown the historical and accelerated nature of the problem with their estimates that illicit capital flight from African countries since 1970 amounted to US$2 trillion, of which almost US$600 billion left after the turn of the century. And, if interest is added on top of that, "the cumulative amount of private wealth held offshore stood at US$2.4 trillion by 2018," and "this was more than three times higher than the stock of external debts owed by the same countries, making Africa a 'net creditor' to the rest of the world" (Ndikumana & Boyce, 2022a, p. 1).

These sums of total IFFs represent a significant leakage of moneys from the African economies and which also increases criminal activities and impede tax collection, among other things, as a West African case study has found (see OECD, 2018b). The largest contributions for money laundering and IFFs in African countries come primarily from fraud or corruption including trade mis-invoicing, human and drug trafficking, and tax evasion (see, for example, Aluko & Bagheri, 2012; Hendriyetty & Grewal, 2017; Miyandazi & Ronceray, 2018; Yikona et al., 2011). In some countries, such as Mali, for example, the proceeds of corruption are also brazenly laundered in the formal economy through real estate, banks, companies, and gold (IMF, 2015). In South Africa, the property environment (including renovation and improvements) and the casino and gambling industry, are often associated with criminal proceeds related to corruption as well as a variety of other predicate offences (Financial Intelligence Centre [FIC], 2019). In other African countries, the enablers generally are Western banks, global consulting and accounting firms, law firms, hedge funds, private equity firms, real estate firms, and transnational networks of plunder (see, for example, Ndikumana & Boyce, 2022b).

In whatever manner enabled and laundered, the resultant effect is that considerable public revenues are lost that could be used to fund sustainable development activities. In that regard, in January 2022, the European Commission (EC) issued an updated list of third countries with strategic deficiencies in their anti-money laundering and counter-terrorist financing frameworks. It included seven African states, namely Burkina Faso, Mali, Morocco, Senegal, South Sudan, Uganda, and Zimbabwe (EC, 2022). The aim of this list is to protect the EU financial system and internal market by better preventing money laundering and terrorist financing risks. As a result of the listing, banks and other financial entities covered by EU anti-money laundering rules can apply increased checks (due diligence) on financial operations involving customers and financial institutions from these high-risk third countries to better identify any suspicious money flows (EC, 2019a).

3.2.4 State Capture

Finally, we have the state capture channel. State capture occurs when the ruling elite and/or powerful business people manipulate policy formation and influence the emerging rules of the game (including laws, rules, and economic regulations) to their own advantage rather than for the public good (Lugon-Moulin, 2010). The captured economy then becomes trapped in a vicious state in which the policy and institutional reforms necessary to improve governance are undermined by collusion between powerful firms and state officials who extract substantial private gains from the absence of a clear rule of law (Lugon-Moulin, 2010). State capture can be further refined by distinguishing between types of institutions subject to capture (legislative, executive, judiciary, regulatory agencies, public works and lands ministries, for example) and the types of actors actively seeking to capture (large private firms, political leaders, high ranking officials, and interest groups, for example) (see, for instance, Hellman et al., 2003; Hellman & Kaufmann, 2001, 2018; Khatri, 2016; Lugon-Moulin, 2010; Martini, 2014).

Powerful individuals and groups are usually associated with state capture and they may include family members of the governing elite, ethnic or religious clans, organized criminal groups, or military cliques, for example. The exercise of state capture also results in the practice of crony capitalism as the collaborative arrangements, between senior public officials and/or politicians on the one hand and private individuals, private companies, and private sector cartels on the other hand, lead to the fixing of tenders, contracts, land sales, administrative decisions/rules and laws, or procurements in favor of those private individuals, companies, and cartels. The intent is to maximize the mutual benefits from such actions, that is, kickbacks for the senior public officials and politicians and profits for their private sector collaborators (Holcombe, 2013).

Much of the past literature and investigative reports on state capture had been primarily focused on the post-communist states of Eastern Europe and countries in Latin America. Africa is still underrepresented in the literature but that is beginning to change due to recent events in South Africa. In fact, most of the current reporting and literature on state capture in Africa is about South Africa as both national and international attention has been drawn to the country's corruption problems, including by a Judicial Commission of Inquiry into Allegations of State Capture, Corruption and Fraud in the Public Sector that was chaired by Chief Justice Raymond Zondo (the Zondo Commission). According to the highly respected (both nationally and internationally) former South African Finance Minister and current Minister of Public Enterprises, Pravin Gordhan, state capture had sucked approximately US$18 billion from his country's fiscal system during the period 2014–2017 alone (Citizen Reporter, 2017).

However, information in other reports suggest that the amount could be at least double that at US$36 billion, especially considering the evidence on the considerable repurposing of public enterprises to become the primary mechanisms for rent-seeking (see, for example, Bertelsmann Stiftung, 2018; Chipkin et al., 2018; Organization Undoing Tax Abuse (OUTA), 2017; Public Protector South Africa (PPSA), 2016). Indeed, it is in that regard that, among other things, state capture, and the role of former President Jacob Zuma and his son in facilitating it with the Gupta family (see Aboobaker et al., 2022; Chipkin et al., 2018; Mkhabela, 2018; PPSA, 2016), ultimately led the ruling party to force Mr. Zuma to resign as President in 2018. At the time of preparation of this book, the now disgraced former President Zuma was on trial, having been separately charged with 16 counts of racketeering, corruption, fraud, tax evasion and money laundering involving a US$5 billion arms deal from the 1990s.

Undoubtedly, over time, corruption became a major factor in the weakening of South Africa's state-owned enterprises (SOEs) and impairing their credibility and public trust in them (see Goodwin, 2022; UNECA, 2021b). In June 2022, the Zondo Commission released its final volumes of its report into state capture corruption during the presidency of Jacob Zuma. The report sets out the case against Mr. Zuma and his cronies and is quite scathing and very determinative also about the role of the ruling party, the African National Congress (ANC), which under Zuma permitted, supported and enabled corruption. Indeed, as Maseko (2022, p. 1) has pointed out, "the evidence revealed how ANC leaders, including former and current government ministers, allegedly participated or encouraged looting at a massive cost to the country," and this "included crippling the country's revenue service, bringing the national carrier South African Airways (SAA) to its knees, looting the agency that runs the country's passenger railways, and interfering with the public broadcaster, the South African Broadcasting Corporation (SABC)."

The Zondo Commission report issued a large number of recommendations including the prosecution, or further investigation for prosecution, of a considerable number of former government officials, ruling party members, and private sector individuals on charges of corruption/bribery, fraud, conspiracy to commit fraud, money laundering, racketeering offences, offences relating to the proceeds of unlawful activities, possession of confidential procurement documentation, influence peddling, defeating or obstructing the course of justice, and tax offences, for example (Zondo Commission, 2022). Other recommendations were also made with respect to parliamentary oversight; recovery of proceeds from fraud and other corrupt activities; the tracing and dissipation of the funds from corrupt activities through offshore money laundering networks; the establishment of a transparent process for the appointment of appropriately qualified and experienced persons of high integrity to the Boards of SOEs and to senior executive positions in those SOEs; the establishment of a permanent Anti-State Capture and Corruption Commission (ASCCC) and a Public Procurement Anti-Corruption Agency (PPACA); and amendment of the Prevention and Combatting of Corrupt Activities Act (PRECCA) (Zondo Commission, 2022).

At the ceremony marking the handover and his receipt of the final report on state capture from Chief Justice Zondo, President Ramaphosa remarked that "state capture was an assault on our democracy and violated the rights of every man, woman and child in this country," and "through the various reports released by the [Zondo] Commission, we have come to understand what happened, who was involved, and what effect state capture has had on our state, our economy and our society" (Ramaphosa, 2022, p. 1). President Ramaphosa further said that "the State of Capture report presented evidence of the abuse of power and of how public institutions were repurposed to enable corrupt activities to take place," and that "the report is [therefore] far more than a record of widespread corruption, fraud and abuse; it is also an instrument through which the country can work to ensure that such events are never allowed to happen again" (Ramaphosa, 2022, p. 1). In a follow-up in a question period in the National Assembly in September 2022, President Ramaphosa further committed that he would implement the Zondo Commission's recommendations, despite the fact that the Commission's recommendations were not binding, and that an implementation plan was being prepared for submission to the Parliament.

For further case studies and assessments of the state capture corruption channel and its absolute or potential impact on socio-economic development in other African countries see, for example, Burgis (2015); Ellis (2016); Hope (2012, 2017); Human Rights Watch (HRW) (2017); Maina (2019); Mariotti et al. (2018); Mbaku (2018); Meirotti and Masterson (2018); Okonjo-Iweala (2018); Page (2018); and Smith and Lee (2018).

3.3 Summary Analysis

From the foregoing, it is quite clear that economic and financial crimes are the primary channels through which corruption is perpetrated in Africa and represents the single greatest obstacle to development progress on the continent. As observed by a former Executive Secretary of the UNECA, "how can we get the Africa we want when we let billions leak out of the continent only to spend time begging for minimal sums because of corruption?" and furthermore, "what this means is that the continent cannot afford to continue to suffer from the kinds of financial leakages it has had to contend with over the past several years through various forms of corrupt acts and practices" (Songwe, 2018, p. 4). Whether determined by empirical academic studies or the eyeball test, where corruption is persistent, socio-economic development is impeded. Generally, economic and financial crimes have a negative impact in emerging and developing countries (see, for example, Saddiq & Abu Bakar, 2019). The loss of government revenues has a host of knock-on effects, including the fact that lower revenues mean that less money is available to fund schools, hospitals and other essential services.

The facilitators of corruption are smart, very well compensated and pervasive in African institutions. They are responsible for the unnecessary leakage from various potential government revenue streams that could be used to fund public services and especially given the existing massive under-funding of those services, and the extent of need (Curtis & O'Hare, 2017). Being aware of the extent and trends related to the economic and financial crimes as corruption channels is a necessary first step toward sustainable policy frameworks for mitigating the negative effects of these crimes. Economic and financial crimes affect everyone and gaining insight into its true magnitude and devastating effects is of paramount importance (Refinitiv, 2018).

Lest it be misunderstood, however, attention must also be drawn to the fact that economic and financial crimes in Africa are also pervasive across the continent's private sector beyond just bribe paying as discussed above. PricewaterhouseCoopers (PwC) has conducted surveys showing that the reported rate of economic (financial) crime increased by 2018 to 62% compared to 57% in 2016 (PwC, 2018). Of the ten countries with the highest rates of economic/financial crime, five of them were African with South Africa and Kenya leading the global list at 77% and 75%, respectively (PwC, 2018). And, Cusack (2020) has estimated that financial criminal markets generated (for 2018) up to US$60 billion in criminal proceeds (excluding fraud, corruption or tax evasion).

Based on the available survey data, Table 3.2 shows some statistics on financial crimes in the African private sector in 2018. Sub-Saharan Africa performs poorly compared to the global indices. For example, as a percentage of global turnover, companies in sub-Saharan Africa spent 3.4% to prevent financial crime issues around their global operations during the 12 months preceding the survey compared to 3.1% across the globe (Refinitiv, 2018). By 2021, some 22% of private firms said that bribery and corruption is the financial crime that posed the greatest risk to their organization while close to a quarter (23%) of them indicated that their organization had fallen victim to bribery and corruption over the past 5 years and 60% said that they had anti-bribery and corruption programs in place (Refinitiv, 2021). However, private firms in sub-Saharan Africa were, nonetheless, found by Ufere et al. (2020)

Table 3.2 Statistics on private sector financial crime in sub-Saharan Africa, 2018 (%)

Turnover lost in the last 12 months due to money laundering	Detected crime reported internally	Regional turnover spent on combating financial crime	Believe money laundering is a common practice in some of the regions in which they operate	Supportive of improving public-private partnerships to fight financial crime	Most common financial crime
3	62	3.4	96	99.5	Theft (34)

Source: Author, based on data derived from Refinitiv (2018)

to voluntarily engage in corruption more as the echoing of the practices of other firms with institutional coercion being the strongest determinant of bribery, while imitation and competitive rivalry routinize the practice. "As such, local firms rely on bribery as a legitimating and rational response to the [environment in which they find themselves]" (Ufere et al., 2020, p. 101).

However, it must also be pointed out here that some African nations have recently been taking actions to maintain the integrity of their financial and banking systems. For example, South Africa, which perhaps has the most advanced banking system in Africa, sanctioned the Deutsche Bank AG—Johannesburg Branch in April 2021. The sanctions by the Prudential Authority (PA) of the country's Reserve (Central) Bank included a fine of 38 million Rand (approximately US$2.5 million) over certain identified weaknesses in Deutsche Bank's money laundering control measures and processes.

Deutsche Bank failed to comply with: (1) customer due diligence and enhanced due diligence requirements; (2) record-keeping requirements in terms of the FIC Act; (3) the governance of anti-money laundering and countering the financing of terrorism (AML/CFT) compliance requirements in terms of the FIC Act; and (4) the provisions outlined in the FIC Act and in its risk management and compliance program (RMCP), all of which inhibited the Bank from proactively detecting potential money laundering and the financing of terrorism (South African Reserve Bank [SARB], 2021). The sanctions were not imposed because the Bank was found to have facilitated transactions involving money laundering or the financing of terrorism. Prior to that, in 2019, the PA had also imposed sanctions on the Standard Bank of South Africa Limited and HBZ Bank Limited for similar weaknesses.

From the perspective of the EC (2019a), the banking system requirements that need to be met are: (1) complying with EU anti-money laundering criteria such as criminalizing money laundering and terrorism financing, customer due diligence requirements, record keeping and suspicious transactions reporting in both the financial and non-financial sectors, transparency of beneficial ownership, and international cooperation; (2) ensuring in practice that information on beneficial owners of companies and trusts is available since opaque structures are regularly involved in money laundering, terrorist financing and tax evasion; and (3) showing positive and tangible progress in improving effectiveness in all areas where significant deficiencies were identified.

In addition, a number of African nations, particularly across the Eastern, Western, and Southern sub-regions have been engaging with their respective private sector to develop and implement anti-fraud measures (AFMs) to counter economic and financial crimes. These AFMs tend to be especially prevalent in the banking and telecommunication sectors (see Mykhalchenko & Wiegratz, 2019, 2021, 2022).

3.4 Conclusion

In general, economic and financial crimes in Africa have been trending upward and their true cost extends far beyond pure economics. In addition to revenue leakage, the consequences include the proceeds being used to fund the financing of terrorism, and human rights abuses such as slavery and child labor (Refinitiv, 2018).

These consequences are also particularly severe for those of the nations that are fragile states as there results a diversion of much needed resources for rebuilding such countries' public services, from security and justice to basic social services such as health and education. Moreover, while financial crime is a distinct category of transnational organized crime, it is also often the catalyst for other forms of organized crime that rapidly adapt to changes in technology and the global financial system (Ewi, 2018). Therefore, for all the reasons, as outlined throughout this book, African nations need to be much more proactive in policy development and implementation to tackle their corruption that is being channeled through economic and financial crimes. This must also consider that the scale of these economic and financial crimes has escalated substantially over the past several years because of diminished state capacity from such corruption (Haysom, 2019).

In addition, there is now an imperative to restoring confidence in African banking systems. Particularly for those individual nations that have been cited by the EC as a third country with strategic deficiencies in their anti-money laundering and counter-terrorist financing frameworks, it absolutely means that a great deal needs to be done to identify and counteract illicit financial transactions and flows. African banking systems therefore need to be improved through better oversight and compliance under any existing sufficient legislation or through new legislation that forces such oversight and compliance. The basic idea, as noted by de Morais (2016), must be to have systems in place that simply make it incredibly difficult—and legally dangerous—for financial transactions of a criminal nature to occur.

In that regard also, sub-regional bodies such as the Eastern and Southern Africa Anti-Money Laundering Group (ESAAMLG) and the Inter-Governmental Action Group against Money Laundering in West Africa (GIABA), for example, have been subscribing to global standards to combat money laundering and the financing of terrorism and proliferation, including taking responsibility for strengthening the capacity of their member states towards prevention and control. In June 2022, G7 leaders also issued a communiqué from their annual meeting that included their intention to do their part on anti-corruption policy as follows: "To hold kleptocrats, criminals and their enablers to account globally, we will broaden our global fight against cross-border corruption, including by supporting African partners in setting up 15 additional beneficial ownership registers" (G7 Leaders' Communiqué, 2022, p. 26). This is indeed an excellent policy approach by the G7 in the context of support for African countries through state parties to recover stolen assets and reduce corruption. As well argued by Munyai and Agbor (2020), and notwithstanding the role and importance of national/regional solutions to Africa's corruption problem, foreign non-African governments have a critical and priceless role to play in the fight against corruption in Africa. This has become necessary as "Africa's fight against corruption cannot be waged by African states themselves only: they need the involvement and participation of non-African states given the fact that the perpetration of corruption itself is sometimes facilitated by financial entities that are located without the African continent" (Munyai & Agbor, 2020, p. 3), as this chapter has also demonstrated.

References

Aboobaker, A., Naidoo, K., & Ndikumana, L. (2022). South Africa: Capital flight, state capture, and inequality. In L. Ndikumana & J. K. Boyce (Eds.), *On the trail of capital flight from Africa: The takers and the enablers* (pp. 149–192). Oxford University Press.

Achim, M. V., & Borlea, S. N. (2020). *Economic and financial crime: Corruption, shadow economy, and money laundering*. Springer Nature.

AfDB. (2013). The cost and extent of corruption and weak governance. *Market Brief–Africa Economic & Financial Brief, 4*(40), 1–7. https://www.afdb.org/fileadmin/uploads/afdb/Documents/Publications/Market_Brief_-_Africa_Economic_Financial_Brief_16-20_September_2013.pdf

AFP. (2022, July 27). Vote bribes leave Kenyan banks short of small notes, *Barron's*. Retrieved from https://www.barrons.com/news/vote-bribes-leave-kenyan-banks-short-of-small-notes-01658934307

Afrobarometer. (n.d.). Round 8 surveys 2019–21. [online data analysis]. Retrieved from https://www.afrobarometer.org/online-data-analysis/

Ali, M., Khan, L., Sohail, A., & Puah, C. H. (2019). The relationship between aid and corruption: A case of selected Asian countries. *Journal of Financial Crime, 26*(3), 692–704. https://doi.org/10.1108/JFC-08-2018-0089

Aluko, A., & Bagheri, M. (2012). The impact of money laundering on economic and financial stability and on political development in developing countries: The case of Nigeria. *Journal of Money Laundering Control, 15*(4), 442–457. https://doi.org/10.1108/13685201211266024

Andersen, J. J., Johannesen, N., & Rijkers, B. (2020). Elite capture of foreign aid: Evidence from offshore bank accounts. [Policy Research Working Paper 9150]. World Bank.

Asongu, S. A., & Nwachukwu, J. C. (2016). Foreign aid and governance in Africa. *International Review of Applied Economics, 30*(1), 69–88.

Bertelsmann Stiftung. (2018). *BTI [Bertelsmann transformation index] 2018 country report–South Africa*. Bertelsmann Stiftung.

Blunt, E. (2002, September 18). Corruption costs Africa billions, *BBC News*. Retrieved from http://news.bbc.co.uk/2/hi/africa/2265387.stm

Breen, M., & Gillanders, R. (2022). Money down the drain: Corruption and water service quality in Africa, *Governance*. [Advance online publication]. https://doi.org/10.1111/gove.12753

Burgis, T. (2015). *The looting machine: Warlords, oligarchs, corporations, smugglers, and the theft of Africa's wealth*. Public Affairs Books.

BusinessTech. (2017, September 1). Corruption costs SA GDP at least R27 billion annually, and 76, 000 jobs, *BusinessTech*. Retrieved from https://businesstech.co.za/news/government/196116/corruption-costs-sa-gdp-at-least-r27-billion-annually-and-76-000-jobs/

CDD-Ghana. (2021). *Democracy capture in Africa: Benin, Ghana, Kenya, Mozambique, Nigeria*. CDD-Ghana.

Cheeseman, N., & Klaas, B. (2018). *How to rig an election*. Yale University Press.

Chingaipe, H. (2022). A decade of governance as "roving banditry": The political economy of public finance mismanagement in Malawi, 2010-2020. In K. R. Ross, A. L. Chiweza, & W. O. Mulwafu (Eds.), *Beyond impunity: New directions for governance in Malawi* (pp. 47–76). University of Cape Town Press.

Chipkin, I., Swilling, M., Bhorat, H., Buthelezi, M., Duma, S., Friedenstein, H., Mondi, L., Peter, C., Prins, N., & Qobo, M. (2018). *Shadow state: The politics of state capture*. Wits University Press.

Citizen Reporter. (2017, September 12). R250bn lost to state capture in the last three years, says Gordhan, *The Citizen*. Retrieved from https://citizen.co.za/news/south-africa/1651069/r250bn-lost-to-state-capture-in-the-last-three-years-says-gordhan/

Curtis, M., & Ngowi, P. (2017). The one-billion-dollar question revisited five years later–how much is Tanzania now losing in potential tax revenues. Retrieved from http://curtisresearch.org/wp-content/uploads/ONE-BILLION-DOLLAR-QUESTION-Final.pdf

Curtis, M., & O'Hare, B. (2017). Lost revenues in low-income countries. Retrieved from http://curtisresearch.org/publications/lost-revenues-in-low-income-countries/

Cusack, J. (2020). Financial crime threat assessment: Sub-Saharan Africa. Retrieved from https://thefinancialcrimenews.com/sub-saharan-africa/

de la Croix, D., & Delavallade, C. (2014). Why corrupt governments may receive more foreign aid. *Oxford Economic Papers, 66*(1), 51–66. https://doi.org/10.1093/oep/gpt004

de Morais, J. P. (2016, January 19). The fight against money laundering–An African perspective. *Financial Times* Retrieved from https://www.ft.com/content/c8184a87-0590-3aa9-b0af-2c6ba5f28c33

EC. (2019a, February 13). European Commission adopts new list of third countries with weak anti-money laundering and terrorist financing regimes. [Press Release]. Retrieved from http://europa.eu/rapid/press-release_IP-19-781_en.htm

EC. (2019b, February 13). Anti-money laundering: Q & A on the EU list of high-risk third countries. [Fact Sheet]. Retrieved from http://europa.eu/rapid/press-release_MEMO-19-782_en.htm

EC. (2022). Commission delegated regulation (EU) 2022/229 of 7 January 2022 on amending Delegated Regulation (EU) 2016/1675 supplementing Directive (EU) 2015/849 of the European Parliament and of the Council. Retrieved from https://eur-lex.europa.eu/legal-content/EN/TXT/PDF/?uri=CELEX:32022R0229&from=EN

EFCC. (2021). *Strategic plan 2021–2025*. EFCC.

Ellis, S. (2016). *This present darkness: A history of Nigerian organized crime*. Oxford University Press.

Epstein, H. (2014, December 4). Colossal corruption in Africa. *New York Review of Books*. Retrieved from https://www.nybooks.com/articles/2014/12/04/colossal-corruption-africa/

Erasmus, M. N. (2020). Placing clientelism and vote buying in context: An African synopsis of the phenomena. *Gender and Behavior, 18*(3), 16173–16181.

Ewi, M. (2018, August 6). Financial crime undercuts Africa's economic growth gains. *ISS Today*. Retrieved from https://issafrica.org/iss-today/financial-crime-undercuts-africas-economic-growth-gains

FIC. (2019). *Typologies and case studies*. Retrieved from https://www.masthead.co.za/wp-content/uploads/2019/04/TYPOLOGIES-CASE-STUDIES-MARCH-2019.pdf

G7 Leaders. (2022). *G7 Leaders' Communiqué*. Retrieved from https://www.g7germany.de/g7-en/g7-documents

GFI. (2018a). *Kenya: Potential revenue losses associated with trade Misinvoicing*. GFI.

GFI. (2018b). *Nigeria: Potential revenue losses associated with trade Misinvoicing*. GFI.

GFI. (2018c). *South Africa: Potential revenue losses associated with trade Misinvoicing*. GFI.

Goodwin, A. (2022). *Strategic organized crime risk assessment: South Africa*. GI-TOC.

Gyimah-Boadi, E. (2021). What is democracy capture? In *CDD-Ghana, democracy capture in Africa: Benin, Ghana, Kenya, Mozambique, Nigeria* (pp. 20–32). Accra, Ghana.

Hardoon, D., & Heinrich, F. (2013). *Global corruption barometer 2013*. TI.

Haysom, S. (2019). The illicit tobacco trade in Zimbabwe and South Africa: Impacts and solutions. [Working paper, the Atlantic Council]. Retrieved from https://www.atlanticcouncil.org/images/publications/The_Illicit_Tobacco_Trade_in_Zimbabwe_and_South_Africa.pdf

Hellman, J., Jones, G., & Kaufmann, D. (2003). Seize the state, seize the day: State capture and influence in transition economies. *Journal of Comparative Economics, 31*(4), 751–773. https://doi.org/10.1016/j.jce.2003.09.006

Hellman, J., & Kaufmann, D. (2001). Confronting the challenge of state capture in transition economies. *Finance & Development, 38*(3), 1–8.

Hellman, J., & Kaufmann, D. (2018, August 31). State capture in transition. [Submission to the Republic of South Africa Judicial Commission of Inquiry into Allegations of State Capture, Corruption and Fraud in the Public Sector Including Organs of State]. Retrieved from https://www.sastatecapture.org.za/site/files/documents/8/Bundle_of_evidence_Hellman_Kaufmann.pdf

References

Hendriyetty, N., & Grewal, B. S. (2017). Macroeconomics of money laundering: Effects and measurements. *Journal of Financial Crime, 24*(1), 65–81. https://doi.org/10.1108/JFC-01-2016-0004

Hoffmann, L. K., & Patel, R. N. (2022). Vote-selling behavior and democratic dissatisfaction in Nigeria: Is democracy really for sale? [Africa Program, Briefing Paper]. Chatham House.

Holcombe, R. G. (2013). Crony capitalism: By-product of big government. *The Independent Review, 17*(4), 541–559.

Hope, K. R. (2012). *The political economy of development in Kenya*. Bloomsbury Publishing.

Hope, K. R. (2014). Kenya's corruption problem: causes and consequences. *Commonwealth & Comparative Politics, 52*(4), 493–512. https://doi.org/10.1080/14662043.2014.955981

Hope, K. R. (2017). *Corruption and governance in Africa: Swaziland (Eswatini), Kenya, Nigeria*. Palgrave Macmillan/Springer.

HRW. (2017). *Manna from heaven? How health and education pay the Price for self-dealing in Equatorial Guinea*. HRW.

IMF. (2015). *Mali: Technical assistance report—Anti-corruption and anti-money laundering*. IMF.

Jensen, P. S., & Justesen, M. K. (2014). Poverty and vote buying: Survey-based evidence from Africa. *Electoral Studies, 33*(March), 220–232. https://doi.org/10.1016/j.electstud.2013.07.020

Jöst, P., & Lust, E. (2022, August 5). Kenya's democracy needs more than campaigns to end vote-buying: Voters attending rallies often expect to receive T-shirts, small amounts of money or other gifts. *The Washington Post*. Retrieved from https://www.washingtonpost.com/politics/2022/08/05/kenya-election-august9-vote-buying/

Justesen, M. K., & Bjørnskov, C. (2014). Exploiting the poor: Bureaucratic corruption and poverty in Africa. *World Development, 58*(June), 106–115. https://doi.org/10.1016/j.worlddev.2014.01.002

Kenny, C. (2017). *Results not receipts: Counting the right things in aid and corruption*. Center for Global Development.

Keulder, C. (2021). Africans see growing corruption, poor government response, but fear retaliation if they speak out. [Afrobarometer dispatch no. 488]. Retrieved from https://www.afrobarometer.org/publication/ad488-africans-see-growing-corruption-poor-government-response-fear-retaliation-if-they/

Khatri, N. (2016). Definitions of cronyism, corruption, and crony capitalism. In N. Khatri & A. K. Ojha (Eds.), *Crony capitalism in India* (pp. 3–7). Palgrave Macmillan.

Kimenyi, M. S., & Mbaku, J. M. (2011). Africa's war on corruption. In *Foresight Africa: The Continent's greatest challenges and opportunities for 2011* (pp. 30–32). Brookings.

Kimeria, C., & Ngila, F. (2022, July 28). Kenya is facing a shortage of small-denomination banknotes due to voter bribery, *Quartz Africa*. Retrieved from https://qz.com/kenya-is-facing-a-shortage-of-small-denomination-bankno-1849341955

Kleinfeld, R. (2019). *A savage order: How the World's deadliest countries can forge a path to security*. Vintage Books/Penguin Random House.

Kramon, E. (2018). *Money for votes: The causes and consequences of electoral Clientelism in Africa*. Cambridge University Press.

Labelle, H. (2009, September 9). Address to the ADB-OECD anti-corruption initiative for Asia and the Pacific regional seminar on political economy of corruption. Retrieved from https://www.oecd.org/site/adboecdanti-corruptioninitiative/meetingsandconferences/44442140.pdf

Leoka, T. (2017). Real-time costs of corruption: A contextual view of the south African economy. In K. Pillay (Ed.), *Annual report 2017* (pp. 24–25). Corruption Watch.

Lugon-Moulin, A. (2010). Understanding state capture. *Freedom from Fear, 6*, 38–39. https://doi.org/10.18356/86a5d3e7-en

Maina, W. (2019). *State capture: Inside Kenya's inability to fight corruption*. Africa Centre for Open Governance (AfriCOG). Retrieved from https://africog.org/wp-content/uploads/2019/05/STATE-CAPTURE.pdf

Mariotti, C., Hamer, J., & Coffey, C. (2018). *Closing the divide in Malawi: How to reduce inequality and increase prosperity for all*. Oxfam GB.

Martini, M. (2014). State capture: An overview. Retrieved from https://www.transparency.org/files/content/corruptionqas/State_capture_an_overview_2014.pdf

Maseko, N. (2022, June 24). South Africa's Zondo commission: Damning report exposes rampant corruption. *BBC News*. Retrieved from https://www.bbc.com/news/world-africa-61912737

Mbate, M. (2018). Who bears the burden of bribery? Evidence from public service delivery in Kenya. *Development Policy Review, 36*(S1), 0321–0340. https://doi.org/10.1111/dpr.12311

Mbaku, J. M. (2018). Rule of law, state capture, and human development in Africa, *American University International Law Review, 33*(4), 4. https://digitalcommons.wcl.american.edu/auilr/vol33/iss4/4.

Meirotti, M., & Masterson, G. (Eds.). (2018). *State capture in Africa: Old threats, new packaging?* Electoral Institute for Sustainable Democracy in Africa.

Menard, A.-R., & Weill, L. (2016). Understanding the link between aid and corruption: A causality analysis. *Economic Systems, 40*(2), 260–272. https://doi.org/10.1016/j.ecosys.2016.01.001

Menocal, A. R., & Others. (2015). Why corruption matters: Understanding causes, effects and how to address them. [Evidence Paper on Corruption]. Department for International Development.

Miyandazi, L., & Ronceray, M. (2018). Understanding illicit financial flows and efforts to combat them in Europe and Africa. [Discussion Paper No. 227]. ECDPM.

Mkhabela, M. (2018). South Africa and the capture of the executive: Undermining transformation? In M. Meirotti & G. Masterson (Eds.), *State capture in Africa: Old threats, new packaging?* (pp. 119–130). Electoral Institute for Sustainable Democracy. in Africa.

Moyo, D. (2009). *Dead aid: Why aid is not working and how there is a better way for Africa*. Farrar, Straus and Giroux.

Munyai, A., & Agbor, A. A. (2020). Delineating the role of foreign governments in the fight against corruption in Africa. *Cogent Social Sciences, 6*(1), 1778988. https://doi.org/10.1080/23311886.2020.1778988

Mykhalchenko, N., & Wiegratz, J. (2019). Anti-fraud measures in southern Africa. *Review of African Political Economy, 46*(161), 496–514. https://doi.org/10.1080/03056244.2019.1660156

Mykhalchenko, N., & Wiegratz, J. (2021). Anti-fraud measures in eastern Africa. *Review of African Political Economy, 48*(168), 289–304. https://doi.org/10.1080/03056244.2020.1866524

Mykhalchenko, N., & Wiegratz, J. (2022). Anti-fraud measures in Western Africa and commentary on research findings across the three regions analyzed. *Review of African Political Economy, 49*(173), 472–486. https://doi.org/10.1080/03056244.2022.2093634

Ndikumana, L., & Boyce, J. K. (2021). Capital flight from Africa, 1970–2018: New estimates with updated trade mis-invoicing methodology. [Research Report]. Political Economy Research Institute, University of Massachusetts-Amherst.

Ndikumana, L., & Boyce, J. K. (2022a). Introduction. In L. Ndikumana & J. K. Boyce (Eds.), *On the trail of capital flight from Africa: The takers and the enablers* (pp. 1–9). Oxford University Press.

Ndikumana, L., & Boyce, J. K. (Eds.). (2022b). *On the trail of capital flight from Africa: The takers and the enablers*. Oxford University Press.

Nichter, S. (2014). Conceptualizing vote buying. *Electoral Studies, 35*(September), 315–327. https://doi.org/10.1016/j.electstud.2014.02.008

Nwagwu, E. J., Uwaechia, O. G., Udegbunam, K. C., & Nnamani, R. (2022). Vote buying during 2015 and 2019 general elections: Manifestation and implications on democratic development in Nigeria. *Cogent Social Sciences, 8*(1), 1995237. https://doi.org/10.1080/23311886.2021.1995237

OECD. (2016). *Preventing corruption in public procurement*. OECD.

OECD. (2018a). *State-owned enterprises and corruption: What are the risks and what can be done?* OECD.

OECD. (2018b). *Illicit financial flows: The economy of illicit trade in West Africa*. OECD.

OECD. (2022). *Assessing tax compliance and illicit financial flows in South Africa*. OECD Publishing.

References

Okonjo-Iweala, N. (2018). *Fighting corruption is dangerous: The story behind the headlines.* The MIT Press.

Olaniyan, K. (2004). Introductory note to African union (AU): Convention on preventing and combating corruption. *International Legal Materials, 43*(1), 1–4. www.jstor.org/stable/20694430

Onuoha, F. C., & Okafor, J. C. (2020). Democracy or moneyocracy? Perspective on vote buying and electoral integrity in Nigeria's recent elections. *Africa Insight, 49*(4), 1–14.

OUTA. (2017). No room to hide: A President caught in the act. Retrieved from https://www.outa.co.za/wp-content/uploads/2017/06/2.-REPORT.pdf

Page, M. T. (2018). *A new taxonomy for corruption in Nigeria.* Carnegie Endowment for International Peace.

Peiffer, C., & Rose, R. (2018). Why are the poor more vulnerable to bribery in Africa? The institutional effects of services. *The Journal of Development Studies, 54*(1), 18–29. https://doi.org/10.1080/00220388.2016.1257121

Poisson, M. (2016). Public expenditure tracking surveys: Lessons from experience. *The IIEP Letter, 32*(1), 8–9.

PPSA. (2016). *The state of capture: A report of the public protector.* PPSA.

Pring, C. (2015). *People and corruption: Africa survey 2015–global corruption barometer.* TI.

Pring, C. (2017). *People and corruption: Citizens' voices from around the world–global corruption barometer.* TI.

Pring, C., & Vrushi, J. (2019). *Global corruption barometer Africa 2019: Citizens' views and experiences of corruption.* TI.

PwC. (2018). *Global economic crime and fraud survey 2018.* Retrieved from https://www.pwc.com/gx/en/forensics/global-economic-crime-and-fraud-survey-2018.pdf

Ramaphosa, C. (2022, June 22). Statement at the handover of the final part of the state capture commission report, Pretoria, South Africa. Retrieved from https://www.gov.za/speeches/president-cyril-ramaphosa-handover-final-part-state-capture-commission-report-22-jun-2022

Refinitiv. (2018). *Revealing the true cost of financial crime–2018 survey report: Focus on sub-Saharan Africa.* Retrieved from http://images.financial-risk-solutions.thomsonreuters.info/Web/ThomsonReutersFinancialRisk/%7B856ab4d8-e758-45fa-9855-0413693a084f%7D_17DD_Regional_Report_Sub-Saharan_Africa_v8.pdf

Refinitiv. (2021). *Financial crime in sub-Saharan Africa 2021.* Retrieved from https://www.refinitiv.com/content/dam/marketing/en_us/documents/gated/reports/re1362546-risk-fc-ssa-1920x1080-v6.pdf

Saddiq, S. A., & Abu Bakar, A. S. (2019). Impact of economic and financial crimes on economic growth in emerging and developing countries: A systematic review. *Journal of Financial Crime, 26*(3), 910–920. https://doi.org/10.1108/JFC-10-2018-0112

SARB. (2021). South African reserve bank imposes administrative sanctions on Deutsche Bank AG-Johannesburg Branch. Retrieved from https://www.resbank.co.za/content/dam/sarb/publications/media-releases/2021/administrative-sanctions-pa-march-2021/South%20African%20Reserve%20Bank%20imposes%20administrative%20sanctions%20on%20Deutsche%20Bank%20AG%20Johannesburg%20Branch.pdf

Smith, J., & Lee, K. (2018). From colonization to globalization: A history of state capture by the tobacco industry in Malawi. *Review of African Political Economy, 45*(156), 186–202. https://doi.org/10.1080/03056244.2018.1431213

Songwe, V. (2018, January 25). Statement on the theme winning the fight against corruption: A sustainable path to Africa's transformation, 30th AU summit, 32nd ordinary session of the AU executive council, Addis Ababa. Retrieved from https://au.int/en/speeches/20180125/statement-vera-songwe-united-nations-under-secretary-general-and-executive

TI. (2017). No sustainable development without tackling corruption: The importance of tracking SDG16. Retrieved from https://www.transparency.org/news/feature/no_sustainable_development_without_tackling_corruption_SDG_16

TI-Kenya. (2017). *The east African bribery index 2017.* TI-Kenya.

TI-Kenya. (2020). *Kenya bribery index 2019.* TI-Kenya.

TI-Zimbabwe. (2022). *Zimbabwe bribe payers index 2021: The dynamics of bribery within Zimbabwe's public sector*. TI-Zimbabwe.

Ufere, N., Gaskin, J., Perelli, S., Somers, A., & Boland, R. (2020). Why is bribery pervasive among firms in sub-Saharan African countries? Multi-industry empirical evidence of organizational isomorphism. *Journal of Business Research, 108*(January), 92–104. https://doi.org/10.1016/j.jbusres.2019.09.060

UN. (2005). *Economic and financial crimes: Challenges to sustainable development*. UN.

UN. (2019). Corruption and the sustainable development goals. In *World public sector report 2019: Sustainable development goal 16: Focus on public institutions* (Vol. chapter 2, pp. 39–83). UN.

UNCTAD. (2020). *Economic development in Africa report 2020: Tackling illicit financial flows for sustainable development in Africa*. UN.

UNCTAD., & UNODC. (2020). *Conceptual framework for the statistical measurement of illicit financial flows*. UNODC.

UNECA. (2018). *A study on the global governance architecture for combating illicit financial flows*. UNECA.

UNECA. (2021a). *Economic governance report I: Institutional architecture to address illicit financial flows*. UNECA.

UNECA. (2021b). *Governance of state-owned Enterprises in South Africa: Enhancing performance, efficiency and service delivery*. UNECA.

UNODC. (2022). *Corruption in Ghana–People's experiences and views*. UNODC.

UNODC., & NBS. (2019). *Corruption in Nigeria: Patterns and trends: Second survey on corruption as experienced by the population*. UNODC.

Vanguard. (2018, January 25). Africa loses $148b to corruption annually. *Vanguard*. Retrieved from https://www.vanguardngr.com/2018/01/africa-loses-148b-corruption-annually/

Vashisht, V. (2017). *Cash, corruption and economic development*. Routledge.

WIN. (2016). *Water integrity global outlook 2016*. WIN.

World Bank. (n.d.). *Enterprise surveys: Corruption*. Retrieved from http://www.enterprisesurveys.org/data/exploretopics/corruption#all-countries

World Bank. (2017). *Brief: Combating corruption*. Retrieved from http://www.worldbank.org/en/topic/governance/brief/anti-corruption

Yikona, S., Slot, B., Geller, M., Hansen, B., & el Kadiri, F. (2011). *Ill-gotten money and the economy: Experiences from Malawi and Namibia*. World Bank.

Yoon, M. Y. (2020). Voters' perceptions of gender differences in vote buying: The case of Tanzania. *Africa Spectrum, 55*(2), 125–147. https://doi.org/10.1177/2F0002039720957010

Zondo Commission. (2022). *Report: Part VI: Vol. 4: Summary of recommendations*. Zondo Commission.

Chapter 4
Revisiting the Corruption and Sustainable Development Nexus in Africa

This chapter quantifies, outlines, and analyzes the nexus between corruption and sustainable development in Africa. It employs the relevant disaggregated data and also complements that with the results of reliable empirical studies to further cross-reference and demonstrate the corruption and sustainable development nexus. The chapter shows that corruption in Africa continues to be negatively associated with development objectives and that, in turn, will continue to affect the continent's progress in achieving sustainable development. Policy implications are also considered and analyzed. Undoubtedly, corruption is very damaging to economies across all nations and regions. However, in Africa, this impact on development has been particularly severe and ongoing.

4.1 Introduction

Across all nations and regions, corruption negatively impacts sustainable development, and this "poses a threat to the legitimacy of both democracies and non-democracies" (International Institute for Democracy and Electoral Assistance [IIDEA], 2021, p. 32). In fact, 18% of democracies contend with high levels of corruption, but democratic systems of government are overall better at tackling corruption than non-democratic governments (IIDEA, 2021). In Africa, the impact of corruption on socio-economic development has been very severe and ongoing. A little more than two decades ago, Hope (2000, p. 17), for example, found that "corruption in Africa is … in fact, so pervasive [a] phenomenon in the region that it … is destroying the future of many societies in the region." Slightly less than a decade after Hope's findings and a little more than a decade ago, the UNECA re-confirmed and reported that "corruption remains the single most important challenge to the eradication of poverty, the creation of a predictable and favourable investment environment and general socio-economic development in Africa" (UNECA, 2009, p. 12). In a 2016 report, the UNECA further lamented that "as both a product and cause of poor governance and weak institutions, corruption is one of the major costs and impediments to structural transformation in Africa" (UNECA, 2016, p. 16). More recently, as discussed below, a number of other studies—both quantitative and qualitative—continue to show that corruption in Africa is negatively associated with development objectives.

Indeed, through various channels, as discussed in Chap. 3, corruption continues to limit sustainable development prospects in Africa. It has been observed that overall corruption is responsible for the continent losing the equivalent of about 25% of its average GDP and up to 50% in lost tax revenues annually. As also referenced in Chap. 3, the UNCTAD, 2020 report on economic development in Africa estimated that illicit capital flight alone from Africa amounts to US$89 billion annually which significantly eclipses the US$54 billion of foreign direct investment as well as the US$48 billion in ODA (foreign aid) that flow into the region (UNCTAD, 2020). These lost resources could all be used to advance development objectives by, among other things, contributing to the funding of the SDGs financing gap.

This chapter revisits the corruption and sustainable development nexus in Africa and offers a contemporary analysis of that relationship on the continent. It employs relevant disaggregated data and draws on the results of credible empirical studies to further demonstrate that, and then discusses some resulting policy implications for controlling corruption to mitigate its negative impact on socio-economic development in the region.

4.2 Corruption and Sustainable Development: Literature Review and Analysis

There are two schools of thought regarding the effects of corruption on sustainable development that have emerged and been identified in the academic literature. In one are the supporters of the efficiency enhancing positive effect of corruption on sustainable development and they are referred to as the "grease in the wheel" advocates. In the other, and far more prominent, school of thought are the proponents of the adverse effects of corruption on development generally, referred to as the "sand in the wheel" advocates (see, for example, Campos et al., 2010; Nur-tegin & Jakee, 2020; Venard, 2013; Xu, 2016). This book, and its author, endorse the latter school of thought and we agree with the historically proven views that corruption results in a diversion or leakage of monetary resources away from the national coffers to private spending purposes. Private spending, by definition, has much lower multiplier effects than expenditures on socio-economic development activities. Corruption therefore strangles sustainable development, with Castro and Pinho (2021) finding that a 1-unit increase in the corruption score decreases sustainable development (which was proxied and measured by adjusted net savings) by 0.12%.

4.2 Corruption and Sustainable Development: Literature Review and Analysis

We can generally summarize the empirical literature—along with the development indicators—as showing that countries with higher levels of corruption also have higher rates of poverty and inequality, and a disproportionate harming of those who are poor and vulnerable (African Union Commission [AUC] and OECD, 2018; Chuah et al., 2020; Lopez-Claros, 2015; Uslaner, 2015; World Bank, 2019); growth rates that are generally lower (Aidt, 2011; Cieślik & Goczek, 2018; d'Agostino et al., 2016; Gründler & Potrafke, 2019; IMF, 2016, 2018a; Uberti, 2022; Ugur, 2014; Wong et al., 2021); average life expectancy that is lower (Lopez-Claros, 2015; Otusanya, 2011); maternal deaths per 1000 births that are higher, average child mortality rates per 1000 live births that are higher, less investment in education and health care, lower average years of schooling, and lower child health and education indicators (Chuah et al., 2020; AU and Child-Focused Agencies [CFAs], 2019); lower overall human development (Dimant & Tosato, 2018; Esona, 2020; Mbaku, 2019; Murshed & Mredula, 2018); higher propensity to experiencing food insecurity (Olabiyi, 2022; Nugroho et al., 2022); lower public policy effectiveness, poor governance and a rise in capital flight (Ganahl, 2013; Hope, 2017b; Osei-Assibey et al., 2018); lower inward foreign direct investment (Cieślik & Goczek, 2018; Qureshi et al., 2021); increased pollution, triggered CO_2 emissions, and natural-resource depletion (IMF, 2016; Murshed & Mredula, 2018); reduced levels of the culture of compliance leading to increased tax evasion and reduced tax revenues (IMF, 2019; Jahnke & Weisser, 2019); sub-standard infrastructure (IMF, 2016; O'Toole & Tarp, 2014; World Bank, 2019); and a higher tendency to facilitate financial and organized crime (International Criminal Police Organization [INTERPOL], 2019).

Despite the complexity of the relationship, there is also some emerging empirical evidence challenging the more or less conventional wisdom that urbanization/modernization ultimately lowers corruption. Adou (2022), for example, has found that, on average, a 1% increase in urbanization in African nations is associated with at least a 0.25–0.5% increase in corruption. This thereby intimates that "urbanization is conducive to corruption in an African context because urbanization is characterized by a more individualistic lifestyle reducing thus the cost of being corrupt as there are fewer social sanctions and peer pressure compared to community-based traditional life" (Adou, 2022, p. 1).

Other empirical results also show that bringing corruption down in a country to the world average levels could increase GDP per capita. In sub-Saharan Africa countries, for example, such a reduction in corruption would increase GDP by 1–2 percentage points (Hammadi et al., 2019). In that regard, a recent country study on Mozambique, for example, by the Centro de Integridade Pública (CIP) and the Chr. Michelsen Institute (CMI), aggregated the monetary value cost of corruption to the country and demonstrated its negative impact on macro-economic aggregates such as GDP. According to the CIP and CMI (2016, p. 7), "the estimated average annual cost of corruption, as observed during the ten years from 2004 to 2014, is up to US$4.9 billion, equivalent to around 30% of the 2014 GDP and 60% of the 2015 budget."

In looking further at both the direct and indirect costs of corruption, the OECD (2015) also found that in developing countries heavily reliant on extractive industries as a driver of economic growth and development (many of which are in Africa), corruption is expected to continue to undermine the performance of their resource sectors. In that same vein, Gillies (2020), in an analysis of corruption trends in Africa's oil sector, noted that in those situations where corruption is enticed by rents, the enabling environment is provided by the rentier state. In Angola, Roque (2021, p. 84) has shown that corruption and rent-seeking in the oil sector has "continued to hijack the country's ability to build a stable socio-economic foundation for growth," with "oil growth [leading] towards greater poverty."

Another area where the literature shows that corruption negatively impacts sustainable development is that of access to, and delivery of, socio-economic services. Freytag and Riaz (2021), for instance, have confirmed that regional or local level country corruption represents a significant barrier to accessing public socio-economic services such as education, health care, water, and paved roads, for example. Budgetary resources that were intended to deliver public services have been pocketed instead and sustainable development is therefore stifled. ONE – which is a global campaigning and advocacy organization that takes action to eliminate extreme poverty and preventable disease, especially in Africa—published an analysis that has estimated the direct impact of corruption on development and concluded that in sub-Saharan Africa, curbing corruption could provide the money to: (1) Educate an additional ten million children per year; (2) Pay for an additional half-million primary school teachers–providing all out-of-school children in 16 of those countries with an education; (3) Provide antiretroviral (ARV) drugs for over 11 million people living with HIV/AIDS; and (4) Pay for almost 165 million vaccines (see McNair et al., 2014). Mbaku (2022) has also provided an excellent analytical review of the impact of corruption on African children's education, welfare, development, and human rights.

Undoubtedly, and as the literature and analysis above demonstrate, corruption is very damaging to any economy. Therefore, corruption can never improve economic efficiency by greasing the wheels (Aidt, 2019; Chuah et al., 2020). Consequently, the views expressed—several decades ago—that corruption can potentially contribute to economic development are not valid and, in fact, have been severally discredited over the years.

4.3 The Corruption and Sustainable Development Nexus in Africa

Basically, the impact of corruption on sustainable development in Africa primarily revolves around, and is influenced by, the front-end loss (diversion) of public resources away from actual or potential development purposes, the capturing of institutions for the back-end diverting of public resources for private gain, and illegal individual or syndicate acts such as bribery and embezzlement and theft. In all cases, the public becomes the loser as the development process eventually becomes impaired because legitimately available, acquired and/or allocated public/private resources are illegitimately re-purposed for the benefit of a private few at the expense of the larger nation-state or even smaller political jurisdiction(s) within the said nation-state.

To demonstrate the impact of corruption on sustainable development, we examine the relationship trends between indicators of corruption and measures of development, where comparative time series data are available for cross-reference. In that regard, and before engaging in cross-referencing the data, including through summarizing and analyzing applicable empirical studies, it is useful to first identify and outline the credible comparative indicators of both overall corruption and/or the key components of corruption, as well as their sources, being utilized in this work. Similarly, the key indicators of sustained development employed in this work are also described below.

4.3.1 The Corruption Indicators

Two sets of corruption indicators, and their respective source, are delineated below. Each indicator is internationally recognized as reliable and both of them are frequently drawn upon and cited in the research and policy literature where measures of corruption are required.

4.3.1.1 The Corruption Perceptions Index

The Corruption Perceptions Index (CPI) has emerged, over the years, as the most popular indicator of corruption at both national and regional levels. Developed and published annually by Transparency International, it scores and ranks countries or territories around the world based on surveys and assessments on how corrupt a country's public sector is perceived to be by experts and business executives (TI, 2020). It utilizes a scale of 0–100, wherein zero implies that a country is perceived as highly corrupt and 100 indicates that a country is regarded as very clean. Each country's score is a combination of at least three data sources drawn from 13 different corruption surveys and assessments that capture perceptions of corruption within the past two years. A country's rank is therefore its position relative to the other countries in the index. The regional scores are the regional average. The data sources are collected by a variety of reputable institutions, including the World Bank (TI, 2021). The CPI is freely available and easily accessible online.

4.3.1.2 The Control of Corruption Indicator in the Worldwide Governance Indicators

The Control of Corruption (CoC) is one of six composite indicators of broad dimensions of governance in the Worldwide Governance Indicators (WGI) developed at the World Bank. The CoC composite indicator, as stated by the World Bank (n.d., p. 1), "captures perceptions of the extent to which public power is exercised for private gain, including both petty and grand forms of corruption, as well as 'capture' of the state by elites and private interests." It also measures how strongly and effectively a country's institutional and policy framework prevents and combats corruption (World Bank n.d.). The CoC indicator is reported out in two ways: (1) in standard normal units, ranging from approximately −2.5 (high corruption) to 2.5 (low corruption); and (2) in percentile rank terms from 0 to 100, with higher values corresponding to higher governance outcomes (World Bank n.d.). The regional scores are also based on the regional average.

According to Hamilton and Hammer (2018), the CoC composite subjective indicator, along with the CPI, are the most appropriate corruption indicators as they represent the best beginning point of any empirical analysis, given that they are more comprehensive and thus more likely to capture all elements of corruption. Similarly, Bello y Villarino (2021, p. 740) concluded that "both the post–2012 CPI and the CoC offer reasonably reliable and minimally valid measurements of perceptions of corruption which can be used with the relevant caveats as proxies for levels of prevalence of corruption in different jurisdictions."

4.3.2 The Development Indicators

Three sets of development indicators are outlined below. Each indicator is also internationally recognized as reliable and is frequently drawn upon and cited in the research and policy literature where measures of development are required.

4.3.2.1 Poverty Rates

Being poor goes beyond not having enough financial and other productive resources to meet basic needs. Poverty can also be seen more holistically as it manifests itself in hunger and malnutrition, and limited access to health care, education, shelter, and other basic services that encompass what is now regarded as multidimensional poverty (Oxford Poverty and Human Development Initiative [OPHI], n.d.).

The two indicators of poverty rates that are employed in this work are: (1) the proportion of the population living below the international poverty line; and (2) the proportion of the population in multidimensional poverty based on the Multidimensional Poverty Index (MPI) which was developed by the UNDP and the OPHI at the University of Oxford and is released annually. On a global scale, the

MPI measures acute multidimensional poverty across more than 100 developing countries. It achieves that by measuring deprivations of each person across 10 indicators in three dimensions that are equally weighted: (1) health; (2) education; and (3) standard of living (OPHI, 2021a). By identifying both who is poor as well as how they are poor, the global MPI also complements the international poverty rate of $US1.90 per day (OPHI, 2021a). By definition therefore, the proportion of people who are multidimensionally poor will always be higher than the proportion of those who are income poor.

4.3.2.2 GDP per Capita

GDP per capita expresses the average economic output (or income) per person in a country, and is a global measure for gauging the prosperity of nations. It is calculated by dividing the nominal (market value or current prices) GDP by the total population of a country. The population statistic used is usually the average (or mid-year) population for the same year as the GDP statistic (see, for example, The Investopedia Team, 2022). GDP is the standard measure used for the value added from the production of goods and services in a country during a certain period. When adjusted for inflation, GDP is referred to as real GDP.

The GDP growth rate measures the percentage change in real GDP from one period to another, typically comparing the most recent quarter or year and the previous one. It can be a positive or negative number (indicating economic expansion or contraction). The real GDP growth rate is often used as an indicator of the general state of performance of an economy. Generally, an increase in real GDP is taken as an indication that the economy is expanding well while the opposite is true of a decrease in real GDP.

4.3.2.3 Public Debt

Public debt (sometimes referred to as government debt, national debt, or even sovereign debt) is the amount a government owes at a given time. It can be regarded as the cumulative sum of all previous fiscal deficits and is basically an indicator of how much public spending is financed by borrowing instead of taxation or other government revenues. The public debt increases when there is a fiscal deficit and can decline when there is a surplus, depending on government priorities. In most African nations, a considerable portion of the fiscal deficit is attributed to corruption and that, in turn, leads to government borrowing to meet the shortfalls which then increases public debt that can become too much of an economic burden to said African nations (see, for example, Madow et al., 2021).

Although the magnitude of a country's public debt is of importance, it is the ability of a nation to service said magnitude that is of greater importance. The tool used to analyze that is referred to as the debt-to-GDP ratio which is measured as public debt as a percentage of GDP. By comparing what a nation owes with the value of the goods and services it produces, the debt-to-GDP ratio indicates that particular nation's ability to pay back its debts. The higher a nation's debt-to-GDP ratio, the greater the potential risk of default and economic hardship. However, a high ratio is both acceptable and manageable if a country is able to pay interest on its debt without having to refinance or adversely impact its economic growth as is the case, for example, with Japan (a G7 nation) where the debt-to-GDP ratio has been exceeding 230% for the past several years (OECD, 2022).

4.3.3 The Contemporary Evidence

Below, we provide some of the contemporary empirical evidence (primarily quantitative) on the relationship/impact of corruption on sustainable development in Africa. That evidence lends support to the "sand in the wheel" perspective, with corruption now being widely acknowledged as a major obstacle to sustainable development as argued in this book.

4.3.3.1 Corruption and Poverty

Figure 4.1 depicts the trends in the relationship between corruption and poverty in sub-Saharan Africa. Although having abundant resources, sub-Saharan Africa is not only the most corrupt region in the world (see Fig. 4.2) but the poorest region in the world as well. Despite the fact that average poverty rates are declining in sub-Saharan Africa, corruption perception indices have not followed the same pattern of improvement and, in fact, have declined slightly since 2015 from a score of 33 and remained fairly stable as an overall average at a score of 32 in 2020, but decreasing significantly in many of the countries while increasing in just a few (TI, 2021).

Corruption not only contributes to poverty by affecting national economic development but it also reinforces the poverty status of those that are already poor and that, in turn, leads to greater inequality in society. For Africa, there are studies that show, for example, that the poor are much more likely to be victims of corruption within their society than the non-poor (Hope, 2017a; Jimada, 2018). For Nigeria, Adebayo (2013, p. 231) found that corruption intensified poverty in that country and remains the biggest barrier to ending extreme poverty by, among other things, "preventing funds reaching healthcare and education, limiting individuals' abilities to access jobs and social benefits, corroding systems of law, and stopping aid working effectively." Similarly, research by ActionAid Nigeria (2015) and the chapters in Àkànle and Nkpe (2022) also found that corruption in Nigeria has been responsible for the diversion of funds away from the employment and wealth generation sectors of the economy, and thereby making the reduction of poverty difficult to accomplish. Also, Yusuf et al. (2014) found that corruption causes poverty in Nigeria but that good governance capabilities is much more likely to provide faster economic growth and reduce both corruption and poverty in Nigeria.

4.3 The Corruption and Sustainable Development Nexus in Africa

Fig. 4.1 Comparative relationship between the corruption perceptions index score and poverty rates (%), at the US$1.90-a-day poverty line and the multidimensional poverty index incidence (%), for sub-Saharan Africa, 2010–2020[a]. *Notes:* [a]The poverty rate, at the US$1.90-a-day Poverty Line, for 2020 is a projection estimate of the author. *Source:* Author, based on data derived from OPHI (2021b); TI (2021); and World Bank (2021a)

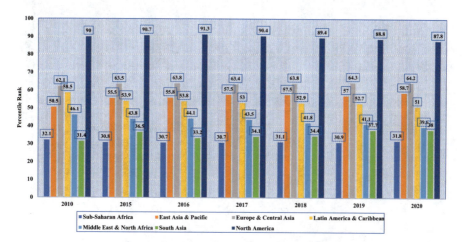

Fig. 4.2 Control of Corruption Indicator by Region (Percentile Rank), 2010–2020. *Source:* Author, based on data derived from World Bank (2021b)

Other examples can be found in studies on South Africa, for instance, where Salahuddin et al. (2020), using data covering the period 1991–2016, showed that corruption increases poverty by its positive long-run effects on the poverty headcount and infant mortality rates. They estimated that, in the long run, a 1% increase in corruption increases the poverty headcount and infant mortality rates by 0.08% and 0.007%, respectively, while a 1% increase in corruption reduces the life expectancy rate by 0.007% (Salahuddin et al., 2020). Corruption therefore intensifies poverty. In The Gambia also, research results from Jeng (2018), for example, show that corruption and poverty have a positive and statistically significant relationship at a 5% confidence level. It therefore suggests that as corruption increases, poverty also tends to increase in The Gambia.

4.3.3.2 Corruption and GDP Growth

In Fig. 4.3, we see the relationship between corruption and GDP per capita growth. Wherein the dismal corruption indices have been holding relatively steady for sub-Saharan Africa, GDP per capita growth has had a much more dreadful performance

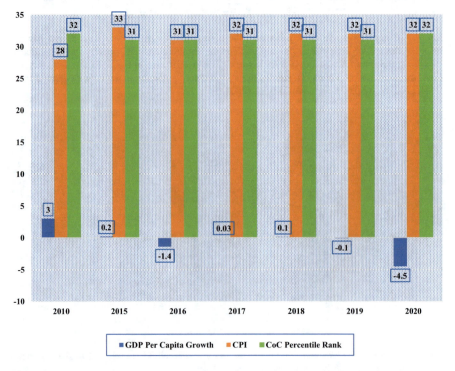

Fig. 4.3 Comparison relationship between corruption and GDP per capita growth for sub-Saharan Africa, 2010–2020. *Source:* Author, based on data derived from TI (2021); and World Bank (2021b, 2021c)

4.3 The Corruption and Sustainable Development Nexus in Africa

since 2010 when it was at 3%. Since 2010, the GDP per capita growth rate has not even reached 1% and, in fact, has been negative in most of the years. Although some exogenous factors, such as the coronavirus disease 2019 (COVID-19), have recently contributed to this state of affairs, over the years it is the endogenous factors, such as rampant corruption and overall bad governance, that have been affecting the growth and sustainable development prospects of African nations.

In their study, Omoteso and Mobolaji (2014) investigated the impact of control of corruption, among other governance indicators, on economic growth in some selected sub-Saharan Africa countries for the period 2002 to 2009 and concluded that a 1-unit change in control of corruption, would lead to a 0.83-unit change in the rate of economic growth in these countries. For East Africa, some empirical results by Jama (2021), for example, showed that corruption has a negative effect on economic development with a finding that a 1% decline in control of corruption will lead to a −0.6407% increase in economic growth. For Ghana, using data covering the period 1984 to 2016, Antwi et al. (2020) reveal a significant negative relationship between corruption and economic growth in both the short-run and the long-run. They determined that "a change in corruption results in a corresponding negative change of 60[%] in growth in the long-term. In the short-term, a change in corruption results in a corresponding negative change of 82[%] in growth" (Antwi et al., 2020, p. 174).

Other studies have also arrived at similar conclusions. For Zimbabwe, the empirical analysis of Muzurura (2017) showed that high levels of corruption/rent-seeking are detrimental to economic growth. For Nigeria, the empirical analysis reveals that the relationship between the level of corruption and economic growth is a long-run one, and that corruption's impact on economic growth in the country is negative (Nwankwo, 2014). The IMF (2018b) has also found that by reducing corruption to the levels of other sub-Saharan African or peer countries, Nigeria could increase its real GDP growth by 0.5 to 1.5 percentage points annually. For the Republic of Congo, Melina et al. (2019) determined that anti-corruption reforms could increase growth by 0.8 to 1.8% per year over a ten-year period. For South Africa, Olamide and Maredza (2023) employed the Autoregressive Distributed Lag (ARDL) technique to time series data running from 1990 to 2019 and concluded that corruption exerts a negative influence on economic growth, and more so in the short-run, with a 1% increase in corruption reducing growth by 0.3%.

Looking at the broader picture across sub-Saharan Africa, Forson et al. (2017) have also provided robust findings that show, overall, both incidental and systematic corruption pose a long-term threat to development. Correspondingly, a review analysis by Mlambo et al. (2019) found that corruption, undoubtedly, hinders Africa's economic growth and development prospects. School (2019) applied four different empirical models using data from 46 African countries, covering the period 2000–2017, that showed that there is a strong negative correlation between corruption and economic growth and that the more corrupt African countries tended to grow at a slower rate than countries that are less corrupt. And, Esona (2020) also applied several econometric models to a panel data set, covering the 2005–2015 period, for a cross-section of 40 sub-Saharan countries and found that corruption has a negative and statistically significant impact on growth. According to the results, a one standard deviation increase in the corruption level results in an expected decrease in the per capita GDP growth rate by 0.45 of its standard deviation. Further, Castro and Pinho (2021) in their empirical analysis of 134 countries (more than 30 of which are African) and covering the period 2000–2018, determined that a 1-unit increase in the corruption score decreases GDP per capita by 5.61%. Also, Spyromitros and Panagiotidis (2022), in their empirical analysis, showed that corruption is a deterrent to growth in sub-Saharan Africa with a 1% increase in corruption deceasing per capita GDP by 1.61%.

By retarding growth, corruption impedes the long-term prospects for socio-economic development in Africa. Economic growth is a pre-requisite for sustained development. However, as the IMF has indicated, the outlook remains extremely uncertain, and risks are tilted to the downside (IMF, 2021, 2022a). Similarly, the African Development Bank has identified headwinds and a number of downside risks to Africa's economic outlook, including wary investor sentiment due to IFFs (AfDB, 2021). Although real GDP in sub-Saharan Africa has been in a positive state over the years, per capita GDP growth, as shown in Fig. 4.4, has been overwhelmed by population growth and other exogenous and endogenous factors as previously noted. In fact, *The Africa Prosperity Report 2019–2020* has observed that much greater prosperity in the region is being inhibited due to a continent-wide decline in the strength of institutions, with governance declining in every sub-region and corruption becoming even more rampant, potentially threatening to hamper growth

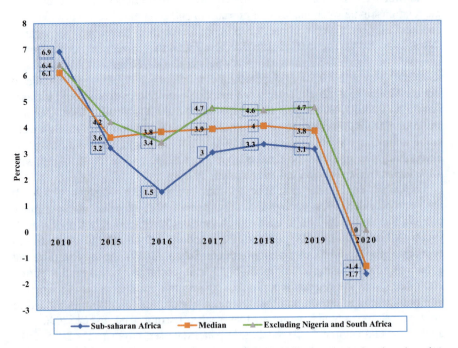

Fig. 4.4 Sub-Saharan Africa real GDP growth (%), 2010–2020. *Source:* Author, based on data derived from IMF (2021)

which, in turn, threatens to intensify existing economic inequalities (The Legatum Institute, 2020).

4.3.3.3 Corruption and Public Debt

Moving on to the fiscal side, we see in Fig. 4.5 that the debt ratio has been increasing in sub-Saharan Africa over the past decade. Clearly then, this was a problem across all income groups of African countries prior to the emergence of COVID-19. Indeed, it is projected that the debt-to-GDP ratio average in Africa will increase significantly over the short-term to more than 70%, and problems with corruption, mismanagement, and overall poor governance have all been identified as major contributors to the debt ordeal episodes that are currently confronting some of the countries (AfDB, 2021).

In Kenya, for instance, one commentator has pronounced that "the real debt burden in Kenya is corruption" with the hemorrhaging of funds through said corruption resulting in budgetary shortfalls which are then filled through borrowing (Ngugi, 2021, p. 1). Similar sentiments about corruption and debt in South Africa have likewise been uttered by Fray (2020), for example. Also, for Zimbabwe, research by Mutondoro (2020), covering the period 2010–2019, concluded that corruption in

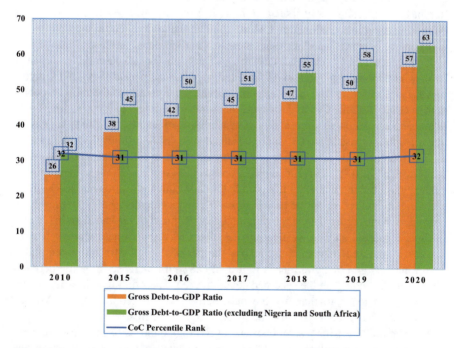

Fig. 4.5 Comparison relationship between the control of corruption percentile ranking and the gross debt-to-GDP ratio for sub-Saharan Africa, 2010–2020. *Source:* Author, based on data derived from IMF (2021); and World Bank (2021b)

the country has culminated in a significant increase in the magnitude of the fiscal deficits and public debt resulting in the off-loading of those debts onto the taxpayers through the Reserve Bank Debt Assumption Bill and the Zimbabwe Asset Management Company (ZAMCO). Continent-wide, the All-Africa Conference of Churches (AACC) has also expressed its concerns about corruption and its effects on public debt (see AACC, 2020, 2021). Based on data from IMF (2021), this work finds that the top five places for countries in terms of highest average debt-to-GDP ratio for the period 2015–2020 are: Eritrea at 185%, Cabo Verde at 132%, Mozambique at 108%, Angola at 91%, and Congo (Republic of) and São Tomé and Príncipe both tied at 86%.

In an empirical analysis using a sample of 29 sub-Saharan Africa countries, and with data covering the period 2000–2015, Henri (2018) found that a 1-unit increase in corruption leads to a 0.64-unit increase in public debt. Likewise, in their empirical study of a panel of 47 African nations covering data for the period 2000–2018, Appiah-Kubi et al. (2022) found that the increasing level of corruption in African countries fosters a rise in public debt levels. Similarly, Owusu-Nantwi and Owusu-Nantwi (2023) measured the effect of corruption and the shadow economy on public debt in 51 African countries, using data covering the period 1996–2015, and found a positive and statistically significant relationship between corruption and public debt with a 1-unit increase in the corruption index increasing public debt by 0.06%. Thiao (2021) has also empirically demonstrated that high levels of corruption have significantly contributed to the reduction of public revenues in the West African Economic and Monetary Union (WAEMU) nations. This, in turn, has led to unnecessary borrowing and resultant increases in their debt burdens.

Cooray et al. (2017) in their study using annual data for 126 countries (more than 30 of which are in sub-Saharan Africa), and covering the period 1996–2012, determined that the greater the corruption in a country the greater is the ratio of public debt to GDP. Both the CPI and the CoC measures were found to have positive coefficients and in all cases were highly statistically significant. The results suggested that a 1-unit increase in the CPI increases the debt-to-GDP ratio by 0.12–0.13% and a 1-unit increase in the CoC indicator increases the debt-to-GDP ratio by 0.11–0.13% (Cooray et al., 2017). Correspondingly, Apergis and Apergis (2019) in their empirical analysis, making use of annual data from 120 countries (more than 30 of which are African) and spanning the period 1999–2015, documented that higher levels of corruption contribute to higher government debt. Similarly, Naz and Yasmin (2021), in their empirical study investigating the effect of corruption on public debt in selected Asian and African countries for the period 1990–2016, estimated that a 1-unit increase in corruption leads to a 0.52–0.81-unit increase in public debt-to-GDP ratio depending on the specified equation used. Their findings show that overall corruption tends to magnify the debt burden in selected Asian and African countries but the effect is found to be much sharper in Africa.

Ibrahim (2021), using a sample of 20 developing countries from various regions across the world (including Africa) that have high levels of corruption and covering the period 1996–2018, provided empirical results that found that corruption increases the debt-to-GDP ratio in the long-run. A 1% increase in corruption was found to increase the debt-to-GDP ratio by 6.28%, with the estimations also showing that high corruption hampers long-term economic growth and increases the adverse effect that public debt has on economic growth in developing countries (Ibrahim, 2021). Likewise, Benfratello et al. (2018) in their cross-country empirical investigation, using a large sample of 164 countries (most of which were African nations) and covering the period 1995–2015, provided evidence that corruption contributes to increased sovereign debt. Their results showed that corruption has a positive coefficient with respect to public debt and is statistically significant at the 5% confidence level. In other words, overall, the estimates reveal that corruption increases public debt (Benfratello et al., 2018).

Corruption increases public debt through such avenues as the lowering of tax revenues which impairs a country's capacity to repay its debts; increases in public expenditures which, in turn, can both increase public debt and require public debt to service those expenditures; and decisions on the structure or composition of public borrowing, which may be riskier, with the result that debt servicing may be needlessly more expensive for the national treasury. For South Africa, for example, Levy et al. (2021) determined that the main causes of the country's debt are due primarily to the costs of corruption (including the costs of refinancing the SOEs damaged by said corruption) and, in some extent, high government expenditures due to salary increases in the public sector. By 2020, South Africa's government debt was 69.4% of GDP compared to 31% in 2010 (IMF, 2022b). This was more than double and represented an increase of 55%.

4.4 Policy Implications and Conclusion

Corruption is, undoubtedly, a very serious impediment to socio-development in Africa as demonstrated above and throughout this book. Among other things, corruption is a barrier to financing sustainable development on the continent, a continent that also faces financial constraints and greater pressure to mobilize domestic resources. The logical policy implications and conclusion that emerge are that improving actions against corruption (the key elements of which are outlined and discussed below) can achieve a significant improvement in development outcomes.

4.4.1 Leadership and Anti-Corruption Institutions

In her remarks at the Ninth Commonwealth Africa Anti-Corruption Agencies Conference, the Commonwealth Secretary-General was moved to urge African leaders "to make tackling corruption a priority of the highest order" as "eliminating corruption brings multiple benefits; poverty is reduced, economic stability and growth are increased, and standards of living raised" (Scotland, 2019, p. 2). In that vein, as recognized for South Africa by President Cyril Ramaphosa, African leaders must also become or remain resolute in leading the fight against corruption, restoring the integrity and capability of public institutions, and overcoming any existence of state capture or attempts to corruptly capture the state (Ramaphosa, 2022).

Consequently, much more needs to be done on the anti-corruption campaign front in Africa. Similar conclusions have been derived from empirical analysis by Amegavi et al. (2022) with the necessary caveat to tailor strategies to individual country circumstances across the spectrum of the relatively least corrupt and the highly corrupt. However, to the extent that corruption continues to be a chronic problem in Africa, it would seem that a greater transformative approach is required. Such a transformation would also need to include and occur at both the national leadership and technocratic levels to accomplish what Spector (2022) refers to as the promotion of sustainable behavioral change. This is necessitated by the fundamental conclusion that an entirely new mind set is required to set the tone and champion new policy frameworks for much better anti-corruption results. The anti-corruption leadership efforts and approach adopted for Singapore by its first, and now late, Prime Minister, Lee Kuan Yew, is instructive here as it made "corruption a high-risk, low reward activity by punishing impartially those found guilty of corruption offences, regardless of their position, status, or political affiliation" (Quah, 2022, pp. 173–174). Corruption in Singapore is almost non-existent. But, perhaps these results may also be related to the setting of the tone and culture from the inception of post-independence rule as we can also point to similar results from similar efforts in Botswana (formerly Bechuanaland Protectorate) under its first Prime Minister/President, Sir Seretse Khama (see, for example, Hern, 2023; Rotberg, 2012; Sebudubudu & Botlhomilwe, 2012). In recent times, we have also seen how such leadership in Rwanda, with the ongoing signaling of zero tolerance for corruption and a solid and consistent enforcement of that policy approach, has considerably reduced corruption in the country. As observed by the World Bank (2020a, p. 9), Rwanda "is one of the rare examples of a poor country that, in only a few years, dramatically reduced the level of corruption." In fact, "the country's experience could yield broader and original lessons for understanding what works against corruption," and "Rwanda's insistence on public sector integrity has been a cornerstone of its development strategy" as "its consistent commitment to holding officials to account for achieving development outcomes is a counterpoint to the more episodic and less successful efforts to stamp out corruption in neighboring countries."

Johnston and Fritzen (2021) have also weighed in on this leadership issue and advocated for the backing of those leaders who, inevitably, take the heat for taking the anti-corruption lead. It also provides the potential to limit what Stephenson (2020) regards as the self-reinforcing aspects of corruption whether the ensuing reform actions are of a big bang nature or incremental over some extended period. This view is further illustrated by the fact, as observed by Senu (2020, p. 676), that "corrupt practices have survived because the numerous anti-corruption laws or development agendas are still founded in negotiations or patterns containing the very impediments against which anti-corruption laws and UNCAC were established."

4.4 Policy Implications and Conclusion

In that respect also, the ACAs—where they exist or need to be established where they do not—must be allowed to pursue their mandates independently but be governed by appropriate legislation so that they do not abuse their power or become powers of their own without regard to the performance standards of fair, apolitical, and impartial functioning. Likewise, they should not be abused or rendered impotent by the political elite. In East Africa, for example, it was determined that while sound legal frameworks for battling corruption exist, there seem to be deliberate efforts by the executive and legislative branches in the respective countries to limit or defeat the abilities of the ACAs to undertake their mandates. This has manifested itself through changes in some laws and a failure to act according to others, as well as in intimidation and the constraining of budgets (AfriMAP, 2016). It is not surprising therefore that those African nations (such as Botswana, Cabo Verde, and Seychelles) that usually have the highest scores in the corruption perception and corruption control indices generally have better and stronger institutions of governance, including their ACAs. So, a first order in the anti-corruption policy framework is to enforce the performance standards through truly independent ACAs. Furthermore, when ACAs are able to function as suggested here, they could also increase possibilities to overcome collective action obstacles thrown their way by politicians and other private interests (Hope, 2017a, 2017b; Martinsson, 2021; Musila, 2019).

4.4.2 Enhancing Asset Recovery

A particularly pertinent implication for policy that has emerged from this work is the importance of enhancing asset recovery. All assets that are deemed and proven to have been acquired through corrupt dealings (either obtained or held in local transactions or through IFFs) must be pursued for recovery and returned to the national treasury. IFFs have been a major source of leakage from African economies in recent years and is now being thoroughly scrutinized by both international and regional development institutions as well as think tanks and academic researchers (see, for example, Gumede & Fadiran, 2019; Ndikumana & Boyce, 2021; Signé et al., 2020; UNCTAD, 2020; UNECA, 2021). Curtailing IFFs through better governance and administrative frameworks locally, and greater repatriation efforts to get funds returned from abroad, must therefore be at the forefront of the anti-corruption efforts of African nations (see also Asongu & Nnanna, 2020). Smith (2021) further argues that plugging such capital leaks would reduce both the need to borrow and the corrupt misuse of such loan proceeds.

However, much more important—than relying on international law, conventions, and foreign relations to get funds repatriated from abroad—is local surveillance and enforcement. Indeed, as argued by Vogl (2022, p. 120), "a quantum upgrade in enforcement capabilities is crucial to curb money laundering." It is this money laundering that primarily leads to IFFs and through currency substitution also as necessary for the safe haven of the looted funds (see, for example, Akinlo, 2022; Maguchu,

2022 in their case studies of Nigeria and Zimbabwe, respectively). As we have seen from past history, and as also noted, for example, by Cooley et al. (2018) and Vogl (2022), central to the increase in the magnitude of IFFs is the complicity of local kleptocrats and the cooperation they receive from enablers in Western nations (including financial institutions, real estate brokers, and luxury goods traders) who aid and abet the kleptocrats for elaborate fees as also discussed in Chap. 3. Consequently, in the first place, a much more local-based approach is required to police the systems to control the laundering of money and its exit out of African borders.

A necessary and urgent consideration in the local-based approach is that of making beneficial ownership transparency, through registration, mandatory. By 2021, only 21% of sub-Saharan Africa countries were asking companies to submit information on beneficial owners (Coste & Meunier, 2021). As of March 2022, according to Knobel and Lorenzo (2022), just 12 African countries had beneficial ownership laws. A beneficial owner is a natural person or persons (i.e., not a corporate vehicle) who ultimately own or control a legal entity or arrangement, such as a company, a trust, or a foundation on whose behalf transactions or activities are being conducted or will be conducted, and who benefit from the income it generates. The lack of beneficial ownership registration leads to anonymity and that, in turn, enables many illegal activities, such as corruption (including money laundering), tax evasion, and financing of terrorism, to occur out of the view of law enforcement authorities (Basel Institute on Governance, 2021; Chatain et al., 2022; Coste & Meunier, 2021).

4.4.3 Emphasizing E-Government Implementation

Finally, another policy implication/conclusion that has arisen from this work is the need for African governments, at all levels, to emphasize or re-emphasize the implementation and application of e-government as a major governance tool that can also be beneficial for the prevention, detection, and prosecution of corruption. E-government (electronic government)—sometimes variously referred to as digital government, e-governance, online government, or smart government—is the utilization of information and communication technologies (ICTs) in government functions and procedures with the intention of improving and increasing transparency, efficiency, service delivery, and citizen empowerment and participation. It is ultimately intended to embrace good government principles and achieve beneficial national policy goals, and therefore provides for important outcomes, especially for government transactions that involve moneys (such as budgeting, tax collection, and procurement contracting, for instance) by, among other things, making it possible to trace and link those who are involved in corrupt activities (see, for example, AU, 2020; Basel Institute on Governance, 2017; IMF, 2020; Park & Kim, 2020; Srivastava et al., 2016; Zhao & Xu, 2015).

4.4 Policy Implications and Conclusion

Adam (2020), in an empirical analysis of 51 African countries, found that e-government significantly has the positive effect of reducing corruption through ICT development. Likewise, a systematic literature review by Inuwa and Ononiwu (2020) points to the overwhelming evidence that e-government can reduce corruption. Also, Walle et al. (2018), in their empirical analysis of 45 sub-Saharan Africa nations based on data covering the period 2012–2016, estimated that digital government development and adoption reduces corruption by as much as 37%. And, Calderón and Cantú (2021, p. 33) provide empirical "evidence that digital technologies have the potential to provide Africa with opportunities to unlock new pathways for rapid economic growth, a more egalitarian distribution of income, and poverty reduction," all of which can reduce corruption. Other studies have also shown that, despite some continuing issues with tax administration (including corruption), digitalization can improve tax collection and increase revenue mobilization (see, for example, Okunogbe & Santoro, 2022). In that regard, according to the UNECA (2009), through digitalization, Rwanda was able to boost tax revenue by 6%, South Africa, lowered the time (by 21.8%) and cost (by 22%) of compliance with the value-added tax (VAT), and Kenya was able to identify data inconsistencies and increase VAT collections by more than US$1 billion between 2016 and 2017.

Moreover, Ouedraogo and Sy (2020), UNECOSOC (2022), and World Bank (2020b) have all summarized and advocated that in countries that start out with a high level of corruption— such as those in Africa—e-government or digitalization is associated with better control of corruption as it decreases opportunities for arbitrary interference by corrupt public officials through the automation of internal bureaucratic processes and thereby also decreasing the reliance on paper-based processes and in-person interactions. Using survey data covering 36 African countries for the period 2014–2015, it was empirically determined that, on average, the adoption of digital tools is correlated with a reduction of corruption perception in tax administration by around 4 percentage points (Ouedraogo & Sy, 2020). In Ghana, as a country case study, for instance, Addo (2021), Ayakwah et al. (2021), and Bala et al. (2022) have outlined that digitalization has decreased corruption and increased efficiency in such public service delivery areas as port and harbor operations; customs clearance processes; the enrolment, renewal and payments for the national health insurance scheme; payment of utility bills; a consolidated database of taxpayers; and location and address systems. It is anticipated that the electronic collection of taxes and fees should help Ghana increase its tax-to-GDP ratio from 12% to about 16% by the end of 2022 (Bala et al., 2022).

To measure the state of e-government development in UN member states, the United Nations Department of Economic and Social Affairs (UNDESA) developed the e-government development index (EGDI). The EGDI, which assesses e-government development at the national level, is a composite index based on the weighted average of three normalized indices based on: (1) one-third from the Telecommunications Infrastructure Index (TII); (2) one-third from the Human Capital Index (HCI); and (3) one-third from the Online Services Index (OSI) (UNDESA, 2022). The score of the EGDI ranges between 0–1. Although Africa's EGDI score has been improving over the years, the continent is still behind other regions and continues to be the region with the lowest score which was 0.4054 in 2022 compared to 0.8305 for Europe, 0.6493 for Asia, 0.6438 for the Americas, 0.5081 for Oceania, and the global average of 0.6102 (UNDESA, 2022). From an individual perspective, only three sub-Saharan Africa countries had EGDI scores above the global average—South Africa at 0.7357, Mauritius at 0.7201, and Seychelles at 0.6793 (UNDESA, 2022). More than one-half of the countries on the African continent (59%) have middle EGDI values (0.25–<0.50), a little less than one-third (30%) have high EGDI values (0.50–<0.75), and a little more than one-tenth (11%) have low EGDI values (0.0–<0.25) (UNDESA, 2022). In sub-Saharan Africa, 12 countries can be classified as having high EGDI values.

Clearly, and as also empirically determined and/or observed by Danowski et al. (2022), Kouladoum (2022), Myovella et al. (2020), and Viik et al. (2018), for example, African nations need to prioritize efforts at e-government development and deployment both as an anti-corruption tool to foster economic growth and to generally improve governance and public sector effectiveness. Castro and Lopes (2022), in their empirical study of the impact of e-government on corruption for 175 countries covering the period 2003–2019, of which the largest portion (27%) are from sub-Saharan Africa, found that an increase by 0.1 in the EGDI improves the CPI score by 0.504 points.

References

AACC. (2020). *Public debt & corruption: A policy brief from all Africa conference of churches*. AACC.
AACC. (2021). *All Africa conference of churches Lusaka statement on public debt, corruption & illicit financial flows in Africa*. AACC.
ActionAid Nigeria. (2015). *Corruption and poverty in Nigeria: A report*. ActionAid Nigeria.
Adam, I. O. (2020). Examining e-government development effects on corruption in Africa: The mediating effects of ICT development and institutional quality. *Technology in Society, 61*(May), 101245. https://doi.org/10.1016/j.techsoc.2020.101245
Addo, A. (2021). Controlling petty corruption in public administrations of developing countries through digitalization: An opportunity theory informed study of Ghana customs. *The Information Society, 37*(2), 99–114. https://doi.org/10.1080/01972243.2020.1870182
Adebayo, A. A. (2013). The nexus of corruption and poverty in the quest for sustainable development in Nigeria. *Journal of Sustainable Development in Africa, 15*(7), 225–235.
Adou, K. D. (2022). The untold story of the modernization thesis: Urbanization and corruption in developing countries. *International Area Studies Review, 25*(3), 214–232. https://doi.org/10.1177/2F22338659221112992
AfDB. (2021). *African economic outlook 2021: From debt resolution to growth: The road ahead for Africa*. AfDB.
AfriMAP. (2016). *Effectiveness of anti-corruption agencies in East Africa: Kenya, Tanzania and Uganda*. African Minds.
Aidt, T. S. (2011). Corruption and sustainable development. In S. Rose-Ackerman & T. Søreide (Eds.), *International handbook on the economics of corruption, volume two* (pp. 3–51). Edward Elgar.
Aidt, T. S. (2019). Corruption. In R. D. Congleton, B. Grofman, & S. Voigt (Eds.), *The Oxford handbook of public choice, volume 1* (pp. 604–627). Oxford University Press.

References

Àkànle, O., & Nkpe, D. O. (Eds.). (2022). *Corruption and development in Nigeria*. Routledge.

Akinlo, A. E. (2022). How does corruption affect currency substitution? Evidence from Nigeria. *Journal of Development Policy and Practice, 7*(2), 221–242. https://doi.org/10.1177/2F24551333221086332

Amegavi, G. B., Quarshie, A., & d'Mensah, J. K. (2022). Mitigating corruption in sub-Saharan Africa: Does heterogeneity in corruption levels matter? *Public Integrity, 24*(2), 229–242. https://doi.org/10.1080/10999922.2021.1917171

Antwi, S. K., Kong, Y., Mohammed, M., Donkor, M., & Kasim, H. (2020). Does corruption grease or sand the wheels of economic growth in Ghana? An ARDL bounds test. *The Economics and Finance Letters, 7*(2), 162–178. https://doi.org/10.18488/journal.29.2020.72.162.178

Apergis, E., & Apergis, N. (2019). New evidence on corruption and government debt from a global country panel: A non-linear panel long-run approach. *Journal of Economic Studies, 46*(5), 1009–1027. https://doi.org/10.1108/JES-03-2018-0088

Appiah-Kubi, S. N. K., Malec, K., Phiri, J., Krivko, M., Maitah, K., Maitah, M., & Smutka, L. (2022). Key drivers of public debt levels: Empirical evidence from Africa. *Sustainability, 14*(3), 1220. https://doi.org/10.3390/su14031220

Asongu, S. A., & Nnanna, J. (2020). Governance and the capital flight trap in Africa. *Transnational Corporations Review, 12*(3), 276–292. https://doi.org/10.1080/19186444.2020.1771123

AU. (2020). *The Digital transformation strategy for Africa (2020–2030)*. Retrieved from https://au.int/en/documents/20200518/digital-transformation-strategy-africa-2020-2030

AU., & CFAs. (2019). *Stolen futures: The impact of corruption on children in Africa*. AU.

AUC., & OECD. (2018). *Africa's development dynamics 2018: Growth, jobs and inequalities*. AU/OECD Publishing.

Ayakwah, A., Damoah, I. S., & Osabutey, E. L. C. (2021). Digitalization in Africa: The case of public programs in Ghana. In J. B. Abugre, E. L. C. Osabutey, & S. P. Sigué (Eds.), *Business in Africa in the era of digital technology: Essays in honor of Professor William Darley* (pp. 7–25). Springer Nature.

Bala, A. R., Behsudi, A., & Owen, N. (2022). Meeting the future: Three countries–Belize, Colombia, and Ghana–Highlight the potential of technology and innovation to strengthen public finances. *Finance and Development, 59*(1), 38–43. https://www.imf.org/en/Publications/fandd/issues/2022/03/Country-cases-meeting-the-future-Belize-Colombia-Ghana

Basel Institute on Governance. (2017). New perspectives in e-government and the prevention of corruption. [Working Paper Series No. 23]. Retrieved from https://baselgovernance.org/publications/working-paper-23-new-perspectives-e-government-andprevention-corruption

Basel Institute on Governance. (2021). *Basel AML index 2021: 10th public edition–ranking money laundering and terrorist financing risks around the world*. Retrieved from https://index.baselgovernance.org

Bello y Villarino, J.-M. (2021). Measuring corruption: A critical analysis of the existing datasets and their suitability for diachronic transnational research. *Social Indicators Research, 157*(2), 709–747. https://doi.org/10.1007/s11205-021-02657-z

Benfratello, L., Del Monte, A., & Pennacchio, L. (2018). Corruption and public debt: A cross-country analysis. *Applied Economics Letters, 25*(5), 340–344. https://doi.org/10.1080/13504851.2017.1321831

Calderón, C., & Cantú, C. (2021). The impact of digital infrastructure on African development. [Policy Research Working Paper 9853]. World Bank.

Campos, N. F., Dimova, R., & Saleh, A. (2010). Whither corruption? A quantitative survey of the literature on corruption and growth. [Discussion Paper no. 5334]. Institute for the Study of labor.

Castro, C., & Lopes, I. C. (2022). E-government as a tool in controlling corruption. *International Journal of Public Administration*. [Advance online publication]. https://doi.org/10.1080/01900692.2022.2076695

Castro, C., & Pinho, C. (2021). Corruption, economic growth and sustainable development—a conditional quantile analysis. *International Journal of Sustainable Development, 24*(3/4), 220–244. https://doi.org/10.1504/IJSD.2021.122714

Chatain, P.-L., van der Does de Willebois, E., & Bökkerink, M. (2022). *Preventing money laundering and terrorist financing: A practical guide for Bank supervisors* (2nd ed.). World Bank.

Chuah, L. L., Loayza, N. V., & Myers, B. (2020). The fight against corruption: Taming tigers and swatting flies. [Research & Policy Briefs, no. 27]. World Bank Malaysia Hub.

Cieślik, A., & Goczek, L. (2018). Control of corruption, international investment, and economic growth–Evidence from panel data. *World Development, 103*(March), 323–335. https://doi.org/10.1016/j.worlddev.2017.10.028

CIP., & CMI. (2016). *The costs of corruption to the Mozambican economy: Why it is important to fight corruption in a climate of fiscal fragility*. CMI.

Cooley, A., Heathershaw, J., & Sharman, J. C. (2018). The rise of kleptocracy: Laundering cash, whitewashing reputations. *Journal of Democracy, 29*(1), 39–53. https://doi.org/10.1353/jod.2018.0003

Cooray, A., Dzhumashev, R., & Schneider, F. (2017). How does corruption affect public debt? An empirical analysis. *World Development, 90*(February), 115–127. https://doi.org/10.1016/j.worlddev.2016.08.020

Coste, C., & Meunier, F. (2021, July 2). Beneficial ownership: Increasing transparency in a simple way for entrepreneurs. [World Bank Blogs]. Retrieved from https://blogs.worldbank.org/developmenttalk/beneficial-ownership-increasing-transparency-simpleway-entrepreneurs

d'Agostino, G., Dunne, J. P., & Pieroni, L. (2016). Corruption and growth in Africa. *European Journal of Political Economy, 43*(June), 1–88. https://doi.org/10.1016/j.ejpoleco.2016.03.002

Danowski, J., van Klyton, A., Peng, T.-Q. W., Ma, S., Nkakleu, R., & Biboum, A. D. (2022). Information and communications technology development, interorganizational networks, and public sector corruption in Africa. *Quality and Quantity. [Advance online publication]*. https://doi.org/10.1007/s11135-022-01508-4

Dimant, E., & Tosato, G. (2018). Causes and effects of corruption: What has past decade's empirical research taught us? A survey. *Journal of Economic Surveys, 32*(2), 335–356. https://doi.org/10.1111/joes.12198

Esona, S. K. (2020). *Essays on the nexus of corruption, economic growth, and human development in sub-Sahara Africa*. [PhD thesis, Middle Tennessee State University].

Forson, J. A., Buracom, P., Chen, G., & Baah-Ennumh, T. Y. (2017). Genuine wealth per capita as a measure of sustainability and the negative impact of corruption on sustainable growth in sub-Sahara Africa. *South African Journal of Economics, 85*(2), 178–195. https://doi.org/10.1111/saje.12152

Fray, P. (2020). South Africa: The bigger pandemic is corruption. Retrieved from https://gga.org/south-africa-the-biggerpandemic-is-corruption/

Freytag, A., & Riaz, M. F. (2021). Corruption and access to socio-economic services in Africa. [CESifo Working Paper no. 8882]. Center for Economic Studies and the ifo Institute.

Ganahl, J. P. (2013). *Corruption, good governance, and the African state: A critical analysis of the political-economic foundations of corruption in sub-Saharan Africa*. Potsdam University Press.

Gillies, A. (2020). Corruption trends during Africa's oil boom, 2005 to 2014. *The Extractive Industries and Society, 7*(4), 1171–1181. https://doi.org/10.1016/j.exis.2020.06.006

Gründler, K., & Potrafke, N. (2019). Corruption and economic growth: New empirical evidence. *European Journal of Political Economy, 60*(December), 101810. https://doi.org/10.1016/j.ejpoleco.2019.08.001

Gumede, V., & Fadiran, D. (2019). Illicit financial flows in southern Africa: Exploring implications for socio-economic development. *Africa Development, 44*(2), 27–52.

Hamilton, A., & Hammer, C. (2018). Can we measure the power of the grabbing hand? A comparative analysis of different indicators of corruption. [Policy Research Working Paper 8299]. World Bank.

Hammadi, A., Mills, M., Sobrinho, N., Thakoor, V. V., & Velloso, R. (2019). A governance dividend for sub-Saharan Africa? [IMF Working Paper No.19/1]. IMF.

Henri, N. N. (2018). Impact of corruption on public debt: Evidence from sub-Saharan African countries. *American Journal of Economics, 8*(1), 14–17.

References

Hern, E. A. (2023). *Explaining successes in Africa: Things Don't always fall apart*. Lynne Rienner Publishers.

Hope, K. R. (2000). Corruption and development in Africa. In K. R. Hope & B. C. Chikulo (Eds.), *Corruption and development in Africa: Lessons from country case-studies* (pp. 17–39). Macmillan Press.

Hope, K. R. (2017a). *Corruption and governance in Africa: Swaziland [Eswatini], Kenya, Nigeria*. Palgrave Macmillan/Springer Nature.

Hope, K. R. (2017b). Fighting corruption in developing countries: Some aspects of policy from lessons from the field. *Journal of Public Affairs, 17*(4), e1683. https://doi.org/10.1002/pa.1683

Ibrahim, C. (2021). Corruption, public debt and economic growth–evidence from developing countries. *International Journal of Development Issues, 20*(1), 24–37. https://doi.org/10.1108/IJDI-12-2019-0208

IIDEA. (2021). *The global state of democracy 2021*. IDEA.

IMF. (2016). *Corruption: Costs and mitigating strategies*. IMF.

IMF. (2018a). *Review of 1997 guidance note on governance – a proposed framework for enhanced fund engagement*. IMF.

IMF. (2018b). *Nigeria: Selected issues*. [IMF Country Report No. 18/64]. IMF.

IMF. (2019). *Fiscal monitor: Curbing corruption*. IMF.

IMF. (2020). Digitalization in sub-Saharan Africa, Chapter 3. In *Regional economic outlook: Sub-Saharan Africa: COVID-19: An unprecedented threat to development*. IMF.

IMF. (2021). *Regional economic outlook: Sub-Saharan Africa: One planet, two worlds, three stories: Background paper: Statistical appendix*. IMF.

IMF. (2022a). *Regional economic outlook: Sub-Saharan Africa: A new shock and little room to maneuver*. IMF.

IMF. (2022b). *Regional economic outlook: Sub-Saharan Africa: A new shock and little room to maneuver: Background paper: Statistical appendix*. IMF.

INTERPOL. (2019). *Corruption as a facilitator for organized crime in the Eastern African Region*. Retrieved from https://enact-africa.s3.amazonaws.com/site/uploads/2019-10-15-interpol-corruption-report.pdf

Inuwa, I., & Ononiwu, C. G. (2020). Traditional and information technology anti-corruption strategies for curbing the public sector corruption in developing economies of sub-Saharan Africa: A systematic literature review. *The African Journal of Information Systems, 12*(2), 5. https://digitalcommons.kennesaw.edu/ajis/vol12/iss2/5

Jahnke, B., & Weisser, R. A. (2019). How does petty corruption affect tax morale in sub-Saharan Africa? *European Journal of Political Economy, 60*(December), 101751. https://doi.org/10.1016/j.ejpoleco.2018.09.003

Jama, A. B. (2021). The effect of corruption on economic growth: Empirical evidence in East Africa. *International Journal of Research and Innovation in Social Science, 5*(6), 717–723. https://www.rsisinternational.org/journals/ijriss/Digital-Library/volume-5-issue-6/717-723.pdf

Jeng, M. A. (2018). *Studying the relationship between corruption and poverty, public debt, and economic growth: A case study of The Gambia (1996–2016)* (MSc thesis, KTH industrial engineering and management). Stockholm.

Jimada, I. S. (2018). Interrogating the issues of corruption and poverty in contemporary Africa. In T. Falola & M. O. Odey (Eds.), *Poverty reduction strategies in Africa* (pp. 78–91). Routledge.

Johnston, M., & Fritzen, S. A. (2021). *The conundrum of corruption: Reform for social justice*. Routledge.

Knobel, A., & Lorenzo, F. (2022). *Beneficial Ownership Registration Around the World 2022*. Retrieved from https://taxjustice.net/reports/the-state-of-play-of-beneficial-ownership-registration-in-2022/

Kouladoum, J.-C. (2022). Technology and control of corruption in Africa. *Journal of International Development*. [Advance online publication]. https://doi.org/10.1002/jid.3723

Levy, B., Hirsch, A., Naidoo, V., & Nxele, M. (2021). *South Africa: When strong institutions and massive inequalities collide*. Carnegie Endowment for International Peace.

Lopez-Claros, A. (2015). Removing impediments to sustainable economic development: The case of corruption. *Journal of International Commerce, Economics and Policy, 6*(1), 1550002. https://doi.org/10.1142/S1793993315500027

Madow, N., Bayale, N., & Kouassi, B. K. (2021). On the robust drivers of public debt in Africa: Fresh evidence from Bayesian model averaging approach. *Cogent Economics & Finance, 9*(1), 1860282. https://doi.org/10.1080/23322039.2020.1860282

Maguchu, P. S. (2022). Challenges of money laundering for sovereign states that use the US dollar. *Journal of Money Laundering Control, 22*(2), 306–312. https://doi.org/10.1108/JMLC-06-2021-0056

Martinsson, J. (2021). Combatting institutional corruption: The policy-centered approach. *Crime Law and Social Change, 75*(3), 267–280. https://doi.org/10.1007/s10611-021-09934-5

Mbaku, J. M. (2019). Corruption and economic development. In E. Nnadozie & A. Jerome (Eds.), *African economic development* (2nd ed., pp. 331–345). Emerald Publishing.

Mbaku, J. M. (2022). International law, corruption and the rights of children in Africa. *San Diego International Law Journal, 23*(2), 195–340. https://digital.sandiego.edu/ilj/vol23/iss2/2

McNair, D., Kraus, J., McKiernan, K., & McKay, S. (2014). *The trillion-dollar scandal.* Retrieved from https://s3.amazonaws.com/one.org/pdfs/Trillion_Dollar_Scandal_report_EN.pdf

Melina, G., Selim, H., & Verdugo-Yepes, C. (2019). *Macro-fiscal gains from anti-corruption reforms in the republic of Congo.* [IMF Working Paper WP/19/121]. IMF.

Mlambo, D. N., Mubecua, M. A., Mpanza, S. E., & Mlambo, V. H. (2019). Corruption and its implications for development and good governance: A perspective from post-colonial Africa. *Journal of Economics and Behavioral Studies, 11*(1), 39–47. https://doi.org/10.22610/jebs.v11i1(J).2746

Murshed, M., & Mredula, F. A. (2018). Impacts of corruption on sustainable development: A simultaneous equations model estimation approach. *Journal of Accounting Finance and Economics, 8*(1), 109–133.

Musila, J. W. (2019). Anticorruption strategies in sub-Saharan Africa: Lessons from experience and ingredients of a successful strategy. *Journal of African Business, 20*(2), 180–194. https://doi.org/10.1080/15228916.2019.1583980

Mutondoro, F. S. (2020). *Nexus between debt and corruption in Zimbabwe's public finance management.* Zimbabwe Coalition on Debt and Development.

Muzurura, J. (2017). Corruption and economic growth in Zimbabwe: Unravelling the linkages. *International Journal of Development Research, 7*(1), 11197–11204. http://www.journalijdr.com/corruption-and-economic-growth-zimbabwe-unravelling-linkages

Myovella, G., Karacukaa, M., & Haucap, J. (2020). Digitalization and economic growth: A comparative analysis of sub-Saharan Africa and OECD economies. *Telecommunications Policy, 44*(2), 101856. https://doi.org/10.1016/j.telpol.2019.101856

Naz, M., & Yasmin, B. (2021). Corruption and public debt in developing countries: Role of institutional quality. *Journal of Economic Cooperation and Development, 42*(3), 59–90. https://jecd.sesric.org/pdf.php?file=ART20090101-2.pdf

Ndikumana, L., & Boyce, J. K. (2021). *Capital flight from Africa 1970–2018: New estimates with updated trade misinvoicing methodology.* [PERI Research Report]. Political Economy Research Institute, University of Massachusetts.

Ngugi, T. (2021, April 16). The real debt problem in Kenya is corruption. *The East African.* https://www.theeastafrican.co.ke/tea/oped/comment/real-debt-burden-in-kenya-is-corruption-3364482

Nugroho, A. D., Cubillos Tovar, J. P., Bopushev, S. T., Bozsik, N., Fehér, I., & Lakner, Z. (2022). Effects of corruption control on the number of undernourished people in developing countries. *Food, 11*(7), 924. https://doi.org/10.3390/foods11070924

Nur-tegin, K., & Jakee, K. (2020). Does corruption grease or sand the wheels of development? New results based on disaggregated data. *The Quarterly Review of Economics and Finance, 75*(February), 19–30. https://doi.org/10.1016/j.qref.2019.02.001

References

Nwankwo, O. (2014). Impact of corruption on economic growth in Nigeria. *Mediterranean Journal of Social Sciences, 5*(6), 41–46. https://www.richtmann.org/journal/index.php/mjss/article/view/2389

OECD. (2015). *Consequences of corruption at the sector level and implications for economic growth and development.* OECD.

OECD. (2022). General government debt (indicator). Retrieved from https://doi.org/10.1787/a0528cc2-en

Okunogbe, O., & Santoro, F. (2022). Increasing tax collection in African countries: The role of information technology. [Policy Research Working Paper 10182]. World Bank.

Olabiyi, O. M. (2022). The effect of bureaucratic corruption on household food insecurity: Evidence from sub-Saharan Africa. *Food Security, 14*(2), 437–450. https://doi.org/10.1007/s12571-021-01231-2

Olamide, E. G., & Maredza, A. (2023). Pre-COVID-19 evaluation of external debt, corruption and economic growth in South Africa. *Review of Economics and Political Science, 8*(1), 19–36. https://doi.org/10.1108/REPS-03-2021-0019

Omoteso, K., & Mobolaji, H. I. (2014). Corruption, governance and economic growth in sub-Saharan Africa: A need for the prioritization of reform policies. *Social Responsibility Journal, 10*(2), 316–330. https://doi.org/10.1108/SRJ-06-2012-0067

OPHI. (n.d.). What is multidimensional poverty. Retrieved from https://ophi.org.uk/policy/multidimensional-poverty-index/

OPHI. (2021a). *Global multidimensional poverty index 2021: Unmasking disparities by ethnicity, caste and gender.* OPHI, University of Oxford.

OPHI. (2021b). Global MPI reports. Retrieved from https://ophi.org.uk/multidimensional-poverty-index/global-mpi-reports/

Osei-Assibey, E., Osei Domfeh, K., & Danquah, M. (2018). Corruption, institutions and capital flight: Evidence from sub-Saharan Africa. *Journal of Economic Studies, 45*(1), 59–76. https://doi.org/10.1108/JES-10-2016-0212

O'Toole, C. M., & Tarp, F. (2014). Corruption and the efficiency of capital investment in developing countries. *Journal of International Development, 26*(5), 567–597. https://doi.org/10.1002/jid.2997

Otusanya, O. J. (2011). Corruption as an obstacle to development in developing countries: A review of literature. *Journal of Money Laundering Control, 14*(4), 387–422. https://doi.org/10.1108/13685201111173857

Ouedraogo, R., & Sy, A. N. R. (2020). Can digitalization help deter corruption in Africa? [IMF Working Paper WP/20/68]. IMF.

Owusu-Nantwi, V., & Owusu-Nantwi, G. (2023). Public debt, corruption and shadow economy in Africa: An empirical analysis. *Journal of Economic and Administrative Sciences, 39*(1), 184–202. https://doi.org/10.1108/JEAS-08-2020-0150

Park, C. H., & Kim, K. (2020). E-government as an anti-corruption tool: Panel data analysis across countries. *International Review of Administrative Sciences, 86*(4), 691–707. https://doi.org/10.1177/2F0020852318822055

Quah, J. S. T. (2022). Lee Kuan Yew's role in minimizing corruption in Singapore. *Public Administration and Policy, 25*(2), 163–175. https://doi.org/10.1108/PAP-04-2022-0037

Qureshi, F., Qureshi, S., Vo, X. V., & Junejo, I. (2021). Revisiting the nexus among foreign direct investment, corruption and growth in developing and developed markets. *Borsa Istanbul Review, 21*(1), 80–91. https://doi.org/10.1016/j.bir.2020.08.001

Ramaphosa, C. [@presidency ZA]. (2022, June 2). Presidency responds to claims by Mr. Arthur Fraser. [tweet]. *Twitter*. https://twitter.com/PresidencyZA/status/1532321007440216064?ref_src=twsrc%5Etfw

Roque, P. C. (2021). *Governing in the shadows: Angola's securitized state.* Oxford University Press.

Rotberg, R. I. (2012). *Transformative political leadership: Making a difference in the developing world.* The University of Chicago Press.

Salahuddin, M., Vink, N., Ralph, N., & Gow, J. (2020). Globalization, poverty and corruption: Retarding progress in South Africa. *Development Southern Africa, 37*(4), 617–643. https://doi.org/10.1080/0376835X.2019.1678460

School, M. (2019). *Corruption and economic growth in Africa* (MSc dissertation, Radboud Universiteit). Nijmegen.

Scotland, P. (2019). Battling corruption in Africa must be top priority. Retrieved from https://thecommonwealth.org/media/news/battling-corruption-africa-must-be-top-priority-says-secretary%E2%80%93general

Sebudubudu, D., & Botlhomilwe, M. Z. (2012). The critical role of leadership in Botswana's development: What lessons? *Leadership, 8*(1), 29–45. https://doi.org/10.1177/2F1742715011426962

Senu, O. (2020). A critical assessment of anti-corruption strategies for economic development in sub-Saharan Africa. *Development Policy Review, 38*(5), 664–681. https://doi.org/10.1111/dpr.12442

Signé, L., Sow, M., & Madden, P. (2020). *Illicit financial flows in Africa: Drivers, destinations, and policy options*. Retrieved from https://www.brookings.edu/research/illicit-financial-flows-in-africa-drivers-destinations-and-policy-options/

Smith, G. (2021). *Where credit is due: How Africa's debt can be a benefit, not a burden*. Hurst Publishers.

Spector, B. I. (2022). *Curbing corruption: Practical strategies for sustainable change*. Routledge.

Spyromitros, E., & Panagiotidis, M. (2022). The impact of corruption on economic growth in developing countries and a comparative analysis of corruption measurement indicators. *Cogent Economics & Finance, 10*(1), 2129368. https://doi.org/10.1080/23322039.2022.2129368

Srivastava, S. C., Teo, T. S. H., & Devaraj, S. (2016). You can't bribe a computer: Dealing with the societal challenge of corruption through ICT. *MIS Quarterly, 40*(2), 511–526.

Stephenson, M. C. (2020). Corruption as a self-reinforcing trap: Implications for reform strategy. *The World Bank Research Observer, 35*(2), 192–226. https://doi.org/10.1093/wbro/lkaa003

The Investopedia Team. (2022). Per capita GDP. Retrieved from https://www.investopedia.com/terms/p/per-capita-gdp.asp

The Legatum Institute. (2020). *The Africa prosperity report 2019–2020*. The Legatum Institute.

Thiao, A. (2021). The effect of illicit financial flows on government revenues in the west African economic and monetary union countries. *Cogent Social Sciences, 7*(1), 1972558. https://doi.org/10.1080/23311886.2021.1972558

TI. (2020). The CPI explained: FAQs. Retrieved from https://www.transparency.org/en/cpi/2020/index/nzl

TI. (2021). *Corruption perceptions index report 2020*. Retrieved from https://www.transparency.org/en/cpi/2020/index/nzl

Uberti, L. J. (2022). Corruption and growth: Historical evidence, 1790–2010. *Journal of Comparative Economics, 50*(2), 321–349. https://doi.org/10.1016/j.jce.2021.10.002

Ugur, M. (2014). Corruption's direct effects on per-capita income growth: A meta-analysis. *Journal of Economic Surveys, 28*(3), 472–490. https://doi.org/10.1111/joes.12035

UNCTAD. (2020). *Economic development in Africa report 2020: Tackling illicit financial flows for sustainable development in Africa*. UN.

UNDESA. (2022). *E-government survey 2022: The future of digital government*. UN.

UNECA. (2009). *African governance report II*. UNECA.

UNECA. (2016). *African governance report IV: Measuring corruption in Africa: The international dimension matters*. UNECA.

UNECA. (2021). *Economic governance report I: Institutional architecture to address illicit financial flows*. UNECA.

UNECOSOC. (2022). *Digital governance challenges and prospects for building forward better: Note by the secretariat*. UN.

Uslaner, E. M. (2015). The consequences of corruption. In P. M. Heywood (Ed.), *Routledge handbook of political corruption* (pp. 199–211). Routledge.

References

Venard, B. (2013). Institutions, corruption and sustainable development. *Economics Bulletin, 33*(4), 2545–2562. http://www.accessecon.com/Pubs/EB/2013/Volume33/EB-13-V33-I4-P240.pdf

Viik, L., Nyman-Metcalf, K., Astok, H., Viiderfeld, T., Kaljurand, K., & Püüa, M. (2018). *The deployment of E-governance Systems in Africa: Final report*. EU.

Vogl, F. (2022). *The enablers: How the west supports Kleptocrats and corruption–endangering our democracy*. Rowman & Littlefield.

Walle, Y. M., Janowski, T., & Estevez, E. (2018). Fighting administrative corruption with digital government in sub-Saharan Africa. In R. Bouzas-Lorenzo & A. C. Ramos (Eds.), *Proceedings of the 18th European conference on digital government ECDG 2018* (pp. 249–256). Academic Conferences and Publishing International Limited.

Wong, Z. W. V., Chen, F., & Yiew, T. H. (2021). Effects of rent-seeking on economic growth in low-income economies. *Bulletin of Monetary Economics and Banking, 24*(2), 205–220. https://doi.org/10.21098/bemp.v24i2.1386

World Bank. (n.d.). Worldwide governance indicators: Documentation. Retrieved from https://info.worldbank.org/governance/wgi/Home/Documents#doc-intro

World Bank. (2019). *Anticorruption initiatives: Reaffirming commitment to a development priority*. World Bank.

World Bank. (2020a). *Republic of Rwanda: Rwanda's anti-corruption experience: Actions, accomplishments, and lessons*. World Bank.

World Bank. (2020b). *Enhancing government effectiveness and transparency: The fight against corruption*. World Bank.

World Bank. (2021a). Regional aggregation using 2011 PPP and $1.90/day poverty line. Retrieved from http://iresearch.worldbank.org/PovcalNet/povDuplicateWB.aspx

World Bank. (2021b). Worldwide governance indicators: Interactive data access. Retrieved from https://info.worldbank.org/governance/wgi/Home/Reports

World Bank. (2021c). GDP per capita growth. Retrieved from https://data.worldbank.org/indicator/NY.GDP.PCAP.KD.ZG?locations=ZG

Xu, X. (2016). Corruption and economic growth: An absolute obstacle or some efficient grease? *Economic and Political Studies, 4*(1), 85–100. https://doi.org/10.1080/20954816.2016.1152097

Yusuf, M., Malarvizhi, C. A., Mazumder, M. N. H., & Su, Z. (2014). Corruption, poverty, and economic growth relationship in the Nigerian economy. *The Journal of Developing Areas, 48*(3), 95–107. http://www.jstor.org/stable/24241230

Zhao, X., & Xu, H. D. (2015). E-government and corruption: A longitudinal analysis of countries. *International Journal of Public Administration, 38*(6), 410–421. https://doi.org/10.1080/01900692.2014.942736

Chapter 5
Police Corruption and Its Security Challenges in Africa: Kenya As a Country Case Study

Where police corruption is persistent, it represents a systemic failure of governance where the principal institutions responsible for ensuring police governance, the observance of ethics and integrity standards, and enforcing the rule of law are compromised and are themselves infested with corrupt individuals and syndicates. This chapter draws on the available data and other research information and synthesizes them to provide a coherent picture and understanding of the police corruption problem and environment in Kenya and across Africa. It serves as an illustration of the police corruption problem in sub-Saharan Africa and its linkage to, influence on, and implications for national security with relevant cross-country comparisons.

5.1 Introduction

The police are the principal institution charged with maintaining internal security and safety (including preventing and controlling terrorist activities) and law and order (including the protection of life, liberty, property, human rights, and dignity of the members of the public while enforcing the law, and preventing, detecting, and investigating criminal activities) in African and all other countries for that matter. These are functions of what is referred to as policing and are intended to be achieved in a disciplined manner by the following and obeying of the rule of law by the police themselves. However, the police in Africa are the most corrupt institution (public or private) and this has historically been the case despite frequent and substantial attempts at state/national police reforms across most of the continent. This police corruption has had, and continues to have, significant negative consequences for ensuring security and contributing to climates of peace and stability which, in turn, provides the environment for sustainable development.

© The Author(s), under exclusive license to Springer Nature Switzerland AG 2023
K. R. Hope, Sr., *Corruption, Sustainable Development and Security Challenges in Africa*, Advances in African Economic, Social and Political Development, https://doi.org/10.1007/978-3-031-32229-7_5

Undoubtedly, a key factor contributing to opportunities for police corruption is the relationship between police and the society. As street-level bureaucrats, the police are imbued with a great deal of autonomy in the execution of their jobs. Unfortunately, too many police officers or police organizations use that autonomy as discretion to engage in corrupt activities. Street-level bureaucrats are public employees (such as police officers, teachers, and public health practitioners) who deal directly with the public and have substantial discretion in the execution of their duties (Lipsky, 1980; Raines, 2009; Tummers et al., 2009). That discretion can be exercised positively in the implementation of public policy in the interests of society, or negatively by ignoring public policy and against the interest of society but for private or organizational gains as police corruption entails.

This chapter discusses and provides an analytical survey of the nature and extent of police corruption in Africa with Kenya as a country case study, and serves as an illustration of the police corruption problem in sub-Saharan Africa and what challenges that poses for security. It draws on the available data and other research information and synthesizes them to provide a coherent picture and understanding of the police corruption problem, and its linkage to, influence on, and implications for national security with African cross-country comparisons. We begin first by setting the stage with a definition of the concept of police corruption. Thereafter, and applying that definition, we provide a cogent survey and examination of the police corruption problem in Kenya and across Africa. It then proceeds to a critical discussion of the relationship between police corruption and its impact on, and challenges to, security. The final section offers some concluding comments based on the analysis in the previous sections.

5.2 What Is Police Corruption?

Although police corruption is a form of police misconduct, corruption is different from other forms of police misconduct because of its principal motivation: achievement of personal/private or organizational gain or advantage. In that regard, it is therefore best to adopt a broad functional approach, rather than seeking to define police corruption in generic terms, and thereby encompass what is popularly understood by police corruption and corrupt police. The advantage of this approach is that it enables many acts and practices that may never show themselves as corrupt to be included within a definition of police corruption. For example, doing what one is duty-bound to do solely for personal advancement or private gain. It considers that motivation is the key to understanding police corruption. The motivation behind an act is corrupt when the primary intention is to further private or organizational advantage.

The functional definition of police corruption being applied in this book is the following: Police corruption is any action or omission, a promise of any action or omission, or any attempt of action or omission, committed by a police officer or a group of police officers, characterized by the police officer's misuse of the official position and motivated in significant part with the achievement of personal/private or organizational gain or advantage (see Hope, 2016a; Kleinig, 1996; Newburn, 1999, 2015; Punch, 1985, 2000).

This way of defining police corruption goes beyond the usual quid-pro-quo assumption and thus allows us to include behavior that could be otherwise classified as extortion, robbery, burglary, theft, or overzealous policing with the aim of personal advancement, for example (Newburn, 1999; Wood, 1997). Moreover, this broad functional definition acknowledges that police corruption can be identified as deviant, dishonest, improper, unethical, or criminal behavior by a police officer (Prenzler, 2009; Roebuck & Barker, 1974).

There has also been a further division of corrupt police officers in general into two lots, and Kenya and the rest of Africa are no different. In one lot, there are the so-called "grass eaters" who are passively corrupt police officers that engage in minor (low-level or petty) corruption such as accepting unsolicited money (Knapp, 1972; Ross, 2012). These kinds of actions are usually reactive (opportunistic ethical violations) and are usually not frowned upon by other police officers. In the other lot, there are the "meat eaters" who are police officers that actively engage in major (grand) corruption, such as drug dealing crimes or participating in shakedowns, on a regular basis, and they are proactive in their endeavors (Knapp, 1972; Ross, 2012). Consequently, police corruption cannot simply be dismissed by the top officials as the product of a few "bad apples" as an easy way out in explaining corruption in a police service (Loree, 2006; Newburn, 1999; Ross, 2012; Swope, 2001).

In fact, from what we now know from the research literature, we can observe that: (1) police corruption is a continuing international problem—there is evidence of corrupt police practices across the globe; (2) police corruption can be pervasive—corrupt practices are found in some form in a great many police services in all societies; (3) police corruption, particularly police bribery, is a social phenomenon with profound roots in social aspects such as education, urbanization, and ethnical separation; (4) police corruption is not simply a problem of the lower ranks—corruption has been found at all levels of a police organization; (5) police corruption can cover a wide number of activities; and (6) there are some forms of policing, or areas of a police organization, which are more at risk of corruption (Gutierrez-Garcia & Rodriguez, 2016; Hope, 2016a; Loree, 2006; Neild, 2007; Newburn, 1999; Punch, 1985;), such as the traffic police across Africa, for example, as this chapter also shows.

5.3 The Nature and Extent of Police Corruption in Kenya and Across Africa

As outlined below, per the constitution and other statutes, the police are one of the three national security organs in Kenya. However, the police in Kenya and across Africa have consistently been ranked as the most corrupt institution in the country and this continues to be the case despite several and ongoing attempts at police reforms. Among the deleterious consequences of this police corruption is its impact on security and sustainable development. Consequently, eradicating police corruption, and the fight against it, remains a key policy agenda of the various governments and some of their international partners.

But, in countries where police corruption is persistent, such as found in most of Africa, it represents a systemic failure of governance where the principal institutions responsible for ensuring police governance, the observance of ethics and integrity standards, and enforcing the rule of law are compromised and may themselves be infested with corrupt individuals and syndicates. The result is that a chain environment of personal and collective impunity prevails and police corruption is therefore both perceived and real as running rampant. That, in turn, has considerable negative impacts on justice or security sector development and performance and is a challenge to nation-building, the maintenance of public order and the rule of law, and to supporting the legitimacy of the state.

5.3.1 Perceptions of Police Corruption

Police corruption is nearly always a function of societal politics, the culture and norms of the people, and larger systemic problems in society caused by the lack of overall transparency, the absence of checks and balances, weak rule of law, fragile institutions, and generally poor governance (see, for instance, Addo, 2023; Hope, 2016a; Neild, 2007). However, there is some recent evidence presented by Hatungimana (2022), for example, that suggests that irrespective of African regime type, the corruption perception of police by the public can also influence the corruption perception of upper-level government officials as the public's information to evaluate the quality of their government is likely to be derived from interactions with police. In any case, by any measure or indicator, Kenya is generally ranked as one of the most corrupt countries in the world (Hope, 2012, 2014, 2017). Consequently, it should not be surprising that a considerable number of reports, studies, surveys, and other publications have observed that corruption is a pervasive and historical part of police functioning in Kenya and across Africa.

Two decades ago, in examining the issue of police accountability and the need for police reform in Kenya, Auerbach (2003, pp. 276–277) had raised the alarm that "the police have been at the nexus of the most serious problems facing Kenyan society: rampant corruption, unacceptably high levels of crime, inter-ethnic violence and vigilantism," and further noted that "through corrupt practices, many police officers have also profited … at the public's expense," and thus, "the police have not only failed to control corruption, a problem so widespread that it appears to be the chief cause of Kenya's economic stagnation, but an unsettling number of the police force have themselves succumbed to corruption." This has continued on and has led to the Kenya police, and other African police institutions as well, remaining somewhat deficient in the areas of professionalism, ethics, integrity, and

5.3 The Nature and Extent of Police Corruption in Kenya and Across Africa

oversight (Hope, 2012, 2016a). Kenya had been ranked third in the top 10 most corrupt police services or forces in the world by 2017 (Hope, 2017), and ranked second, along with Uganda, as being perceived as having the most corrupt police in Africa for 2019–2021 (Logan et al., 2022). Other previously compiled indices by Transparency International, for example, had also shown that the perceptions of corruption by institution, further confirm that the Kenya police are among the most corrupt with a perceptions index score of 4.8, based on a score scale of 1–5, where 1 means not at all corrupt, and 5 means extremely corrupt (TI, 2013).

Indeed, as (Hope, 2015, p. 96) has noted, "survey after survey continue to rank the Kenya police as [one of] the most corrupt institutions in the country and one of the most corrupt in East Africa," with corruption arising as routine in the daily work of the Kenya police and now a matter of some concern with Kenyans having a considerably negative perception of their police (see also Ethics and Anti-Corruption Commission [EACC], 2018; Osaleh, 2016). For example, in a report by the Commonwealth Human Rights Initiative (CHRI) and the Kenya Human Rights Commission (KHRC), it was observed that:

> Kenyans view their police… in one of two ways. First, they see it as an organization in such a corrupt state that it is little more than an institutionalized extortion racket, that uses illegal and violent methods to uphold the status quo and is only paying lip service to reform initiatives. Alternatively, they see it as an institution that is struggling to reform itself and to overcome its history, to become a disciplined and law-abiding police service more suited to the democracy in which it now exists (CHRI and KHRC, 2006, p. 19).

Other research surveys have also found that Kenyans estimate that large numbers of the police service are corrupt. In fact, the 2019 *Global Corruption Barometer Africa* published by Transparency International found the Kenya police, overall, leading government departments and institutions perceived to be very corrupt by 66% of the respondents compared to 75% in 2015 (Pring & Vrushi, 2019). According to Afrobarometer (n.d.-a) and Logan et al. (2022), and as also shown in Table 5.1, this perception was climbing back up and stood at 68% of Kenyan respondents in 2021. More recent survey data from the Institute for Development Studies (IDS)/ University of Nairobi (IDS-UON) (2022) showed that this perception remained at 68% of respondents who thought that most or all of the Kenya police were corrupt in 2022, with 60% saying that the police did not operate in a professional manner.

Similarly, across the rest of Africa, the police services or forces continue to be the public institution most likely to engage in corrupt activities and other misconduct with survey findings showing just that (Hope, 2017; Logan et al., 2022; Pring & Vrushi, 2019). In the most recent surveys with comparative data covering the period 2019–2021, the police rank as more corrupt than three other key institutions (judges/magistrates, parliament, and the presidency) in 23 of 34 African countries (Logan et al., 2022). As a police corruption indicator, across the entire continent, an average of almost one-half (47%) of respondents perceive "most" or "all" of the police as being corrupt (Afrobarometer, n.d.-a; Logan et al., 2022). Table 5.1 shows the available comparable time-series data, covering 2015–2021, of the proportion of citizens in sub-Saharan Africa countries that consider their police to be corrupt. This corruption undermines public trust in the police. For example, less than one-half

Table 5.1 Police corruption indicator—perceptions: proportion of citizens in sub-Saharan Africa countries who perceive their police to be corrupt, 2015–21 (%)

Country	2015	2019	2021
Benin	54	55	46
Botswana	34	39	30
Burkina Faso	28	29	30
Cabo Verde	19	23	22
Cameroon	55	63	61
Côte d'Ivoire	49	49	58
Eswatini	42	30	53
Gabon	63	75	69
Ghana	64	59	60
Guinea	38	57	50
Kenya	75	66	68
Lesotho	38	34	46
Liberia	77	62	67
Malawi	39	54	49
Mali	53	55	55
Mauritius	22	19	26
Mozambique	43	47	48
Namibia	40	42	37
Niger	27	33	29
Nigeria	72	69	63
Senegal	31	29	47
Sierra Leone	59	56	61
South Africa	48	49	55
Sudan	42	34	36
Tanzania	50	36	23
Togo	44	55	51
Uganda	63	70	68
Zambia	51	54	54
Zimbabwe	58	57	59
Regional average	**47.5**	**48.3**	**49**

Source: Author, based on data derived from Afrobarometer (n.d.-a, n.d.-c); Logan et al. (2022); and Pring and Vrushi (2019)

(49%) of respondents in the Afrobarometer 2019–2021 surveys say they trust the police "somewhat/a lot" (Afrobarometer, n.d.-a).

Further, and comparatively, in empirical studies conducted on Nigeria by Akinlabi (2022) and on South Africa by Bello (2021), for example, among other things, it was concluded that personal experience of police corruption was also a statistically significant predictor of perceived lack of confidence in police professionalism and effectiveness, and the resultant unwillingness to cooperate with police. Indeed, perceptions of corruption and other forms of police misconduct have significant negative effects on trust in the police. The obvious implication is that as people observe the police engaging in rampant corruption, the less likely those people are to perceive the police as effective in undertaking their duties. In slightly more exhaustive dives covering a wider cross-section of African countries, we further glean that, beyond the lack of trust, professionalism and effectiveness, police corruption has also contributed to a relationship between the public and their police that is marked by suspicion and discontent which, in turn, calls into question police legitimacy as the possibility of procedural fairness is jeopardized (see, for example, Addo, 2023; Boateng, 2018a, 2018b; Boateng et al., 2022; Gyamfi, 2022; Harris & Katusiimeh, 2020; Nivette & Akoensi, 2019; Usman, 2019).

5.3.2 The Bribery Menace

Another prominent indicator of police corruption in Kenya, and the rest of Africa as well, is bribery. The *East African Bribery Index* (EABI) by TI-Kenya—one of the most credible, accurate and frequently published reports and data sets—showed that, in its most recent survey available (2019), the police in Kenya remarkably came in at second place after the judiciary as the two sectors most affected by bribery. The 2019 police aggregate bribery index was scored at 64 compared to a score of 69 for the judiciary (TI-Kenya, 2020). The aggregate bribery index value ranges between 0 and 100 with 100 being the worst score, and the aggregation is a composite index of the individual scores of five indicators. The five indicators are (1) likelihood of encountering a bribery incidence; (2) prevalence of bribery; (3) average size of bribe; (4) share of "national" bribe; and (5) impact of bribery. The aggregate bribery index serves to capture an overall reflection of the bribery pattern in an institution (TI-Kenya, 2020). On average, the majority of respondents interacting with the police (75%) were asked (implicitly and explicitly) or offered to pay a bribe to access the services they sought (TI-Kenya, 2020). Historically, a failure or refusal to comply with such a bribe demand would result in a failure to access the service or in the incurring of punishment (Hope, 2017; TI-Kenya, 2020). In fact, as noted by the Truth, Justice, and Reconciliation Commission (TJRC) of Kenya: "Those who cannot bribe police officers are the ones who are arrested and charged" (TJRC, 2013, p. 355).

The average size of the police bribe amount by 2019 was equivalent to US$30 compared to US$239 for the judiciary (TI-Kenya, 2020). The police also accounted for the second largest share of the national bribes paid at 19% compared to 30% in 2017, while the judiciary had the largest share at 24% compared to 15% in 2017 (TI-Kenya, 2020). So, here again we see the two key arms of the justice system (police and judiciary) representing the most corrupt institutions in Kenya with the data reflecting public perception of the judiciary based on a number of recent corruption scandals that have plagued members of the judiciary, including Supreme Court justices. However, paying these bribes imposes a direct financial cost, a rent-seeking tax burden, on Kenyans. These are extortion payments that the police collect from their victims, often times, as per a survey conducted by Andvig and Barasa

(2011, p. 74), "using imprisonment or the threats of it as their major instrument … [and] these extortion forms constitute more than 80% of the police corruption incidences reported."

Consequently, these bribes and extortion payments to the Kenya police have now become par for the course. All of this amounts to predatory policing, however, and one frequently used mode of such predatory policing comes in the form of police roadblocks and unnecessary pullovers where motorists are subject to extortion and shakedowns. Indeed, some 81% of survey respondents have indicated that the police stop drivers without good reason (IDS-UON, 2022). One result of this state of affairs, according to research by Onyango (2022), for example, is that the police bribery corruption at traffic checkpoints and roadblocks has become an art form. Police behavior at these encounters occurs within a well-established and expansive syndicated network where "motorists pay bribes to circumvent traffic regulations or be on the right terms with corrupt police officers. [At the same time], the police are more attentive to maximizing illicit incomes for personal and institutional gains" (Onyango, 2022, pp. 3–4). In fact, so lucrative is the bribery business for the Kenya police that one former police officer negotiated with the EACC to turnover to the government the sum of KES26 million (approximately US$238,000) that had been frozen in that former officer's bank account (Kiplagat, 2021). The EACC had originally sought KES47 million (approximately US$427,000).

In relationship to other African countries, and similarly for Nigeria, for example, Adisa et al. (2020) have shown that bribery and extortion by the police have become a plague on motorists, especially commercial drivers. And, in Ghana, it was intimated that the experiences of commercial vehicle drivers with police bribery corruption were not only prevalent but also contributed to traffic violations, thereby leading to the suggestion that the police can reduce traffic violations by curbing bribery corruption among traffic officers (Tankebe & Boakye, 2020; Tankebe et al., 2020). In the DRC, Alexandre (2018) found that there are cooperative arrangements both internally and externally that facilitate the police bribery process with taxi drivers in the city of Bukavu. Internally, there is a well- organized arrangement between traffic police officers and their superiors whereby said traffic officers are requested to submit weekly, unofficial bribe amounts to the traffic police headquarters in Bukavu, while externally there is an amicable arrangement whereby taxi drivers are not forced to pay bribes but with the full knowledge of all players that the bribe represents protection for the taxi drivers, otherwise they will be stuck and not be able to work as taxi drivers (Alexandre, 2018).

Looking further at the available comparable and credible data on police bribery rates covering sub-Saharan Africa, we see in Fig. 5.1 the averages of the proportion of people who, during the previous 12 months, paid a bribe to the police after seeking assistance from said police over the period 2013–2021. By 2021, the average had reached 36%, increasing steadily since 2013. However, as to be expected, there is considerable variation across countries ranging from the high of more than three-quarters of Nigerians (80%) and Ugandans (76%) who sought police assistance and paid these bribes to get that assistance, as did more than two-thirds (68%) of Liberians compared to the single digit lows of 1% in Cabo Verde, 4% in Mauritius,

5.3 The Nature and Extent of Police Corruption in Kenya and Across Africa

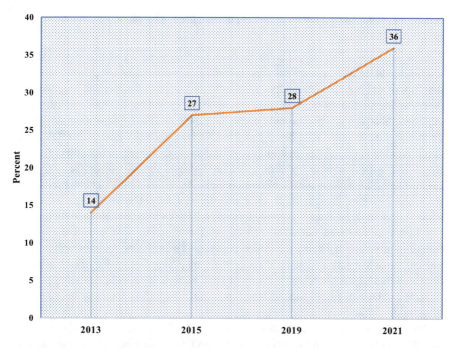

Fig. 5.1 Police corruption indicator—bribery rates: averages of the proportion of people in sub-Saharan Africa who, during the previous 12 months, paid a bribe to the police for police assistance, 2013–2021[a] (%). *Notes:* [a]Data for 2013 represents the bribery rate for avoiding problems with the police. *Source:* Author, based on data derived from Afrobarometer (n.d.-a, n.d.-b, n.d.-c); Pring (2015); Pring and Vrushi (2019)

5% in Namibia, 7% in Botswana, and 9% in Lesotho (Afrobarometer, n.d.-a; Logan et al., 2022).

A further demonstration of the pan-African police bribery menace can be gleaned from Malawi where in June 2022, among other actions, the President of Malawi, Lazarus Chakwera, fired the Malawi Police Service (Malawi-PS) Inspector-General (Police Chief), George Kainja, who was also subsequently arrested, based on evidence provided by the Malawi Anti-Corruption Bureau (MACB) in a report that contained audio recordings of the Inspector-General discussing procurement deals, bribes and kickbacks with a British businessman and the soliciting of advantage with respect to contracts (see MACB, 2022). This was the second Chief of Police to be removed since President Chakwera took office on a 2020 political campaign ticket of zero-tolerance for corruption.

5.3.3 Criminality and Other Misconduct Abuses of Power

The concerns raised about police corruption in Africa tend to be primarily about, but not limited to, police officers actively misbehaving rather than about any omissions, incompetence, negligence, or poor performance in controlling crime. Accordingly, it seems that police criminality, plain and simple, is fueling the most negative perceptions about the police. Recent survey data indicate that 66% of Kenyan respondents consider the police to be engaged in criminal or illegal activities (IDS-UON, 2022; Kamau et al., 2022). In addition to bribery as discussed above, that criminality includes the perversion of the criminal process, illegal use of force, general police abuse, as well as abuse of due process. As defined by Bonner et al. (2018, p. 2), police abuse "can include arbitrary arrest, selective surveillance and crowd control, harassment, sexual assault, torture, killings, or even disappearances," and "its persistence is understood to reflect weak democratic institutions and poorly functioning police institutions." Police brutality is an extreme form of police abuse and can be defined as the use of violent tactics by police that violate the civil and/or human rights of the victim or victims of such tactics. It includes excessive and/or unwarranted use of force, such as beatings, torture, or killings, against an individual or group.

The report by the retired Justice Philip Ransley (The Ransley Report), released in 2009 is considered the definitive source and analysis (and rightly so) of what ailed the Kenya police and what reforms were needed then—and still needed now—to improve the organization's performance overall and for democratic/ethical policing. Among other things, the report found or observed the following: (1) corruption amongst junior and senior police officers was rife and had a debilitating impact on policing and on public trust; (2) there is corruption and nepotism in the recruitment and promotion process perpetrated through interference by influential individuals and instances where recruits paid substantial sums to join the police services. This then presented a basic contradiction in values in that a police officer, who is expected to uphold law and order, would have entered the police force on a corruption platform; (3) corruption within the police services was widespread and endemic with the tolerance levels for corruption for all ranks being unacceptably high and bribery appearing to be blamed on poor salaries and working conditions of the officers. Allegations of links and collusion with organized criminal groups and drug cartels were also raised by the public as a major concern; (4) the public and other stakeholders accused the Traffic Department of corruption and complained about the numerous roadblocks, some of which had become permanent features on the roads and which were used by traffic police officers to extort money from motorists and other members of the public. Many police officers were categorical that a majority of police officers manning road blocks and many others performing traffic duties knew nothing about traffic management and operations while those who had been trained with the objective of taking up traffic duties, were deployed elsewhere to perform duties that were completely irrelevant to their training. Nepotism and ethnicity had significantly contributed to corruption in the Traffic Department; (5) the low salary paid to the police officers contributed highly to their predisposition to corruption, lethargy, and inefficiency in the execution of their duties; (6) the performance of the police had been consistently poorly rated by the public, particularly on violation of human rights, abuse of power and corruption. This was a matter of great concern to the government, hence the focus of police reforms; and (7) a major security challenge was found to be emanating from the Northern part of the country, through the then Eastern Province of Kenya, and originating from Ethiopia and from Somalia through the North Eastern and Coast regions of Kenya. The immigration personnel had not coordinated well with the police and there were allegations of rampant corruption in facilitating trafficking (Republic of Kenya, 2009).

Other official country reports such as those by the United Nations Committee Against Torture (UNCAT), for example, have also observed that corruption in the police service in Kenya was hindering efforts to deal with violations of human rights and arbitrary arrest by the police. In a 2009 report, UNCAT stated:

> The Committee urges the State Party [Kenya] to address the problem of arbitrary police actions including unlawful and arbitrary arrests and widespread police corruption particularly in slums and poor urban neighborhoods, through clear messages of zero tolerance to corruption from superior officers, the imposition of appropriate penalties and adequate training. Arbitrary police action must be promptly and impartially investigated and those found responsible punished (UNCAT, 2009).

Also in 2009, the United Nations Special Rapporteur on Extra Judicial, Arbitrary and Summary Executions accused the Kenya police of having death squads that hunted down and killed people arbitrarily and brutally (United Nations Human Rights Council [UNHRC], 2009). In 2012 and 2013, the United Nations Human Rights Committee (UN-HRC) and the UNCAT, respectively, raised concerns about the slow pace of investigations and prosecutions for allegations of torture and extrajudicial killings by the Kenya police and also recommended that the government of Kenya "should take all necessary measures to determine cases where vulnerable persons are prone to arbitrary arrest, prevent such acts and put in place systems to ensure that police corruption is promptly, effectively and impartially investigated," and with "perpetrators being suspended from duties while under investigation and brought to justice" (UNCAT, 2015, p. 5; UNHRC, 2012). The failure to prosecute police officers responsible for corruption and human rights violations remains a serious challenge for governance in Kenya. Extrajudicial killings, which are executions, refer to the arbitrary deprivation of life by government authorities or individuals without the sanction of any judicial or legal process. These executions include, among others, deaths resulting from torture or ill-treatment in prison or detention, death resulting from enforced disappearances, and deaths resulting from the excessive use of force by law-enforcement officials. Extrajudicial killings often target political opponents, activists, or marginalized groups.

In 2013, Kenya's Independent Policing Oversight Authority (IPOA) conducted and released a *Baseline Survey on Policing Standards and Gaps in Kenya* to gather first hand data/information and experiences of Kenyans, including police officers, on policing standards and factors/challenges affecting effective and efficient policing in Kenya. The Survey found, among other things, that:

- Thirty percent of respondents had experienced police malpractice including: assault/brutality, falsification of evidence, bribery, and threat of imprisonment within 12 months prior to the survey. The incidence of police malpractice was higher in rural areas at 61% than in urban areas; higher among men (62%) compared to 38% of women; and higher among younger people aged less than 35 years (64%) than those aged above 35 years (34%).
- Among police officers, 53% admitted to have experienced incidences of police misconduct that included bribery (36%); assault (25%); use of excessive force (25%); injuries from a weapon (14%); falsification of evidence (14%); threats of imprisonment (14%); and unwarranted shooting (9%).
- Among the police officers who had witnessed incidences of misconduct, only 32% of them reported such cases to the relevant authorities. Police officers who did not report cases of malpractice by their colleagues indicated that they did not do so for fear of reprisals (56%); threats of being transferred (18%); fear of losing their job (13%); because not much action will be taken (5%); and being unaware of where to report (5%).
- For police officers, the most important factors affecting police performance in Kenya was low pay and incentives (54.6%); limited resources including transportation to fight crime (24.7%); corruption (3%); discrimination, ethnicity, nepotism, and favoritism (2.7%); lack of ICT infrastructure (1.6%); lack of proper training (1.2%); and other factors (2.6%).
- About 34.3% of the public expressed confidence in the IPOA's ability to effectively hold the police accountable for their misconduct while 13.7% had no such confidence.
- The majority of the police officers (62.5%) had confidence in the IPOA and believed that it could deliver on its mandate while 29.3% were somewhat confident. Only 6% were not confident while 2.1% were not sure (IPOA, 2013).

Over time, the evidence continues to show the damning nature and extent of police corruption and misconduct in the country. In a 2014 monitoring report by the IPOA—on a police security operation undertaken in areas of Kenya perceived to be hideouts for immigrants and intended to flush out terrorists and search for weapons and explosives as well as disrupt and deter terrorism and other criminal activities—found that "the operation was marred by widespread allegations of corruption where members of the public were allegedly forced to part with bribes to avoid being arrested and/or detained in unclear circumstances [and] arbitrary arrests, harassment, assault, unlawful detentions and deportation of individuals" (IPOA, 2014a, p. 3).

Also in 2014, in a report published by the Independent Medico-Legal Unit (IMLU) in which they examined 1873 deaths resulting from gunshot wounds over the period 2009–2013, it was found that (1) police use of firearms accounted for 67% of those deaths; (2) inadequate documentation did not allow for perpetrator identification in more than 200 cases; (3) the circumstances of police involvement were unclear or absent in over 60% of these fatal shootings; and (4) the reason for the police resorting to deadly force was not given in over 65% of the shootings (IMLU, 2014).

The Kenya National Commission for Human Rights (KNCHR) has further reported that, together with its partners, it has documented 1005 cases of extrajudicial killings and enforced disappearances attributed to the security agencies during the period 2013–2019, with the majority (80%) of the victims being young men aged 15–35 years (KNCHR, 2020). Enforced disappearance is used here as defined in the International Convention for the Protection of All Persons from Enforced Disappearance (see UN, 2010), which Kenya signed in 2007 but has since failed to ratify. More currently, available data show that during the period 2019–2021, the Kenya police killed close to 500 people (by shooting or torturing them) and more than 40 have disappeared while in police custody and therefore considered to be victims of enforced disappearance (Missing Voices, n.d.). However, according to IPOA, during the period for which comparative data are now available (2018–2020), it received 428 complaints classified as deaths from police action, 121 complaints classified as deaths while in police custody, and 65 complaints classified as enforced disappearances (IPOA, 2019a, 2019b, 2020a, 2020b, 2021a, 2021b).

In October 2021, the Kenya Senate Standing Committee on Justice, Legal Affairs and Human Rights released its report on its inquiry into extrajudicial killings and enforced disappearances in the country which, among other things, acknowledged that extra-judicial killings and enforced disappearances in Kenya have been of grave concern for quite a while, despite the country having put in place legal and institutional frameworks to address the two issues. It was noted that "extrajudicial killings and enforced disappearances present a grave affront to the Constitution and the administration of justice," due to the fact "that persons profiled or suspected to have committed crimes are summarily executed without being subjected to the benefit of a fair trial, where evidence may be presented against them and the opportunity to rebut such evidence granted" (Republic of Kenya, The Senate, 2021, p. 7). To effectively address extrajudicial killings and enforced disappearances in the country, the report concluded with a number of recommendations on actions that need to be taken by government actors that were categorized as (1) legislative; (2) policy; and (3) administrative.

In May 2022, UNCAT adopted and released its report on its concluding observations on the third periodic assessment of Kenya. Among other things, the Committee expressed its concerns that its recommendations on extrajudicial killings and disproportionate use of force have not yet been fully implemented. The Committee remains seriously concerned at the allegations received of extrajudicial killings, enforced disappearances and excessive use of force by the police (UNCAT, 2022). Among its recommendations were that the Kenyan government should: (1) Ensure that prompt, impartial and effective investigations are undertaken into all allegations relating to extrajudicial killings, enforced disappearances and excessive use of force by law enforcement officers and military personnel, and ensure that the alleged perpetrators are prosecuted and the victims adequately compensated; (2) Revise the legal framework to ensure that all forms of enforced disappearance are clearly defined in criminal law with associated penalties that are proportionate to the severity of the offence; (3) Review the Sixth Schedule of the National Police Service (NPS) Act (Act No. 11 of 2011) to ensure that it is fully compliant with the basic principles on the use of force and firearms by law enforcement officials, and adequately train all relevant state officers, particularly police officers, on the use of force; and (4) Expedite the establishment of the National Coroners Service to ensure that any investigation into allegations of extrajudicial executions entails independent forensic examination, including, if necessary, an autopsy, in line with the Minnesota Protocol on the Investigation of Potentially Unlawful Death (UNCAT, 2022).

Figure 5.2 shows statistics on complaints to the IPOA regarding police corruption/extortion (C/E) and unethical practices/abuse of office (UP/AO) as a proportion of total complaints. Unfortunately, good comparative time series data are only currently available for 2019 and 2020. As can be seen, in both years an average of one-fifth of all complaints were in the nature of C/E and UP/AO combined. However, based on what we know about the predatory nature of policing in Kenya as well as the incidence of bribery demands and payments to the police in the country, as discussed above, these C/E and UP/AO complaints against the police that have been compiled by the IPOA are a drop in the bucket compared to the scale of the problem as reported by the media and other monitoring entities (see also Hope, 2019; Probert

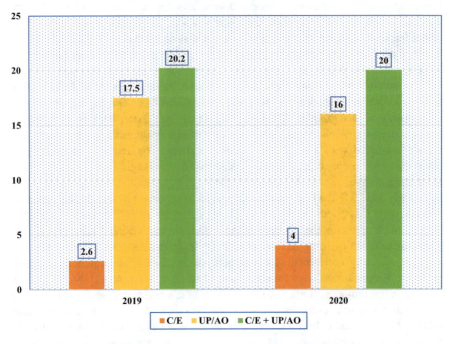

Fig. 5.2 Complaints to the IPOA about police corruption/extortion and unethical practices/abuse of office as a proportion of total complaints, 2019–2020 (%). *Notes:* C/E = corruption/extortion; UP/AO = unethical practices/abuse of office. *Source:* Author, based on data derived from IPOA (2020a, 2020b, 2021a, 2021b)

5.3 The Nature and Extent of Police Corruption in Kenya and Across Africa

et al., 2020). The great majority of Kenyans who are victims of police corruption do not file complaints or cases against the police. Moreover, the United States (US) Department of State (2022a, p. 2) has also noted that "impunity at all levels of government continued to be a serious problem" as "the governmental Independent Policing Oversight Authority, established to provide civilian oversight of police, investigated numerous cases of misconduct" but "the government took limited and uneven steps to address cases of alleged unlawful killings by security force members, although the Independent Policing Oversight Authority continued to refer cases of police misconduct to the Office of the Director of Public Prosecutions for prosecution."

In comparison to South Africa—which is currently the only other African country with independent civilian oversight of the police—Tshoose and Rapatsa (2022) concluded that the weakness of police accountability systems in the country contributes to widespread criminality and brutality by law enforcement officers with far-reaching consequences for society extending to offences including execution-style killings in custody; deaths linked to torture or other assaults, reckless or accidental shootings, including killings during demonstrations; unlawful detention of suspects involved in petty offences; other non-fatal assaults on persons at the point of arrest or outside of custody; cases of rape and other assaults on persons in custody and even those reporting cases to the police; and other cases of brutality in dealing with rowdy crowds. Corruption Watch (2019) has also shown that the police and their accomplices are accused of a number of criminal and corrupt activities, ranging from procurement irregularities, sexual harassment and sextortion, threatening of witnesses and whistle-blowers on behalf of their criminal syndicates' benefactors such as drug dealers, to exerting pressure through violence, if necessary, when a bribe is sought.

According to the available data, the number of public complaints reported to South Africa's Independent Police Investigative Directorate (IPID) increased by approximately 11% between 2015–2016 and 2020–2021 from 5519 to 6122 (IPID, 2016, 2021). Of the total complaints reported against the South African police, the majority continued to be related to allegations of assault. For the period 2020–2021, more than two-thirds (69%) were about assault, followed by complaints of discharge of an official firearm (14%), death as a result of police action (6%), death in police custody (4%), torture (4%), rape by police officer(s) (1%), and non-systemic corruption as defined in the statutes (1%) (IPID, 2021). In the breakdown of the corruption complaints, the highest number were for extortion or soliciting bribes (85%), followed by sale, theft and/or disposal of exhibits (11%), aiding escape from custody (3%), and abuse of power (1%) (IPID, 2021).

In Rwanda, during the period 2012–2021, more than 2000 police officers, including some in the most senior ranks, have been fired and/or charged for engaging in corruption, other gross misconduct or professional malpractice (Kashaka, 2021; Mwasa, 2021; World Bank, 2020). In Lesotho, according to Amnesty International (2022, p. 1), the police are "facing a number of legal claims over crimes ranging from murder, cover-up and defeating the ends of justice, to assault, torture and death in police custody," with "one law firm in Maseru (the capital city) pursuing 58 cases of police brutality recorded since 2018." Consequently, amid a growing sense of insecurity, a majority of the citizens of Lesotho say the police routinely torture or abuse people in their custody, use excessive force in dealing with criminals, and engage in criminal activities (see Malephane & Salau, 2022).

In October 2022, the newly elected President of Kenya, William Ruto, ordered the disbandment of the Special Service Unit (SSU) of the Directorate of Criminal Investigations (DCI) of the NPS because it had been used to spread terror against Kenyans. As reported by the press, President Ruto said that the SSU—which has been accused of engaging in extra-judicial killings—had made the country very insecure as the police changed and became killers instead of protectors of ordinary Kenyans and were killing Kenyans arbitrarily (see, for example, Kiage, 2022). President Ruto further said that these "extrajudicial killings must come to an end," as "it is illegal, it is unconstitutional, [and] it offends every principle of the right to life" (see Amunga, 2022, p. 1). He also challenged the IPOA to develop a plan and provide it to the Interior Ministry as a roadmap on how to end extra-judicial killings in Kenya. At least in theory, if not in practice, going forward this disbandment of the SSU, along with a credible plan from IPOA to prevent or counteract these extrajudicial killings, offers an opportunity to rid the Kenya police of at least some of its criminal elements and introduce accountability for the multiple police killings and enforced disappearances recorded in the past.

In that regard, the country's Director of Public Prosecutions (DPP) also announced in October 2022 that several police officers, most of them in the senior ranks, were charged with murder and other crimes against humanity including some of the offences stemming from a crackdown on post-election protests back in 2017. However, we will be able to gauge in the near future if these actions by the newly elected President and his government represent permanent good policies in the national interest or just a public relations stunt intended as appeasement (temporarily) to national and international human rights concerns before an eventual return to the police again either being used, or going rogue, as instruments for extrajudicial killings and enforced disappearances.

5.3.4 *Recruitment for Sale*

Another contributing factor to the police corruption problem in Kenya, and across Africa as well, is that of recruitment for sale. A good and well publicized example in the Kenya case can be gleaned from the July 2014 attempt by the National Police Service Commission (NPSC) to recruit 10,000 police trainees in one day. This exercise was troubled with allegations of much shameless bribery and tribalism that moved one commentator to describe it as reaching a new low when it comes to corruption in the police service with the security services having become even more corrupt, politicized and tribalized since 2013 when a new government was sworn in (Warah, 2014a). It had previously been noted by the Ransley Report and, subsequently, the TJRC Kenya that "during the recruitment exercise, money changes hands. If you cannot part with [KES] 60,000 [approximately US$680], your son cannot be employed" (TJRC Kenya, 2013, p. 102).

The resultant effect of this botched corrupt recruitment of 10,000 police trainees was that a number of institutions and individuals went to court to prevent the selection results from being implemented and that included candidates who were not selected. Among the institutions that moved to the courts was the IPOA. The IPOA filed a case in the High Court seeking to have this police recruitment exercise nullified on the grounds that the exercise was marred by maleficent irregularities, was conducted in a manner that was not in compliance with the constitution and hence led to the great hue and cry from members of the public and aggrieved participants (IPOA, 2014b).

In a much more elaborate and dramatic statement, entitled *Police Recruitment: A National Shame and a Sham*, the IPOA outlined its findings and subsequent verdict on the recruitment exercise as its rationale for taking the matter to court. Among its findings was that:

> There were reported incidents of influence peddling and conflict of interest. The involvement of NPS [National Police Service] senior officers and the Deputy County Commissioners from the stations within or near the recruitment exercise appeared to complicate the exercise. Given the manner in which many of these officers conducted the exercise, it was easy to conclude that these officers could have been compromised long before the exercise (IPOA, 2014c, p. 2).

Based on its findings, the verdict by the IPOA was stated as follows:

> Therefore, it is the position of IPOA that the recruitment exercise was not transparent and accountable. There were complaints of discrimination on the basis of ethnicity and undefined criteria which disqualified the candidates in the final stage. The exercise was marred by widespread irregularities and, therefore, could not pass muster in the test of a free and fair undertaking including promoting public confidence in policing. Arising from this, we recommend the cancelation of the entire exercise, and its repeat with a more transparent process owned by as many stakeholders as possible, before commencement of the exercise. We are confident that the process when started afresh, will create a viable relationship between the public and the police, and further, improve the policing function, and this can only start at the recruitment and selection stage. No other way (IPOA, 2014c, p. 2).

In an attempt to head off court action, the NPSC annulled the recruitment in 36 of the 289 centers suspected to have had malpractices in the exercise and to repeat the process. The 36 centers affected 1215 recruits representing 12% of the total 10,000 recruits. According to the NPSC, the results were annulled for reasons including acts which are criminal in nature, corruption, and professional misconduct (NPSC, 2014). The High Court eventually ruled in favor of the IPOA, annulled the entire recruitment process and ordered that recruitment be started afresh. In a precedent-setting ruling, the High Court said that the July 2014 hiring was tainted with corruption, irregularities, and blatant violation of the constitution. According to court reporting by Lucheli and Weru (2014), the High Court found and held "that the National Police Service Commission failed itself, it failed Kenyans, it failed the recruits, it failed the constitution and it must be told so." Consequently, "the orders that are appropriate in the circumstances is an order quashing the recruitment exercise conducted on July 14 this year. [The Court is] satisfied that drastic action must be taken, painful or unpopular as it may be." And, it was indeed quite interesting and refreshing to notice that the IPOA was vigorously and studiously exercising its civilian oversight role. Perhaps this augurs well for the future as a sign that the policing institutions will be made to comply with the constitution and all existing policing statutes that have now been put in place in support of said constitution to bring about a professionalization of the police that significantly eschews corruption. Indeed, the control of police corruption and the professionalization of the NPS must begin at the recruitment and training stages in the quest for the transformation of the NPS into an efficient, effective, accountable, and transparent organization (Hope, 2013).

However, in April 2015 the IPOA, the court ruling, and the rule of law were all undermined when the then President of Kenya irresponsibly ordered the NPS to ignore the court and accept and begin training the 10,000 police recruits. This was one of the actions taken by the government in response to a terrorist attack in a northeastern county that killed more than 145 students on a university campus. The President blamed the insecurity in the country on a shortage of police officers and directed that the recruits start their training immediately. As also observed by Ng'ulia (2015), this directive was not only a blow to the war against corruption but also a boost to impunity by further institutionalizing corruption in the recruitment of police officers and inspiring them to work corruptly. Fortunately, after considerable public outrage, the directive was rescinded and, subsequently, in May 2015, the Court of Appeal upheld the nullification of the recruitment. It is also interesting to note here that the new NPS recruitment exercise conducted in April 2015 was deemed by the IPOA to be "a major improvement compared to the July 2014 exercise. In centers monitored there was semblance of adherence to the principles of transparency, accountability and public participation. Generally, the exercise was not marred by manifest flaws and can pass the test of being free and fair" (IPOA, 2015, p. 26). Nonetheless, the 2016 recruitment process seemed to have reverted back to business as usual. Monitoring conducted by the KNCHR found, among other things, that although "the levels of bribery allegations witnessed during this process were not blatant and exposed as had been experienced in the previous exercises." However, "there were many cases of bribery of various amounts ... with members of the public being used to pass the money to the police officers" (KNCHR, 2016, pp. 22–23). Recent reports also determined that police recruitment officers pocketed close to KES500 million (approximately US$4 million) in the recruitment exercise that was conducted across the country on 24 March, 2022 (Angira, 2022).

With respect to, and in comparison, with other, African countries, in South Africa, for example, the Independent Policing Union of South Africa (IPUSA) has also expressed its concerns about the recruitment of new police officers being open to corruption due to prospective police recruits paying money to be admitted to the police training college (Tshuma, 2022). In Nigeria, there are similar problems with recruitment exercises resulting in frequent warnings not to bribe police recruitment officials. For example, the government had approved and budgeted for the recruitment of 40,000 police constables (10,000 per year) over the period 2019–2022.

However, only about 10,000 had been recruited by the end of 2022, and many of those applicants individually paid N700,000 (approximately US$1590) and above to secure the job (see Sahara Reporters, 2022a). Other investigative reporting further show that some senior Nigeria police officers have been accused of issuing fake appointment letters after collecting huge amounts of money from applicants for the post of constable in the country's police force (Sahara Reporters, 2022b).

Also, apart from the selling and buying of police employment, police recruitment in Africa is also influenced by ethnicity, nepotism, and the "godfather" principle which is addressed below. Consequently, according to Aremu (2021, p. 319), for instance, "most [police] recruits in Nigeria arrive 'dirty' and then serve to perpetuate a culture of corruption in the police. Similarly, corruption thrives in the police because the culture of the organization inadvertently promotes it."

5.3.5 The Retention Vetting Realities

Given the need to control police misconduct, and in the context of necessary policies to reform the police and modify police behavior, Kenya also recognized, and then codified, following on from the 2010 constitution, that the existing members of the NPS needed to be vetted for retention or release from the NPS. Vetting (whether transitional or for new employment) is a significant element of human resource management which includes recruiting, hiring, deploying, and managing an organization's employees. The retention vetting process was rolled out in Kenya in November 2013. Section 7 of the NPS Act of 2011 provides the legal basis for the vetting of all police officers by the NPSC as well as for the removal from the NPS of any officer who fails the vetting. Vetting of police officers is mandated to be conducted to determine the suitability and competence of the officers—serving before the commencement of the NPS Act of 2011, which for all practical purposes would be those serving before the promulgation of the 2010 constitution—to remain in the NPS. Any officer who is found unsuitable to continue serving could seek redress in the courts or file an appeal with the NPSC requesting consideration of a review on grounds consistent with Regulation 33 of the NPS Vetting Regulations. The NPSC considered any degree of the lack of "Integrity and/or Respect for Human Rights" as areas of zero tolerance in the vetting process, and officers found culpable under these areas were to be removed from the NPS (NPSC, 2018).

In an October 2015 speech on the police vetting process, the then Chairperson of the NPSC revealed that the NPSC had fired 63 senior police officers for corruption and integrity issues based on investigations undertaken for the vetting of police officers, as mandated (Kavuludi, 2015). Those investigations, to date, have brought to the fore some of the complex police corruption networks and the interface between junior officers and their seniors in those networks. For example, "through a scrutiny of Mpesa [mobile money] statements, the Commission was able to establish that junior officers working in the traffic department regularly transferred fixed amounts of money to some of their seniors, suggesting that they had been given targets" (Kavuludi, 2015, p. 2; see also Aglionby, 2016; Mukinda, 2015; Okebiro, 2016; Wachira, 2016).

In addition, "it also emerged that most Mpesa [mobile money] kiosks within and around police stations are either owned or contracted by police officers for purposes of facilitating direct money transfers in order to cover their tracks." And, "the depositors are mostly motorists or junior officers making transfers to their seniors" (Kavuludi, 2015, p. 3). These senior officers have been referred to as "godfathers" who ensure protection for their chosen and/or collaborating juniors (Mutahi et al., 2023). In that regard, the police often function like pyramid schemes, with an expectation that corruption passes from the lower-level ranks to the top (Kleinfeld, 2019). In June 2016, the NPSC announced that another 302 police officers had been fired for corruption (Omollo, 2016; Odula, 2016). The officers had refused to be vetted consistent with the mandatory requirements of the law and as well as being an integral part of the police reforms process.

Moreover, the Kenyan newspapers are almost daily replete with investigative reports of police corruption. Recently, these reports have been concerned with internal police corruption and misconduct such as the rampant cases of victimization, widespread graft, unexplained salary deductions, and dismissals perpetrated by senior officers against the junior ones. Teyie and Menya (2014), for example, reported that junior police officers who do not cooperate in corrupt activities with their seniors, or so-called self-declared "godfathers," are being arbitrarily dismissed, transferred, or demoted on questionable grounds. This has led some junior officers to question "if expertise in corruption is a qualification for one to be promoted in the police service" (Teyie & Menya, 2014, p. 28).

Indeed, the retention vetting process also found that "many police officers had served in the same rank for many years yet some of their colleagues had been promoted very frequently," and "this led to lack of morale among officers who felt that they needed to 'know someone in the senior ranks' to obtain a promotion, or to some extent there were reports of bribery to obtain promotion or to be selected for promotion courses" (NPSC, 2018, p. 52). This state of affairs ultimately led the NPSC to develop Promotions Regulations in a bid to provide uniform standards for promotion for the NPS. Complementarily, the NPSC also developed Career Progression Guidelines to address the officers' career progression, redress problems of stagnation and conduct training needs (NPSC, 2018).

Unfortunately, the police vetting process came to a standstill some time in 2019. Based on available data at time of writing, the total number of police officers in Kenya stood at 100,481 in 2020 (NPS, 2020). The publicly available data indicates that at the time vetting was halted only 5993 police officers had undergone the process, and of which 445 (approximately 7.5%) of them were found to be unsuitable and terminated from the NPS (NPSC, 2018, 2019). Not surprisingly, the majority of officers terminated were traffic police. Of the 2640 traffic officers vetted, 318 (12%) of them were removed from the NPS (NPSC, 2018). The total number of police officers vetted (5993) represents only 6% of the total number of Kenya police. It would seem that the entire operation may have been a bit too ambitious with a NPSC that lacked the underlying capacity to organize and undertake an exercise of this order of magnitude. Moreover, and in fairness, there were also other factors that were beyond the control of the NPSC.

In an Opinion Editorial document on their website, the NPSC has set out its reasons why the vetting process was halted and the way forward as they see it (see NPSC, n.d.). They acknowledged that, inevitably, there were unforeseen gaps, miscalculations and unmet expectations as factors which contributed to the delay, and there were no lessons available to be learnt from previous country experiences to guide the process. In addition, there were also issues related to insecurity in the nation due to terrorist attacks and the lack of funds to conduct the investigations that were required to address the large volume of serious public complaints against some officers (NPSC, n.d.).

However, in a research report and a briefing paper facilitated and published through the International Center for Transitional Justice (ICTJ) and the Van Vollenhoven Institute for Law, Governance and Society (VVI), an analytical critique was offered on why the vetting process went from optimism to disillusionment as perceived by civil society; as well as views on the general obstacles encountered, the pitfalls that emerged, and the identifiable challenges and problems related to decision-making that need to be addressed (see Blocq et al., 2020; Blocq & Duthie, 2020). The key reasons elucidated for the optimism to disillusionment thesis regarding the vetting process can be summarized as resulting from flaws in the design and implementation of the process which exhibited many problematic elements, including the disparate compositions and behavior of the commissioners and panelists, the failure to collect and corroborate evidence, the insecurity of those within and outside of the commission, poor communication, a lack of transparency, and the failure to focus on human rights violations instead of focusing mostly on corruption (see Blocq et al., 2020; Blocq & Duthie, 2020).

To counteract the problems and criticisms encountered, and based on the vetting experience acquired along the way, the NPSC has decided to move to a "targeted vetting" model whereby only officers with significant issues touching on their suitability and competence will be subjected to face-to-face interviews to fulfil the requirements of due process. Essentially, the strategy on vetting is being shifted from a supply to a demand driven process, as and when necessary (NPSC, n.d., 2019). Moreover, instead of vetting officers based on their ranks, the process will be conducted according to formations with priority being accorded to formations such as traffic police and the criminal investigations department, for example, that highly interact with the public. It was projected that the number of officers that would now require a face-to-face interview should not exceed 6% of the total number in service (NPSC, n.d.). This approach will be further supported by the use of new ICT software that will reduce processing times to a fraction of the current amount of time it now takes to process a vetting file, and "the Commission is confident that these adjustments will expedite the vetting process while at the same time enhancing its integrity" (NPSC, n.d., p. 2).

Perhaps, the NPSC may also want to take a look at the police reforms vetting processes that have occurred in Georgia and Honduras, for example, where rampant police corruption was attacked through the investigation/evaluation of police officers and the subsequent purging of significant numbers of those that were found to be unfit to serve, including many in the top ranks. Despite the ongoing problems with police corruption in both countries, and the now overwhelming violence and criminal gang activities in Honduras in particular, the police vetting and purging exercises were universally hailed as successful.

5.3.6 Super Cops: The Dirty Harry Syndrome

Despite the perceived, potential, and real negative consequences of police abuse, brutality, violence, and general police misconduct, it must also be noted that some events have shown that there are pockets of members of Kenyan society that support and promote such police behavior as a means that justify the ends of stamping out neighborhood crime and insecurity. The police officers engaging in such "Dirty Harry" type of misconduct are bad apples who are generally referred to as "Super Cops" in Kenya as well as in other African countries such as Nigeria, for instance (see, for example, Kabir, 2022; Omanga et al., 2021; O'Rukevbe, 2022; Wairuri, 2022).

These so-called "Super Cops" are police officers (vigilantes) "who take a violent approach to policing that often goes beyond the legal limits of their power. They often emerge in contexts marked by high levels of fear of crime and popular frustration with the formal criminal justice system" (Wairuri, 2022, p. 76). "Super-Cops" therefore "describe an unorthodox form of policing where specific policemen (mostly male), through a mix of public consent and state sanction, use extrajudicial means to confront suspected criminals" (Omanga et al., 2021, p. 1). In most cases, these "Super Cops" present themselves as incorruptible. However, among other things, they ("Super Cops") either collect protection money from small business owners and others, extort ordinary citizens, or they engage in outright criminal activities including, and beyond, even their extra-judicial policing (see Kabir, 2022; Omanga et al., 2021; O'Rukevbe, 2022; Princewill, 2022; Wairuri, 2022).

At the time of writing, one so-called Nigerian "Super Cop," Abba Kyari, a decorated Deputy Commissioner of Police (DCP), was suspended, arrested, and being prosecuted by the National Drug Law Enforcement Agency (NDLEA) on drug-related charges. DCP Kyari was also being pursued by the US Department of Justice (DOJ) for extradition on a warrant of arrest on charges that included conspiring to commit fraud and money laundering. However, a Federal High Court in Abuja subsequently dismissed the extradition action. Police teams under Kyari's direction have been accused of torturing and killing innocent people. In fact, according to Ratliff and Clowes (2022), Kyari's teams routinely targeted businesspeople for arrest, extorted money from suspects and their families, and in some cases committed extrajudicial killings. Undoubtedly, "Super Cops" are part of the problem of police corruption and the generally bad policing in Africa that this chapter discusses and analyzes.

5.4 The Security Challenges of Police Corruption in Kenya and Across Africa

One of the primary purposes of the government of any nation is the provision of security of life, property, and the national interest. In Kenya, this function of the national government is embedded in the country's 2010 constitution which defines national security as "the protection against internal and external threats to Kenya's territorial integrity and sovereignty, its people, their rights, freedoms, property, peace, stability and prosperity, and other national interests" (Republic of Kenya, 2010, p. 144). The constitution also established three national security organs including the NPS with the other two being the Kenya Defence Forces, and the National Intelligence Service (Republic of Kenya, 2010), similar to what obtains in the 1996 constitution of South Africa. The Heads of Kenya's three national security organs are also, necessarily, members of the country's National Security Council (NSC) which was democratized in the country's 2010 constitution by placing it under civilian control and oversight with the country's President presiding at its meetings (see Republic of Kenya, 2010; Mwachofi, 2022). Civilian oversight and control are further guaranteed by the constitutional requirement that the NSC "shall report annually to Parliament on the state of the security of Kenya" (Republic of Kenya, 2010, Article 240).

In most other African countries, their respective constitution provides the police with prescribed powers, duties, and procedures to secure internal security and public tranquility, among other functions.

5.4.1 Contributor to Crime

As shown above, the endemic culture of police corruption still remains a critical problem in Kenya despite attempts at some police reforms, with the Kenya NPS being described as a bribe factory (Mageka, 2015). In fact, so pervasive has police corruption become in Kenya that Mageka (2015, p. 2) also reported that even some "top [police] commanders referred to the police services as an institution that is turning into a criminal enterprise where tribalism, favoritism, and the search for bribes has replaced the vaunted motto of providing service to all." This police corruption criminal enterprise now has serious implications for security in the country.

From a general standpoint, police corruption increases the crime rate and may even contribute to the development of large-scale organized crime (Williams, 2002). The police corruption-crime nexus allows increased consumption of illegal services (such as prostitution) and goods (such as drugs, illegal alcohol, and weapons) (Andvig & Fjeldstad, 2008). Furthermore, this nexus can have a negative impact on economic growth by discouraging foreign direct investment (FDI), as is indeed the case in Kenya (Hope, 2012), and staining the country's international reputation by painting it as an unstable and non-secure environment.

Moreover, as also discussed above, police corruption at any level, but especially low-level corruption by the individual officers in Kenya, affects other unit or team members who do not agree but who feel the cultural pressure of the "code of silence" not to speak out since loyalty to fellow officers tends to be a key feature of police culture, irrespective of whether criminality is involved (see, for example, Prenzler, 2009; Quinn, 2011; Skolnick, 2008; Westmarland, 2005; Williams, 2002). The work of the police is then compromised as individuals lose trust and confidence in each other. In the worst case, others may be drawn into the process, thereby exacerbating the problem for the entire police service and for community and national security. The KNCHR, for instance, claimed to have "information [that] confirms that organized criminal gangs [in Kenya] have infiltrated the police service making it difficult for the police to respond to the challenge of national and transnational crime" (KNCHR, 2014, p. 31). Similarly, in Nigeria, the police have also been infiltrated by drug gangs culminating in a police extortion and complicity enterprise that has become a key motivation for raids on drug hotspots by the police. The creation of these criminal alliances effectively redirected policing from the goals of crime control and public order to personal enrichment and self-preservation of police officers (see, for example, Nelson, 2023; Nelson & Brown, 2020).

5.4.2 Safe Haven for Terrorists and Radicalization Influences

One key implication of police corruption vis-á-vis national security is related to the governance weakness of the Kenyan state. Corruption in the police, and other security services for that matter, is a major feature of "weak" or "failing states" that often then become safe havens for terrorists. In fact, corruption in security services is a key factor at the core of the reasons that terrorist actors thrive. As correctly observed by Sewall (2016, pp. 20–23), "by undermining state effectiveness, corruption creates openings for these dangerous actors," and "also gives them a tool to infiltrate and influence the state itself, further weakening governance and expanding terrorist and criminal reach." Kreiman and Espadafor (2022, p. 350) have also provided some preliminary empirical evidence showing that, in sub-Saharan Africa as well as in South East Asia countries, "terrorism deteriorates state capacity and state legitimacy… and organized crime groups take advantage of this in order to expand their activities."

Generally, terrorist networks have found safety in Kenya judging by the country's inability to secure its territory and ensure safety for its citizens from these agents of insecurity, and the same applies for other weak, corrupt states (Odula, 2014; Ombaka, 2015; Schwartz, 2015; Shelley, 2014). For Kenya, the terrorism that had hit the country as early as 1998—when Al-Qaeda bombed US embassies in twin attacks on Nairobi and Dar es Salaam—is now being wreaked by Al-Shabaab (the Somali terrorist group). Kenya's security situation has also continued to deteriorate since the September 2013 attack on Nairobi's Westgate Mall, where 67 people were reported killed and more than 175 others injured (Anderson & McKnight, 2015a;

IEP, 2015a), and this has had devastating consequences, not only in terms of lives lost, but other economic consequences such as reductions in tourist arrivals with the concomitant loss of revenues to the country.

From 1998 to the present, thousands of people have been killed in Kenya from terrorist activities and several thousand more have been wounded. Indeed, Kenya has experienced severe and fatal attacks since the 1998 bombing of the US embassy in Nairobi as the terror attacks have intensified with the highest threat peaking with the entry of the Kenya Defence Forces into Somalia in 2011 which have stirred retaliatory and sporadic attacks in Kenya by Al-Shabaab and occasioning an unprecedented era of insecurity characterized by constant threats of attacks, radicalization, bombings, and kidnappings. The KNCHR has reported that "the police reforms notwithstanding, Kenya witnessed a surge in the levels of crime and insecurity during the review period [2010-14]. Notably, the biggest challenge during this period was terrorism" (KNCHR, 2015, p. 42). Overall, according to the available information from the KNCHR, some 3060 Kenyans (both civilian and law enforcement officers) lost their lives and 180,300 people were displaced from their places of habitual residence due to insecurity during the period 2010–2014 (KNCHR, 2014). And, based on data from the Global Terrorism Database of the National Consortium for the Study of Terrorism and Responses to Terrorism (START), between 1998 and 2015 there were about 1458 fatalities from terrorism in Kenya with almost 6000 injured (START, n.d.). In that regard, Warah (2014b) was moved to declare that Kenyans were slowly realizing that endemic fraud—among public officials, the police, and politicians—had left them unprotected and alone.

The currently available data shows that in sub-Saharan Africa there were 9863 terrorist attacks resulting in 30,557 deaths, during the period 2007–2021, which was the third largest number of deaths following behind the Middle East and North Africa (MENA) that had 49,764 deaths and South Asia with 37,001 deaths (IEP, 2022). However, sub-Saharan Africa had the most lethal terrorist attacks, averaging three people killed per attack, compared to two people killed per attack in the both the MENA and South Asia regions, respectively (IEP, 2022). In Kenya, the current publicly available data indicate that, during the period 2007–2020, there were 753 terrorist attacks resulting in 1540 fatalities and 2161 people injured (START, n.d.). In Fig. 5.3, we see the number of terrorist attacks in Kenya and the fatalities and injuries resulting from those attacks for the period 2010–2020.

In addition, "there have been various reports of members of Al-Shabaab easily buying their passage into Kenya by bribing police as well as immigration officials" (Gibendi, 2015, p. 1). In fact, in 2012, several police officers were dismissed for accepting bribes in exchange for granting safe passage to Al-Shabaab terrorists who were carrying explosives that were destined to be used for terror bombings in Nairobi, and a member of Kenya's Anti-Terrorism Police Unit (ATPU) was reported to have helped Al-Shabaab smuggle the weapons used during a June 2014 massacre in two coastal towns in the country (Meservey, 2015; Some, 2012). One investigation into the massacre of non-Muslims that occurred at a quarry in Mandera County in December 2014 revealed that the terrorist attackers not only roamed freely in the area but were also assisted by the police and immigration officers to cross the

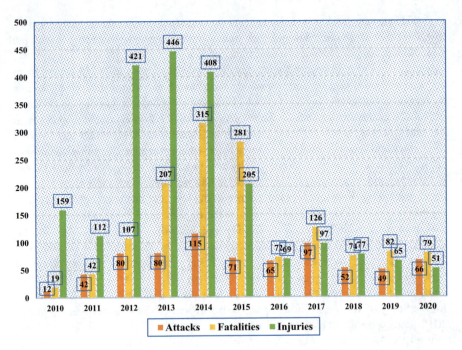

Fig. 5.3 Terrorist attacks, fatalities and injuries in Kenya, 2010–2020. *Source:* Author, based on data derived from START (n.d.)

Kenya-Somalia border by paying corrupt border police and security officers (New African, 2015).

Entrenched corruption in the security system has therefore allowed Al-Shabaab and other criminal elements to move freely in and out of Kenya and carry out terrorist attacks with ease (Gilchrist & Eisen, 2019; Higgins, 2015; KNCHR, 2014). It has long been pointed out that criminal and terrorist groups depend on unimpeded cross-border movements, and so the police and other border guards, customs officers, and immigration personnel are their notable targets of corruption despite enhanced border measures (Mann, 2011; Mogire et al., 2018; Thachuk, 2005). For such figures, the bribes need not be very high, as much of what is required of them is to look the other way when contraband and people pass. Notably, police personnel are just as susceptible to bribery as civilians, but the potential consequences are more serious in an environment of active terrorism (Mann, 2011; Thachuk, 2005). Terror masterminds have also capitalized on persistent graft to advance their agenda. Terror suspects have, for instance, walked to freedom after bribing Kenyan police officers (Misiko, 2014; Ombaka, 2015). "Endemic corruption, in particular, is [therefore] a huge blight on the success of Kenya's [police and other] security agencies in countering terrorism" (Ndung'u, 2015, p. 1).

Consequently, as observed by Mboya (2014, p. XII):

5.4 The Security Challenges of Police Corruption in Kenya and Across Africa 111

…Kenya has become a favored target for terrorists. This is largely the case due to the fact that terrorists are aware that our corrupt nature guarantees any indulgence for a small fee. Indeed, many have been able to secure their freedom from the clutches of our security services in precisely this manner!

Senior government officials have also expressed their dismay and concern about the relationship between police corruption and its security challenges in Kenya. Joseph Nkaissery who, until his death in July 2017, was the Cabinet Secretary of the Ministry of Interior and Coordination of National Government, and under whose remit the NPS fell, was quoted as saying that "there is a positive correlation between the increased corruption among our security officers and the rising insecurity in Kenya. It is a … problem that we have been grappling with for some time" (Kapchanga, 2015, p. 1). Others, including retired senior police officers, have expressed that Al-Shabaab is becoming stronger day after day despite the authorities in Kenya devoting massive resources to combat terrorism. This is because of the endemic corruption that is deeply ingrained in the police whose officers provide haven and logistical support to the terrorist group as they avert their eyes in exchange for a bribe (Chayes, 2015; Pyman, 2015). The terrorists can therefore easily acquire identification documents such as passports, identity cards, and birth certificates, among others, from state offices in Kenya provided that they pay some bribe to the police and other officials (Kapchanga, 2015). Chayes (2015, pp. 184–185) has informed that in the capital city, Nairobi, "residents joke about the 'Shebab [Shabaab] bribe'—double the normal rate—that allowed attackers to infiltrate the Westgate Mall in September 2013, in a siege that claimed more than sixty lives."

John Githongo, a former Kenyan government anti-corruption czar and whose trials and tribulations in that regard have been chronicled by Wrong (2009), has steadfastly argued that it was corruption in public contracting for security kits and other items that led to what in Kenyan parlance is known as "eating" (looting and gorging on state resources) by the elite that opened the door to Al-Shabaab, which now poses a significant threat to the Kenyan state (see Githongo, 2015). He explained that "the door was opened because the kit that was supposed to safeguard the Kenyan borders, to ensure national security, simply wasn't in place to interdict terrorists. 'Eaten' were the contracts for a robust immigration control system, or for basic police communication equipment" (Githongo, 2015, p. 1). Corruption has therefore become a terror problem in Kenya with Al-Shabaab or other criminals being able to buy passage, visas and other useful items from the police and other governmental services, making the border to Somalia highly porous, and terrorists able to avoid the police (Burite & Gridneff, 2015).

In November 2015, during his tenure, the immediate past President of Kenya, Uhuru Kenyatta, said, in a Statement on a National Call to Action Against Corruption, that: "I believe that corruption is a standing threat to our national security. The bribe accepted by an official can lead to successful terrorist attacks that kill Kenyans," and "it can let a criminal off the hook for them to return to crime and harming Kenyans. Terrorism itself is a national security threat" (Kenyatta, 2015, p. 4). The former President had also made it known to his fellow Kenyans that "the damage to our economy puts millions of lives at peril and undermines our very aspirations as a nation," and that he was "therefore declaring with immediate effect corruption as a national security threat. I direct all the security agencies, the Ethics and Anti-Corruption Commission, the Asset Recovery Agency and the Financial Reporting Centre to take cognizance of this" (Kenyatta, 2015, p. 4). He further said that the National Intelligence Service should pursue information and intelligence on corruption and bring it to the attention of the relevant investigating and prosecution bodies and that "the National Security Advisory Committee should add corruption, particularly that which impacts security, to its agenda and advise the National Security Council [accordingly]" (Kenyatta, 2015, p. 4).

One other terrorism-related aspect of the relationship between police corruption and the security challenge in Kenya that gets little attention has to do with the frequent police shakedowns of certain neighborhoods where large numbers of ethnic Somalis and Muslims reside. Instead of providing safety and security to these neighborhoods, the police engage in corrupt shakedowns where they pick-up ethnic Somali residents and threaten them with jail unless they hand over money. The scene has become so normal, the neighborhoods are known as police "ATM[s] [automatic teller] machines" (Schifrin & Fannin, 2016, p. 1). These neighborhoods are targeted for bribe collection because their "mostly Somali Muslim population lacks the political power to withstand extortion," and the police admit that "they're more focused on getting cash than keeping the peace" as extortion rings are police policy where "[police] superiors expect a certain cut of illicitly obtained cash at the end of each shift. It's right from the junior officer to the higher-most" (Schifrin & Fannin, 2016, p. 1).

However, one chilling result from such police corruption through the ethnic targeting of Somalis and the victimization of Muslims is that it has created a dominant narrative of the reasons for the radicalization and terrorist recruitment of many Kenyan youths as it is not a huge leap for the latter to become mercenary soldiers against the state (see, for example, Anderson & McKnight, 2015b; Botha, 2014; Hellsten, 2016; Meleagrou-Hitchens, 2015). In fact, according to the OECD, "Al-Shabaab has shown itself adept at stoking deeply entrenched grievances among Kenya's ethnic Somali, Muslim and coastal populations, in effect localizing its transnational conflict in Kenya" (OECD, 2016, p. 46). Moreover, this radicalization is further aided and abetted by the conduct of the ATPU which has been accused of acting with impunity in the harassment of Kenyan Muslim youth, restricting their movements through tactics such as frequently checking their identification, imposing curfews, and meting out physical violence, or accusing these youths of being suspected Al-Shabaab violent extremists to justify their murder (see, for example, Al-Bulushi, 2021; Biegon & Songa, 2018; Mesok, 2022).

One outcome of this behavior by the ATPU is that "they set their mind so that our youth say, these police are calling us Al-Shabaab. Let us just go and join Al-Shabaab" (Mesok, 2022, p. 726; see also Breidlid, 2021). In other words, as Papale (2022), has shown, the indiscriminate repression of targeted populations in Kenya has increased the motivation of those populations to mobilize into terrorism while, at the same time, such repression shapes the conducive conditions enabling these targeted groups to do so through emerging connections with Al-Shabaab. Similarly, in their research interviews, Speckhard and Shajkovci (2019) found that many Muslim youth become radicalized due to their anger over what they regard as harassment and arrests and even extrajudicial killings in their communities by the police and other security forces. Al-Shabaab, in turn, makes full use of this victim narrative in its recruitment strategies. This, in turn, leads to further insecurity in the country with "radicalization still [remaining] one of the most significant threats to security" [as fuel for violent extremism] (NPS, 2016, p. 4; see also Antwi-Boateng, 2017; Atta-Asamoah, 2015; KNCHR, 2019; Onuoha & Nwangwu, 2021). In fact, as confirmed in the President of Kenya's *Annual Report to Parliament on the State of National Security* covering 2019, the threat of radicalization and recruitment of youth by terrorist groups was a major concern in some parts of the country, not only especially in the coastal areas but also in the capital, Nairobi, as well (Republic of Kenya, 2020).

Undeniably, there is a strong link between corruption and insecurity. Indeed, police corruption is widely recognized as a threat to peace and security from both national/regional (as this work shows for Africa) and global perspectives with associations between corruption on the one hand, and political instability and violent conflict on the other, being increasingly commonplace in research documents, policy statements, and recent events (Pyman et al., 2014). When a country's institutions are weak, its security forces, such as the police, tend to be untrusted and its borders weak, as is the case in Kenya, giving terrorist and other criminal organizations, for example, room to flourish (Musau, 2018). This was similarly found to be the case in the Mali-Niger-Burkina-Faso Borderlands areas where porous borders have also benefitted Jihadist operations (see, for example, de Montclos, 2021; Stanicek & Betant-Rasmussen, 2021). Also, in Nigeria, Ojo et al. (2023) have shown that weak border management—along with the existing police extortion that contributes to armed banditry—is also part of the challenges of Nigeria's weak security architecture which has resulted in, among other things, spill-over effects of armed conflict in the region.

Furthermore, with the police being corrupt, and even predatory, instead of serving the public they are often sources of insecurity themselves rather than providers of security and they then become people to avoid, not to seek out, in the event of trouble (Downie, 2013). Generally, as this work shows, the police are one of the most dysfunctional, underperforming institutions in Africa and the consequences of this failure are severe as "insecurity affects the ability of people to go about their daily lives" (Downie, 2013, p. 1). "In addition, a country that cannot deal with its internal security challenges, or control its borders, can quickly become a base for criminal networks, terrorists, and other groups that … pose a threat to national or even regional security" (Downie, 2013, p. 1), as is the case for Kenya and other African nations such as Nigeria with respect to Boko Haram, and the Sahel region with respect to Jihadists, for example. On Nigeria, research by Transparency International-Defense and Security (TI-DS) has shown that the individual humiliations wrought by corrupt, brutal police officers contributed to a swell of initial support for Boko Haram which, not surprisingly, began its activities with attacks on police stations (TI-DS, 2017). Indeed, as outlined by Hansen (2022, p. 418), "in some cases, as in Kenya and Nigeria, outright police brutality has been claimed to be a major cause of radicalization," with such brutality of the police representing a structural factor fertilizing the soil for said radicalization.

Moreover, as Diallo (2019, pp. 298–299) has so elegantly put it, "the police, in the current context, [in Africa] are a toxic factor to both the security of individual citizens and to sound security sector governance" and, as such, "despite police reform initiatives … the picture of police remains grim. Reforms initiated in these countries have not really transformed the police from villains to heroes, from predators to professional, service-oriented, accountable and effective police." Resultantly, and as argued by the UNDP (2023), deep-seated perceptions of impunity and distrust in security actors, notably the police as well as the military, continue to fuel grievances leading to radicalization.

5.4.3 Tourism Impact

The biggest consequence of terrorist attacks in Kenya, besides the obvious loss of life, is its impact on tourism. Undoubtedly, terrorism negatively affects tourism demand. Although tourism has been and continues to be an important source of revenue for Kenya, and a source of livelihood for many, its dynamics have changed in the wake of terrorism and increased competition. The tourism industry in Kenya has suffered from a raft of security advisories that were issued from countries whose citizens traditionally make up a large percentage of Kenya's target market for tourism, putting pressure on visitor numbers and hospitality revenues, which in turn have led to the closing down of hotels and the laying off of staff (International Crisis Group [ICG], 2014; KNCHR, 2014; Oxford Business Group [OBG], 2016). There was also one tour operator, the TUI Group, that evacuated 500 holidaymakers under armed guard in 2014 (Manson, 2014). To this time period (2022), there are travel advisories being issued by tourist origin nations such as the US, for example, for travelers to "exercise increased caution in Kenya due to crime, terrorism, civil unrest, and kidnapping" with "terrorist attacks having occurred with little or no warning, targeting Kenyan and foreign government facilities, tourist locations, transportation hubs, hotels, resorts, markets/shopping malls, and places of worship. Terrorist acts have included armed assaults, suicide operations, bomb/grenade attacks, and kidnappings" (US Department of State, 2022b, p. 1). Furthermore, due to terrorism concerns, U.S. government personnel are still prohibited from traveling to some specific Kenya-Somalia border counties and coastal areas.

The country also continues to face increased competition from alternative safer tourist destinations such as South Africa, the Far East, and Asia (OBG, 2016; PwC, n.d.). An empirical analysis by Buigut (2018), covering the period 2010–2013, found that terrorism, proxied by the number of fatalities, negatively and significantly affects the number of visitors to Kenya from developed countries with a 1% increase in fatalities decreasing arrivals in Kenya by about 0.082%, and this translates to an annual loss of about US$1.8 million in tourism revenue per unit increase in fatality per quarter. Other, and more recent, empirical research by Fauzel and

Seetanah (2023), covering the period 1995–2017, found that a 1% increase in terrorism incidents reduces tourist arrivals in African countries, including Kenya, by 2.5%. These empirical, and other findings, have led to the conclusion that terrorism is the main security threat affecting inbound tourism in Kenya and other African countries but not the rest of the world, or not to the same extent (see, for example, Krajňák, 2021; Santana-Gallego & Fourie, 2022).

5.5 Concluding Comments

As this chapter shows, police corruption erodes public trust in the police. This undermines day-to-day security as citizens avoid interacting with the police with the resultant effect that states become easily destabilized and sustainable development falters. As Bello (2021, p. 155) has eloquently stated: "Policing should not be for personal gains, or aggrandizement; but is for collaborating with the public in addressing pressing security challenges." Furthermore, as noted by Logan et al. (2022, p. 27):

> Security is a foundation on which citizens build productive lives and livelihoods. Popular perceptions and experiences of the police as corrupt, untrustworthy, and unhelpful hold back national development while providing fertile soil for protest. Even without the high-profile reports of police brutality that have sent Nigerians, Kenyans, South Africans, and others into the streets, poor police service and demands for bribes make everyday victims of citizens from all walks of life, especially among the poor and most vulnerable.

As in this chapter, and as Hidalgo (2015, p. 1) has also noted, "Kenya's [police] services are acknowledged as the most corrupt institution in one of the most corrupt countries in the world" and "the entrenched system of nepotism, bribery, and tribal affiliation has led observers to conclude that, in practice, the forces decrease security more than increase it." Despite the police reforms aimed at transforming the police service, police corruption still arises in the daily work of the Kenya police and has emerged as a significant problem and a matter of concern that now has significant implications for security in the country (ICG, 2014). In fact, there is still a major police reform program underway in the country which aims, among other things, to control police corruption and its negative societal consequences (Hope, 2015). That reform program was initially being spearheaded by the former and first NPS Inspector-General, Mr. David Kimaiyo, who had observed in that respect that:

> Police are the most visible manifestations of government authority responsible for public security. In Kenya, this manifestation has previously been associated with high-handedness, brutality and corruption. This led to the unequivocal call for police reforms … to come up with pragmatic measures to make the police service more responsive and accountable to the people they serve (Kimaiyo, 2013, p. 1).

The country's former President, Uhuru Kenyatta, had also recognized the importance of controlling police corruption, and corruption in general for that matter, as a national security issue. In that regard, among his speeches he had exhorted graduating police recruits as follows:

> ... I want to make it perfectly clear to you that my government, and the people of Kenya whom we serve, simply will not tolerate corruption. For corruption is an evil in itself, but when it infects those who are supposed to guard us from its effects, then we are speaking of a special kind of wickedness. It has been said that the corruption of the best is the worst. That saying is certainly true when dishonesty compromises the finest of our youth, charged with the protection of our common safety. I urge you not to fall victim to it, and I assure you that those who succumb, especially at this critical time, will suffer the most severe penalties that our law can impose (Kenyatta, 2014).

In February 2016, the then President Kenyatta returned to this theme in another speech to another batch of graduating police recruits where he said very sternly:

> The National Police Service you will enter has undertaken a number of reforms to conform to the requirements of the new constitution. Much has been done, and yet much remains to be done. I want to challenge the leadership of the Service to aggressively deal with integrity aspects of the reform agenda. However much we invest in the Service, it will count for little in the eyes of Kenyans if the failures and shortcomings in integrity that still trouble the Service are not handled decisively. Failures of integrity weaken any organization that tolerates them — and, if left untreated, they will destroy the service. Failures of integrity also rob us of the public support we must have if we are to protect Kenyans. While I appreciate all the work that has been done, I think it is fair to say that the Police Service has yet to solve these problems. They had better be solved, and quickly (Kenyatta, 2016).

Undoubtedly, there is a causal connection between police corruption and the continued security threat a country faces, and "recognizing the linkages between corruption and security in sub-Saharan Africa is an important first step toward confronting the challenges [such linkages present]" (Forest, 2022, p. 379). As argued by Aghedo (2010, p. 127), "any security-undermining phenomenon in a political community is nefarious." More specifically, it has been empirically determined that corrupt police systems are a key factor in undermining prospects for long term peace within a society (IEP, 2015b). And, therefore, "insecurity can hardly be averted when national security institutions are deeply implicated in corruption" (Hellsten, 2016, p. 5). As observed by Pkalya (2015, p. 1), "Kenya has suffered from violent extremism and terrorism in the region [more] than any other Al-Shabaab front line state; thanks to corruption within the security and law enforcement agencies."

Consequently, "the security challenges within Kenya are evident to Kenyans. There is need to pre-empt terror attacks, end localized violence, avert insurgencies and reduce crime" (Goldman, 2015, p. 1). For Kenya to achieve that, it will require all Kenyans to take responsibility for the fight against police corruption and corruption in general for that matter. It cannot, at this stage, be left entirely to the government. The lessons of history learned have demonstrated that the incubated police corruption in the country has broken out into the lawlessness and the insecurity Kenyans must now confront (Mwandia, 2014). It is a confrontation Kenyans cannot afford to lose. As had been recognized by Wagner (2014), the stakes are high because Al-Shabaab has become stronger, in spite of all the resources devoted to fighting against it.

5.5 Concluding Comments

In addition, we also know that "police corruption depends in part on the complicity or tacit consent of the fellow officers of the corrupt. So, controlling police corruption is a collective moral responsibility [that] is fundamental to the design of an integrity system for police organizations" (Miller, 2016, p. 35), and this also entails the involvement and cooperation of the public. In that regard, the NPS has recently publicly stated that the measures being put in place to curb police corruption, in addition to "public-police partnerships like community policing," include "enhanced management and supervision; sensitization of officers through weekly lectures on issues of integrity and code of ethics; and arrest of suspects" (NPS, 2016, pp. 9–10). Hopefully, these measures will take hold, and soon, as it was found that the challenges to national security continue to be exacerbated by [police and other] "security agency corruption at multiple levels" (US Department of State, 2017, p. 33). Indeed, also according to the US Department of State (2021, p. 24), although the Kenyan police and other security forces have begun to "demonstrate improved procedures in line with [their] obligations and commitments for protection of human rights in response to terrorist threats and attacks," there are still "reports [that] human rights violations and abuses by the police and other security forces during counter-terrorism operations [have] continued, including allegations of extrajudicial killings, forced disappearances, and torture."

In that regard also, looking across Africa, Lamb (2021, p. 102) reported that in South Africa even the Head of the country's police oversight authority—the IPID—testified to the Police Portfolio Committee of Parliament that the South African Police Service (SAPS) was being governed by a "matrix of corruption," which had become the "biggest threat to national security," as it had drastically eroded the ability of the police "to contain serious and violent crime." A greater elaboration of this view can be found in Parliamentary Monitoring Group ([PMG], 2018) and a more general review of South African policing (including police corruption, in its various forms discussed in this chapter, and the security problem) can be found in Govender and Pillay (2022) and Ivković et al. (2020). Indeed, Nyawasha and Mokhahlane (2017, p. 111), for example, have been very steadfast in their view that "instead of entrenching democratic and civil ideals based on the respect and preservation of human life and security, policing in South Africa is associated with the use of physical violence and in some cases a mere disregard of human lives." Similarly, for Nigeria, research by Enweremadu (2019, p. 345) also determined that "although the police force is the preeminent public institution established to assure the security of lives and property within the country, the institution has ironically functioned more as an enabler of corruption and insecurity." Indeed, these observations further underscore the importance and need for strong police oversight as discussed in Chap. 8.

5.5.1 Further Readings and Information on Police Corruption and Security Challenges in Africa

For other detailed contemporary country case studies and surveys discussing the police corruption problem and the historical police misconduct generally across Africa, and the security and peace challenges confronting the continent, see, for example, Akinlabi (2023); Appiahene-Gyamfi (2021); Corruption Watch (2019); Darga and Hurroo (2022); Diallo (2019); Emerson and Solomon (2018); Garcia (2019); Hope (2016b); Inspectorate of Government [IOG] (2020); Ivković et al. (2020); Karbo and Virk (2018); Kuwali (2022); Lekunze (2020); Logan et al. (2022); Marc et al. (2015); Matunhu and Matunhu (2021); Oarhe and Aghedo (2010); and Taylor (2019).

Also, much of the data used in this chapter, especially for the continental and country comparable comparisons, are derived from the Afrobarometer surveys database, either directly or from other Afrobarometer publications utilizing the surveys' data covering "Security, Crime, and the Police." In the view of this book's author, Afrobarometer collects and is the custodian of the most credible and comprehensive data on African police interactions with the public including, among other things, requested assistance; encounters at checkpoints, during identity checks, during traffic stops, or during an investigation; and payments of bribes to either get needed assistance or to avoid a problem during encounters with the police. Further details about Afrobarometer are provided in Chap. 7.

References

Adisa, W. B., Alabi, T., & Adejoh, S. (2020). Corruption on the road: A test of commercial drivers' encounters with police extortion in Lagos metropolis. *Journal of Police and Criminal Psychology, 35*(3), 389–399. https://doi.org/10.1007/s11896-018-9289-6

Addo, K. O. (2023). An exploratory study of police corruption in Ghana: Why does it exist? *International Criminology, 3*(1), 52–62. https://doi.org/10.1007/s43576-022-00078-7

Afrobarometer. (n.d.-a). Round 8 surveys 2019–21. [online data analysis]. Retrieved from https://www.afrobarometer.org/online-dataanalysis/

Afrobarometer. (n.d.-b). Round 5 surveys 2011–13. [online data analysis]. Retrieved from https://www.afrobarometer.org/online-dataanalysis/

Afrobarometer. (n.d.-c). Round 6 surveys 2014–15. [online data analysis]. Retrieved from https://www.afrobarometer.org/online-dataanalysis/

Aglionby, J. (2016, August 30). Corruption in Kenya evolves for a digital age. *Financial Times*. https://www.ft.com/content/1a734368-6911-11e6-ae5b-a7cc5dd5a28c

Akinlabi, O. M. (2022). *Police-Citizen Relations in Nigeria: Procedural Justice, Legitimacy, and Law-Abiding Behavior*. Palgrave Macmillan/Springer Nature.

Akinlabi, O. M. (Ed.). (2023). *Policing and the rule of law in Sub-Saharan Africa*. Routledge/Taylor and Francis.

Al-Bulushi, S. (2021). Citizen-suspect: Navigating surveillance and policing in urban Kenya. *American Anthropologist, 123*(4), 819–832. https://doi.org/10.1111/aman.13644

References

Alexandre, A. B. (2018). Perception of corruption by traffic police and taxi drivers in Bukavu DR Congo: The limits of moral analysis. *Journal of Contemporary African Studies, 36*(4), 563–574. https://doi.org/10.1080/02589001.2019.1583323

Amnesty International. (2022, September 28). Lesotho: Authorities must tackle police brutality, torture and unlawful killings before and after election. [News]. Retrieved from https://www.amnesty.org/en/latest/news/2022/09/lesotho-authorities-must-tackle-policebrutality/#:~:text=Legal%20action%20against%20the%20police,police%20brutality%20recorded%20since%202018

Amunga, V. (2022, October 31). Kenya's president demands end to extrajudicial killings by police. *VOAnews*. Retrieved from https://www.voanews.com/a/kenya-s-president-demands-end-to-extrajudicial-killings-by-police-/6813570.html

Anderson, D. M., & McKnight, J. (2015a). Kenya at war: Al-Shabaab and its enemies in Eastern Africa. *African Affairs, 114*(454), 1–27. https://doi.org/10.1093/afraf/adu082

Anderson, D. M., & McKnight, J. (2015b). Understanding Al-Shabaab: Clan, Islam and insurgency in Kenya. *Journal of Eastern African Studies, 9*(3), 536–557. https://doi.org/10.1080/17531055.2015.1082254

Andvig, J. C., & Barasa, T. (2011). Cops and crime in Kenya: A research report. [Norwegian Institute of International Affairs (NUPI) Working Paper 794]. NUPI.

Andvig, J. C., & Fjeldstad, O.-H. (2008). Crime, poverty and police corruption in developing countries. [WP 2008: 7]. Retrieved from https://www.cmi.no/publications/file/3076-crime-poverty-police-corruption-in-developing.pdf

Angira, Z. (2022, April 11). Police took home Sh500m in bribes from recruitment fields. *People Daily*. Retrieved from https://www.pd.co.ke/news/police-took-home-sh500m-in-bribes-from-recruitment-fields-122756/

Antwi-Boateng, O. (2017). The rise of Pan-Islamic terrorism in Africa: A global security challenge. *Politics & Policy, 45*(2), 253–284. https://doi.org/10.1111/polp.12195

Appiahene-Gyamfi, J. (2021). Policing in Ghana. In J. M. Mbuba (Ed.), *Global Perspectives in Policing and Law Enforcement* (pp. 3–23). Lexington Books.

Aremu, O. (2021). The effectiveness of self-efficacy in the reduction of police attitude to corruption in Nigeria. In J. F. Albrecht & G. den Heyer (Eds.), *Enhancing police service delivery: Global perspectives and contemporary policy implications* (pp. 315–328). Springer Nature.

Atta-Asamoah, A. (2015). The nature and drivers of insecurity in Kenya, *East Africa Report*, Issue 2. Retrieved from https://issafrica.org/research/east-africa-report/the-nature-and-drivers-of-insecurity-in-kenya

Auerbach, J. N. (2003). Police accountability in Kenya. *African Human Rights Law Journal, 3*(2), 275–313.

Bello, P. O. (2021). Do people still repose confidence in the police? assessing the effects of public experience of police corruption in South Africa. *African Identities, 19*(2), 141–159. https://doi.org/10.1080/14725843.2020.1792827

Biegon, J., & Songa, A. (2018). Kenya: The impact of counter-terrorism measures on police reform. In E. E. O. Alemika, M. Ruteere, & S. Howell (Eds.), *Policing reform in Africa: Moving towards a rights-based approach in a climate of terrorism, insurgency and serious violent crime* (pp. 197–220). African Policing Civilian Oversight Forum (APCOF).

Blocq, D., & Duthie, R. (2020). Hearings and decision making during transitional vetting processes: Insights from Kenya. [ICTJ Briefing]. Retrieved from https://www.ictj.org/sites/default/files/ICTJ_Briefing_Kenya_Police_Vetting_Web.pdf

Blocq, D., Mwikali, M., & Ndonga, A. (2020). *From optimism to disillusionment: Examining civil society perceptions of police vetting in Kenya*. Retrieved from https://www.ictj.org/publication/optimism-disillusionment-examining-civil-society-perceptions-police-vetting-kenya

Boateng, F. D. (2018a). Institutional trust and performance: A study of the police in Ghana. *Australian & New Zealand Journal of Criminology, 51*(2), 164–182. https://doi.org/10.1177/2F0004865817712335

Boateng, F. D. (2018b). Police legitimacy in Africa: A multilevel multinational analysis. *Policing and Society, 28*(9), 1105–1120. https://doi.org/10.1080/10439463.2017.1280034

Boateng, F. D., Pryce, D. K., & Abess, G. (2022). Legitimacy and cooperation with the police: Examining empirical relationship using data from Africa. *Policing and Society, 32*(3), 411–433. https://doi.org/10.1080/10439463.2022.2037554

Bonner, M. D., Kempa, M., Kubal, M. R., & Seri, G. (2018). Introduction. In M. D. Bonner, G. Seri, M. R. Kubal, & M. Kempa (Eds.), *Police abuse in contemporary democracies* (pp. 1–27). Palgrave Macmillan/Springer Nature.

Botha, A. (2014). Radicalization in Kenya: Recruitment to Al-Shabaab and the Mombasa Republican Council. [ISS Paper 265]. Institute for Security Studies.

Breidlid, T. (2021). Countering or contributing to radicalization and violent extremism in Kenya? a critical case study. *Critical Studies on Terrorism, 14*(2), 225–246. https://doi.org/10.1080/17539153.2021.1902613

Buigut, S. (2018). Effect of terrorism on demand for tourism in Kenya: A comparative analysis. *Tourism and Hospitality Research, 18*(1), 28–37. https://doi.org/10.1177/2F1467358415619670

Burite, J., & Gridneff, I. (2015, April 7). Corruption, lack of political will for reform weaken Kenya's ability to fight terrorists, *Mail & Guardian Africa*.

Chayes, S. (2015). *Thieves of state: Why corruption threatens global security.* W. W. Norton & Company.

CHRI., & KHRC. (2006). *The police, the people, the politics: Police accountability in Kenya.* CHRI/KHRC.

Corruption Watch. (2019). *Corruption in uniform: When Cops become criminals.* Retrieved from https://www.corruptionwatch.org.za/cw-reveals-grim-state-of-corruption-in-policing/

Darga, L. A., & Hurroo, N. (2022). Distrust, corruption, and favoritism: Mauritians' negative perceptions of their police. [Afrobarometer Dispatch No. 526]. Retrieved from https://www.afrobarometer.org/publication/ad526-distrust-corruption-and-favouritism-mauritians-negativeperceptions-of-their-police/

de Montclos, M. A. P. (2021). Rethinking the response to Jihadist groups across the Sahel. [Africa Program, Research Paper]. Chatham House.

Diallo, F. S. (2019). *State policing in Sub-Saharan Africa: The weakest link of security sector governance.* L' Harmattan.

Downie, R. (2013). *Building police institutions in Fragile States: Case studies from Africa.* Center for Strategic and International Studies.

EACC. (2018). *National ethics and corruption survey, 2017.* EACC.

Emerson, S., & Solomon, H. (2018). *African security in the twenty-first century: Challenges and opportunities.* Manchester University Press.

Enweremadu, D. U. (2019). Understanding police corruption and its effect on internal security in Nigeria. In O. O. Oshita, I. M. Alumona, & F. C. Onuoha (Eds.), *Internal security management in Nigeria: Perspectives, challenges and lessons* (pp. 327–350). Palgrave Macmillan/Springer Nature.

Fauzel, S., & Seetanah, B. (2023). Assessing the impact of terrorism on African tourism demand. *Tourism Analysis, 28*(1), 1–11. https://doi.org/10.3727/108354223X16746729371991

Forest, J. J. F. (2022). Crime-terror interactions in sub-Saharan Africa. *Studies in Conflict & Terrorism, 45*(5–6), 368–388. https://doi.org/10.1080/1057610X.2019.1678881

Garcia, F. P. (2019). Africa and the threats to its security. *Austral: Brazilian Journal of Strategy & International Relations, 8*(16), 242–262. https://doi.org/10.22456/2238-6912.84807

Gibendi, R. (2015, October 31). Four reasons why Al-Shabaab hits Kenya with ease, *Tuko*. Retrieved from https://tuko.co.ke/4294-fourreasons-why-al-shabaab-hits-kenya-with-ease.html

Gilchrist, N., & Eisen, N. (2019, August 22). Corruption and terrorism: The case of Kenya. [Brookings Order from Chaos Blog]. Retrieved from https://www.brookings.edu/blog/order-from-chaos/2019/08/22/corruption-and-terrorism-the-case-of-kenya/

References

Githongo, J. (2015, March 19). Corruption has opened door to Al-Shabaab in Kenya, *The Guardian*. https://www.theguardian.com/world/2015/mar/19/corruption-has-opened-door-to-al-shabaab-in-kenya.

Goldman, D. (2015, January 20). Tackling security challenges. [Strategic Intelligence Briefs]. Retrieved from http://intelligencebriefs.com/tackling-security-challenges/.

Govender, D., & Pillay, K. (2022). Policing in South Africa: A critical evaluation. *Insight on Africa, 14*(1), 40–56. https://doi.org/10.1177/2F09750878211048169

Gutierrez-Garcia, J. O., & Rodriguez, L.-F. (2016). Social determinants of police corruption: Toward public policies for the prevention of police corruption. *Policy Studies, 37*(3), 216–235. https://doi.org/10.1080/01442872.2016.1144735

Gyamfi, G. D. (2022). Exploring public trust in policing at a community in Ghana. *Security Journal, 35*(4), 1249–1262. https://doi.org/10.1057/s41284-021-00325-y

Hansen, S. J. (2022). "Forever wars"? Patterns of diffusion and consolidation of Jihadism in Africa. *Small Wars & Insurgencies, 33*(3), 409–436. https://doi.org/10.1080/09592318.2021.1959130

Harris, D., & Katusiimeh, M. W. (2020). Public administration and corruption: A comparative case study of the police services in Ghana and Uganda. In A. Graycar (Ed.), *Handbook on corruption, ethics and integrity in public administration* (pp. 255–273). Edward Elgar Publishing Limited.

Hatungimana, W. (2022). How people appraise their government: Corruption perception of police and political legitimacy in Africa. *Journal of Modern African Studies, 60*(1), 1–22. https://doi.org/10.1017/S0022278X21000392

Hellsten, S. (2016). Radicalization and terrorist recruitment among Kenya's youth. [Policy Note No. 1]. The Nordic Africa Institute.

Hidalgo, P. (2015, April 12). Kenya's own worst enemy: Al-Shabaab isn't the real problem, *Foreign Affairs*. https://www.foreignaffairs.com/articles/kenya/2015-04-12/kenyas-own-worst-enemy

Higgins, A. (2015, April 4). Kenyans blame corrupt government for escalating Al-Shabaab violence, *Time*. http://time.com/3771445/kenyansblame-corrupt-government-al-shabaab-violence/

Hope, K. R. (2012). *The political economy of development in Kenya*. Bloomsbury Publishing.

Hope, K. R. (2013). Tackling the corruption epidemic in Kenya: Toward a policy of more effective control. *The Journal of Social, Political, and Economic Studies, 38*(3), 287–316.

Hope, K. R. (2014). Kenya's corruption problem: Causes and consequences. *Commonwealth & Comparative Politics, 52*(4), 493–512. https://doi.org/10.1080/14662043.2014.955981

Hope, K. R. (2015). In pursuit of democratic policing: An analytical review and assessment of police reforms in Kenya. *International Journal of Police Science and Management, 17*(2), 91–97. https://doi.org/10.1177/2F1461355715580915

Hope, K. R. (2016a). An analytical perspective on police corruption and police reforms in developing societies. In K. R. Hope (Ed.), *Police corruption and police reforms in developing societies* (pp. 3–31). CRC Press/Taylor and Francis.

Hope, K. R. (Ed.). (2016b). *Police corruption and police reforms in developing societies*. CRC Press/Taylor and Francis.

Hope, K. R. (2017). *Corruption and governance in Africa: Swaziland [Eswatini], Kenya, Nigeria*. Palgrave Macmillan/Springer Nature.

Hope, K. R. (2019). The police corruption "crime problem" in Kenya. *Security Journal, 32*(2), 85–101. https://doi.org/10.1057/s41284-018-0149-y

ICG. (2014). Kenya: Al-Shabaab–closer to home. [Africa Briefing No. 102]. https://www.crisisgroup.org/africa/horn-africa/kenya/kenya-alshabaab-closer-home

IDS-UON. (2022). *Summary of results: Afrobarometer round 9 survey in Kenya, 2022*. Afrobarometer.

IEP. (2015a). *Global terrorism index 2015: Measuring and understanding the impact of terrorism*. Retrieved from https://www.visionofhumanity.org/resources/?type=research

IEP. (2015b). *Peace and corruption 2015: Lowering corruption—a transformative factor for peace*. IEP.

IEP. (2022). *Global terrorism index 2022: Measuring the impact of terrorism*. IEP.

IMLU. (2014). *Guns: Our security, our dilemma! enhancing accountability for police use of firearms*. IMLU.
IOG. (2020). *The fourth national integrity survey report, 2019*. IOG/Republic of Uganda.
IPID. (2016). *Annual report 2015/16*. IPID.
IPID. (2021). *Annual report 2020/21*. IPID.
IPOA. (2013). *Baseline survey on policing standards and gaps in Kenya*. IPOA.
IPOA. (2014a). *Monitoring report on operation sanitization Eastleigh: Publicly known as 'Usalama Watch'*. IPOA.
IPOA. (2014b, August 5). The independent policing oversight authority (IPOA) files a case to nullify the just concluded police recruitment exercise. [Press Release]. IPOA.
IPOA. (2014c). *Police recruitment: A national shame and a sham*. IPOA.
IPOA. (2015). *IPOA monitoring report on the recruitment of police constables: April 2015*. IPOA.
IPOA. (2019a). *Performance report: January–June 2018*. IPOA.
IPOA. (2019b). *Performance report: July–December 2018*. IPOA.
IPOA. (2020a). *Performance report: January–June 2019*. IPOA.
IPOA. (2020b). *Performance report: July–December 2019*. IPOA.
IPOA. (2021a). *Performance report: January–June 2020*. IPOA.
IPOA. (2021b). *Performance report: July–December 2020*. IPOA.
Ivković, S. K., Sauerman, A., Faull, A., Meyer, M. E., & Newham, G. (2020). *Police integrity in South Africa*. Routledge/Taylor and Francis.
Kabir, A. (2022, February 14). Growing scandals of Nigeria's "Super Cop" show accountability gaps in security sector, *Humangle Media*. Retrieved from https://humanglemedia.com/growing-scandals-of-nigerias-super-cop-show-accountability-gaps-in-security-sector/
Kamau, P., Onyango, G., & Salau, T. (2022). Kenyans cite criminal activity, lack of respect, and corruption among police failings. [Afrobarometer Dispatch No. 552]. Retrieved from https://www.afrobarometer.org/wp-content/uploads/2022/09/AD552-Kenyans-citecriminal-activity-and-corruption-among-police-failings-Afrobarometer-16sept22-1.pdf
Kapchanga, M. (2015, July 1). How corruption makes terror easy in Kenya, *New African Magazine*. http://newafricanmagazine.com/howcorruption-makes-terror-easy-in-kenya/
Karbo, T., & Virk, K. (Eds.). (2018). *The Palgrave handbook of peacebuilding in Africa*. Palgrave Macmillan/Springer Nature.
Kashaka, U. (2021, December 17). Over 480 police officers dismissed in Rwanda, *New Vision*. Retrieved from https://www.newvision.co.ug/category/news/over-480-police-officers-dismissed-in-rwanda-122569
Kavuludi, J. (2015, October 15). Speech by the chairman of the national police service commission, Johnston Kavuludi, during the release of the results of SSPS, SPS, ASPS and IAU Officers, Sky Park Plaza, Westlands. NPSC.
Kenyatta, U. (2014, April 4). Speech by His Excellency Hon. Uhuru Kenyatta on the Kenya Police Service recruits passing-out parade, Kiganjo Police Training College. Retrieved from https://www.scribd.com/document/216423985/President-Uhuru-Kenyatta-s-Speech-duringthe-Kenya-Police-Service-Recruits-Passing-out-Parade-at-Kiganjo-Police-Training-College
Kenyatta, U. (2015, November 23). Statement by his excellency Hon. Uhuru Kenyatta, C. G. H., President and Commander in Chief of the Defense Forces of the Republic of Kenya on a national call to action against corruption, State House, Nairobi, Kenya. Retrieved from http://www.president.go.ke/2015/11/23/statement-by-his-excellency-hon-uhuru-kenyatta-c-g-h-president-and-commander-in-chief-of-thedefence-forces-of-the-republic-of-kenya-on-a-national-call-to-action-against-corruption-state-house/
Kenyatta, U. (2016, February 12). Speech by His Excellency Hon. Uhuru Kenyatta, C.G.H., President and Commander in Chief of the Defense Forces of the Republic of Kenya, during the National Police Service recruits passing out parade, Kenya Police College, Kiganjo, Kenya. Retrieved from http://www.president.go.ke/2016/02/12/speech-by-his-excellency-hon-uhuru-kenyatta-c-g-h-president-andcommander-in-chief-of-the-defence-forces-of-the-republic-of-kenya-during-the-national-police-service-recruits-passing-out-parade-at/

References

Kiage, N. (2022, October 19). How elite "killer" squad drew Ruto's anger and earned a date with DCI investigators, *Nation*. Retrieved from https://nation.africa/kenya/news/how-elite-killer-squad-drew-ruto-s-anger-and-earned-a-date-with-dci-investigators%2D%2D3990166

Kimaiyo, D. M. (2013, May 13). Remarks by the Inspector-General of Police during the launching ceremony of the county police reforms forums, Hilton Hotel, Nairobi, Kenya.

Kiplagat, S. (2021, November 3). Traffic police gives up Sh26m bribes to state, *Business Daily*. https://www.businessdailyafrica.com/bd/news/traffic-police-gives-sh26m-bribes-state-3605792

Kleinfeld, R. (2019). *A savage order: How the world's deadliest countries can forge a path to security*. Vintage Books/Penguin Random House.

Kleinig, J. (1996). *The ethics of policing*. Cambridge University Press.

Knapp, W. (1972). *Report of the commission to investigate alleged police corruption*. George Braziller.

KNCHR. (2014). *A country under siege? The state of security in Kenya: An occasional report (2010–2014)*. KNCHR.

KNCHR. (2015). *The fourth state of human rights report: Post Promulgation 2010–2014*. KNCHR.

KNCHR. (2016). *Disservice to the service: Report of the monitoring of the 2016 recruitment of police constables to the national police service*. KNCHR.

KNCHR. (2019). *Guarding the coast: A report of the public inquiry on insecurity & its impact on the enjoyment of human rights in the coastal Region of Kenya*. KNCHR.

KNCHR. (2020). *Submission to Parliament on extrajudicial killings, enforced disappearances and related human rights violations*. KNCHR.

Krajňák, T. (2021). The effects of terrorism on tourism demand: A systematic review. *Tourism Economics, 27*(8), 1736–1758. https://doi.org/10.1177/2F1354816620938900

Kreiman, G., & Espadafor, M. C. (2022). Unexpected allies: The impact of terrorism on organized crime in sub-Saharan Africa and South-East Asia. *Studies in Conflict & Terrorism, 45*(5–6), 348–367. https://doi.org/10.1080/1057610X.2019.1678877

Kuwali, D. (Ed.). (2022). *The palgrave handbook of sustainable peace and security in Africa*. Palgrave Macmillan/Springer Nature.

Lamb, G. (2021). Safeguarding the republic? the South African Police Service, legitimacy and the tribulations of policing a violent democracy. *Journal of Asian and African Studies, 56*(1), 92–108. https://doi.org/10.1177/2F0021909620946853

Lekunze, M. (2020). *Inherent and contemporary challenges to African security*. Palgrave Macmillan/Springer Nature.

Lipsky, M. (1980). *Street-level bureaucracy: Dilemmas of the individual in public services*. Russell Sage Foundation.

Logan, C., Sanny, J., & Katenda, L. (2022). Perceptions are bad, reality is worse: Citizens report widespread predation by African police. [Afrobarometer Dispatch No. 512]. Retrieved from https://www.afrobarometer.org/publication/ad512-perceptions-are-bad-reality-is-worseciti-zens-report-widespread-predation-by-african-police/

Loree, D. J. (2006). *Corruption in policing: Causes and consequences: A review of the literature*. Research and Evaluation Branch, Community, Contract and Aboriginal Policing Services Directorate, Royal Canadian Mounted Police.

Lucheli, I., & Weru, J. (2014, November 1). High court nullifies police recruitment, *Standard Digital*. http://www.standardmedia.co.ke/article/2000140061/high-court-nullifies-police-recruitment.

MACB. (2022, June 23). ACB arrests former Inspector-General of police Dr. George Kainja and Mwabi Kaluba in Lilongwe and Mzuzu, respectively. [Press Release]. Retrieved from https://acbmw.org/acb-arrests-former-inspector-general-of-police-dr-george-kainja-and-mwabika-luba-in-lilongwe-and-mzuzu-respectively/

Mageka, A. (2015). Police reform in Kenya: Challenges and opportunities. [Center for Security Governance Insights]. Retrieved from https://www.ssrresourcecentre.org/2015/10/09/police-reform-in-kenya-challenges-and-opportunities/?utm_source=feedburner&utm_medium=feed&utm_campaign=Feed%3A+ssrresourcecentre+%28Security+Sector+Reform+Resource+Centre%29

Malephane, L., & Salau, T. (2022). Basotho cite brutality, lack of professionalism, and corruption among police failings. [Afrobarometer Dispatch No. 555]. Retrieved from https://www.afrobarometer.org/publication/ad555-basotho-cite-brutality-lack-of-professionalism-andcorruption-among-police-failings/

Mann, C. (2011). Corruption in justice and security [U4 Expert Answer Number 285]. Retrieved from www.u4.no/publications/corruption-injustice-and-security/downloadasset/2517

Manson, K. (2014, June 17). Kenya's tourism industry faces renewed threat from Al-Shabaab, *Financial Times*. http://www.ft.com/cms/s/0/f51cc380-f5fb-11e3-83d3-00144feabdc0.html

Marc, A., Verjee, N., & Mogaka, S. (2015). *The challenge of stability and security in West Africa*. World Bank.

Matunhu, J., & Matunhu, V. (2021). Policing and law enforcement in Zimbabwe. In J. M. Mbuba (Ed.), *Global perspectives in policing and law enforcement* (pp. 43–58). Lexington Books.

Mboya, T. (2014, August 16/17). The role we play in a corrupt society, *Weekend Star*.

Meleagrou-Hitchens, A. (2015, July 27). Crime and punishment in Kenya: Terrorism and Obama's visit, *Foreign Affairs*. https://www.foreignaffairs.com/articles/kenya/2015-07-27/crime-and-punishment-kenya

Meservey, J. (2015, May 29). The cost of Kenyan corruption. [Atlantic Council Blog]. Retrieved from http://www.atlanticcouncil.org/blogs/new-atlanticist/the-cost-of-kenyan-corruption

Mesok, E. (2022). Counterinsurgency, community participation, and the preventing and countering violent extremism agenda in Kenya. *Small Wars & Insurgencies, 33*(4–5), 720–741. https://doi.org/10.1080/09592318.2022.2037908

Miller, S. (2016). *Corruption and anti-corruption in policing—philosophical and ethical issues*. Springer Nature.

Misiko, H. (2014, June 17). How Kenya made itself vulnerable to terror, *The Washington Post*. https://www.washingtonpost.com/news/worldviews/wp/2014/06/17/how-kenya-made-itself-vulnerable-to-terror/

Missing Voices. (n.d.). Statistics. Retrieved from https://missingvoices.or.ke/statistics/

Mogire, E., Mkutu, K., & Alusa, D. (2018). Policing terrorism in Kenya: The security-community interface. In K. M. Agade (Ed.), *Security governance in East Africa: Pictures of policing from the ground* (pp. 79–104). Lexington Books.

Mukinda, F. (2015, August 15). M-Pesa the bribe, and other tricks traffic police use, *Daily Nation*. http://www.nation.co.ke/news/M-Pesa-Bribes-Traffic-Police-Officers-Corruption/1056-2834614-1ml46v/index.html

Musau, S. (2018). Combating terrorism and upholding human rights in Kenya. [APCOF Research Paper 21]. APCOF.

Mutahi, N., Micheni, M., & Lake, M. (2023). The godfather provides: Enduring corruption and organizational hierarchy in the Kenyan police service. *Governance, 36*(2), 401–419. https://doi.org/10.1111/gove.12672

Mwachofi, S. S. (2022). Kenya's National Security Council: Balancing democratic control and executive power. In P. O'Neill (Ed.), *Securing the state and its citizens: National security councils from around the world* (pp. 123–132). Bloomsbury Academic.

Mwandia, J. (2014, August 16/17). Systemic corruption and embezzlement began at independence, *Weekend Star*.

Mwasa, F. (2021, March 28). In past two years, police have dismissed more than 1,300 officers, *The Chronicles*. Retrieved from https://www.chronicles.rw/2021/03/29/in-past-two-years-police-has-dismissed-more-than-1300-officers/

Neild, R. (2007). *USAID program brief: Anticorruption and police integrity*. USAID.

Nelson, E. E. (2023). Police extortion and drug dealers' negotiation strategies: Exploring the accounts of street-level dealers in Nigeria. *International Criminal Justice Review*, [Advance online publication]. https://doi.org/10.1177/10575677231154865

Nelson, E. E., & Brown, A. S. (2020). Extra-legal policing strategies and HIV risk environment: Accounts of people who inject drugs in Nigeria. *Drugs: Education Prevention and Policy, 27*(4), 312–319. https://doi.org/10.1080/09687637.2019.1684446

References

New African. (2015, July 1). How corruption makes terror easy in Kenya, *New African*. Retrieved from https://newafricanmagazine.com/11042/

Newburn, T. (1999). Understanding and preventing police corruption: Lessons from the literature. [Police Research Series Paper 110]. Home Office.

Newburn, T. (2015). *Literature review–police integrity and corruption*. Her Majesty's Inspectorate of Constabulary.

Ndung'u, I. (2015, October 9). To fight terrorism, fight corruption first, *ISS Today*. https://www.issafrica.org/iss-today/to-fight-terrorismfight-corruption-first

Ng'ulia, T. (2015, April 3). How police can redeem tainted image, *Daily Nation*. http://www.nation.co.ke/oped/Opinion/How-police-canredeem-tainted-image/-/440808/2675318/-/p1dg8h/-/index.html

Nivette, A. E., & Akoensi, T. D. (2019). Determinants of satisfaction with police in a developing country: A randomized vignette study. *Policing and Society, 29*(4), 471–487. https://doi.org/10.1080/10439463.2017.1380643

NPS. (2016). *Crime situation report: 2015*. NPS.

NPS. (2020). *Annual report: 2020*. NPS.

NPSC. (n.d.). Vetting of police officers–the way forward. [NPSC Opinion Editorial]. Retrieved from https://www.npsc.go.ke/download/vetting-of-police-officers-the-way-forward/

NPSC. (2014). *Statement by the national police service commission on the audit of the police constables recruitment exercise held on 14th July 2014*. NPSC.

NPSC. (2018). *Inaugural commissioners' Exit report: October 2012–October 2018*. NPSC.

NPSC. (2019). *Strategic plan for financial years (2019–2022): A strategy for transformation of the commission to better serve the human resource and welfare needs of police officers*. NPSC.

Nyawasha, T. S., & Mokhahlane, P. M. (2017). The paradox of civil policing in contemporary South Africa. *Insight on Africa, 9*(2), 109–125. https://doi.org/10.1177/2F0975087817707448

Oarhe, O., & Aghedo, I. (2010). The open sore of a nation: Corruption complex and internal security in Nigeria. *African Security, 3*(3), 127–147. https://doi.org/10.1080/19392206.2010.503854

OBG. (2016). *The report: Kenya 2016*. OBG.

Odula, T. (2014, May 29). Experts: Corruption exposing Kenya to terrorism, *Associated Press*. Retrieved from https://www.ksl.com/article/30085666/experts-corruption-exposing-kenya-to-terrorism

Odula, T. (2016, June 9). Kenya fires 302 police officers as it fights corruption, *AP News*. https://apnews.com/article/25c3ba17d3454c54a0dedfa9e2f0330e

OECD. (2016). *States of fragility 2016: Understanding violence*. OECD Publishing.

Ojo, J. S., Oyewole, S., & Aina, F. (2023). Forces of terror: Armed banditry and insecurity in North-West Nigeria. *Democracy and Security*. [Advance online publication]. https://doi.org/10.1080/17419166.2023.2164924

Okebiro, G. N. (2016). Corruption in the Kenya traffic police and leadership. Retrieved from https://papers.ssrn.com/sol3/papers.cfm?abstract_id=2850881

Omanga, D., Mainye, P., & Kashara, E. J. (2021). Policing gangs: Facebook, extra-judicial killings and popular imaginaries of super-cop Hessy in Eastlands, Nairobi. *Politeia, 40*(2), 1–20. https://doi.org/10.25159/2663-6689/10609

Ombaka, D. M. (2015). Explaining Kenya's insecurity: The weak state, corruption, banditry and terrorism. *International Journal of Liberal Arts and Social Science, 3*(3), 11–26. https://ijlass.org/data/frontImages/gallery/Vol._3_No._3/2._11-26.pdf

Omollo, K. (2016, June 10). 302 Traffic police officers sacked for evading vetting, *Standard Digital*. http://www.standardmedia.co.ke/article/2000204656/302-traffic-police-officers-sacked-for-evading-vetting

Onuoha, F. C., & Nwangwu, C. (2021). Radicalization, violent extremism, and de-radicalization in Africa. In U. A. Tar (Ed.), *The Routledge handbook of counterterrorism and counterinsurgency in Africa* (pp. 100–115). Routledge/Taylor and Francis.

Onyango, G. (2022). The art of bribery! analysis of police corruption at traffic checkpoints and roadblocks in Kenya. *International Review of Sociology, 32*(2), 311–331. https://doi.org/10.1080/03906701.2022.2038845

O'Rukevbe, H. (2022, March 9). Super cop, super fall, *The Guardian Nigeria*. Retrieved from https://guardian.ng/opinion/super-cop-superfall/

Osaleh, L. (2016). Tackling corruption in Kenyan judiciary & police. Retrieved from https://www.igi-integrity.com/wpcontent/uploads/2018/01/AGM2015-Workshop-on-JudiciaryPolice-Background.pdf

Papale, S. (2022). Fueling the fire: Al-Shabaab, counterterrorism and radicalization in Kenya. *Critical Studies on Terrorism, 15*(2), 356–380. https://doi.org/10.1080/17539153.2021.2016091

Pkalya, D. (2015, December 1). Yes, Corruption is a security threat, *Standard digital*. https://www.standardmedia.co.ke/article/2000184092/yes-corruption-is-asecurity-Threat

PMG. (2018). *High profile cases & Marikana progress report: IPID briefing: DPCI 2016/17 annual report*. Retrieved from https://pmg.org.za/committee-meeting/26095/

Prenzler, T. (2009). *Police corruption: Preventing misconduct and maintaining integrity*. CRC Press/Taylor and Francis.

Princewill, N. (2022, February 14). Nigeria hero "Supercop" arrested in cocaine smuggling case. *CNN*. Retrieved from https://www.cnn.com/2022/02/14/africa/nigeria-supercop-declared-wanted-intl/index.html

Pring, C. (2015). *People and corruption: Africa survey 2015: Global corruption barometer*. TI.

Pring, C., & Vrushi, J. (2019). *Global corruption barometer Africa 2019: Citizens' views and experiences of corruption*. TI.

Probert, T., Kimari, B., & Ruteere, M. (2020). *Strengthening policing oversight and investigations in Kenya: Study of IPOA investigations in deaths resulting from police action*. Retrieved from https://apcof.org/wp-content/uploads/apcof-study-of-ipoa-deaths-from-police-action-kenya-eng-041-3.pdf

Punch, M. (1985). *Conduct unbecoming: The social construction of police deviance and control*. Tavistock.

Punch, M. (2000). Police corruption and its prevention. *European Journal on Criminal Policy and Research, 8*(3), 301–324. https://doi.org/10.1023/A:1008777013115

PwC. (n.d.). *Overview of the tourism sector in Kenya*. Retrieved from http://www.pwc.com/ke/en/industries/tourism.html

Pyman, M. (2015, 25 June). Corruption, insecurity and terrorism. [Security in Complex Environments Group (SCEG) Conference]. Retrieved from http://www.sceguk.org.uk/wp-content/uploads/sites/24/2015/07/SCEG-Conference-25th-June-2015-Mark-Pyman-address-oncorruption.Pdf

Pyman, M., Bock, T., de la Blache, E. V., Mustafa, S., & Zaum, D. (2014). *Corruption as a threat to stability and peace*. Transparency International Deutschland eV.

Quinn, M. W. (2011). *Walking with the devil: The police code of silence: What bad cops don't want you to know and good cops won't tell you*. Quinn and Associates Publishing and Consulting.

Raines, J. (2009). *Ethics in policing: Misconduct and integrity*. Jones & Bartlett Learning.

Ratliff, E., & Clowes, W. (2022, February 16). How Instagram's "Billionaire Gucci Master" sank Nigeria's "Super Cop." *Bloomberg*. Retrieved from https://www.bloomberg.com/news/features/2022-02-16/how-instagram-s-billionaire-gucci-master-hushpuppi-sank-nigerian-super-cop-kyari

Republic of Kenya. (2009). *Report of the national task force on police reforms (The Ransley Report)*. Republic of Kenya.

Republic of Kenya. (2010). *The Constitution of Kenya, 2010*. Republic of Kenya.

Republic of Kenya. (2020). *Annual report to parliament on the state of national security*. Government Printer.

References

Republic of Kenya (The Senate). (2021). *Report on the inquiry into extrajudicial killings and enforced disappearances in Kenya.* The Senate, Republic of Kenya.

Roebuck, J. B., & Barker, T. (1974). A typology of police corruption. *Social Problems, 21*(3), 423–437. https://doi.org/10.2307/799909

Ross, J. I. (2012). *Policing issues: Challenges and controversies.* Jones and Bartlett Learning.

Sahara Reporters. (2022a, November 7). How policemen at force headquarters sold constable recruitment slots for N700,000 each, colluded with National Identity Agency officials to illegally reduce applicants' ages, *Sahara Reporters.* Retrieved from https://saharareporters.com/2022/11/07/exclusive-how-policemen-force-headquarters-sold-constable-recruitment-slots-n700000-each

Sahara Reporters. (2022b, November 11). How police officers at force headquarters sold fake constable job slots for N200,000, issued forged appointment letters to job seekers, *Sahara Reporters.* Retrieved from https://saharareporters.com/2022/11/11/exclusive-how-police-officersforce-headquarters-sold-fake-constable-job-slots-n200000

Santana-Gallego, M., & Fourie, J. (2022). Tourism falls apart: How insecurity affects African tourism. *Tourism Economics, 28*(4), 995–1008. https://doi.org/10.1177/2F1354816620978128

Schifrin, N., & Fannin, Z. (2016, May 29). Police officers treat this Nairobi neighborhood like an "ATM Machine," residents say. *The World.* https://theworld.org/stories/2016-05-23/police-officers-treat-nairobi-neighborhood-atm-machine-residents-say

Schwartz, M. (2015). Policing and (in)security in fragile and conflict-affected settings: A review of perspectives on policing in sub-Saharan Africa. [Global Center on Cooperative Security]. Retrieved from http://www.globalcenter.org/wp-content/uploads/2015/05/policing-and-insecurity-in-fragile-and-conflict-affected-settings.pdf

Sewall, S. (2016). Corruption: A 21st-century security challenge. *The Foreign Service Journal, 93*(5), 20–23.

Shelley, L. I. (2014). *Dirty Entanglements: Corruption, Crime, and Terrorism.* Cambridge University Press.

Skolnick, J. H. (2008). Corruption and the blue code of silence. In A. Millie & D. K. Das (Eds.), *Contemporary issues in law enforcement and policing* (pp. 45–60). CRC Press.

Some, K. (2012, September 24). How corrupt police officers undermine war on terrorism, *Daily Nation.*

Speckhard, A., & Shajkovci, A. (2019). The Jihad in Kenya: Understanding Al-Shabaab Recruitment and terrorist activity inside Kenya—in their own words. *African Security, 12*(1), 3–61. https://doi.org/10.1080/19392206.2019.1587142

Stanicek, B., with Betant-Rasmussen, M. (2021). Jihadist networks in sub-Saharan Africa: Origins, patterns and responses. [Briefing, European Parliamentary Research Service]. Retrieved from https://www.europarl.europa.eu/thinktank/en/document/EPRS_BRI(2021)698048

START. (n.d.). Global terrorism database. Retrieved from http://www.start.umd.edu/gtd/search/Results.aspx?expanded=no&casualties_type=&casualties_max=&success=yes&country=104&ob=GTDID&od=desc&page=1&count=20#results-table

Swope, R. (2001). Bad apples or bad barrel? *Law and Order, 49*(1), 80–85.

Tankebe, J., & Boakye, K. E. (2020). Police-public interactions during COVID-19: Assessing the experiences of commercial vehicle drivers in Ghana. [Research Brief Series No. 4]. Retrieved from https://africpgr.org/wp-content/uploads/2020/11/Africpgr-Research-Brief-Series_No-4.pdf

Tankebe, J., Boakye, K. E., & Amagnya, M. A. (2020). Traffic violations and cooperative intentions among drivers: The role of corruption and fairness. *Policing and Society, 30*(9), 1081–1096. https://doi.org/10.1080/10439463.2019.1636795

Taylor, W. A. (2019). *Contemporary Security Issues in Africa.* Praeger/ABC-CLIO.

Teyie, A., & Menya, W. (2014, August 17). GSU officers accuse seniors of harassment and corruption, *Sunday Nation,* 28.

Thachuk, K. (2005). Corruption and international security. *SAIS Review, 25*(1), 143–152.

TI. (2013). *Global corruption barometer 2013.* TI.

TI-DS. (2017). *The Fifth Column: Understanding the relationship between corruption and conflict*. Transparency International UK.
TI–Kenya. (2020). *Kenya bribery index 2019*. TI–Kenya.
TJRC Kenya. (2013). *Report of the truth, justice and reconciliation commission: Volume IIB*. TJRC Kenya.
Tshoose, C. T., & Rapatsa, M. (2022). Who will watch the watchers? a critical perspective on police brutality in post-apartheid South Africa. *International Human Rights Law Review, 11*(2), 221–244. https://doi.org/10.1163/22131035-11020003
Tshuma, N. (2022, May 31). IPUSA calls out SAPS for alleged flawed recruitment drives, *Independent Online*. Retrieved from https://www.iol.co.za/capeargus/news/ipusa-calls-out-saps-for-alleged-flawed-recruitment-drives-d86907cd-ef8c-45c2-8071-89a6b3ecfed6
Tummers, L., Bekkers, V., & Steijn, B. (2009). Policy alienation of public professionals: Application in a new public management context. *Public Management Review, 11*(5), 685–706. https://doi.org/10.1080/14719030902798230
UN. (2010). *International convention for the protection of all persons from enforced disappearance*. Retrieved from https://www.ohchr.org/en/instruments-mechanisms/instruments/international-convention-protection-all-persons-enforced
UNCAT. (2009). *Consideration of reports submitted by states parties under article 19 of the convention: Concluding observations of the committee against torture: Kenya*. UN.
UNCAT. (2015). *Concluding observations on the second periodic report of Kenya, adopted by the committee at its fiftieth session (6 to 31 May 2013)*. UN.
UNCAT. (2022). *Concluding observations on the third periodic report of Kenya*. UN.
UNDP. (2023). *Journey to Extremism in Africa: Pathways to Recruitment and Disengagement*. Retrieved from https://www.undp.org/publications/journey-extremism-africa-pathways-recruitment-and-disengagement
UN-HRC. (2012). *Consideration of reports submitted by states parties under article 40 of the covenant: Concluding observations adopted by the human rights committee at its 105th Session Kenya*. UN-HRC.
UNHRC. (2009). *Promotion and protection of all human rights, civil, political, economic, social and cultural rights, including the right to development: Report of the special rapporteur on extrajudicial, summary or arbitrary executions: Addendum: Mission to Kenya*. UN General Assembly.
US Department of State. (2017). *Country reports on terrorism 2016*. US Department of State.
US Department of State. (2021). *Country reports on terrorism 2020*. US Department of State.
US Department of State. (2022a). *Kenya 2021 human rights report*. US Department of State.
US Department of State. (2022b, July 22). Kenya travel advisory. Retrieved from https://travel.state.gov/content/travel/en/traveladvisories/traveladvisories/kenya-travel-advisory.html
Usman, D. J. (2019). *Public perceptions of trust in the police in Abuja, Nigeria*. [PhD thesis, University of Glasgow].
Wachira, M. (2016, May 26). Corrupt police bosses exposed by juniors, *Kenyans.co.ke*. https://www.kenyans.co.ke/news/corrupt-police-bosses-exposed-juniors
Wagner, D. (2014, August 18). Kenya, corruption, and terrorism. [The Blog-Huff Post]. Retrieved from http://www.huffingtonpost.com/daniel-wagner/kenya-corruption-and-terr_b_5505869.html
Wairuri, K. (2022). Thieves should not live amongst people: Under-protection and popular support for police violence in Nairobi. *African Affairs, 121*(482), 61–79. https://doi.org/10.1093/afraf/adac006
Warah, R. (2014a, August 4). Corruption, politics and tribalism have neutered our security services. *Daily Nation*.
Warah, R. (2014b, December 9). Corruption is costing Kenyans their lives–no one is safe. *The Guardian*. https://www.theguardian.com/commentisfree/2014/dec/09/corruption-kenyans-fraud

References

Westmarland, L. (2005). Police ethics and integrity: Breaking the blue code of silence. *Policing and Society: An International Journal, 15*(2), 145–165. https://doi.org/10.1080/10439460500071721

Williams, H. (2002). Core factors of police corruption across the world. *Forum on Crime and Society, 2*(1), 85–99.

Wood, J. R. T. (1997). *Final report of the royal commission into the New South Wales police service: Volume 2: Reform.* Government of the State of New South Wales.

World Bank. (2020). *Republic of Rwanda: Rwanda's anti-corruption experience: Actions, accomplishments, and lessons.* World Bank.

Wrong, M. (2009). *It's our turn to eat: The story of a Kenyan whistle-blower.* Harper Collins.

Chapter 6
Peace, Justice, and Inclusive Institutions: Overcoming Challenges to the Implementation of Sustainable Development Goal 16 in Africa and Beyond

This chapter provides an analysis of the importance of SDG 16 (Peace, Justice, and Inclusive Institutions) in achieving all the SDGs, the progress on implementation of SDG 16 to date, the principal challenges that countries in Africa and beyond are encountering in the implementation of SDG 16, and then proposes a set of policy solutions to overcome those challenges. It argues that progress on SDG 16 is critical to progress on the other SDGs and, therefore, it is imperative that countries vigorously attempt to overcome those SDG 16 challenges to meet the targets indicated for all goals.

6.1 Introduction

The SDGs are a universal call to action to end poverty, protect the planet, and ensure that all people enjoy peace and prosperity. As shown in Table 6.1, there are 17 SDGs that came into effect in January 2016, after being approved by UN member states in September 2015. These goals represent the scale and breadth of the *2030 Agenda for Sustainable Development* which is a plan of action for people, the planet and prosperity. The SDGs are intended to be universal in the sense of embodying a universally shared common global vision of progress towards a safe, just, and sustainable space for all human beings to thrive on the planet. They reflect the moral principles that no one and no country should be left behind, and that everyone and every country should be regarded as having a common responsibility for playing their part in delivering the global vision.

African nations have also developed and ratified the previously referred to *Agenda 2063* that is intended to be a shared strategic framework for inclusive growth and sustainable development and a global strategy to optimize the use of Africa's resources for the benefit of all Africans (AU, 2015). *Agenda 2063*, which is also

Table 6.1 The 17 Sustainable development goals

Sustainable development goals	
1 No poverty	10 Reduce inequality
2 Zero hunger	11 Sustainable cities and communities
3 Good health and well-being	12 Responsible consumption & production
4 Quality education	13 Climate action
5 Gender equality	14 Life under water
6 Clean water and sanitation	15 Life on land
7 Affordable and clean energy	16 Peace, justice, and strong institutions
8 Decent work and economic growth	17 Partnership for the goals
9 Industry, innovation, and infrastructure	

Source: Author, derived from information in UN (2015)

aligned with *Agenda 2030*, is comprised of seven aspirations encompassing 20 goals. Aspiration 3 (An Africa of Good Governance, Respect for Human Rights, Justice, and the Rule of Law) and Aspiration 4 (A Peaceful and Secure Africa) are correlated with SDG 16.

This chapter is concerned with Goal 16 of the *2030 Agenda for Sustainable Development* which is officially titled: "*Promote peaceful and inclusive societies for sustainable development, provide access to justice for all and build effective, accountable and inclusive institutions at all levels.*" The chapter provides an analysis of the importance of SDG 16 in achieving all the SDGs, the progress on implementation of SDG 16 to date, the principal challenges that African countries, in particular, are encountering in the implementation of SDG 16, and proposes a set of policy solutions to overcome those challenges. It argues that progress on SDG 16 is critical to progress on the other SDGs and, therefore, it is imperative that all countries vigorously attempt to overcome those SDG 16 challenges to meet the targets indicated for all goals.

6.2 SDG 16: Peace, Justice, and Inclusive Institutions

One innovation of the overall SDGs, and noted by many policy-makers and analysts, is the shift in focus away from a set of goals that only relate to developing countries to a set of goals that are global and therefore applicable to all countries, developed and developing alike. SDG 16 is one of the more innovative aspects of the development framework, focusing on advancing government accountability, building trust, and sustaining peace. It provides an insight into how we might actually hold leaders to account, and achieve all the SDGs by 2030. There are 12 targets of SDG 16 along with 24 associated official indicators as of mid-2022 (see UN, 2015, 2017; United Nations Statistical Commission [UNSC], 2022).

6.2.1 Why SDG 16 Matters to Sustainable Development and the Overall SDGs

There is a wealth of evidence linking development to peace. The IMF, UN, and the World Bank, for example, have all published research showing that insecurity and conflict are major development challenges and can set back development gains (see, for example, IMF, 2019, 2022; UN and World Bank, 2018; World Bank, 2011). Similarly, the IEP, has found that higher levels of violence greatly affect economic development by reducing foreign direct investment and the broader macroeconomic environment (IEP, 2019). In turn, "this affects poverty, economic development, life expectancy and education outcomes, as well as indicators which are essential for longer-term development such as infant mortality and access to services" (IEP, 2019, p. 6). In that regard also, the Africa Center for Strategic Studies (ACSS) has published research showing that some 81% of the record more than 135 million Africans facing acute food insecurity are in conflict-affected countries, thereby underscoring the development impact fact that conflict continues to be the primary driver of Africa's food crisis (ACSS, 2022). As also previously argued by Lucey (2015), the link between peace, security and development is well recognized although discussions about the nature of this link remain prevalent in current policy circles, such as those surrounding the SDGs.

As also noted in Chap. 2 of this book, *Agenda 2030* states, and reaffirms that wealth of evidence, that "there can be no sustainable development without peace and no peace without sustainable development" (UN, 2015, p. 6). Peace is identified as one of five areas of critical importance for humanity—along with people, prosperity, the planet, and partnership. *Agenda 2030* recognizes the need to build peaceful, just, and inclusive societies that provide equal access to justice and which are based on respect for human rights (including the right to development); on effective rule of law and good governance at all levels; and on transparent, effective, and accountable institutions. There was a clear acknowledgement, therefore, that political goals— ensuring inclusion, entrenching good governance, and ending violent conflict—must find a place alongside the economic, social, and environmental ones. SDG 16 therefore emerged as an "enabler" for the entire *Agenda 2030*.

Accordingly, SDG 16 is a key element to achieve the transformative *Agenda 2030*. This applies to all goals whether related to education, health, economic growth, climate change, and so on. In other words, as Nygård (2017, p. 4) expresses it, "meeting any of the other SDGs fundamentally rests on the shoulders of SDG 16." Without sustained peace, which goes beyond the mere absence of violence and includes respect for human rights and the rule of law, development gains will be reversed. And, without inclusion and access to justice for all, inequalities in poverty reduction and socio-economic development will increase and countries' commitments to leaving no one behind will not be met (see Global Alliance for Reporting Progress on Peaceful, Just and Inclusive Societies, 2019; Hope, 2019). SDG 16 therefore "represents the international community's recognition that peace and security are the prerequisite for sustainable development" (Mustafayeva, 2020, p. 267).

To further demonstrate the importance of SDG 16 in meeting the SDGs and achieving comprehensive sustainable development, we can look at one of the targets as an example and this is explored in greater detail in the next chapter. Target 16.5 is to: "Substantially reduce corruption and bribery in all their forms." Sustainable development thrives best in a climate of good governance, peace, and security. However, corruption has a corrosive impact on sustainable development and it (corruption) often leads to civil unrest and instability.

Consequently, SDG 16 underpins the other sixteen SDGs, all of which also rest on institutions that are inclusive and capable of responding to the needs of the public transparently and accountably. A commitment to human rights, justice, accountability, and transparency—which are all recognized as prerequisites to ensuring an enabling environment in which people are able to live freely, securely, and prosperously—is therefore evident throughout the SDG 16 targets. From anti-corruption and the rule of law, to participatory decision-making, violence reduction and the promotion of peace, SDG 16 touches on all aspects of society and across *Agenda 2030*. While all aspects of *Agenda 2030* must be seen as mutually reinforcing and interdependent, if we are to achieve sustainable development, building solid and strong institutions, together with peace, just and inclusive societies, are key steps to delivering on all goals and to achieve sustainability. As observed by the Global Alliance for Reporting Progress on Peaceful, Just and Inclusive Societies (2018), effectively, SDG 16 cannot be seen in isolation because it impacts the likelihood of achieving all other targets across the SDGs and has very strong links to the economic, social, and environmental goals of *Agenda 2030*. Moreover, it provides a strong rationale to insist on the centrality of justice in any sustainability effort, but with an awareness of the complexities of doing so. As argued elsewhere, sustainability without some consideration of justice would be nonsensical from a normative perspective and even difficult to achieve strategically (see Klinsky & Golub, 2016; Pérez et al., 2018).

Furthermore, a growing number of countries have been addressing—with varying degrees of detail in their Voluntary National Reviews (VNRs)—the relevance and enabling role of SDG 16 for sustainable development (see, for example, Pathfinders for Peaceful, Just and Inclusive Societies, 2019). VNRs document how countries are tackling the transformative challenge of *Agenda 2030* and their primary purpose is to enable countries to assess their own progress and draw lessons learned on their way to achieving the SDGs. The reviews complement the broader thematic reviews of progress that also take place at the High-Level Political Forums (HLPFs), the central platform for follow-up and review of *Agenda 2030*, and have shown that positive change can be achieved. Countries have made concrete commitments on preventing violence, increasing access to justice, strengthening institutions, and promoting greater inclusion (Pathfinders for Peaceful, Just and Inclusive Societies, 2019). Countries such as Cabo Verde, Eritrea, Ethiopia, Ghana, Rwanda, Saint Lucia, Spain, and Vanuatu, for example, have underlined that SDG 16 is a vital enabling goal for the entire sustainable development agenda (UN, 2019a; UNDESA,

2018; UNECOSOC, 2022). They have also stressed that just, peaceful, and inclusive societies are crucial for the realization of the SDGs, while the role of inclusive, democratic governance, with responsive institutions, and access to justice for all is paramount (UN, 2019a; UNDESA, 2018, 2021a).

Several other countries (among them Australia, Bahrain, Ecuador, Egypt, Guinea, pre-coup Mali (ironically), and Sri Lanka, for example) have elaborated on the compelling need to promote good governance, protection of human rights, and the eradication of violence—especially against women and children. The importance of upholding the rule of law; ensuring universal access to justice as well as to government and information; building effective, accountable, and inclusive institutions; and the delivery of public services have also been highlighted by several countries (among them Armenia, Bhutan, Canada, Greece, Grenada, Hungary, Ireland, Latvia, pre-coup Mali [surprisingly], Malta, Senegal, Singapore, Spain, and Viet Nam) (UNDESA, 2018, 2021a).

6.3 Progress on SDG 16 and Its Impact Relationship to Other SDGs

Significant attempts have been made, and continue to be made, by UN member states and several organizations (UN, non-governmental organizations [NGOs], other multilateral institutions, donor agencies, and academic research institutions) in tracking progress toward meeting the SDGs. Particularly, as noted above, many countries have been increasingly producing VNRs to track their SDGs progress overall as well as other specific reports related to SDG 16. In addition, given the nature of SDG 16, and the fact that there can be no sustainable development without peace and effective institutions, progress on SDG 16 is intuitively necessary for progress on the other SDGs. However, almost all the progress reports that are publicly available are primarily concerned with progress vis-à-vis each goal and their targets and there is very little information linking the performance data from each goal's targets to other goals.

While people overall are living better lives than they were a decade ago, progress to ensure that "no one is left behind" has not been rapid enough to meet the targets of *Agenda 2030*. In fact, the rate of global progress is not keeping pace with the ambitions of *Agenda 2030*, necessitating immediate and accelerated action by countries and stakeholders at all levels. Using the median composite SDG Index score—a measure that tracks performance across all SDG areas—we can determine that, on average, countries with higher per capita income have better SDG outcomes, yet none are on track to achieve all 17 SDGs (Sachs et al., 2022). For the high-income countries (HICs) and OECD economies, the overall performance outcome is 78% and 77%, respectively, which implies they are 22% and 23%, respectively, short of reaching the SDGs. In contrast, the median score for sub-Saharan Africa countries is 54% and means that they are 46% behind in reaching the SDGs. The composite

SDG Index score is drawn from the 2022 edition of the *Sustainable Development Report* which includes the SDG Index and Dashboards. It reflects the performance of countries in all 17 SDGs and ranges between the worst (0) and the best or target (100) outcomes (Sachs et al., 2022). The index measures the gap in achieving the SDGs, and it is built using indicators underlying the SDGs, with data drawn from both official and non-official data sources (Sachs et al., 2021, 2022).

A key aspect of measuring, monitoring, and understanding the performance of the SDGs is that of spillover effects. International spillover effects occur when one country's actions generate benefits or impose costs on another country that are not reflected in market prices (Sachs et al., 2022). International spillovers are said to fall into four categories: (1) environmental and social spillovers embodied into trade; (2) direct cross-border flows in air and water; (3) spillovers related to economic and financial flows; and (4) peacekeeping and security spillovers (for greater details, see Sachs et al., 2022). The HICs tend to generate the largest negative spillover effects, thereby undermining the progress of other countries toward achieving the SDGs. The International Spillover Index (ISI) includes indicators (currently 14 in 2022) that are already included in the total SDG Index score, and used to generate a stand-alone ISI (Sachs et al., 2022). The ISI score ranges from the worst (0) and the best (100). For sub-Saharan Africa, the ISI score in 2022 was 98.3 while for the OECD economies it was 70.7 (Sachs et al., 2022).

With specific respect to SDG 16, progress in promoting peace and justice, and in building effective, accountable, and inclusive institutions remains uneven across and within regions. Many regions of the world continue to suffer untold horrors because of armed conflict or other forms of violence that occur within societies and at the domestic level (UN, 2019b; 2022). Advances in promoting the rule of law and access to justice are also uneven. However, progress is being made in regulations to promote public access to information, albeit slowly, and in strengthening institutions upholding human rights at the national level. In their VNRs, several countries (among them Australia, Bahrain, Egypt, Ecuador, pre-coup Mali [but surprisingly], Guinea, and Sri Lanka) have also elaborated on measures to promote good governance, protection of human rights, and the eradication of violence—especially against women and children.

Several countries have also reported on their efforts to combat organized crime, money laundering and terrorist financing, and corruption and bribery (UNDESA, 2018, 2021a). Ecuador, for example, is seeking through education and training to generate a society with ethical and civic values that promote rejection of corruption. Antigua and Barbuda is now requiring all public officials to declare all their assets to an investigative commission. Namibia promulgated a Whistle Blowers Act that aims to encourage people to come forward and denounce corrupt practices. To curtail illicit financial flows into Switzerland from developing countries, Switzerland is helping these countries to better manage their revenue from commodities transactions and institute effective taxation.

Many other countries (including Armenia, Canada, Bhutan, Greece, Hungary, Ireland, Latvia, pre-coup Mali [again surprisingly], Malta, Senegal, Singapore, Spain, and Viet Nam) have highlighted the importance of upholding the rule of law;

6.3 Progress on SDG 16 and Its Impact Relationship to Other SDGs

ensuring universal access to justice as well as to government and information; building effective, accountable, and inclusive institutions; and the delivery of public services (UNDESA, 2018, 2021a). Figure 6.1 shows the SDG 16 Index performance score by regional/income classification. The 12 highest scoring countries are all high-income nations being only between 6%–12% short of reaching full compliance with SDG 16. On the other hand, the 12 lowest scoring countries are all developing with ten in Africa, one in Latin America and the Caribbean (Venezuela), one in the Middle East and North Africa (Yemen), and they are all between a range of 55%–70% behind on compliance with the goal. Figure 6.2 shows the SDG 16 performance score for the ten African countries among the 12 lowest scoring countries globally, along with their overall SDG Index performance score.

The quest for global peace has been setback as violent conflicts have been increasing and, by 2020, had reached their highest levels since 1945 (UN, 2022a). These conflicts have, in turn, resulted in more than 88 million people being displaced globally by mid-2022, compared to 84 million in mid-2021, with a broad impact being in sub-Saharan Africa where more than 1% of the population has been forcibly displaced in 17 of that region's nations during the period 2021–2022 (IEP,

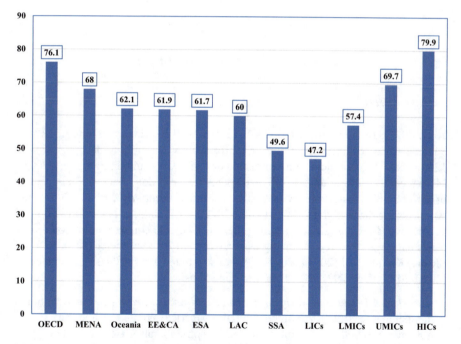

Fig. 6.1 SDG 16 index performance score by regional/income classification, 2022. *Notes:* Abbreviations are as follows: *OECD* = Organization for Economic Cooperation and Development, *MENA* = Middle East and North Africa, *EE&CA* = Eastern Europe and Central Asia, *ESA* = East and South Asia, *LAC* = Latin America and Caribbean, *SSA* = sub-Saharan Africa, *LICs* = Low Income Countries, *LMICs* = Lower Middle-Income Countries, *UMICs* = Upper Middle-Income Countries, *HICs* = High Income Countries. *Source:* Author, based on data derived from the online database for Sachs et al. (2022)

138 6 Peace, Justice, and Inclusive Institutions: Overcoming Challenges…

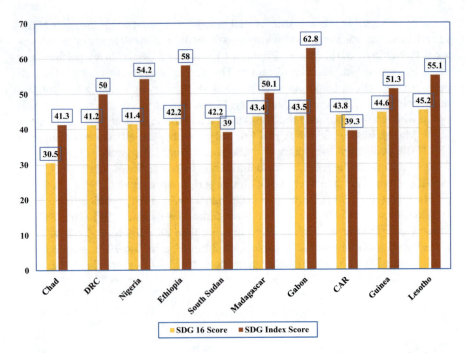

Fig. 6.2 SDG 16 index performance score and overall SDG index performance score for the ten lowest scoring African countries, 2022. *Notes: DRC* = Democratic Republic of the Congo, *CAR* = Central African Republic. *Source:* Author, based on data derived from the online database for Sachs et al. (2022)

2021, 2022). In the period 1980–2005, there were 126 armed conflicts in 32 sub-Saharan Africa countries resulting in approximately one million deaths, and with 120 of these 126 conflicts being intrastate or civil wars (Fukuda-Parr et al., 2008). More recently, "five coups as well as disputes over election results and allegations of corruption led to a rise in civil unrest and *political instability* across [sub-Saharan Africa during the period mid-2021 to mid-2022]" (IEP, 2022, p. 21). From a regional perspective, for each target for which there is available comparable regional time series data, we know the following as derived from Afrobarometer (n.d.); Keulder (2021); Kukutschka (2021a, 2021b); Kukutschka and Vrushi (2019); Sachs et al. (2021, 2022); UN (2021, 2022b, 2022c); and Vrushi (2020):

- *Target 16.1 (Reduce all forms of violence and related death rates)* – Intentional homicide rates (2020) are highest in Latin America and the Caribbean at 21 victims per 100,000 population, followed by sub-Saharan Africa at a rate of 13.3 victims per 100,000 population and Oceania (excluding Australia and New Zealand) at a rate of 7.8 victims per 100,000 population. The world average rate was 5.6 victims per 100,000 population. East and South Asia had the lowest rate at 0.9 victims per 100,000 population.

6.3 Progress on SDG 16 and Its Impact Relationship to Other SDGs

- *Target 16.2 (End abuse, exploitation, trafficking and all forms of violence against and torture of children)* – (a) The proportion of children aged 1–14 years who experienced any physical punishment and/or psychological aggression by caregivers in the past month (2021) was highest in sub-Saharan Africa at 85%, followed by Northern Africa and Western Asia at 82%. The world proportion was 79%; and (b) The proportion of young women aged 18–29 years who experienced sexual violence by age 18 (2020) was highest in Oceania (excluding Australia and New Zealand) at 6.8% followed by sub-Saharan Africa at 5.5%, which is followed by Central and Southern Asia at 1.5%. The world average proportion was 3%.
- *Target 16.3 (Promote the rule of law at the national and international levels and ensure equal access to justice for all)* – Unsentenced detainees as a proportion of the overall prison population remained steady worldwide at 30% in 2020 compared to 2015. The region with the highest proportion of such detainees in 2020 was Central and Southern Asia at 57% which was an increase from 51% in 2015, followed by sub-Saharan Africa at 42% which was an increase from 39% in 2015. Latin America and the Caribbean had the third highest proportion at 34% in 2020 which was a decrease from 41% in 2015. Oceania (excluding New Zealand and Australia) and Eastern and South Eastern Asia are in the next two places at 29% and 27%, respectively, in 2020. For Oceania this was a decrease from 32% in 2015, while for Eastern and South Eastern Asia, it was a slight decrease from 28%.
- *Target 16.5 (Substantially reduce corruption and bribery in all their forms)* – The average bribery rates for public services (2019–2021) was highest in sub-Saharan Africa at 28% which was an increase from 23% in 2017. In the Middle East and North Africa region the bribery rate was 22% in 2019 which was a decline from 30% in 2017. In Latin America and the Caribbean, the 2019 bribery rate was 21%. For Asia-Pacific, the bribery rate was 26% in 2020–2021 while for the EU the bribery rate for public services was 7% in 2021 compared to 9% in 2017. For business firms, the average bribery incidence (proportion of firms experiencing at least one bribe payment request) during the period 2006–2021 was 30% in Eastern and South Eastern Asia, 22% in Oceania (excluding Australia and New Zealand), 21% in Central and Southern Asia and sub-Saharan Africa, 9% in Latin America and the Caribbean, and with a world average of 16%.
- *Target 16.9 (By 2030, provide legal identity for all, including birth registration)* – The proportion of children under five years of age whose births have been registered with a civil authority globally was 75% in 2021 which is two points higher than it was during the period 2010–2018. North America and Europe remain at 100%. Oceania as a whole was at 70% in 2021 compared to an average of 98% in 2010–2018 increasing from 57% in 2010–2016, while Australia and New Zealand remain at 100%. Latin America and the Caribbean was at 95% in 2021 compared to 94% in 2010–2018. In South East Asia, the proportion was 85% in 2021, representing a slight increase from 82% in 2010–2018, and in sub-Saharan Africa it was only 45% in 2021 compared to 46% in 2010–2018.

- *Target 16.10 (Ensure public access to information and protect fundamental freedoms, in accordance with national legislation and international agreements)* – The number of countries that have adopted and implemented constitutional, statutory and/or policy guarantees for public access to information (2021) was 135 globally out of a total of 193 UN member states. In Latin America and the Caribbean, it was 23 countries; and in both sub-Saharan Africa and Asia it was 21 countries, respectively.
- *Target 16.A (Strengthen relevant national institutions, including through international cooperation, for building capacity at all levels, in particular in developing countries, to prevent violence and combat terrorism and crime)* – (a) The proportion of countries with independent National Human Rights Institutions in compliance with the Paris Principles has increased globally from 40% in 2019 to 43% in 2021. In sub-Saharan Africa, there was an increase from 40% in 2019 to 48% in 2021; in Eastern and Southeastern Asia there was no change in 2021 from 35% in 2019; and in Latin America and the Caribbean there was a decline in 2021 to 38% from 41% in 2019; and (b) The proportion of countries that applied for accreditation as independent National Human Rights Institutions in compliance with the Paris Principles has slightly increased globally from 60% in 2019 to 62% in 2021. In sub-Saharan Africa, there was no increase in 2021 from 58% in 2019; in Central and Southern Asia there was an increase from 71% in 2019 to 79% in 2021; in Eastern and South Eastern Asia there was no change in 2021 from 53% in 2019; and in Latin America and the Caribbean there was also no change in 2021 from 59% in 2019.

Incorporating *Agenda 2063* here also, Figs. 6.3 and 6.4, respectively, show the comparative performance of Aspirations 3 and 4 (which are aligned with SDG 16 as noted above) against their targets for 2019 and 2021. The data suggest that East Africa had the best performance on both Aspirations 3 and 4 while Southern Africa was the worst performer for Aspiration 3 and North Africa had the worst performance for Aspiration 4.

Looking at the uneven SDG 16 progress and outcomes, to date, as shown above, we can also trace some of the impacts on, and links to, other SDGs. For example, intentional homicide rates are higher in countries with high income inequality and this is a phenomenon that cuts across countries and regions. Countries with higher income inequality had, on average, a homicide rate that was nine times greater than countries where income was more evenly distributed and there are significant gender implications related thereto. Homicides and violence, generally, are crimes that fall within the crime-development nexus that is an important element of SDG 16 (see, for example, Blaustein et al., 2022).

Statistics from the database of the United Nations Office on Drugs and Crime (UNODC) show that homicide represents the most extreme form of violence against women, a lethal act on a continuum of gender-based discrimination and abuse. Gender-related killings of women and girls therefore remain a grave problem across regions, in countries rich and poor. While the vast majority of homicide victims are men, killed by strangers, women are far more likely to die at the hands of someone

6.3 Progress on SDG 16 and Its Impact Relationship to Other SDGs

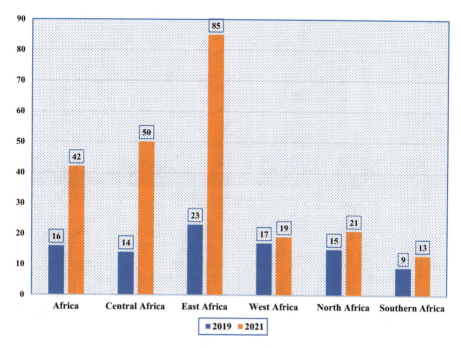

Fig. 6.3 Continental and sub-regional performance of Agenda 2063 Aspiration 3 against its targets, 2019–2021 (%). *Source:* Author, based on data derived from AU (2020, 2022)

they know. Women killed by intimate partners or family members account for 58% of all female homicide victims reported globally in 2020, and little progress has been made in preventing such murders (UNODC, 2021). While Asia is the region with the largest absolute number of killings, Africa is the region with the highest level of violence relative to the size of its female population. In 2020, the female intimate partner/family-related homicide rate in Africa was estimated at 2.7 per 100,000 female population, compared with 1.6 in Oceania, 1.4 in the Americas, 0.8 in Asia, and 0.7 in Europe (UNODC, 2021). Research on the Pacific region has identified a number of risk factors behind the high rates of gender-based violence. These include economic dependence and poverty, the low social status of women and girls, sexual double standards, and a lack of sexual and reproductive health education (Ackman et al., 2018; Biersack et al., 2016).

When income inequality is combined with gender-inequality homicides, then we have an obvious impact on gender and development. This, in turn, delays the necessary achievement of gender equality and the empowering of all women and girls (SDG 5, SDG 10), as gender inequality continues to hold women back and deprive them of basic rights and opportunities. Furthermore, gender inequalities, in turn, have a large and wide-ranging impact on society. For example, they can contribute to gender inequities in health and access to health care (SDG 3), opportunities for employment and promotion (SDG 8), levels of income (SDG 10), and education (SDG 4), for instance.

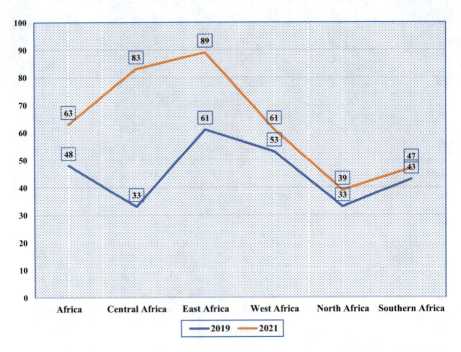

Fig. 6.4 Continental and sub-regional performance of Agenda 2063 Aspiration 4 against its targets, 2019–2021 (%). *Source:* Author, based on data derived from AU (2020, 2022)

Another example of SDG 16 outcome impact being noted here is that pertaining to unsentenced detainees. The decision to detain a person before he/she is found guilty of a crime is one of the most draconian a nation or individual can make (see Berry and English 2011; Schönteich, 2014). A decision made in an instant by the arresting officer can have a severe, lasting, and adverse impact. Whether or not it is justified, and regardless of whether due process is followed, the arrest is likely to have a traumatic effect on the detainee and those who love and depend on him/her (Berry and English 2011; Schönteich, 2014; Wakefield & Andersen, 2020). Pretrial detention is one of the worst things that can happen to a person: the detainee immediately loses his/her freedom, and can also lose his/her family, health, home, job, and community ties (Berry and English 2011; Schönteich, 2014).

Rates of pretrial detention suggest that progress with respect to the rule of law and access to justice has been slow. Globally, the proportion of people held in detention without being tried or sentenced for a crime has basically remained unchanged since 2000 (UN, 2022a). This indicates that no significant progress has been made in the ability of judicial systems to process and try an accused in an efficient manner. In turn, it means that human rights and rule of law concerns emerge. Many pretrial detainees are exposed to torture, extortion, and disease. They are subject to the arbitrary actions of police, corrupt officials, and even other detainees (Berry and English 2011; Schönteich, 2014). The socio-economic impact of excessive pretrial detention is profound, affecting not just the individuals detained, but their families, communities, and even the nation as a whole. That impact is felt most keenly by the poor (SDG 1). In summary, excessive pretrial detention impacts poor detainees and increases poverty (SDG 1); exposes detainees to disease (SDG 3); increases inequalities in society (SDG 10); interrupts education (SDG 4); and reduces income-earning opportunities and leads to loss of jobs (SDG 8).

One more example is the outcomes impact stemming from violent forms of child discipline. Violent forms of discipline, including methods that rely on physical punishment, verbal intimidation, and psychological aggression, are pervasive. Different forms of violent discipline tend to overlap and frequently occur together, exacerbating the short- and long-term harm they inflict. Such harm ranges from immediate effects to long-term damage that children carry well into adulthood. Despite their detrimental and long-lasting impact, violent forms of discipline are widespread. According to the World Health Organization (WHO), one billion children globally experience some form of physical, sexual, or emotional violence every year and one child dies as a result of violence every five minutes (WHO, 2018, 2020).

Gender, sexual orientation, disability, poverty, national or ethnic origin are some of the factors that expose children to a high risk of violence. Children also continue to be victims of torture, trafficking, slavery and forced labor. In addition, hundreds of millions of girls have undergone female genital mutilation and millions more are at risk of undergoing the procedure every year (SDG 5). The United Nations Children's Fund (UNICEF) has noted that violent discipline at home is the most common form of violence experienced by children (UNICEF, 2022).

The Global Initiative to End All Corporal Punishment of Children has also provided overwhelming evidence that shows violent punishment of children is associated with a variety of negative health and behavioral outcomes—including poorer mental health (SDG 3); cognitive development and educational outcomes (SDG 4, SDG 5); and increased aggression and involvement in criminal behavior in children and adults (SDG 4, SDG 5) (Global Initiative to End All Corporal Punishment of Children, 2018). While the long-term effects of violence in families and society are felt by all, they can disproportionately affect low- and middle-income countries, where its impact can be severe in terms of slowing economic growth (SDG 8); undermining personal and collective security (SDG 1, SDG 5); and impeding social development (SDG 10). Also, as noted by Mbaku (2022), corruption is at the core of some of the most important violations of human rights, including those of children in Africa. Furthermore, Mbaku (2022, p. 258) states that:

> In many countries in Africa, corruption allows state- and non-state agents to engage in behaviors that violate the rights of children. For example, families force their children into underage marriage; children are subjected to significant levels of physical and mental abuse, as well as neglect or negligent treatment; young girls are sold into prostitution, as well as for use in pornography and illegal adoptions and organ transplantation. These crimes, which constitute major human rights violations, are being committed while highly corrupt national enforcement agencies standby and do nothing.

Consequently, "government corruption and dysfunction continue to reinforce or make possible pervasive violence and the customary and traditional practices that harm children" (Mbaku, 2022, p. 338).

A final example of SDG 16 outcomes impact linkage, with respect to other SDGs, has to do with climate change (SDG 13). Climate change not only impacts the sustainability of cities and communities (SDG 11) but it also affects, to a significant degree, peace and security. In fact, climate change is regarded, by the UN Security Council also, as one of the most pervasive global threats to peace and security in the 21st century (UN News, 2019). Climate change touches all areas of security, peace building, and development, and its impacts are already adversely affecting vulnerable communities, as well as stretching the capacities of societies and governments.

Climate change is best understood as a "threat multiplier," i.e., something that interacts with existing pressures (such as social conflict, poverty, economic inequality, large-scale migration, or competition for resources) and further compounds these issues—increasing the likelihood of instability or violent conflict. It increases the human insecurity of people dependent on natural or agricultural resources for their livelihoods. Recent research by Baptista et al. (2022) and Adesete et al. (2022), for example, have shown that climate change is intensifying food insecurity across sub-Saharan Africa with lasting adverse effects, especially on economic growth and poverty. Pearce and Andrijevic (2022) have calculated that even if governments across the world live up to the 2015 Paris Agreement to limit global temperature rise to 1.5C, the average hit to GDP per capita across African countries will be 14% up to 2050, growing to 34% by the end of this century.

Rising human insecurity, in turn, can induce people to migrate or seek out alternative resources or illegal sources of income, which in turn can also drive conflict, increasing humanitarian need (see, for example, Craig et al., 2021; The White House, 2022). Good examples of these impacts can be seen across Africa, especially the Lake Chad Basin, the Horn of Africa, and the Sahel (see, for example, Brunero et al., 2022; Hope, 2009, 2011a; Lamarche, 2023; Lindvall, 2021; Schaar, 2018). In societies where there is conflict or potential for conflict, climate change can therefore only exacerbate such conflicts. A quantitative study, for example, by Diallo and Tapsoba (2022), covering a broad sample of 51 African countries over the period 1990–2018, found evidence that climate change, as captured through weather shocks, increases the likelihood of domestic conflicts by as much as up to 38%. Similarly, an econometric analysis by Cappelli et al. (2023), based on a panel of 2653 georeferenced cells for the African continent between 1990 and 2016, found that changes in climatic conditions are important factors for risk and propensity of conflict, and their influence stretches over large spatial ranges. Perhaps it is relevant to note here that Africa is the most vulnerable continent to climate change impacts, significantly because of greenhouse gas emissions from outside of the region as the continent has the lowest rate of global greenhouse gas emissions, accounting for only 2%–3% (World Meteorological Organization [WMO], 2022).

6.4 Challenges to SDG 16 Progress and Implementation

Many of the challenges in achieving SDG 16, and all the other SDGs for that matter, are not new. In fact, even during the implementation of the Millennium Development Goals (MDGs), there were a set of challenges, particularly faced by developing countries, that persist until today. In addition, because of the sensitive nature of SDG 16, as it relates to issues of justice and peace, some countries cling to the notion of strongly upholding their sovereignty and government dominance without internal or external interference. The principal challenges to progress on outcomes and implementation of SDG 16, and therefore on the other SDGs, are discussed below.

6.4.1 Inadequate Capacity

Although there have been significant accomplishments toward capacity development in most African and other developing countries over the past several decades, there is still inadequate implementation capacity in too many countries. Some countries suffer terribly from the emigration of their highly skilled workforce (brain drain). This inadequate capacity, in turn, leads to the overall weakness of institutions as they are unable to meet their obligations to implement policies and programs, either in total or in a timely manner, to sufficiently influence progress in meeting SDG16 and the other SDGs for that matter. For example, insufficiently trained judicial officers or an insufficient number of them leads to failure in the justice system with long delays in investigation and disposition of cases, high rates of unsentenced or pretrial detainees, and an environment where bribery and corruption runs rampant.

Beyond human resource capacity, many countries also suffer from lack of capacity at the physical institutional level. Most of this lack of institutional capacity is related to deficient information technology and systems processes as is found in Africa, for instance (see, for example, Jaiyesimi, 2016). In many African nations, despite the efforts to increase Internet connectivity, there are still many government offices, especially in rural areas that lack such connectivity. It means that many tasks are still being conducted manually, and that in turn means it is being done in a time-consuming and inefficient manner. This, ultimately, hampers the effectiveness of the institutions in delivering not just on SDG 16 but all the other SDGs also. If the courts and police stations, for instance, are still places where tasks have to be done manually only, then the justice system will lack the capacity to meet the needs of the citizenry in a timely manner. Such gaps in local delivery capacity are a major factor in determining the success—or failure—of efforts to reach the SDGs. The uptake of the use of information technology, or the promotion of e-government, can therefore be instrumental in reducing the cost of SDG implementation and promote development and good governance as previously discussed in Chap. 4.

6.4.2 Poor Data and Information

Good data and its availability have been improving over the years as more and more countries are receiving technical assistance to beef up their national statistics capabilities. Data, and especially data of good quality, are essential for national governments and institutions to accurately plan, fund and evaluate sustainable development activities. However, there are still too many countries (and especially in Africa and Asia) where, due to lack of capacity, data is of poor quality, insufficient, and mostly outdated. Yet, basic development data are essential for an accurate picture of a country's development status. This includes a country's progress towards specific development goals and improving its citizens' socio-economic conditions. In fact, solutions to social and economic problems are often inseparable from the statistics. A country cannot, for example, end abuse, exploitation, trafficking, and all forms of violence against, and torture of, children (Target 16.2) without knowing how many children are being catered for and their regional distribution.

While laws on access to information exist in many countries, not all have been implemented effectively. Major issues include non-compliance, the lack of enforcement, and poor monitoring of implementation. In many countries, requests for information are often denied. The main challenges to implementation are: (1) unclear legal frameworks; (2) the lack of independence of oversight bodies; (3) the lack of political will to implement the laws; (4) the lack of human and financial resources; (5) ineffective management systems; and (6) low public awareness about the rights of citizens (UN, 2019c).

Furthermore, as a recent report by the IEP found, although there is a clear conceptual link between SDG 16 and the other SDGs, the empirical link cannot be clearly established and the lack of data offers a potential explanation for this (IEP, 2019). If more data were available the link may be more easily shown. IEP conducted a comprehensive data audit in 2019 which found at that time that of the indicators in other SDGs that are related, or linked, to SDG 16 (SDG 16+), there is official data for only 15 of them, with only six of these having coverage for more than 100 countries and only 44 of the 56 total indicators having any data available at all—from either official or unofficial sources (IEP, 2019). Also, a total of 30 countries were excluded from the 2022 SDG Index due to insufficient data with six of those countries being from sub-Saharan Africa (Sachs et al., 2022).

6.4.3 Inadequate Delivery Systems

Service delivery is a key element of sustainable development implementation and the last decade has witnessed significant government focus on service delivery in developing nations such as South Africa, Philippines, India, and Malaysia, for example. Research conducted notes that this movement towards efficient public service delivery in developing nations (versus developed nations) has required a significant shift in institutional thinking and institutional capacity for the governments (UN, 2019d). Where public service delivery is inadequate, the citizenry (clients) are robbed of their fundamental rights to efficiently access public goods and services. This means, for instance, that governments would not be able to appropriately ensure public access to information and protect fundamental freedoms, in accordance with national legislation and international agreements or significantly reduce all forms of violence and related death rates everywhere.

A key factor influencing the inadequacy of service delivery is the lack of accountability mechanisms in public institutions leading to a cycle of poor performance and an increase to the risk of collapse of public services. Accountability exists when there is a relationship where an individual or body, and the performance of tasks or functions by that individual or body, are subject to another's oversight, direction, or request that they provide information or justification for their actions (see Guerin et al., 2018). It means ensuring that officials in public sector organizations are answerable for their actions and that there is redress when duties and commitments are not met. According to the Transparency and Accountability Initiative (TAI), accountability may be classified as horizontal (internal), vertical (external), or diagonal (TAI, 2017).

Horizontal or internal accountability refers to the existence of public agencies that are legally enabled and empowered, and willing and able, to take actions that span from routine oversight to checking abuses, to criminal sanctions or impeachment in relation to actions or omissions by other public agents or agencies that may be regarded as unlawful. Vertical or external accountability is the means through which citizens and their civil associations play direct roles in holding the powerful to account by seeking to enforce standards of good performance on officials. Diagonal accountability operates in a domain between the vertical and horizontal dimensions. It refers to the phenomenon of direct citizen engagement with horizontal accountability institutions when promoting better oversight of state actions (TAI, 2017). By allowing for the provision of more adequate service delivery, accountability mechanisms also enhance human development.

6.4.4 Insufficient Financing

Financing is a critical ingredient for implementing and achieving *Agenda 2030* as it is for all development processes. The available data related to the SDG 16 targets show, for example, that (1) violence and conflict (including persecution and human rights violations) have resulted in almost 88 million individuals being forcibly displaced worldwide by mid-2022, with the global economic impact of violence estimated at being US$16.5 trillion (purchasing power parity terms) in 2021, equivalent to 10.9% of global GDP, and for sub-Saharan Africa the economic impact was estimated at US$581 billion representing a 10.2% increase from 2020 (IEP, 2022); (2) child marriage will lead to losses in welfare of over US$560 billion by 2030, according to recent research published by the Economic Impacts of Child Marriage project

(Wodon et al., 2017); and (3) the cost of bribery is estimated at US$1.5–2 trillion, or around 2% of GDP, with much larger economic and social costs when all forms of corruption are considered according to the IMF (2016). Overall, the SDGs will have very significant resource implications across the developed and developing world. The estimates in 2015 for total investment needs in developing countries alone had ranged from US$3.3 trillion to US$4.5 trillion per year, for basic infrastructure (roads, rail, and ports; power stations; water and sanitation), food security (agriculture and rural development), climate change mitigation and adaptation, health, and education (UNCTAD, 2015). The OECD (2020) has now estimated that the SDG annual unmet financing needs before COVID-19 was US$2.5 trillion while during the pandemic the SDG financing gap could increase by at least 70% to US$4.2 trillion.

African countries, and most other developing economies as well, are financially constrained as a result of their lower-level development (and that is why they are referred to as developing countries). Many developing economies therefore do not have sufficient financial capital to engage in public or private investment and there are several reasons advanced in the economic development literature for this, including the following: (1) low growth (growth is not sufficient to increase tax revenues or to allow scarce financial resources to be freed up for non-current expenditure); (2) lack of savings (a general lack of savings is often seen as the key reason why financial capital is in short supply); (3) debt overhang (spare public funds are often used to repay previous debts, so there are less available funds for capital investment by government); (4) crowding out (because many developing economies have large public sectors, private investment may be *crowded out* by public sector borrowing. This means that a government may borrow from local capital markets, if indeed they exist, which causes a relative shortage of capital and raises interest rates); and (5) absence of credit and financial markets (this discourages both lenders and borrowers) (Economics Online, 2020).

6.4.5 Lack of Political Will and Leadership

Without political will and leadership there can be no credible and significant push for policy development and implementation. In other words, political leaders have to be at the forefront of anything that a government gets done. Political will is the extent of committed support among key decision-makers for a particular policy solution to a particular problem. It therefore implies that a bureaucratic or political actor is willing to commit precious time, effort, and political capital and incur opportunity costs to achieve change, in this case, change to implement *Agenda 2030*.

All the evidence shows that in Africa and Asia as well, for instance, the lack of political will and leadership is a major factor influencing: (1) the uneven promotion of the rule of law at the national and international levels and ensuring equal access to justice for all; (2) the insignificant reduction in illicit financial and arms flows, or any strengthening of the recovery and return of stolen assets and combating of all forms of organized crime; (3) any substantial reduction in corruption and bribery in all their forms; and (4) the erosion of civil society participation for responsive, inclusive, participatory and representative decision-making and human rights observance.

Particularly, civil society organizations (CSOs) are under threat across the globe. The deterioration and shrinking of the civic space in Africa, Asia-Pacific, and beyond have a pervasive impact on the realization of SDG 16, and especially when coupled with the various forms of undermining and "erosion of democratic institutions" being observed, including "populism," "oligarchy," and "growing levels of corruption" diverting development resources and negatively affecting electoral processes (Ulaanbaatar Democracy Forum [UBDF], 2019). Since 2015 some 50–90, countries worldwide have introduced restrictive laws aimed at curtailing civil society activities and their funding (Amnesty International, 2019; Global Alliance of National Human Rights Institutions [GANHRI], 2018). Legal and administrative restrictions have been introduced in the areas of the registration of NGOs, the receipt of (foreign) funding, hiring of foreigners, financial auditing, taxation, and on the scope of activities that CSOs can pursue, especially political advocacy and human rights work (Amnesty International, 2019; GANHRI, 2018). In all the world's regions, there are governments that have implemented measures limiting the rights to freedom of expression, peaceful assembly and association, such as restrictive laws and policies introduced in the name of counter-terrorism and national security (GANHRI, 2018). In Africa, such restrictions have been regarded as being "part of a broader strategy adopted by regimes to narrow space for democratic activity and prevent challenges to the rule of strongmen and governing parties" (Musila, 2019, p. 3). Perhaps, this is a bit over the top and can only lend credence to the anti-NGO/CSO rationales being advanced by some governments as they (NGOs/CSOs) should not be profiling or behaving as if they are opposition political parties.

6.5 Overcoming the Challenges to SDG 16 Progress and Implementation

Overcoming the challenges to progress on SDG 16 is, of course, a critical necessity as the implementation process moves forward. The identification and acceptance of the nature of the challenges are important first steps and provide the platform from which to launch policies and processes to overcome them to accelerate SDG overall implementation.

Based on best practices, the research literature, and field practice, this work suggests below some policy approaches to overcoming the challenges to a more rapid and efficient implementation of SDG 16 targets. These approaches will also result in the promotion of processes that are gender-sensitive and responsive to the needs of minorities and those most left behind.

6.5.1 Capacity Development

Capacity development (sometimes referred to as capacity building, capacity enhancement, or capacity strengthening in some of the literature) has become recognized as a necessity for underpinning a number of critical prerequisites for sustaining development in the developing world. High on the list of those prerequisites is good governance. Without good governance, the quest for sustainable development is a fruitless goal. Consequently, capacity development has taken on added importance as a vital aspect of policy change for sustainable development (UN, 2017; UNDESA, 2021b). Where capacity is weak, countries will lack the capability to undertake basic public management functions. Institutions then hamper entrepreneurship, corrupt officials impede efficiency, and economic growth would be obstructed, all of which would affect the SDG 16 agenda and the rest of the SDGs as well.

The aim of capacity development in the context of SDG 16 should be to rectify such things as an insufficient pool of qualified workforce, dysfunctional organization structures, outdated procedures, dilapidated infrastructure, archaic equipment, flawed incentive structures, as well as corruption. Consequently, this means more than just training. Too frequently, capacity development has been regarded as synonymous with training (Hope, 2011b; Venner, 2015). In other words, the recommended approach to capacity development also entails a focus on all the potential elements that influence a fundamental increase in national capacity, including using diaspora knowledge networks (DKNs) to strengthen the domestic knowledge base. DKNs consist of groups of highly-skilled expatriate professionals who are interested in helping to advance structural transformation in their countries of origin. Capacity development is therefore much more comprehensive than mere technical training as also recognized in some of the VNRs. For example, the reviews of several countries including Niger and Paraguay have referred to donor assistance for the dissemination of statistics as part of their capacity development needs (UNDESA, 2018).

The following are the key areas in which most African and other developing countries appear to suffer from serious capacity gaps and deficiencies with respect to implementation of the SDGs, and for which sustainable capacity development is therefore required, among both their state and non-state actors:

The legislative bodies, which are experiencing difficulties in exerting their oversight and control functions due to their limited capacity in terms of policy analysis and review, budget control, initiation of new bills, and the development and enforcement of codes of ethics and conduct.

The justice systems, which require reforms to address their burdensome judicial procedures, inadequate human-resource recruitment and management methods, and issues of judicial independence.

The electoral systems, which need to improve their competence to deliver credible, politically neutral, and transparent services and elections to voters, candidates, and political parties.

The civil services, which require reforms to fill existing gaps in capacity in the executive branch where flawed incentive structures and employment methods, weak leadership and management, dysfunctional organizational structures, outdated procedures, archaic equipment, poor expenditure management and policy-analysis skills, and corruption are adversely affecting the implementation of government policies and the delivery of public services.

The local governments, which need to respond better to the citizens' needs, particularly in those countries where decentralization efforts have been undertaken or are being contemplated.

The CSOs (including the media) and *private enterprises*, both of which need to improve their respective productive, analytical, strategic, goods and services delivery, policy advocacy, and partnership capabilities related to SDG 16.

6.5.2 Data and Information Sharing

As we approach the halfway point in the implementation of *Agenda 2030*, more than ever, high-quality and trustworthy data are needed to inform evidence-based decision-making and to measure the progress towards achieving the SDGs. Data and information are key ingredients for development. Therefore, they are a bridge through which we gain understanding about development processes and outcomes. Sustainable development is not possible without data and information to guide the process (see Espey, 2019). In addition to the obvious need to better fund national data collection efforts and enhance the capacity and autonomy of national statistics bureaus, data needs to be freely shared and made available across all available platforms, including print and via electronic means.

Developing countries must also accept that just collecting data is not enough. It must be analyzed and converted into information and knowledge, then shared widely within and between countries and stakeholders to focus attention on SDG 16 problems across all scales for it to be meaningful (SDG 16 Data Initiative, 2019). It is only when the data have been collected and analyzed that we can properly understand systems affecting SDG 16.

Also, as observed about African nations but relevant to all countries, the collection of data relevant to SDG 16 must not be limited both in terms of content and the institutions with responsibility for such collection (Laberge, 2019). For example, governments should not shy away from collecting data that may be embarrassing, such as data related to corruption and bribery. Also, the collection of non-official data on SDG 16 can complement and fill gaps left by official sources, particularly in non-democratic contexts, where government data may not be trustworthy (SDG 16 Data Initiative, 2021). Countries should therefore fully support the SDG 16 Data Initiative, the Cape Town Global Action Plan for Sustainable Development Data (CTGAP), and the Data for Now (Data4Now) initiative as the focus for developing the capacities of countries to strengthen their national statistical systems, so that they can collect, process, analyze, and disseminate disaggregated data on peaceful, just, and inclusive societies. This continues to be absolutely essential despite, for example, the fact that peace has been only gradual progress made by national statistical offices (NSOs) towards the strategic areas proposed in the CTGAP due primarily to considerable capacity gaps in the national statistical systems (see World Bank, 2022). Access to information is also a critical ingredient for participatory decision-making as has been also stressed in the Dubai Declaration (announced in 2018) and the Bern Data Compact (announced in 2021), both of which support, promote, and reinforce the importance of the implementation of the CTGAP.

Readers who are interested in obtaining greater details on the SDG 16 Data Initiative, the Data4Now, and the CTGAP can consult the respective websites of these initiatives. A common element of all these initiatives, in concert with their partner and collaborating organizations, is the recognition of statistical capacity deficits in most developing countries, hence the emphasis on building capacity to improve the delivery timeliness, coverage, and quality of SDG data.

6.5.3 Improved Delivery Systems

Improving delivery systems to meet the SDG 16 targets needs to take on added urgency in most developing countries. One recurring theme in this regard is the need to engage with local communities more effectively. In other words, greater efforts in working with and through decentralized and local governance structures. Indeed, local governments have a central role in the implementation of SDG 16 as well as the other SDGs. The *Agenda 2030* with its emphasis on local ownership and participation, provides an ideal planning framework for municipalities.

National governments must therefore empower and leverage the potential of local governments in delivering peace, justice, and inclusion. Among other things, local governments are instrumental in preventing conflicts and in building bridges and channels for dialogue. Emphasizing this role, the United Cities and Local Governments (UCLG) has launched a "Peace Prize" to incentivize and showcase inspiring examples of local governments building inclusive and peaceful societies (UCLG, n.d.). It is an award that celebrates successful initiatives for conflict prevention, peace-building and post-conflict reconstruction undertaken by local governments and stimulates others to follow suit (UCLG, n.d.). Also, while the role of the national governments is crucial, decentralization and delegation of authority to make change to a more grassroots level may ensure that the context of the reform, as well as local interests, are considered, thus preventing possible failures and lags.

In addition to the role of local governments, service delivery can also be improved to accomplish SDG 16 by countries recognizing that SDG 16 cannot be seen in isolation. SDG16 impacts the likelihood of achieving all other targets across the SDGs and has strong links to the economic, social, and environmental goals of the Agenda. As such, it is useful to look for "accelerators" —SDG 16 targets which will help achieve other targets throughout the Agenda. For example, failing to reduce violence (Target 16.1) impacts negatively on environmental degradation (SDG 15), thwarts entrepreneurship and job creation (SDG 8) and even impacts knowledge-sharing between countries in conflict and others (SDG 4 and SDG 17). When reporting on SDG 16, countries should draw attention to these interlinkages to guide the allocation of resources in areas where they can unleash the "catalytic effects" of SDG 16 across A*genda 2030*.

However, identifying interlinkages between goals and targets requires cooperation and information-sharing between government agencies and ministries, which may not always be a given. One proposal toward progress in this regard, and for improving public service delivery also, is for countries to fully embrace ICT. Technology has become one of the most important factors in determining possibilities in the field of sustainable development. In that regard, E-government needs to be fully supported as was discussed in Chap. 4. E-government has made significant strides across the globe, but developments are still strikingly uneven across regions and countries, especially the most vulnerable, particularly the African countries, the least developed countries, small island developing states, and the landlocked developing countries (UNDESA, 2022).

6.5.4 *Meeting the Financing Requirements*

Like the SDGs' objectives, their financing must also be sustainable if their targets are to be met, especially in developing countries. The OECD (2020) has estimated that the COVID-19 pandemic level of investment, in SDG-related sectors in developing countries, has an annual overall funding shortfall of some US$4.2 trillion. Bridging such a gap is a daunting task, but it is achievable given a global GDP of approximately US$115 trillion, and especially given what achieving the SDGs would mean for unleashing human and economic potential and ensuring planetary safety. As also indicated in the UN's *Secretary-General's Strategy for Financing the 2030 Agenda for Sustainable Development (2018–2021)*, governments, international financial institutions, and private financial markets should direct adequate flows of resources into sustainable investment (UN, 2018). They must also take steps to reduce the flow of resources into unsustainable uses by shifting the structure of incentives and the thrust of legislation and regulation to lower the attractiveness of, and returns from, such investments (UN, 2018).

Undoubtedly, domestic public finance is key, especially to providing public goods and essential services. African governments, for example, would need to find innovative ways to increase the fiscal space, particularly through increased government revenues by implementing fiscal reforms (UNECA, 2019). Similarly, in the Asia-Pacific region, it was found that fiscal policy, through taxation, is a critical element for sustainable development and equality (UN, Asian Development Bank [ADB], and UNDP, 2019. But, in many developing countries, the mobilization of domestic public resources still falls well short of requirements; and external public resources, including ODA, remain essential in many countries (see UN-ITFFD, 2022). It is, therefore, important to make progress towards meeting the ODA commitments of the Addis Ababa Action Agenda (AAAA) (see UNDESA, 2015 for greater details on the AAAA). However, the public sources of funding in all countries, rich and poor alike, clearly still do not suffice to fund the SDGs. Hence, private finance is also an essential component of the financing of *Agenda 2030*.

More specifically, domestic budgets supported by tax reforms (for enhancing the tax base and strengthening tax administration and tax compliance), and including subsidy removals to increase revenue generation for improving services in health, water, education, are fundamental. Countries need to strengthen enabling environments to reduce investment risks and encourage funding for capacity development and institution-building. These include predictable and rational policies and regulations; stronger public institutions and the rule of law; efforts to deepen still embryonic domestic financial systems; and a financial regulatory and supervisory regime that strengthens stability while avoiding the inadvertent deepening of the short-termism of private capital markets (UN, 2018). Governments should also, where appropriate, strengthen the capacity of the domestic private business sector to develop pipelines of sustainable investable projects into which private capital can flow. The successful experiences of other countries will be a tremendous support to these efforts (UN, 2018).

In specifically targeting SDG 16 to fill the financing gap, governments must now consider re-allocating resources, for example, from crisis response to the prevention of violence, while increasing investments in justice and inclusion, and reducing resources lost to corruption and illicit flows. The UNCTAD (2020), for example, has determined that curbing Africa's annual illicit capital flight of US$89 billion could bridge close to one-half of the continent's SDGs financing gap. Improved governance will also increase the efficiency with which resources are spent for all SDGs, while strengthening domestic resource mobilization (DRM). DRM is the process through which countries raise and spend their own funds for public goods and services, such as schools, hospitals, clean water, electricity, and roads, for example, which are all critical to helping people rise out of poverty and to accelerate national economic growth. DRM is the long-term path to sustainable development finance and is therefore also a critical step on the path out of aid dependence. The bulk of DRM is comprised of tax revenues. However, Africa remains the region with the lowest median tax-to-GDP ratios. With 2020 median tax revenue remaining below 13%, the continent has the largest number of economies below what is considered the minimum desirable tax-to-GDP ratio of 15% which is typically associated with accelerated growth and development (see Aslam et al., 2022; Gaspar et al., 2016; UN-ITFFD, 2022).

6.5.5 *Enhancing Political Will and Good Leadership*

Lessons of field experience suggest that the political will deficit in developing countries is related to the lack of good leadership and/or leadership initiative for good governance and sustainable development generally. What is therefore required is the emergence of transformational leadership. By definition, where transformational leadership exists, there will also be political will. Transformational leadership can be seen when leaders and followers make each other advance to a higher level of morality and motivation. Through the strength of their vision and personality, transformational leaders can inspire followers to change expectations, perceptions, and motivations to work toward common goals. In fact, the worst-performing countries, naturally, have been led over the years by dictators, despots, and kleptocrats. Nothing seems to matter more than quality leadership. But much more importantly, quality leadership improves the lives of ordinary citizens.

In this framework, the role of civil society looms large for holding the local political leadership to account on its commitments to peace and security and the other SDGs as well. This will also further promote the necessity to nationalize and localize *Agenda 2030* to create true ownership of the Agenda by all stakeholder groups as envisioned also in the Agenda. Civil society stakeholders can spur government action through persistent advocacy and act as watchdogs holding governments accountable to their commitments. They can advise governments on concrete implementation measures to take, building on their experience on the ground, often working with marginalized communities. CSOs can also directly support implementation through the role they often play in service delivery, including in the area of sexual and reproductive health; and have an important role in supporting data collection efforts, including on marginalized groups; and in the promotion and advocacy for observance of all human rights.

Transformational leadership, as defined here, will recognize and accept the importance of civil society and human rights as key pillars of the good governance and accountability elements of the SDGs as expressed primarily through SDG 16. Furthermore, *Agenda 2030* affirms that "it is guided by the purposes and principles of the Charter of the UN, including full respect for international law" (UN, 2015, Article 10), and is grounded in, amongst others, the Universal Declaration of Human Rights and international human rights treaties. The responsibilities of all countries to respect, protect and promote human rights and fundamental freedoms for all is therefore also fundamental to the implementation of *Agenda 2030*. In that regard also, the International Covenant on Economic, Social and Cultural Rights, as a core UN human rights treaty, is thus a fundamental pillar of *Agenda 2030*.

6.6 Concluding Comments

As this book demonstrates, both the mantra and the reality is that there can be no sustainable development without peace and no peace without sustainable development. SDG 16 is a tool to foster resilience, safeguard development gains, and ultimately lead to a more lasting peace. Sustained peace requires more than an end to poverty and discrimination, it also necessitates a shift towards more inclusive forms of decision-making and stronger accountability mechanisms across public institutions—at all levels of government.

SDG 16 cannot be considered in an isolated context. It touches on cross-cutting issues that require peace and peacebuilding to be also contemplated in connection with the other goals for progress to be made. The call for an integrated approach to all the SDGs therefore reflects the need to connect SDG 16 with the other SDGs through the recognition that, for example, tackling poverty, inequality or injustice is essential to addressing the underlying causes of violence. Societies that provide access to employment, sustainable livelihoods, justice, human rights, basic security and services, and that have some form of political inclusion and respect for the rule of law are far more likely to be peaceful.

Sustainable development cannot take hold in countries where there is conflict. In Africa and Asia, for example, conflict and violent extremism continue to threaten future development and security. This chapter shows that implementation progress on SDG 16 has been uneven. As we move forward, all stakeholders must keep in mind what was so eloquently stated by Doug Frantz, then a Deputy Secretary General of the OECD:

> The SDGs are nothing less than a blueprint for a better world. A roadmap to get from the world we have to the world we want to have. It's a bumpy road but it is a vital journey, and we will all be held to account in 2030 for what we have achieved collectively and individually (OECD, 2017, p. 3).

In that regard, this chapter has also proposed and outlined a set of policy approaches to assist in the attempts to overcome the challenges to purposeful implementation of SDG 16 and the rest of the SDGs, in turn. The importance and significance of SDG 16 cannot be over-emphasized. As also found by Egbende et al. (2023), in a case study of the DRC, SDG 16 had the strongest promoting influence on other goals and was identified as a key priority for that country to attain the SDGs.

References

Ackman, M., Hammond, D., Cooney, C., & Liu, L. (2018). *SDG 16 in the Pacific: Strengthening and legitimizing institutions to achieve sustainable development.* Institute for Economics & Peace.

ACSS. (2022). Conflict remains the dominant driver of Africa's spiraling food crisis. [Infographics]. Retrieved from https://africacenter.org/spotlight/conflict-remains-the-dominant-driver-of-africas-spiraling-food-crisis/

Adesete, A. A., Olanubi, O. E., & Dauda, R. O. (2022). Climate change and food security in selected sub-Saharan African countries. *Environment, Development and Sustainability.* [Advance online publication]. https://doi.org/10.1007/s10668-022-02681-0

Afrobarometer. (n.d.). Round 8 surveys 2019–21. [online data analysis]. https://www.afrobarometer.org/online-data-analysis/

Amnesty International. (2019). *Laws designed to silence: The global crackdown on civil society organizations.* Amnesty International.

Aslam, A., Delepierre, S., Gupta, R., & Rawlings, H. (2022). Revenue mobilization in sub- Saharan Africa during the pandemic. Retrieved from https://www.imf.org/-/media/Files/Publications/covid19-special-notes/en-covid-19-special-series-revenue-mobilization-in-ssa-during-the-covid-19-pandemic.ashx

References

AU. (2015). *Agenda 2063: The Africa we want*. AU.
AU. (2020). *First continental report on the implementation of agenda 2063*. AUDA–NEPAD.
AU. (2022). *Second continental report on the implementation of agenda 2063*. AUDA–NEPAD.
Baptista, D., Farid, M., Fayad, D., Kemoe, L., Lanci, L., Mitra, P., Muehlschlegel, T., Okou, C., Spray, J., Tuitoek, K., & Unsal, F. (2022). *Climate change and chronic food insecurity in sub-Saharan Africa*. IMF.
Berry, D., & English, P. (2011). *The socioeconomic impact of pretrial detention*. Open Society Foundations.
Biersack, A., Jolly, M., & Macintyre, M. (Eds.). (2016). *Gender violence and human rights: Seeking justice in Fiji, Papua New Guinea and Vanuatu*. ANU Press.
Blaustein, J., Chodor, T., & Pino, N. W. (2022). *Unravelling the crime-development nexus*. Rowman & Littlefield.
Brunero, M., Stuart, M. B., Guiryanan, O., Hull, D., & Roberti, A. (2022). *Perceptions of climate change and violent extremism: Listening to local communities in Chad*. United Nations Interregional Crime and Justice Research Institute (UNICRI).
Cappelli, F., Conigliani, C., Consoli, D., Costantini, V., & Paglialunga, E. (2023). Climate change and armed conflicts in Africa: Temporal persistence, non-linear climate impact and geographical spillovers. *Economia Politica, 40*(2), 517–560. https://doi.org/10.1007/s40888-022-00271-x
Craig, C. M., Overbeek, R. W., & Niedbala, E. M. (2021). A global analysis of temperature, terrorist attacks, and fatalities. *Studies in Conflict & Terrorism, 44*(11), 958–970. https://doi.org/10.1080/1057610X.2019.1606992
Diallo, Y., & Tapsoba, R. (2022). Climate shocks and domestic conflicts in Africa. [IMF Working Paper, WP/22/250]. IMF.
Economics Online. (2020). *Development constraints*. Retrieved from https://www.economicsonline.co.uk/Global_economics/Development_constraints.html
Egbende, L., Helldén, D., Mbunga, B., Schedwin, M., Kazenza, B., Viberg, N., Wanyenze, R., Mapatano, M. A., & Alfvén, T. (2023). Interactions between health and the sustainable development goals: The case of the Democratic Republic of Congo. *Sustainability, 15*(2), 1259. https://doi.org/10.3390/su15021259
Espey, J. (2019). The missing ingredient for a better world: Data. *Nature, 571*(7765), 299. https://www.nature.com/magazine-assets/d41586-019-02139-w/d41586-019-02139-w.pdf
Fukuda-Parr, S., Ashwill, M., Chiappa, E., & Messineo, C. (2008). The conflict-development nexus: A survey of armed conflicts in sub-Saharan Africa 1980-2005. *Journal of Peacebuilding & Development, 4*(1), 1–16. https://doi.org/10.1080/15423166.2008.700972482539
GANHRI. (2018). *Space for civil society participation in SDG implementation*. GANHRI.
Gaspar, V., Jamarillo, L., & Wingender, P. (2016). Tax capacity and growth: Is there a tipping point?. [IMF Working Paper No. 16/294]. IMF.
Global Alliance for Reporting Progress on Peaceful, Just, and Inclusive Societies. (2018). *Meeting report*. Retrieved from https://www.sdg16hub.org/node/91
Global Alliance for Reporting Progress on Peaceful, Just and Inclusive Societies. (2019). *Enabling the Implementation of the 2030 Agenda Through SDG 16+: Anchoring Peace, Justice and Inclusion*. Retrieved from https://www.sdg16hub.org
Global Initiative to End All Corporal Punishment of Children. (2018). *Ending legalized violence against children by 2030*. Global Initiative to End All Corporal Punishment of Children.
Guerin, B., McCrae, J., & Shepheard, M. (2018). *Accountability in modern government: What are the issues?* [Discussion Paper]. Institute for Government.
Hope, K. R. (2009). Climate change and poverty in Africa. *International Journal of Sustainable Development & World Ecology, 16*(6), 451–461. https://doi.org/10.1080/13504500903354424
Hope, K. R. (2011a). Climate change in the context of urban development in Africa. In B. Yuen & A. Kumssa (Eds.), *Climate change and sustainable urban development in Africa and Asia* (pp. 37–55). Springer Science+Business Media.
Hope, K. R. (2011b). Investing in capacity development: Towards an implementation framework. *Policy Studies, 32*(1), 59–72. https://doi.org/10.1080/01442872.2010.529273

Hope, K. R. (2019). *Realizing SDG 16 interlinkages: A background report*. [commissioned by the UNDP Oslo Governance Center].
IEP. (2019). *SDG16+ Progress report 2019: A comprehensive global audit of Progress on SDG 16 indicators*. IEP.
IEP. (2021). *Global peace index 2021: Measuring peace in a complex world*. IEP.
IEP. (2022). *Global peace index 2022: Measuring peace in a complex world*. IEP.
IMF. (2016). *Corruption: Costs and mitigating strategies*. IMF.
IMF. (2019). *Regional economic outlook: Sub-Saharan Africa: Recovery amid elevated uncertainty*. IMF.
IMF. (2022). *Regional economic outlook: Sub-Saharan Africa: A new shock and little room to maneuver*. IMF.
Jaiyesimi, R. (2016). The challenge of implementing the sustainable development goals in Africa: The way forward. *African Journal of Reproductive Health [Special Edition on SDGs], 20*(3), 13–18.
Keulder, C. (2021). Africans see growing corruption, poor government response, but fear retaliation if they speak out. [Afrobarometer dispatch no. 488]. Retrieved from https://www.afrobarometer.org/publication/ad488-africans-see-growing-corruption-poor-government-response-fear-retaliation-if-they/
Klinsky, S., & Golub, A. (2016). Justice and sustainability. In H. Heinrichs, P. Martens, G. Michelsen, & A. Wiek (Eds.), *Sustainability science: An introduction* (pp. 161–173). Springer Science+Business Media.
Kukutschka, R. M. B. (2021a). *Global corruption barometer Pacific 2021: Citizens' views and experiences of corruption*. TI.
Kukutschka, R. M. B. (2021b). *Global corruption barometer European Union 2021: Citizens' views and experiences of corruption*. TI.
Kukutschka, R. M. B., & Vrushi, J. (2019). *Global corruption barometer Middle East and North Africa 2019: Citizens' views and experiences of corruption*. TI.
Laberge, M. (2019). *Is Africa measuring up to its goal 16 commitments? The road to HLPF 2019 and beyond*. Retrieved from https://www.sdg16hub.org/system/files/2019-06/SAIIA_SDG16_A4_Brochure_V9_LD.pdf
Lamarche, A. (2023). *Climate-fueled violence and displacement in the Lake Chad Basin: Focus on Chad and Cameroon*. Refugees International.
Lindvall, D. (2021). Democracy and the challenge of climate change. [International IDEA Discussion Paper 3/2021]. IIDEA.
Lucey, A. (2015). Implementing the peace, security and development nexus in Africa. *Strategic Analysis, 39*(5), 500–511. https://doi.org/10.1080/09700161.2015.1069970
Mbaku, J. M. (2022). International law, corruption and the rights of children in Africa. *San Diego International Law Journal, 23*(2), 195–340. https://digital.sandiego.edu/ilj/vol23/iss2/2
Musila, G. M. (2019). *Freedoms under threat: The spread of anti-NGO measures in Africa*. Freedom House.
Mustafayeva, A. (2020). Promoting peace and security through sustainable development goal 16. In F. O. Hampson, A. Özerdem, & J. Kent (Eds.), *Routledge handbook of peace, security and development* (pp. 264–274). Routledge/Taylor and Francis.
Nygård, H. M. (2017). *Voluntary supplemental indicators for goal 16 on inclusive, just and peaceful societies*. Community of Democracies. Retrieved from https://community-democracies.org/app/uploads/2018/06/Framework.-Voluntary-Supplemental-Indicators-SDG16-1-1-1.pdf
OECD. (2017). *Getting governments organized to deliver on the sustainable development goals*. OECD.
OECD. (2020). *Global outlook on financing for sustainable development 2021: A new way to invest for people and planet*. OECD Publishing.
Pathfinders for Peaceful, Just and Inclusive Societies. (2019). *Joint Statement by a Group of Member States in Support of SDG 16+*. Retrieved from https://docs.wixstatic.com/ugd/6c192f_ab0ce8ccc4a744f8baee7ac83767f2e0.pdf
Pearce, O., & Andrijevic, M. (2022). *The Cost to Africa: Drastic Economic Damage from Climate Change*. Retrieved from https://www.christianaid.org.uk/resources/get-involved/cost-africa

References

Pérez, B. F., Márquez, D. I., & Hernández, L. M. (Eds.). (2018). *Rethinking sustainable development in terms of justice*. Cambridge Scholars Publishing.

Sachs, J., Kroll, C., Lafortune, G., Fuller, G., & Woelm, F. (2021). *The decade of action for the sustainable development goals: Sustainable development report 2021*. Cambridge University Press.

Sachs, J., Lafortune, G., Kroll, C., Fuller, G., & Woelm, F. (2022). *From crisis to sustainable development: The SDGs as roadmap to 2030 and beyond: Sustainable development report 2022*. Cambridge University Press.

Schaar, J. (2018). The relationship between climate change and violent conflict. [Working Paper]. Sida.

Schönteich, M. (2014). *Presumption of guilt: The global overuse of pretrial detention*. Open Society Foundations.

SDG 16 Data Initiative. (2019). *2019 Global Report*. Retrieved from https://www.sdg16.org/reports/2019/07/08/the-third-annual-global-report.html

SDG 16 Data Initiative. (2021). *SDG 16 Data Initiative Report 2021: Impact of the Pandemic on Measuring Progress Towards SDG 16: Looking Forward, Tackling Obstacles*. Retrieved from https://www.sdg16.org/reports/

TAI. (2017). How do we define key terms? transparency and accountability glossary. Retrieved from https://www.transparency-initiative.org/blog/1179/tai-definitions/

The White House. (2022). *National Security Strategy*. The White House.

UBDF. (2019). Final report. Retrieved from https://www.sdg16hub.org/system/files/2019-03/2019%20UBDF%20rapporteurs%20final%20report_13%20March%202019.pdf

UCLG. (n.d.). About the UCLG peace prize. Retrieved from https://peaceprize.uclg.org/about/

UN. (2015). *Transforming our world: The 2030 agenda for sustainable development*. UN.

UN. (2017). *Successfully achieving the sustainable development goals: What is to be done?* UN.

UN. (2018). *The Secretary-General's strategy for financing the 2030 agenda for sustainable development (2018–2021)*. UN.

UN. (2019a). *Compilation of the Main messages for the 2019 voluntary National Reviews*. UN.

UN. (2019b). *Special edition: Progress towards the sustainable development goals: Report of the secretary-general*. UN.

UN. (2019c). *Progress on institutional aspects of sustainable development goal 16: Access to information, transparency, participation and accountability*. UN.

UN. (2019d). *Sustainable Development Goal 16: Focus on Public Institutions–World Public Sector Report 2019*. UN.

UN. (2021). *Progress towards the sustainable development goals: Report of the secretary-general: Supplementary information*. UN.

UN. (2022a). *Progress towards the sustainable development goals: Report of the secretary-general*. UN.

UN. (2022b). *Progress towards the sustainable development goals: Report of the secretary-general: Supplementary information*. UN.

UN. (2022c). *The sustainable development goals report 2022*. UN.

UN., ADB., & UNDP. (2019). *Accelerating Progress: An empowered, inclusive and equal Asia and the Pacific: Theme report for the Asia-Pacific forum on sustainable development*. UN.

UN., & World Bank. (2018). *Pathways for peace: Inclusive approaches to preventing violent conflict*. World Bank.

UNCTAD. (2015). *Investing in sustainable development goals: Part 1 – Action plan for private investment in SDGs*. UN.

UNCTAD. (2020). *Economic development in Africa report 2020: Tackling illicit financial flows for sustainable development in Africa*. UN.

UNDESA. (2015). *Addis Ababa Action Agenda of the Third International Conference on Financing for Development*. Retrieved from https://www.un.org/esa/ffd/publications/aaaa-outcome.html

UNDESA. (2018). *Voluntary National Reviews: Synthesis report*. UNDESA.

UNDESA. (2021a). *2021 voluntary National Reviews Synthesis Report*. UNDESA.

UNDESA. (2021b). *World public sector report 2021: National Institutional Arrangements for implementation of the sustainable development goals: A five-year stocktaking*. UNDESA.

UNDESA. (2022). *E-government survey 2022: The future of digital government*. UN.
UNECA. (2019). *Economic report on Africa 2019: Fiscal policy for financing sustainable development in Africa*. UNECA.
UNECOSOC. (2022). *Compilation of Main messages for the 2022 voluntary National Reviews*. UNECOSOC.
UNICEF. (2022). Violent discipline. Retrieved from https://data.unicef.org/topic/child-protection/violence/violent-discipline/
UN-ITFFD. (2022). *Financing for sustainable development report 2022: Report of the interagency task force on financing for development*. UN.
UN News. (2019, 25 January). Climate change recognized as "threat multiplier," UN Security Council Debates its Impact on Peace. https://news.un.org/en/story/2019/01/1031322
UNODC. (2021). *Killings of women and girls by their intimate partner or other family members: Global estimates 2020*. UNODC.
UNSC. (2022). *Global indicator framework for the sustainable development goals and targets of the 2030 agenda for sustainable development*. UN.
Venner, M. (2015). The concept of "capacity" in development assistance: New paradigm or more of the same? *Global Change, Peace & Security, 27*(1), 85–96. https://doi.org/10.1080/14781158.2015.994488
Vrushi, J. (2020). *Global corruption barometer Asia 2020: Citizens' views and experiences of corruption*. TI.
Wakefield, S., & Andersen, L. H. (2020). Pretrial detention and the costs of system overreach for employment and family life. *Sociological Science, 7*(14), 342–366. https://doi.org/10.15195/v7.a14
WHO. (2018). *World health statistics 2018: Monitoring health for the SDGs–sustainable development goals*. WHO.
WHO. (2020). Violence against children. Retrieved from https://www.who.int/news-room/fact-sheets/detail/violence-against-children
WMO. (2022). *State of the climate in Africa 2021*. WMO.
Wodon, Q., Male, C., Nayihouba, A., Onagoruwa, A., Savadogo, A., Yedan, A., Edmeades, J., Kes, A., John, N., Murithi, L., Steinhaus, M., & Petroni, S. (2017). *Economic impacts of child marriage: Global synthesis report*. The World Bank and International Center for Research on Women.
World Bank. (2011). *World development report 2011: Conflict, security, and development*. World Bank.
World Bank. (2022). *Survey on the implementation of the Cape Town global action plan for sustainable development data*. World Bank.

Chapter 7
Reducing Corruption and Bribery in Africa As a Target of the Sustainable Development Goals: Applying Indicators for Assessing Performance

This chapter draws on the data from Chaps. 3 and 4 which assessed the corruption and bribery trends in Africa through the official indicators for achieving Target 16.5 of the SDGs; and recommends other indicators for assessing ethical behavior in African political, administrative, and business leadership and institutions for achieving sustainable development and improved ethical performance toward significant reductions in all manifestations of bribery and corruption on the continent potentially by 2030.

7.1 Introduction

As shown in previous chapters, corruption remains an inescapable problem in Africa with harmful consequences on sustainable development across the continent. Warf (2019, p. 135) has also observed that "corruption is, unfortunately, a pronounced feature on the African political and economic landscape" with "many of the world's most corrupt governments [being] found in Africa." As this book shows, such sweeping corruption is hindering Africa's economic, political, and social development, and it is a major barrier to peace, security, and stability. The scale of corruption in Africa, and throughout most developing countries as well, hinders development performance and escalates poverty, robbing the most vulnerable populations of fair access to crucial public goods and services required to sustain development. Generally, corruption represents an infection on any society. It undermines the core activities of the state and the ability of governments to deliver effective policies and services that promote equitable sustainable development and growth (see, also, Medas, 2022). Also, Jay S. Albanese, in his address upon receipt of the Freda Adler Distinguished International Scholar Award at the 2021 meeting of the American Society of Criminology (ASC), correctly reminded us that "it is clear from [the] empirical research that the world's largest problems, as captured by the SDGs, have been either created or worsened by corruption" (Albanese, 2022, pp. 104–105).

Consequently, there is need to tackle corruption for meeting the SDGs. In that respect, Target 16.5 of the SDGs is to *Substantially reduce corruption and bribery in all their forms*. This target does not require that corruption be totally stamped out. That is not possible anywhere in the world for the same human nature reasons that we cannot stamp out people lying. However, the requirement is for there to be a significant reduction of corruption in those countries (such as found in Africa) with historically high levels of corruption and bribery. In fact, as this book has proclaimed and demonstrated, controlling corruption is a prerequisite for meeting the targets of the 2030 *Agenda*.

To measure and monitor progress toward achieving this target, two indicators have been approved: (1) Indicator 16.5.1—the proportion of persons who had at least one contact with a public official and who paid a bribe to a public official, or were asked for a bribe by those public officials, during the previous 12 months; and (2) Indicator 16.5.2—the proportion of businesses that had at least one contact with a public official and that paid a bribe to a public official, or were asked for a bribe by those public officials during the previous 12 months (UN, 2017; UNSC, 2022a). Undoubtedly, recognizing and then including bribery and corruption among the SDGs are laudable and necessary as corruption, including bribery, has become one of the most pressing challenges in developing countries, especially those in Africa.

This chapter assesses the trends in the region through the official indicators for achieving Target 16.5 of the SDGs; and recommends other indicators for assessing ethical behavior in African political, administrative, and business leadership and institutions for achieving sustainable development and improved ethical performance toward significant reductions in all manifestations of bribery and corruption on the continent by 2030. However, before proceeding, two things need to be noted in the context of this chapter's focus as just outlined.

First, it is recognized and fully understood that Target 16.4 of the SDGs also makes reference to a channel of corruption to the extent that it is partially concerned with IFFs and stolen assets. Target 16.4 states that: *By 2030, significantly reduce illicit financial and arms flows, strengthen the recovery and return of stolen assets and combat all forms of organized crime* (UN, 2017; UNSC, 2022a). However, in the view of this book's author, the relevant Indicator 16.4.1—which is: Total value of inward and outward illicit financial flows (in current US dollars)—does not require any further consideration of additional or alternative indicators as it directly measures the values of IFFs moving in and out of a country. It is therefore not of relevance to this chapter. The UNCTAD is the designated official focal point for Indicator 16.4.1, and it partners with the UNODC as the indicator's custodian agencies (UNSC, 2022b, 2022c).

Second, to facilitate the application of the SDGs indicators, the Inter-Agency and Expert Group on SDGs (IAEG-SDGs) created an indicator classification system resulting in three tiers of indicators based on the level of methodological development and the availability of data at a global level (UNSC, 2022b). The three tiers are the following: Tier 1—the indicator is conceptually clear, has an internationally established methodology and standards are available, and data are regularly produced by countries for at least 50% of countries and of the population in every region where the indicator is relevant; Tier 2—the indicator is conceptually clear, has an internationally established methodology and standards are available, but data are not regularly produced by countries; and Tier 3—the indicator has no internationally established methodology or standards available, but these are being (or will be) developed or tested (UNSC, 2022b). Indicator 16.5.1 is classified as Tier 2 while Indicator 16.5.2 is classified as Tier 1 (UNSC, 2022b).

7.2 Assessing Corruption and Bribery Reduction in Africa As a Target of the SDGs

Measuring progress towards the targets of the SDGs and the overall implementation of *Agenda 2030* requires not only appropriate indicators but also credible statistical data and estimates produced by credible institutions. These data and estimates are generally derived from national data compiled—through various statistical methods—by NSOs, international agencies, NGOs (national and international), think tanks, and research outfits according to their respective mandates and specialized expertise. However, as discussed in Chap. 6, and noted by UN (2022, p. 3), "while considerable progress has been made in building stronger data and statistical systems for Sustainable Development Goal monitoring, significant data gaps still exist." These gaps are more pronounced with respect to geographical coverage, timeliness of compilation and distribution, and disaggregation levels of the global indicators.

7.2.1 Applying the Official Bribery/Corruption Indicators

As previously indicated, and per UN (2017) and UNSC (2022a), the official global-level indicators that have been approved to monitor and measure progress toward Target 16.5 are the following:

- Indicator 16.5.1—Proportion of persons who had at least one contact with a public official and who paid a bribe to a public official, or were asked for a bribe by those public officials, during the previous 12 months.
- Indicator 16.5.2—Proportion of businesses that had at least one contact with a public official and that paid a bribe to a public official, or were asked for a bribe by those public officials during the previous 12 months.

The data for each of these two indicators, with respect to Africa, seem to be sufficiently available. Despite being classified as Tier 2, on a global basis, there is now a growing amount of data on African nations pertaining to Indicator 16.5.1 as bribery has become one form of corruption that is being frequently captured by country research surveys that are conducted by both national and international organizations. These two global-level indicators (16.5.1 and 16.5.2) were selected as the basis for measuring and monitoring progress toward achieving Target 16.5, irrespective of the anti-corruption/bribery policies that each nation-state is implementing. For Indicator 16.5.1, the most widely consulted global source currently are the Global/Regional Corruption Barometers published by TI, while for Indicator 16.5.2 the source is the Enterprise Surveys conducted and published by the World Bank.

In applying the two indicators, using the available data, we can see from Chaps. 3 and 6 some of the resulting statistics that are also being used for monitoring performance vis-à-vis Target 16.5 and we do not need to duplicate that discussion here save to say that the Africa region is one of the worst performers with respect to the bribery indicators. In terms of Indicator 16.5.1, the bribery rate for the public sector stood at 28% by 2021. However, there is also recent research and monitoring reviews by the AU that found that "the proportion of persons [in Africa] who reported to have paid a bribe to a public official at least once or were asked for a bribe in the preceding 12 months increased from 9.5% in 2013 to 31.4% in 2021" (AU, 2022, p. 36). For Indicator 16.5.2, the bribery rate average for businesses was 22% compared to the global average of 16% during the period 2010–20 (World Bank, n.d.).

However, the two agreed and approved indicators for Target 16.5 do not capture other forms of systemic corruption—as opposed to just the transactional bribery type—that also have a significant negative bearing on sustainable development. In that regard, each country needs to apply other indicators depending on what types of corruption are prevalent within its borders. Despite TI and the World Bank currently producing the official indicators, as discussed above, the UNODC and the UNDP have developed a manual—mainly targeted at anti-corruption agencies, national statistical bodies, relevant national institutions, research centers, NGOs, and private sector entities—that offers specific guidance and support to establish methodological and operational guidelines for developing and implementing sample data collection surveys, both among the population and businesses, to measure the prevalence of bribery at a national level and to collect other relevant information on corruption (see UNODC, UNDP, and UNODC-INEGI Center of Excellence in Statistical Information on Government, Crime, Victimization and Justice, 2018). "A particular goal of [the] manual is to support countries in their measurement of their progress towards achieving Sustainable Development Goal 16, Target 5" (UNODC, UNDP, and UNODC-INEGI Center of Excellence in Statistical Information on Government, Crime, Victimization and Justice, 2018, p. 11).

7.2.2 Proposed Other Indicators

Notwithstanding the existing official indicators and efforts to create others, below are outlined five other approaches to indicators—as also shown in a summary table list (Table 7.1)—that this work proposes that African nations can *immediately* apply for monitoring performance and compiling relevant progress reports with respect to meeting Target 16.5. These are supplemental indicators and are based on already available, reliable, and credible databases that produce the appropriate indicators and, as also observed by Laberge (2019), they can help prevent Target 16.5 from dropping off the national agenda. In addition, as we have also been reminded by Nygård (2017), *Agenda 2030* encourages member states to complement the global indicators by developing indicators at regional and national levels. These proposed

Table 7.1 Summary list of proposed other indicators for assessing progress in reducing corruption and bribery in Africa and their sources

Proposed other indicators	Source
Political corruption index • *Executive corruption index* • *Public sector corruption index* • *Judicial corruption decision* • *Legislature corruption activities* • *Regime corruption index*	V-Dem Institute indicators (Varieties of Democracy Institute, University of Gothenburg)
Security and rule of law • *Anti-corruption* • *Absence of corruption in state institutions* • *Absence of corruption in the public sector* • *Absence of corruption in the private sector* • *Anti-corruption mechanisms* • *Public procurement procedures*	Ibrahim Index of African governance (Mo Ibrahim Foundation)
The index of public integrity • *Administrative transparency* • *Online services* • *Budget transparency* • *Judicial independence* • *E-citizenship* • *Freedom of the press*	European Research Center for Anti-Corruption and State-Building (Hertie School of Governance)
The corruption risk forecast	European Research Center for Anti-Corruption and State-Building (Hertie School of Governance) and the Anti-Corruption & Governance Center, the Center for International Private Enterprise (an Institute of the National Endowment for Democracy and an affiliate of the United States Chamber of Commerce)
Institutions, leadership, and governance • *Corruption* • *Central government performance* • *Handling fighting corruption*	Afrobarometer (pan-African, non-partisan survey research network)

Source: Author compilation

indicators have to be compiled or generated and therefore cannot be directly or automatically constructed by countries. Although, as indicated above, there are other ongoing initiatives to produce harmonized statistics on governance issues, including corruption, they all lack the comprehensive coverage and availability across all African nations as also reported by Razafindrakoto and Roubaud (2018), for example.

Moreover, it must be noted here that, in this necessary pursuit of other appropriate indicators to monitor progress toward the reduction of corruption and bribery in Africa, it is also recognized that such indicators must also be primarily non-perception based. Despite the fact, and as also stated in this book, that there is considerable correlation between actual reported corruption and citizen and expert perceptions of corruption (see, also, Bello y Villarino, 2021; Charron, 2016), perception-based corruption indicators have been argued to have limitations (see, for example, Gilman, 2018; Németh et al., 2019). Taking all of that into consideration, we therefore also understand the need to have a much more diverse set of indicators that are both objective and actionable (see, also, Mungiu-Pippidi & Fazekas, 2020).

The five indicator approaches suggested below offer comprehensive, objective, and actionable coverage. Another important benefit feature provided by the use of the other indicators proposed here is that it eliminates the concern that the SDGs indicators on corruption are overly focused on the easiest aspect of corruption to be measured—bribery—instead of addressing corruption in all its forms (see, also, Andersson, 2017; Mugellini & Villeneuve, 2019; Mugellini et al., 2021) as required for Target 16.5. This bias is also reflected in the fact that bribery is much more prevalent in developing countries as opposed to the grand corruption found in developed nations. Another benefit for African countries, and all countries for that matter, is that the proposed indicators are already accessible, whereas official data require costly and lengthy collection and compilation processes.

These five further sets of indicators being recommended, and described here, are derived from some of the governance indicators developed and/or held as custodians by: (1) the Varieties of Democracy (V-Dem) Institute at the University of Gothenburg, Sweden; (2) the Mo Ibrahim Foundation (an African foundation) headquartered in London, United Kingdom (UK); (3) the European Research Center for Anti-Corruption and State-Building (ERCAS) at the Hertie School of Governance, Berlin, Germany; (4) the ERCAS and the Anti-Corruption & Governance Center (ACGC) at the Center for International Private Enterprise (CIPE), the latter is one of the four core institutes of the National Endowment for Democracy—and also an affiliate of the US Chamber of Commerce—that works to support democracy and strengthen the private sector; and (5) Afrobarometer, which has its headquarters in Ghana, is a non-profit, pan-African, non-partisan survey research network that conducts public surveys on democracy, governance, the economy, and society.

These recommended sets of indicators allow for a much deeper dive into a broader set of key corruption components for judging progress in reducing overall bribery and corruption. Moreover, they further provide for having a much more quantitative or evidence-based set of indicators as also suggested as necessary by the World Bank (2020). Indeed, in that regard, we likewise agree with the World Bank (2020, p. 347) that "sustaining the momentum for corruption mitigating reforms is [challenging] but it could be aided by having better ways to measure their impact." Furthermore, having additional and much more visible and relevant indicators supports and suggests the use of better data. Good or better data enable governments to understand the impact of policies and improve service delivery and sustainable development performance. Good data are key ingredients for sustainable development. In fact, without strong data to draw on, much of the potential for data to improve outcomes will not be realized (World Bank, 2021).

7.2.2.1 V-Dem Institute Indicators

The V-Dem Institute has one of the larger (and freely available) social science databases with world-wide coverage of indicators on democracy and political systems. This data collection, which originated in 2011 at the Kellogg Institute (KIIS) at Notre Dame University, has been centralized on an international basis at the V-Dem Institute since mid-2014 (KIIS, 2022). Among the V-Dem indicators that would be useful to African nations in measuring corruption is the Political Corruption Index (PCI) and its sub-components which include: (1) the executive corruption index; (2) the public sector (bureaucratic) corruption index; (3) judicial corruption decision; and (4) legislature corrupt activities (Olin, 2017), as well as the regime corruption index.

The PCI, with its sub-components, includes measures of corruption that envelop different areas and levels of the polity realm, with a distinction between executive, legislative and judicial corruption. The PCI is derived through a calculation of the mean of the indices of public sector corruption and executive corruption; and the indicators for legislative and judicial corruption. In other words, each of these four spheres of government are given equal weight in the derived index (McMann et al., 2016). The PCI, therefore, indicates how prevalent political corruption is, linking its sub-components to corruption in the public sector, and the executive, legislative, and judicial branches.

The executive corruption index indicates how commonly members of the executive branch accept bribes, kickbacks, or other material inducements in exchange for granting favors, and how frequently they steal, embezzle, or misappropriate public monies or other government resources for their own, or family or other use (Olin, 2017).

The public sector corruption index captures the degree to which government employees take bribes, kickbacks, or other material inducements, in exchange for granting favous, and how frequently they steal, embezzle, or misappropriate public monies or other government resources for their own, or family or other use (Olin, 2017).

Judicial corruption decision specifies the frequency with which the judiciary accepts bribes or undocumented extra payments from individuals or businesses in exchange for expediting or delaying processes or to provide favorable outcomes from judicial processes (Olin, 2017).

Legislature corrupt activities shows whether members of the legislature misuse their roles and activities for material benefits. This includes, for instance, soliciting and taking bribes, assisting in the steering of government procurement awards to businesses owned by legislators, doing favors for firms in exchange for employment opportunities upon departing the legislature, or pilfering national resources or campaign funds for personal or other uses (Olin, 2017).

The regime corruption index indicates to what extent do political actors use political office for private or political gain? The distinction here is that in systems of neopatrimonial rule (as found still in some African nations), politicians use their offices for private and/or political gain. This index relates closely to V-Dem's political corruption index, but it is focused more on a specific set of actors—those who occupy political offices—and a more specific set of corrupt acts that relate more closely to the conceptualization of corruption in the literature on neopatrimonial rule (see Coppedge et al., 2022).

7.2.2.2 The Ibrahim Index of African Governance Indicators

The Ibrahim Index of African Governance (IIAG), as the name implies, is an index tool that is produced by the MIF. It was first published in 2007 and constitutes the most comprehensive dataset measuring African governance, providing scores and trends for African countries on a whole spectrum of thematic governance dimensions (MIF, 2020a). It is also freely available online, and the Founder and Chair of the MIF board regards it as "the most accurate picture of what is going on in Africa, based on data, not personal views or political bias" (Ibrahim, n.d.). The IIAG constructs a set of indicators in four categories or components: (1) Security and Rule of Law; (2) Participation, Rights, and Inclusion; (3) Foundations for Economic Opportunity; and (4) Human Development. According to the MIF (2020a), each of these categories contains sub-category levels of the IIAG framework and providing specific scores and trends of various indicators on the thematic and overarching dimensions of governance.

Among the relevant IIAG indicators that African countries can use in relationship to monitoring progress in meeting Target 16.5 are: (1) Absence of corruption in state institutions; (2) Absence of corruption in the public sector; (3) Absence of corruption in the private sector; (4) Anti-corruption mechanisms; and (5) Public procurement procedures. All these indicators fall under the sub-category "Anti-Corruption" which, in turn, falls under the category of Security and Rule of Law (see MIF, 2020a). It is interesting to note here that the MIF data shows that over the ten-year period 2010–19, "Anti-Corruption" still constitutes sub-Saharan Africa's lowest scoring IIAG sub-category just ahead of "Accountability and Transparency" with average annual scores of 38.3 and 38.6, respectively, in a scale of 0–100 (see MIF, 2020b). However, according to the MIF (2020a), there has been an upward movement in anti-corruption scores both over the past ten-year and five-year periods, with the strides of improvement even quickening within the last five years.

As defined by the MIF (2020c), the *absence of corruption in state institutions* indicator shows how commonly members of the executive, and/or their agents, engage in the granting of favors in exchange for bribes or other rewards, and how frequently they embezzle, steal, or misappropriate national finances for personal or other use; whether members of the legislature abuse their position for financial gain; and how frequently individuals or business firms make informal payments or engage in bribery to accelerate or impede government processes or to derive a favorable decision from the judiciary.

The absence of corruption in the public sector indicator is focused on capturing the extent to which public sector employees accept bribes, kickbacks, or other rewards to grant favors, and how frequently do they embezzle, steal, divert or misappropriate public monies or other national resources for personal or other use; and the prevalence of the illegal transfer of public resources to private actors. It gauges how common corruption is among government officials including the police and military personnel (MIF, 2020c).

The MIF (2020c) definition of the *absence of corruption in the private sector* indicator states that it focuses on the pervasiveness of informal payments or bribes by business firms and the risk that individuals and/or companies will face bribery or other corrupt practices to undertake business, including the winning of sizable contracts to being allowed permits to import and/or export products or secure general documents.

The *anti-corruption mechanisms* indicator, as defined by the MIF (2020c), basically determines the degree to which a government successfully develops and implements policies to control corruption, whether appropriate institutional arrangements are in place to implement anti-corruption strategies and if there is successful engagement in competent investigations and prosecutions of corruption.

The indicator for *public procurement procedures*, as defined by the MIF (2020c), captures both the extent to which competitive bidding in procurement exists and gauges the policies for and extent of exclusion of incriminated companies from procurement.

7.2.2.3 The ERCAS Index of Public Integrity

The Index of Public Integrity (IPI) was created by the ERCAS in 2017 (ERCAS, n.d.-a). It represents one of a new generation of corruption indicators that allow for understanding of where a country stands on control of corruption. It is a composite index that uses six fact-based indicators that measure the balance between opportunities for corruption versus constraints on corruption. The original components for opportunities were the extent of administrative discretion, the level of trade openness, and the degree of budget transparency while for constraints it was the degree of judicial independence, the endowment of citizens with electronic means (e-citizenship), and the degree of freedom of the press (see Mungiu-Pippidi &

Dadašov, 2016). Beginning with the 2021 edition, the extent of administrative discretion and the level of trade openness have been replaced by administrative transparency and online services, due to unavailable alternative data in the original components as data for those components were no longer available from their original source (ERCAS, n.d.-b). The values for the IPI have been normalized to range between 1 (less control of corruption) and 10 (more control of corruption) and it correlates well with a variety of corruption measures including the World Bank's and Transparency International's measures of control of corruption and perception of corruption, respectively.

Administrative transparency pertains to the public availability of information such as the existence of a centralized public procurement portal where both tenders and contract awards are posted. It consists of the standardized sum of individual scores for four items in the de facto (real) index of transparency: public procurement, land cadaster, register of commerce, and the Auditor General's annual report (ERCAS, n.d.-b; Mungiu-Pippidi, 2022a).

The online services component is derived from the OSI of the EGDI of the UN. The OSI assesses access to information on each country's national website in the native language, including the national portal, e-services portal and e-participation portal, as well as the websites of the related ministries of education, labor, social services, health, finance and environment, as applicable (ERCAS, n.d.-b).

Budget transparency covers transparency of the executive's budget proposals. It is based on the simple mean value of the scores resulting from 14 specific questions from the Open Budget Survey (OBS) of the International Budget Partnership (IBP) (see Mungiu-Pippidi, 2022a; Mungiu-Pippidi & Dadašov, 2016). The IBP is a global partnership of budget analysts, community organizers, and advocates working to advance public budget systems that work for people, not special interests (IBP, n.d.). The OBS is part of the IBP's Open Budget Initiative (OBI), a global research and advocacy program to promote public access to budget information and the adoption of inclusive and accountable budget systems. The OBS seeks to help civil society partners advocate for improvements in budget transparency, participation, and accountability. Ministries of Finance ministries development practitioners around the world also use the survey to identify baselines and trends in country practices and to implement reforms in line with identified gaps and recommendations (IBP, n.d.).

Judicial independence refers to what extent a country's judiciary is independent from influences of members of government, citizens, or firms. This indicator is derived from the Executive Opinion Surveys (EOSs) of the global competitiveness data assembled by the World Economic Forum (WEF) (Mungiu-Pippidi & Dadašov, 2016; ERCAS, n.d.-b).

E-citizenship captures the endowment of citizens to use online tools and social media and thereby exercise social accountability. It is based on the simple mean of standardized values of fixed broadband subscriptions (% population); Internet users (% population); and Facebook users (% population) (Mungiu-Pippidi & Dadašov, 2016; ERCAS, n.d.-b).

The freedom of the press component measures the degree of media independence thereby capturing the national legal, political, and economic environment in which print, broadcast, and Internet-based media operate (Mungiu-Pippidi & Dadašov, 2016). The score is currently derived from the World Press Freedom Index (WPFI) compiled by Reporters Without Borders (RWB) also known as Reporters Sans Frontières (RSF). Prior to 2019, the source used was the Freedom of the Press Report from Freedom House (ERCAS, n.d.-b).

7.2.2.4 The ERCAS and CIPE Corruption Risk Forecast

The Corruption Risk Forecast (CRF) was developed through a collaboration of the ERCAS with the ACGC of the CIPE in 2020 (ERCAS, n.d.-a). It yields forecasting of trends (stationary, improving, and declining) at a country level and therefore provides insight about future corruption risks, allowing for government officials, development institutions, activists, and international donors to target those areas where interventions can have the greatest impact (see Mungiu-Pippidi, n.d., 2022b).

The CRF draws from data on control of corruption, including five components from the IPI: administrative transparency, budget transparency, judicial independence, freedom of the press, and e-citizenship. It is based on the "aggregated, fact-based indicators of the IPI, which models corruption risk as an interaction between enablers and disablers of corruption and traces these indicators as far back as they go without missing values for a core group" of more than 120 countries (Mungiu-Pippidi, 2022b, p. 1; see, also, Hertie School, 2022). It therefore can be regarded as a complement to the IPI which offers only a snapshot in one moment in time.

7.2.2.5 Afrobarometer Survey Data on Corruption

Afrobarometer advertises itself as the world's leading source of high-quality data on what Africans are thinking and, to that end, it provides reliable, timely data on the views of ordinary Africans to inform development and policy decision making (Afrobarometer, n.d.-a, n.d.-b). Its goals are to: (1) Produce high-quality survey data and analysis on African attitudes, experiences, and aspirations; (2) Widely disseminate findings to key stakeholders, including policy actors and advocates, researchers, and media, as well as ordinary African citizens; and (3) Build capacity for survey research, analysis, and communication on the continent (Afrobarometer, n.d.-a). Its data are freely available online.

The data it produces of relevance here are categorized under Institutions, Leadership, and Governance with two related sub-categories of "Corruption" and "Central Government Performance" (see Afrobarometer, n.d.-c). Among the data indicators that can be accessed by African nations are (1) Perceptions of corruption in various public institutions; (2) Payments of bribes for various services in various public institutions; (3) Government effectiveness in combating corruption; (4) Public trust in anti-corruption agencies; and (5) Ordinary people being able to report corruption without fear.

Afrobarometer also partners with TI in the latter's production and publication of the Global Corruption Barometer (GCB)-Africa which presents the largest and most detailed set of public opinion data on citizens' views on corruption and direct experiences of bribery in Africa (Pring & Vrushi, 2019). The GCB-Africa is based on fieldwork conducted in more than 30 countries by Afrobarometer.

7.3 Concluding Remarks

This chapter has pinpointed the use and performance of the official indicators for Target 16.5 and recommended other indicators for assessing ethical behavior in African political, administrative, and business leadership for achieving sustainable development and improved ethics performance toward substantially reducing all forms of corruption and bribery on the continent by 2030.

As illustrated, sustainable development will be elusive where corruption and bribery are prevalent. Indeed, corruption results in more sand than grease in the wheels. Therefore, where corruption is persistent, sustainable development is impeded and the development imperative therefore makes the case that addressing corruption is essential (UNDP, 2017; World Bank, 2019). As also noted by Trapnell et al. (2017, p. 2), "corruption affects all SDG-related sectors, undermining development outcomes and severely compromising efforts to achieve health, education, gender equality, climate action, water and sanitation and other goals."

Consequently, prioritizing corruption reduction—including from money laundering, bribery, and other illegal activities—is a necessary requirement for achieving good governance, building effective and inclusive institutions as required by SDG 16, and funding the achievement of the SDGs (see, also, Akenroye et al., 2018; Cardamone, 2019; Ericson, 2019; UN, 2019). In fact, the Sustainable Development Goals Centre for Africa (SDGCA) had estimated the pre-COVID-19 annual financing gap for all the SDGs in Africa to be between US$500 billion and US$1.2 trillion, and that it could be easily met by the continent substantially reducing corruption and bribery (SDGCA, 2019). However, due to the COVID-19 pandemic, the resultant slowdown of domestic economic performance has certainly led to revenue shortfalls, and the financing gap for the SDGs in Africa has therefore been widened.

This book has also shown that the facilitators of corruption in Africa now include professional money launderers (PMLs) and enablers of economic crime (see, also, Duri, 2020; Financial Action Task Force [FATF], 2018; Windridge, 2022). Therefore, if the SDGs are to be a vehicle for poverty eradication in Africa, then the continent needs to do more for itself (Nhamo, 2017), including engaging a robust anti-corruption policy framework, as advocated by Hope (2017a, 2017b), for example, and creating new partnerships to yield the data needed for SDG 16 reporting in order to facilitate the process toward realizing solid performances in meeting Target 16.5 (Laberge, 2019).

Finally, we must also acknowledge here that despite any rosy forecasting on economic recovery, the COVID-19 pandemic has definitively posed a major challenge to progress in achieving the SDGs in Africa and elsewhere (see, for example, AfDB, 2020; OECD, 2020; SDGCA, 2020; UN, 2020; UNECA, 2020). Due to this pandemic, an unprecedented health, economic, and social crisis remains a threat to life expectancy and with negative impacts on livelihoods also. Consequently, pursuing Target 16.5 may become less of a priority and many corruption prevention and enforcement mechanisms may be further suspended due to health emergency scenarios as, among other factors, new disease cases and fatality rates can potentially emerge; health and social safety net systems may continue to get overburdened; employment and income-generating opportunities may continue to decline resulting in increased poverty rates; and the already constrained budgets and further declining resources of the various African nations may be re-purposed to protect lives and economies. However, as a result of increased procurement, including for vaccines and medicines in the near future, and other spending by governments arising from the need to ameliorate some ongoing and future residual impacts of the COVID-19 and other emerging infectious diseases, African governments must also take the necessary steps, including measures for strong institutional and governance processes, to ensure future non-corrupt use of such expenditures as well as for any health-related external financial assistance, debt forgiveness, or borrowing.

We have seen, from experience for example, that despite Africa escaping the worst health impacts of the COVID-19 pandemic, the disease presented another opportunity for corruption in the region. Aikins (2022), for instance, has compiled a list of some of the COVID-19- related corruption that has occurred across the continent. It includes Cameroon, where an estimated US$333 million which was meant to help with the pandemic, was misappropriated in 2020. In Kenya, some US$400–$500 million that was meant to procure medical equipment was embezzled through the Kenya Medical Supplies Authority (KEMSA) (see, also, Ochieng-Springer & Odhiambo, 2022). In Malawi, there were issues pertaining to government officials colluding with the private sector, through procurement irregularities, to misappropriate US$1.3 million of funds intended to fight COVID-19. In Nigeria, there was misuse of funds, by officials in the Federal Ministry of Health, in the purchase of face masks. In Uganda, four top government officials were arrested and charged for overpricing COVID-19 food relief items leading to a loss of approximately US$528,000. In Zimbabwe, the Minister of Health was fired for illegally awarding a contract and inflating the cost of medical equipment.

Consequently, and consistent with the recommendations in this book, there is an obvious imperative for African countries to establish anti-corruption, transparency, and accountability (ACTA) structures and mechanisms as sustained efforts to reduce corruption and improve transparency and accountability in their health systems and ensure that all health financing and resources are used for their intended purposes. A good practice in this regard can be gleaned from the approach used to prevent health sector corruption by the Global Fund to Fight AIDS, Tuberculosis and Malaria and other international organizations, such as the UNDP, WHO, and the World Bank, as outlined and assessed by Chang et al. (2021) and Koller et al. (2020), for instance. That approach to ACTA must include, among other things, frameworks that address risk management as well as ethics and integrity.

References

AfDB. (2020). *African economic outlook 2020–Supplement: Amid COVID-19*. AfDB.
Afrobarometer. (n.d.-a). About. Retrieved from https://www.afrobarometer.org/about/
Afrobarometer. (n.d.-b). What we do. Retrieved from https://www.afrobarometer.org/about/what-we-do/
Afrobarometer. (n.d.-c). Institutions, leadership, and governance. Retrieved from https://www.afrobarometer.org/topics/institutions-leadership-governance/
Aikins, E. R. (2022, May 19). Corruption in Africa deepens the wounds of COVID-19. *ISS Today*. Retrieved from https://issafrica.org/iss-today/corruption-in-africa-deepens-the-wounds-of-covid-19
Akenroye, T. O., Nygård, H. M., & Eyo, A. (2018). Towards implementation of sustainable development goals (SDGs) in developing nations: A useful funding framework. *International Area Studies Review, 21*(1), 3–8. https://doi.org/10.1177/2F2233865917743357
Albanese, J. S. (2022). Why corruption is the largest problem in the world. *International Criminology, 2*(2), 103–110. https://doi.org/10.1007/s43576-022-00060-3
Andersson, S. (2017). Beyond unidimensional measurement of corruption. *Public Integrity, 19*(1), 58–76. https://doi.org/10.1080/10999922.2016.1200408
AU. (2022). *Second continental report on the implementation of agenda 2063*. AUDA–NEPAD.
Bello y Villarino, J.-M. (2021). Measuring corruption: A critical analysis of the existing datasets and their suitability for diachronic transnational research. *Social Indicators Research, 157*(2), 709–747. https://doi.org/10.1007/s11205-021-02657-z
Cardamone, T. (2019, July 9). Need funds for the SDGs? Tackle trade fraud. [GFI blog]. https://gfintegrity.org/need-funds-forthe-sdgs-tackle-trade-fraud/
Chang, Z., Rusu, V., & Kohler, J. C. (2021). The Global Fund: Why anti-corruption, transparency and accountability matter. *Globalization and Health, 17*(108), 1–11. https://doi.org/10.1186/s12992-021-00753-w
Charron, N. (2016). Do corruption measures have a perception problem? Assessing the relationship between experiences and perceptions of corruption among citizens and experts. *European Political Science Review, 8*(1), 147–171. https://doi.org/10.1017/S1755773914000447
Coppedge, M., Gerring, J., Knutsen, C. H., Lindberg, S. I., Teorell, J., Altman, D., Bernhard, M., Cornell, A., Fish, M. S., Gastaldi, L., Gjerløw, H., Glynn, A., Grahn, S., Hicken, A., Kinzelbach, K., Marquardt, K. L., McMann, K., Mechkova, V., Paxton, P., Pemstein, D., … Ziblatt, D. (2022). *V-Dem codebook v12*. [V-Dem Project]. Retrieved from https://www.v-dem.net/static/website/img/refs/codebookv12.pdf
Duri, J. (2020). *Professional enablers of economic crime during crises*. Retrieved from https://www.u4.no/publications/professional-enablers-of-economic-crime-during-crises.pdf
ERCAS. (n.d.-a). A new generation of corruption indicators. Retrieved from https://corruptionrisk.org/about/
ERCAS. (n.d.-b). Index of public integrity methodology. Retrieved from https://corruptionrisk.org/ipi-methodology/
Ericson, S. (2019, July 8). Illicit financial flows inhibit development. *BORGEN Magazine*. https://www.borgenmagazine.com/illicit-financial-flows-inhibit-development/
FATF. (2018). *Professional money laundering*. FATF.
Gilman, S. C. (2018). To understand and to misunderstand how corruption is measured: Academic research and the corruption perception index. *Public Integrity, 20*(sup1), S74–S88. https://doi.org/10.1080/10999922.2018.1472974
Hertie School. (2022, May 25). Alina Mungiu-Pippidi and co-researchers develop in-depth corruption index. [News and Events]. Retrieved from https://www.hertie-school.org/en/news/allcontent/detail/content/alina-mungiu-pippidi-develops-in-depth-indexcomparing-corruption-in-120-countries-over-12-years
Hope, K. R. (2017a). *Corruption and governance in Africa: Swaziland [Eswatini], Kenya, Nigeria*. Palgrave Macmillan/Springer Nature.

References

Hope, K. R. (2017b). Fighting corruption in developing countries: Some aspects of policy from lessons from the field. *Journal of Public Affairs, 17*(4), e1683. https://doi.org/10.1002/pa.1683

IBP. (n.d.). About us. Retrieved from https://internationalbudget.org/about-us/

Ibrahim, M. (n.d.). Statement. Retrieved from https://mo.ibrahim.foundation/iiag

KIIS. (2022). Varieties of democracy project. Retrieved from https://kellogg.nd.edu/research/major-research-initiatives/varietiesdemocracy-Project

Koller, T., Clarke, D., & Vian, T. (2020). Promoting anti-corruption, transparency and accountability to achieve universal health coverage. *Global Health Action, 13*(sup1), 1700660. https://doi.org/10.1080/16549716.2019.1700660

Laberge, M. (2019). *Is Africa Measuring up to its Goal 16 Commitments? The Road to HLPF 2019 and Beyond*. Retrieved from https://www.sdg16hub.org/system/files/2019-06/SAIIA_SDG16_A4_Brochure_V9_LD.pdf

McMann, K., Pemstein, D., Seim, B., Teorell, J., & Lindberg, S. I. (2016). Strategies of validation: Assessing the varieties of democracy corruption data. [Working Paper Series]. Varieties of Democracy Institute, University of Gothenburg.

Medas, P. (2022). The macro-fiscal benefits of eliminating corruption in government. In M. Newiak, A. Segura-Ubiergo, & A. A. Wane (Eds.), *Good governance in sub-Saharan Africa: Opportunities and lessons* (pp. 11–26). IMF.

MIF. (2020a). *2020 Ibrahim index of African governance: Index report*. MIF.

MIF. (2020b). Explore the data. Retrieved from http://iiag.online/downloads.html

MIF. (2020c). IIAG metadata. Retrieved from http://iiag.online/downloads.html

Mugellini, G., & Villeneuve, J. P. (2019). Monitoring the risk of corruption at international level: The case of the United Nations sustainable development goals. *European Journal of Risk Regulation, 10*(1), 201–207. https://doi.org/10.1017/err.2019.16

Mugellini, G., Villeneuve, J.-P., & Heide, M. (2021). Monitoring sustainable development goals and the quest for high-quality indicators: Learning from a practical evaluation of data on corruption. *Sustainable Development, 29*(6), 1257–1275. https://doi.org/10.1002/sd.2223

Mungiu-Pippidi, A. (n.d.). Trend analysis and forecast methodology: Can we trace change in corruption using perception indicators? Retrieved from https://corruptionrisk.org/forecast-methodology/

Mungiu-Pippidi, A. (2022a). Transparency and corruption: Measuring real transparency by a new index. *Regulation & Governance*. [Advance online publication]. `https://doi.org/10.1111/rego.12502

Mungiu-Pippidi, A. (2022b, May 17). New corruption risk forecast uses fact-based indicators, transparent methodology. [The FCPA Blog]. Retrieved from https://fcpablog.com/2022/05/17/new-corruption-risk-forecast-uses-fact-based-indicatorstransparent-methodology/

Mungiu-Pippidi, A., & Dadašov, R. (2016). Measuring control of corruption by a new index of public integrity. *European Journal on Criminal Policy and Research, 22*(3), 415–438. https://doi.org/10.1007/s10610-016-9324-z

Mungiu-Pippidi, A., & Fazekas, M. (2020). How to define and measure corruption. In A. Mungiu-Pippidi & P. M. Heywood (Eds.), *A research agenda for studies of corruption* (pp. 7–26). Edward Elgar Publishing Limited.

Németh, E., Vargha, B. T., & Pályi, K. A. (2019). The scientific reliability of international corruption rankings. *Public Finance Quarterly, 64*(3), 319–336. https://doi.org/10.35551/PFQ_2019_3_1

Nhamo, G. (2017). New global sustainable development agenda: A focus on Africa. *Sustainable Development, 25*(3), 227–241. https://doi.org/10.1002/sd.1648

Nygård, H. M. (2017). *Voluntary supplemental indicators for goal 16 on inclusive, just and peaceful societies*. Retrieved from https://community-democracies.org/app/uploads/2018/06/Framework.-Voluntary-Supplemental-Indicators-SDG16-1-1-1.pdf

Ochieng-Springer, S., & Odhiambo, H. (2022). Governance during COVID-19: Kenya's graft practices. *The Round Table, 111*(4), 489–505. https://doi.org/10.1080/00358533.2022.2105537

OECD. (2020). *COVID-19 in Africa: Regional socio-economic implications and policy priorities*. OECD.

Olin, M. (2017). Measuring corruption in sustainable development target 16.5 with V-Dem data. [Policy Brief No. 13]. Retrieved from https://www.v-dem.net/en/publications/briefing-papers/

Pring, C., & Vrushi, J. (2019). *Global corruption barometer Africa 2019: Citizens' views and experiences of corruption*. TI.

Razafindrakoto, M., & Roubaud, F. (2018). Responding to the SDG 16 measurement challenge: The governance, peace and security survey modules in Africa. *Global Policy, 9*(3), 336–351. https://doi.org/10.1111/1758-5899.12559

SDGCA. (2019). *Africa 2030: Sustainable development goals three-year reality check*. SDGCA.

SDGCA. (2020). *COVID-19: Unprecedented risk to SDGS in Africa*. SDGCA.

Trapnell, S., Jenkins, M., & Chêne, M. (2017). *Monitoring corruption and anti-corruption in the sustainable development goals–a resource guide*. TI.

UN. (2017). *Resolution adopted by the general assembly on 6 July 2017: Work of the statistical commission pertaining to the 2030 agenda for sustainable development*. UN.

UN. (2019). Corruption and the sustainable development goals. In *World public sector report 2019: Sustainable development goal 16: Focus on public institutions (chapter 2)* (pp. 39–83). UN.

UN. (2020). Policy brief: impact of COVID-19 in Africa. Retrieved from https://unsdg.un.org/resources/policy-brief-impactcovid-19-africa

UN. (2022). *Progress towards the sustainable development goals: Report of the secretary-general*. UN.

UNDP. (2017). Corruption, an impediment to SDGs achievement: What must Africa do? *Maendeleo policy forum*. [7th ed.]. Retrieved from http://www.africa.undp.org/content/dam/rba/docs/undp_rba_7th%20Mandeleo%20Policy%20Forum%20-%20FINAL%20Report.pdf

UNECA. (2020). *COVID-19 in Africa: Protecting lives and economies*. UNECA.

UNODC, UNDP, & UNODC-INEGI Center of Excellence in Statistical Information on Government, Crime, Victimization and Justice. (2018). *Manual on corruption surveys*. UNODC.

UNSC. (2022a). *Global indicator framework for the sustainable development goals and targets of the 2030 agenda for sustainable development*. UN.

UNSC. (2022b). Tier classification for global SDG indicators as of 9 June 2022. Retrieved from https://unstats.un.org/sdgs/iaegsdgs/tier-classification/

UNSC. (2022c). SDG indicators: Data collection information & focal points. Retrieved from https://unstats.un.org/sdgs/dataContacts/

Warf, B. (2019). *Global corruption from a geographic perspective*. Springer Nature.

Windridge, O. (2022), Constructing corruption: Identifying the enablers helping build violent kleptocracies. [Sentry Briefing]. Retrieved from https://thesentry.org/reports/enablers-violent-kleptocracies/

World Bank. (n.d.). Enterprise surveys: Corruption. Retrieved from http://www.enterprisesurveys.org/data/exploretopics/corruption#all-countries

World Bank. (2019). *Anticorruption initiatives: Reaffirming commitment to a development priority*. World Bank.

World Bank. (2020). *Enhancing government effectiveness and transparency: The fight against corruption*. World Bank.

World Bank. (2021). *World development report 2021: Data for better lives*. World Bank.

Chapter 8
Civilian Oversight for Democratic Policing and Its Challenges: Overcoming Obstacles for Improved Police Accountability and Better Security in Africa and Beyond

This chapter provides an analytical review of formal civilian oversight for democratic policing, outlining the benefits as well as the key challenges such oversight encounters. It extends the comparative analysis about formal civilian oversight for democratic policing by providing a much more international perspective, beyond Africa, including examples of the use of the various classifications and approaches to such oversight. Currently, only two African nations (Kenya and South Africa) have mechanisms of independent civilian oversight of police accountability. Drawing on the author's field experience, it then offers some insights on the required framework and environment for overcoming the civilian oversight challenges in pursuit of much more improved police accountability and better internal security in Africa.

8.1 Introduction

In Africa, there are only two countries with mechanisms of statutorily created independent civilian oversight of police accountability. These are Kenya with its IPOA and South Africa with its IPID, as discussed in Chap. 5. Such a state of affairs is obviously problematic as it challenges democratic norms and especially so in a continent where police corruption and other forms of bureaucratic misconduct run rampant with similar impunity at the expense of the poor and marginalized. Notwithstanding that, and although like for all public institutions we can also identify performance issues with the IPOA and the IPID, African nations need to establish independent institutions of civilian oversight in the pursuit of democratic policing and the general deepening of democracy (Hope, 2017; Mugari, 2023).

The basic tenets or principles of ideal democratic policing require the police to, among other things: be guided by government institutions and monitored by a vigilant civil society; uphold the law embodying values respectful of human dignity, rather than the wishes of a powerful leader or political party; be accountable to democratic oversight institutions outside their organization that are specifically designated and empowered to regulate police activity; be accountable to the communities they serve; be ethical and transparent in their activities; give the highest operational priority to protecting the safety, security, and rights of individuals; be representative of the communities they serve; and to seek to build professional skills and conditions of service that support efficient and respectful service delivery to the public (Bayley, 2001, 2006; Fichtelberg, 2013; Hope, 2015, 2019a; Manning, 2010; Organization for Security and Cooperation in Europe [OSCE], 2009; Pino & Wiatrowski, 2006; Prasad, 2006; Sen, 2010; Wiatrowski & Goldstone, 2010).

More recently, Bonner (2020) proposed that democratic policing be considered as a multidimensional, multilevel, and contested concept rooted in political ideology that is not singular or politically neutral but grounded in four typologies: right (neo-populist), center-right (conservatism), center-left (social democratic/liberal socialism), and left (populist). As with all typologies, including the use of typologies as applied in this work, these are ideal types in which governments will fit in gradations, reflecting particular political and economic ideas about governance (Bonner, 2020).

Police accountability is a key element of democratic policing given that the latter is "based on the concept of the police as protector of the rights of citizens and rule of law, while ensuring the safety and security of the citizens" (Sen, 2010, p. 8). Many scholars and others have all contributed to the notion that democratic policing cannot survive without accountability and encompassing transparency (see, for example, Bittner, 1980; den Boer et al., 2011; Ellison, 2007; Harris, 2013; Prasad, 2006; Rogers, 2014; Rowe, 2020; Scheye, 2018; Sklansky, 2008). According to the UNODC (2011), accountability pertains to a system of internal and external checks and balances aimed at ensuring that police perform the functions expected of them to a high standard and are held responsible when they fail to do so. "It aims to prevent the police from misusing their powers, to prevent political authorities from misusing their control over the police, and most importantly, to enhance public confidence and (re-) establish police legitimacy" (UNODC, 2011, p. 9). As also noted by Jones and van Steden (2013, p. 563), "democratically accountable policing is not only morally desirable, but also instrumentally superior to unaccountable policing."

Accordingly, police accountability functions at two levels. At the first, it refers to holding the police agencies accountable for the services they deliver (such as crime control, maintaining order in society, providing for security of property and people, and other community services). At the second level, it refers to holding individual police officers accountable for how they treat citizens including use of brutal or deadly force, discriminatory or disrespectful behavior, and other conduct that tramples on human dignity and rights (Walker & Archbold, 2014). Police accountability therefore includes both what the police do and how they go about doing it. "Hence, accountability refers to being accountable for police conduct, oversight of policing activities and evaluation of those activities" (Feys et al., 2018, p. 226).

Despite making major headway in the citizens' desire to bring accountability to policing in their respective political jurisdiction or country, civilian oversight for democratic policing has encountered, and continues to suffer from, a number of challenges. This chapter provides an analytical review of formal civilian oversight for democratic policing, outlining the benefits as well as the key challenges such oversight encounters. It extends the comparative analysis about formal civilian oversight for democratic policing by providing a much more international perspective including examples of the use of the various classifications and approaches to such oversight. Drawing on the field experience of this book's author, it then offers some insights on the required framework and environment for overcoming the civilian oversight challenges in pursuit of much more improved police accountability in Africa and beyond.

8.2 What Is Civilian Oversight for Democratic Policing?

Civilian oversight of a police service or force has also been interchangeably referred to as citizen oversight, citizen review, external review, external oversight, civilian review, or civilian/citizen monitoring. In the view of this book's author, the term civilian oversight is more appropriate as it differentiates purpose, given that (in most countries) the public police are being organizationally structured and regarded as a military/paramilitary force and they are increasingly employing military/paramilitary tactics in the exercise of their routine police activities, duties and functions (see, for example, Flores-Macías & Zarkin, 2021; Roziere & Walby, 2018; Stuurman, 2020; Tabassi & Dey, 2016). In addition, it is recognized and now well-known, as emphasized by Rowe (2020, p. 86), that "modern policing has been organized as a 'disciplined service', following a military model with a uniformed hierarchical structure with a rule-based bureaucracy." Moreover, the police are an integral component of the security sector. "The security sector is [comprised] of all the structures, institutions and personnel responsible for security provision, management and oversight at national and local levels" (DCAF, 2015a, p. 2). It includes both actors that use force (such as the military, paramilitary, and the police) and those responsible for controlling how force is used through management and oversight (DCAF, 2015a).

In addition, it is duly noted that the two prominent associations of law enforcement oversight also use the term civilian oversight, rather than citizen oversight, in their names. These are the Canadian Association for Civilian Oversight of Law Enforcement (CACOLE) and the National Association for Civilian Oversight of Law Enforcement (NACOLE). Both these associations are concerned with the development and promotion of independent civilian oversight entities that seek to make their local law enforcement agencies more transparent, accountable, and responsive to the communities they serve.

Civilian oversight entails individuals outside the sworn chain of command of a police department undertaking the task of holding that department and its members accountable for their actions (City of Austin, Office of the Police Monitor, 2018). Ideally, civilian oversight should include on-scene investigation/monitoring of critical incidents, such as officer-involved shootings, and/or any other matters related to police conduct/misconduct that negatively or can potentially negatively impact members of the public. It therefore involves the scrutiny of the police by a citizen/civilian group to ensure the police act within the law, use resources efficiently, and fulfill their mandates with integrity, discipline, accountability, transparency, independence, and professionalism (Hope, 2019a, 2020). Civilian oversight of the police can be accomplished through an agency and/or procedures that involve participation by persons—who are not sworn police officers (citizens/civilians)—in the assessment of public complaints against the police and/or other allegations of misconduct by police officers (De Angelis et al., 2016a; Walker, 2001).

Generally, in practice, civilian oversight of police is the oversight of police activities by people who are not in the majority active members of either the police that they are overseeing or any other police service. It involves a network of multiple checks and balances on the police by civilians (citizens) to maintain a set of standards primarily geared to preventing and/or investigating and remedying misconduct and enhancing police accountability, integrity, transparency, and independence. It can also be seen as a public good given that it provides a manner in which the police may reinforce and rationalize their public function as protectors of democracy (Hope, 2019a, 2020; Hryniewicz, 2011; Miller and Merrick, 2002).

As observed by Hope (2019a, 2020), civilian oversight of the police has come into vogue across the globe as a preferred approach to hold the police accountable on behalf of the public or civilian population. It is a more public-facing mechanism of police accountability for democratic policing. Countries and/or political jurisdictions within countries as varied as Australia, Belgium, Canada, the Cayman Islands, Czech Republic, Denmark, the Hong Kong Special Administrative Region of the People's Republic of China, Israel, Jamaica, Kenya, Malta, Mauritius, New Zealand, Norway, Republic of Ireland, Scotland, Republic of South Africa, Trinidad and Tobago, the UK, and the US, for example, have civilian oversight bodies. However, while civilian oversight for police accountability can commonly be found in police agencies in Western countries, this concept is fairly new to many emerging democracies in other regions such as Asia, for example (Kang & Nalla, 2011; Nalla & Mamayek, 2013), and other nations evolving from conflict such as some in Africa (Hope, 2016).

Although in most countries, members of the public can file a complaint over police misconduct directly with the police or with the justice authorities (who often have a symbiotic relationship with the police), it is not a sufficient condition in the pursuit of natural justice and police accountability (Kessing, 2018; Mugari & Obioha, 2022). In recognition of that, a senior police officer with a police department in California was moved to point out "the fact that more and more major cities are voting for some form of civilian review of police is a great indicator that this is a path to improve police and community relations as well as build legitimacy" (Seyffert, 2017, p. 7).

8.2 What Is Civilian Oversight for Democratic Policing?

As a consequence, there are several reasons for establishing civilian oversight—and preferably through an independent police oversight body—but primary among them are the twin aims of (1) the need to ensure democratic police accountability through impartial, prompt, unbiased, accountable, and non-corrupt handling of complaints against the police; and (2) achieving the rule of law (Kunetski & Barkway, 2014). The onset of civilian oversight of the police beckoned that police services had lost their monopoly to determine whether they were treating citizens in the appropriate manner and being held accountable in that regard (Boghani, 2016). Therefore, "the culture of police organizations everywhere is facing a monumental change; [and] for many of them, that means accepting civilian oversight so that they can maintain or regain legitimacy in the communities they serve" (Seyffert, 2017, p. 5). As observed by Decker and Shjarback (2020 p. 114), "the [original] rationale behind civilian oversight is simple: when the police are left to investigate officer misconduct or to review critical incidents themselves, the community perceives a lack of accountability."

8.2.1 Extant Model Types of Civilian Oversight of the Police

Civilian oversight of the police can take a wide variety of forms and operate under a wide range of frameworks. In a recent study, Fairley (2020) reported on her research survey of the civilian oversight entities in the 100 most populous U.S. cities, and has identified and classified seven model types of civilian oversight of police—Investigative, Review, Audit, Adjudicative, Appeals, Supervisory, and Advisory—stemming therefrom. This documents that civilian oversight has become sufficiently prevalent among the largest U.S. cities as to now be considered a "normative" element within the police accountability infrastructure (Fairley, 2020). However, and drawing from Hope (2019a, 2020), as well as other current literature on the subject, this work identifies and categorizes five distinct comparative model types of civilian oversight of the police that can be found across nations in the globe. These are outlined below as described and summarized in Table 8.1 in a typology by features and characteristics.

8.2.1.1 Independent Investigation

The independent investigation model type of civilian oversight, which is also referred to as the external investigatory type or the external investigative type, is a form of oversight that operates separately from the police service and is primarily focused on conducting independent investigations of allegations of misconduct against police officers and remove or reduce the risk of sabotage of such investigations by the police (Clarke, 2009; De Angelis et al., 2016b; Prenzler & Ronken, 2001). In this model type, entities investigate police incidents independently from the police department and employ at least one professional investigator (Fairley,

Table 8.1 Typology of models of civilian oversight of police by features and characteristics

Investigation
- Based on independence from law enforcement agencies
- Directly receives complaints from the public about police misconduct
- Power to conduct independent investigations of complaints against police officers
- Power to replace, parallel, or duplicate police internal affairs investigations and processes
- Staffed by non-police, civilian investigators
- Reports and provides findings to the police and public at large

Review
- Receives complaints from the public directly or indirectly
- Police conduct the investigations
- Reviews reports and records of completed police investigations
- Makes recommendations to the police regarding findings on investigations
- Requests that further investigations be conducted, if deemed necessary
- Holds public meetings to get public input, and facilitate police-community communication and outreach

Appeals
- Complaints are received directly by the police
- Complaints are scrutinized and investigated by the police
- Complainants and accused officers not satisfied with outcomes can appeal
- Appeals body may comprise both civilian(s) and police

Auditor/monitor
- Examines broad patterns in complaint investigations including their quality, thoroughness, fairness, accuracy of findings, and discipline meted out
- Some auditors/monitors may be able to actively participate in or monitor open internal investigations
- Conducts systematic reviews of police policies, practices or training and recommends reforms
- Promotes broad organizational change by making recommendations for improvement

Hybrid/mixed
- Merges features and characteristics of two or more different civilian oversight model types into a unique insider/outsider approach

Source: Author compilation

2020). Oversight institutions applying this type of civilian oversight, are empowered to conduct each aspect of the process from original complaint intake to investigation and recommendations for sanctions, if any.

The key features and characteristics of the contemporary police oversight bodies or agencies that employ this model type are that they are: (1) Based on independence from law enforcement agencies; (2) Have the authorization to directly receive complaints from the public about police misconduct; (3) Have unfettered power to conduct independent investigations of complaints against police officers; (4) Have the power to replace, parallel, or duplicate police internal affairs investigations and processes; (5) Staffed by non-police, civilian investigators; and (6) Have the authorization to report and provide findings to the police and public at large. And, although it is the most expensive type of oversight body, the investigation-focused type of civilian oversight is also regarded as best equipped to enforce police accountability, because this type has the expertise, authority, and independence necessary to conduct credible and thorough investigations (Ajilore, 2018; De Angelis et al., 2016a;

8.2 What Is Civilian Oversight for Democratic Policing?

Finn, 2001; King, 2015; Miller and Merrick, 2002; Stephens et al., 2018; Walker, 2001).

In their study of select independent investigative agencies from around the world, including Kenya's IPOA and South Africa's IPID, and under the premise that the obligation to investigate police and other state agents' use of excessive force and allegations of torture and deaths in custody is established by international human rights and criminal law, Scott and Lisitsyna (2021, p. 71) conclude that "the goal of independent investigative agencies is to bring to justice those state agents who allegedly commit serious offenses against members of the public, a goal that may only be achieved through independent, effective, thorough, and transparent investigations."

In addition to the expensive nature of this type of civilian oversight, other potential shortcomings can include the civilian investigators facing strong resistance from police personnel, and police executives developing less of an incentive to create effective police accountability/integrity systems and simply cast blame on the civilian oversight body (De Angelis et al., 2016a).

There are many examples of this investigation model type of civilian oversight being deployed across the globe. They include Kenya, where it is operationalized through the IPOA; the Republic of South Africa, operationalized through its IPID; the City of San Francisco, California, US, operationalized through its Department of Police Accountability (DPA), originally the Office of Citizen Complaints (OCC); the Province of British Columbia, Canada, operationalized through its Independent Investigations Office (IIO) and the Office of the Police Complaint Commissioner (OPCC); New Zealand, where it is operationalized through the Independent Police Conduct Authority (IPCA-New Zealand); Trinidad and Tobago, operationalized through its Police Complaints Authority (PCA); the Cayman Islands, operationalized through the Office of the Ombudsman (the successor agency of the Office of the Complaints Commissioner); the State of New South Wales, Australia, through its Law Enforcement Conduct Commission (LECC); Jamaica, operationalized through the Independent Commission of Investigations (INDECOM); and Denmark, operationalized through its Independent Police Complaints Authority (IPCA-Denmark). However, and as also noted by Rosenthal (2019-20), notwithstanding the many commonalities to this model type of civilian oversight worldwide, it tends to be uniquely operationalized to its jurisdiction's political, social, and cultural environment.

8.2.1.2 Review

This model type of civilian oversight is primarily focused on reviewing the quality of the work outputs of investigations that are completed internally by the police. Rather than conducting independent investigations, the review-focused bodies or agencies evaluate completed investigations done internally. Therefore, there is a reliance on the information about the investigative process and its outcomes that is provided by the police. In some cases, the review-focused bodies may monitor police investigations as they proceed but in no case do they have powers to conduct independent investigations (Mehta, n.d.).

The major features and characteristics of police oversight bodies or agencies that are based on this type are that they: (1) Receive complaints directly from the public or indirectly through referral from some other institution(s); (2) Review reports and records of completed police investigations of public complaints; (3) Make recommendations to the police regarding findings on investigations reviewed; (4) Request that further investigations be conducted, if deemed necessary; and (6) Hold public meetings to get public input, and facilitate police-community communication and outreach (De Angelis et al., 2016a; Fairley, 2020; Seyffert, 2017; Stephens et al., 2018; UNODC, 2011). It is considered the least expensive type of civilian oversight as it generally relies on volunteers as members of the review bodies.

The principal potential shortcomings of this model type of civilian oversight, in its institutional application, have been identified as: (1) Having both limited organizational resources and limited authority; (2) Being less independent than other types; and (3) Having Review Board members with insufficient expertise to undertake their duties (De Angelis et al., 2016a). Examples of the application of this type of civilian oversight of the police include the City of San Diego, California, US, through its Community Review Board on Police Practices (CRBPP); the Province of Alberta, Canada, through its Law Enforcement Review Board (LERB); the Hong Kong Special Administrative Region of the People's Republic of China, through its Independent Police Complaints Council (IPCC-Hong Kong); Canada, through its Civilian Review and Complaints Commission for the Royal Canadian Mounted Police (CRCC); and Scotland, UK, through its Police Investigations and Review Commissioner (PIRC).

In Hong Kong, for example, its IPCC observes, monitors, and reviews the handling and investigation by the Complaints Against Police Office (CAPO) of reportable complaints against the police. Unlike CAPO, which is an internal affairs unit of the police, the IPCC-Hong Kong is a civilian body not linked with the police that reports directly to the office of the Chief Executive of Hong Kong.

8.2.1.3 Appeals

In this model type of civilian oversight, the primary focus is on appeals of outcomes. Complaints are first received, scrutinized, and investigated by the police and they recommend disciplinary action, if so determined, to the police top officials. Under this type, the entire complaint process is handled by the police. However, in the event a complainant is not satisfied with the outcome of his or her case, a board that may include police officers hears the complainant, undertakes scrutiny of how the case was originally investigated, confers with the police and/or the investigative file, and makes recommendations to the police top officials. In some jurisdictions, particularly in the US, accused and disciplined police officers are also allowed to utilize this appeals process.

8.2 What Is Civilian Oversight for Democratic Policing?

The key features and characteristics of this type of civilian oversight are that: (1) Complaints against the police are received directly by the police; (2) Complaints are scrutinized and investigated by the police; (3) Complainants and accused officers who are not satisfied with outcomes of investigations can appeal those outcomes; and (4) The appeal body can be comprised of both civilians and sworn officers (International Association of Chiefs of Police [IACP], 2000; Mehta, n.d.; Wilson, 2014). Potential shortcomings of the application of this type are the length of time it can take to get from investigation to appeal, and the lack of trust the process may engender in cases where there may be police officers as members of the review body. Examples of the application of this type include the City of Richmond, Virginia, US, through its Community Police Review Commission (CPRC); the City of Urbana, Illinois, US, through its Civilian Police Review Board (CPRB); and the Province of Newfoundland and Labrador, Canada, through its Royal Newfoundland Constabulary Public Complaints Commission.

8.2.1.4 Auditor/Monitor

This model type of civilian oversight of the police is primarily focused toward identifying patterns and practices of police misconduct and the systemic failure(s) that contribute to them so that they can be remedied. Auditors/monitors usually have unfettered access to all materials and relevant police investigations and reviews and may contact complainants to assess satisfaction with outcomes. They also make findings on the fairness and thoroughness of the process and may present recommendations as to how it can be improved if necessary.

The features and characteristics of this model type of civilian oversight are that it: (1) Examines broad patterns in complaint investigations including their quality, thoroughness, fairness, accuracy of findings, and discipline meted out; (2) Enables some auditors/monitors to actively participate in or monitor open internal investigations; (3) Conducts systematic reviews of police policies, practices or training and recommends reforms; and (4) Promotes broad organizational change by making recommendations for improvement (see, for example, De Angelis et al., 2016a; Evenson, n.d.; Fairley, 2020; King, 2015; Mehta, n.d.; Sen, 2010; Stephens et al., 2018; Walker & Archbold, 2014). The use of this type is generally less expensive to execute than the investigation type but more expensive than the review and appeal types.

The major shortcomings in the use of the auditor/monitor model type are that (1) considerable expertise is required to meet the mandate of an auditing/monitoring program for a police service; and (2) only a sample of misconduct cases or investigations gets audited or monitored. Examples of the use of this type include the City of Edmonton, Alberta, Canada, through its Edmonton Police Commission (EPC); the City of San Jose, California, US, through its Office of the Independent Police Auditor (OIPA); and the Hong Kong Special Administrative Region of the People's Republic of China, through its IPCC.

8.2.1.5 Hybrid/Mixed

In this final model type of civilian oversight, oversight bodies/agencies may use a combination of two or more of the primary focus types/approaches described above or some of their functional elements. The key feature and characteristic of the hybrid/mixed type is that it merges features and characteristics of two or more different civilian oversight types into a unique approach to civilian oversight (Cintrón Perino, 2004; Evenson, n.d.; UNODC, 2011).

Hybrids particularly allow for the development and application of oversight processes that entail the use of authority and power structures that are considered fitting for a given political jurisdiction or country. Whatever combination of types/approaches used, the ultimate goal is to derive governance and accountability mechanisms that hold the police accountable and satisfy community concerns about police misconduct and policing processes. The primary potential shortcoming of the use of this type is derived from the possibility that the body employing its use may be overwhelmed by the volume of work occasioned by the hybrid nature of its mandate and the lack of the appropriate expertise to handle the workload.

Examples of the use of this type of civilian oversight include the Province of Ontario, Canada, through its Office of the Independent Police Review Director (OIPRD); the City of Denver, Colorado, US, through its Citizen Oversight Board (COB); the Hong Kong Special Administrative Region of the People's Republic of China, through its IPCC; Scotland, UK, through its PIRC; England and Wales, UK, operationalized through their Independent Office for Police Conduct (IOPC); the State of Queensland, Australia, through its Crime and Corruption Commission (CCC); and Belgium, through its Standing Committee of Supervision of Police Services (SCSPS) also known as Committee P.

8.2.2 Benefits of Civilian Oversight of the Police: Accountability/Transparency/Independence

Civilian oversight of the police champions the principles of accountability, transparency, as well as independence in policing because the powers given to the public police to protect, such as the ability to arrest, detain, and use force, are significantly different than for any other profession. Indeed, both in symbol and in practice, the police personify the sovereign state and have the power to use force against their fellow citizens in ways not available to other public servants (Rowe, 2020). When those police powers are abused, they can have serious impacts on people's lives (Bourke, n.d.; Diaz, 2009; Wentkowska, 2016). Since policing, at all levels of government, has become the most powerful intrusion into the lives of citizens, oversight of the police needs to be transparent and independent of the police. As previously recognized by Greene (2007, p. 747), "simply put, those who guard the guardians should not be left to guarding themselves."

8.2 What Is Civilian Oversight for Democratic Policing?

Consequently, civilian oversight of policing also needs to be seen as consistent with the principles of democratic policing, as previously outlined, given the significant power the police have over citizens and the fact that it is the latter who suffer the consequences of the former's conduct/misconduct (see, for example, Goldsmith & Lewis, 2000; Hope, 2019a, 2020; Wentkowska, 2016). In fact, as argued by Friedman and Ponomarenko (2015, p. 1827), "it is fundamentally unacceptable for policing to remain aloof from the ordinary processes of democratic governance." Therefore, "all police practices … should be legislatively authorized, subject to public rulemaking, or adopted and evaluated through some alternative process that permits democratic input" (Friedman & Ponomarenko, 2015, p. 1827).

Essentially, there are five common goals of civilian oversight that benefit a society: (1) Discourage police misconduct; (2) Ensure an accessible complaint process; (3) Deliver fair and thorough investigations; (4) Enhance transparency; and (5) Improve public trust. The gist of civilian oversight is to accomplish these goals to reach an impact that is deterrence-based by preventing or limiting police misconduct and improving the fairness and thoroughness of investigations of complaints of such misconduct and the resultant recommendations for remedies such as the enforcement of rules and disciplinary actions (Hope, 2019a, 2020; Livingston, 2004; Porter, 2013).

Civilian oversight of the police is critical for any democracy or an emerging one. As convincingly argued by Roach (2014, p. 29), "any state that does not hold its police accountable can become a police state in which those entrusted with the state's most coercive powers can defy the rule of law with impunity." Simultaneously, "democracies can legitimately expect that the police perform to higher standards than not committing criminal or regulatory offences or even actionable civil wrongs" (Roach, 2014, p. 29). Oversight for democratic policing is required not only to ensure the fair and impartial application of existing standards of good conduct and behavior, but to also create standards and impose democratic expectations on the police (Hope, 2019a, 2020; Roach, 2014). Furthermore, "such oversight is consistent with democratic conceptions of the rule of law, where the law is visible, transparent, and managed through overlapping institutions that provide sufficient checks and balances to ensure legal compliance and democratic consensus" (Greene, 2007, pp. 747–748).

By employing civilian oversight of the police, a framework is thereby provided that offers access to all citizens to register any concerns they may have about police conduct/misconduct. Therefore, civilian oversight is becoming popular around the globe because it meets a societal need (Diaz, 2009; Hope, 2019a, 2020). Where the police conduct internal investigations of themselves, such investigations are often perceived as biased and spurious (Clarke, 2009). In fact, the need for civilian oversight is, in part, further justified due to the reality that internal police complaints systems do not offer reliable and transparent checks and balances for citizens against police misconduct (see, for example, Attard, 2010; Hryniewicz, 2011; Jerome, 2006; Prateeppornnarong & Young, 2019; Sajor, 2015; Terrill & Ingram, 2015). In turn, those impacted by police misconduct desire and prefer an independent civilian review of complaints that provides the opportunity for fellow citizens to have transparency and be able to move past any code of silence culture exhibited by officers investigating their own (Hope, 2019a, 2020; Sajor, 2015).

Civilian oversight of the police has therefore come to the fore as the preferred approach to monitor and enforce police accountability, independence, and transparency within a policing framework that is either based, or aspiring to be based, on the previously discussed principles of contemporary democratic policing and that functions in a professional manner. In addition to primarily promoting accountability, independence, and transparency, civilian oversight of the police also helps to restore frayed relations between the public and the police by contributing to the rebuilding of mutual trust and respect (Bobb & Pearsall, 2010; Calderon & Hernandez-Figueroa, 2013; Evenson, n.d.; Hope, 2019a, 2020; Vitoroulis et al., 2021). Any police service that is indeed accountable, independent, and respects and protects transparency and human rights will be able to build constructive relations with the public and society as part of the democratization process (see, for example, Aydin-Aitchison & Mermutluoğlu, 2020; Bayley, 2015; Goold, 2016; Hope, 2019a, 2020; Ivković & Borovec, 2018; Kessing, 2018). Undoubtedly, "the police should be held accountable in all stages of their operations before, during and after police operations" (Kessing, 2018, p. 5).

Although it is now a diverse and growing practice, civilian oversight of the police has too frequently been reduced to public complaints against the police (Hope, 2019a, 2020). However, it is absolutely much more than that. It tends to fall along a continuum classification of reactive and proactive approaches. The reactive approaches—which are applicable for after an incident has occurred—includes complaints, investigations, justifications, and sanctions. Here, the focus tends to be on identifying a specific bad apple while ignoring what may be larger systemic and structural problems that may have led to the incident in the first place (Bourke, n.d.). At the other end of the continuum are the proactive approaches which seek to directly influence policies that promote standards of ethics and professionalism. Instead of reacting when an incident occurs, measures are taken to attempt to avoid and deter misconduct (Bourke, n.d.).

Furthermore, irrespective of jurisdiction or country, but as also advocated for the US by the President's Task Force on 21st Century Policing (2015, p. 26), "some form of civilian oversight of law enforcement is important in order to strengthen trust with [a] community." From the perspective of this book's author, this is a universal truth in pursuit of the principles of democratic policing as previously outlined. Each policed community must take responsibility for fashioning a system that fits its local situation and unique needs and should therefore delineate the appropriate form and structure of civilian oversight to meet those requirements (President's Task Force on 21st Century Policing, 2015). In addition, it is also very questionable when the police have to investigate their own, especially given the conflict of interest between the demanded obligations of police officers to their colleagues and the public they are sworn to serve. As stated factually by Walker and Archbold (2014, p. 54), the "police are inherently unable to police themselves, as a result of both bureaucratic self-interest and the power of the police subculture."

This is a conflict of interest that is both inappropriate and counterproductive for democratic policing. In Taiwan, there was a transition from authoritarian policing under martial law to democratic policing under greater civilian and local control, with democratization weakening the top-down power of the authoritarian center—which had functioned as a source of power for the police—and it strengthened the bottom-up power of the local community (Cao et al., 2014; Choi, 2015). In Australia and New Zealand, as Prenzler (2011) and den Heyer and Beckley (2016), respectively, have pointed out, the repeated failures of internal investigations and discipline drove the evolution towards civilian oversight. Similarly, in Kenya (see Hope, 2015, 2020) and Jamaica (see Hall, 2017), civilian oversight of the police was instituted to counteract what was then the failing procedures for police accountability. In Canada, civilian oversight of police grew out of a serious and sustained public and political concern and frustration that the police, especially in metropolitan centers, were not being controlled by their senior officers and that instances of brutality and misconduct were being underplayed and going unpunished (CRCC, 2009; Murphy & McKenna, n.d.). In other words, "the police [had] not been able to demonstrate either the willingness or the ability to govern the behavior of their members at least in ways that create public and political confidence" (CRCC, 2009, p. 9).

In the Republic of South Africa, having the police under civilian authority has subjected them (the police) to political and constitutional accountability (Berg, 2013, 2021; IPID, 2013; Pruitt, 2010). In the UK (England and Wales) and the Netherlands, the introduction of local levels of civilian oversight of the police was justified as a means of increasing police accountability and transparency and, thereby, democratic control of the police (Jones & van Steden, 2013; Mawby & Smith, 2017; Rowe, 2020; van Sluis & Devroe, 2020). In Thailand, despite some shortcomings, moving to civilian oversight of the police has benefited the country (Prateeppornnarong, 2019). In Ghana, recent empirical research by Amagnya (2023) has also shown that a lack of oversight measures (deterrence) was a constant predictor or factor of support for corruption by police officers. In other words, an absence of oversight and accountability create and promote an environment for police corruption to thrive. Therefore, the key to restoring or enhancing public confidence in the police is openness to civilian oversight and external review (Byrne & Priestley, 2017).

Also, as observed in other research, oversight should be treated as an activity integral to the efforts of policing itself (Rowe, 2020; Stageman et al., 2018). Indeed, "a consensus [has emerged] that the traditional models of police investigating police are no longer defensible, either as an effective model for addressing public complaints or as a method that satisfies public demands for accountability" (CRCC, 2009, p. 11). Therefore, "the independence and civilian leadership of police oversight [have become] a procedural necessity rather than a functional one, designed to ensure that oversight decision-making is guided by community standards and universal ideals rather than factionally defined, narrow self-interest" (Stageman et al., 2018, pp. 124–125). At the top among those benchmarks and ideals are the principles of democratic policing. Some research on Asia, for example, found that countries that use some type of civilian oversight tended to represent a higher degree of democratic governance and as also demonstrated by their scores on global governance indicators (Nalla, 2016; Nalla & Mamayek, 2013).

Moreover, as summarized by New Zealand's IPCA, given that effective, efficient policing services are the cornerstone of a free and democratic society, independent oversight provides assurance for both the public and police that allegations of misconduct or neglect of duty will be appropriately dealt with (IPCA-New Zealand, n.d.). Independent oversight therefore: (1) Exposes misconduct; (2) Provides public accountability; (3) Protects citizens against abuse of police powers, including excessive force; (4) Improves police practice and policy; (5) Encourages discipline within the police; (6) Protects against politicization of the police; (7) Protects against corruption; (8) Enhances public trust and confidence in the overall justice system; and (9) Contributes towards the justice sector outcomes of a safe and just society (IPCA-New Zealand, n.d.).

Similarly, the OPCC of British Columbia, Canada (which is independent of government and the police) has found that transparent and impartial civilian oversight promotes accountable policing and enhances public confidence in law enforcement based on the guiding principles of integrity, independence, and excellence (OPCC, 2019). Civilian oversight is seen as holding police accountable, providing an impartial place for the public to make complaints, helping to educate the public about police, fostering improvements in police operations, and increasing the transparency around police disciplinary actions (OPCC, 2019). In addition, the Commissioner of the OPCC has further pronounced that "accountability to civilian authority is an immutable tenet of policing in a democratic society" (OPCC, 2019, p. 6).

Also, the INDECOM of Jamaica has made the case that independent oversight of the police was essential to the beginning of a change in Jamaican policing culture and the security of Jamaicans (INDECOM, n.d.). The Commission had stated that "the introduction of the Independent Commission of Investigations (INDECOM) Act and the resultant authority of the Commission would have greater influence on policing, as culpable and discreditable conduct would be exposed" (INDECOM, n.d., p. 1), and the data shows that has indeed been the case since it began operations in 2011 (see INDECOM, n.d.).

Likewise, the NACOLE in the US has set out persuasive reasoning which shows that "civilian oversight provides a mechanism to bring together the many stakeholders involved in supporting trusted, respectful, and effective law enforcement efforts" (NACOLE, 2015, p. 1). Accordingly, "citizen oversight of law enforcement is a critical facet of any well-founded effort to strengthen the relationship between police and communities and to build public trust, all while promoting effective [democratic] policing" (NACOLE, 2015, p. 2). In addition to other things, such as independent oversight, it (1) builds legitimacy and public trust, through increased police transparency and accountability to the public served; (2) fosters additional accountability through independent investigations, reviews, or auditing of police misconduct complaints; (3) can identify needed changes in police practices and training; (4) provides a meaningful voice or forum for the public, and forms a crucial bridge between the public and the police; (5) supports and vigorously protects the rights of minority and marginalized communities; (6) promotes procedural

8.2 What Is Civilian Oversight for Democratic Policing?

justice; and (7) offers an independent source and a repository of qualitative and quantitative data on policing and policing conduct (NACOLE, 2015).

However, we must also note that civilian oversight of the police is not a particularly unfamiliar idea for any country. In African nations, for example, although not generally acknowledged formally as such, the police have always had civilian oversight through the ruling elite such as foreign governors in colonial times to native leaders in the post-colonial period. Basically, as pointed out by Marenin (2014), what transpired was the swapping of white faces for black ones but with the institutional practices and occupational cultures, that preserved colonial norms, continuing past independence. Anyway, in both periods, none of that oversight was truly independent and it was randomly exercised to use the police as a force of control and for protection of those ruling elite as the police were made to do the bidding of the ruling elite through brutality and any other suppressive, repressive, or corrupt means—such as extrajudicial killings, torture, arbitrary detention, suppression of dissent and fomenting ethnic violence—as deemed required and primarily guided by the principle of maintaining power and hegemony rather than to the advancement of the public interest (Addo, 2022; Alemika, 2011, 2018; Auerbach, 2003; Bangura, 2018; Berg & Howell, 2016; Bierschenk, 2017; Hope, 2017, 2020; Jibrin & Yandaki, 2022; Roque, 2021; Stapleton, 2011). The police therefore became alienated from citizens because of their exclusive focus on securing social order and defending ruling interests including their own.

Indeed, across the African continent, and in Latin America as well, a number of the police forces and services can still be viewed as the primary agents of repression, abuse, violence, insecurity, corruption, criminality, extra-judicial killings, human rights violations, and a major component of state securitization rather than as institutions and promoters of safety and security (see, for instance, Alemika, 2018; Berg & Howell, 2016; Bonner et al., 2018; Cruz, 2015; Diallo, 2019; Harris & Katusiimeh, 2019; Hills, 2017; Hope, 2016, 2017, 2020; Prado et al., 2012; Roque, 2021). In fact, many of these police services are frequently, and correctly, described as predatory, corrupt, and violently abusive (see, for example, Alemika, 2018; Berg & Howell, 2016; Bonner et al., 2018; Cruz, 2015; Diallo, 2019; Hope, 2016, 2017, 2018, 2020; Newham & Faull, 2011; Ungar, 2011). In Africa, for instance, and as discussed in Chap. 5, "many people see the police as a predatory force at the service of elites and political leaders instead of as a service-oriented body with the mandate to protect civilians against violence, crime and criminals" (Diallo, 2019, p. 23). On Latin America, Ortega (2018, p. 1), reported that "looking into policing in [the region] often feels like looking into a well of misconduct, abuse, and derision." In other words, most post-colonial and post-authoritarian governments have failed to essentially change the roles, functions, culture and mission of contemporary policing in the majority of African and Latin American nations (see, for example, Bonner et al., 2018; Cruz, 2015; Diallo, 2019; Hope, 2016, 2019b; Prado et al., 2012; Ungar, 2011).

Resultantly, it is of utmost benefit to society that the police be subject to oversight by civilian bodies (preferably independent ones) to prevent, detect and provide remedies for the consequences of their excesses. Indeed, democratic policing is too important a matter to be left exclusively in the hands of the police. This is also an undisputed fact that applies globally across both developing and developed nations. As noted by Haberfeld and Gideon (2008, p. 8), "police forces, throughout the history, served and protected the ruler, the king, the politician, and never the public. The safety and security of the public was always secondary to the safety and security of the ruler, king, politician." It is therefore in that regard that Alemika (2019, p. 20) also eloquently observed with respect to Africa:

> History indicated moments in which police powers were abused by the police, political rulers and economic powerholders with impunity. Holding police accountable is therefore imperative for democratic governance and the protection of the security, welfare, rights and freedom of citizens. Effective accountability and oversight institutions and processes are necessary for the institutionalization of democratic policing culture and practices.

To further demonstrate the demand by citizens for civilian oversight of the police as they (the citizens) recognize the benefits of such an approach, and in general pursuit of the ideal of civilian oversight for democratic policing and thereby holding the police accountable for their bad behavior and general misconduct, recent survey research by Mugari and Olutola (2022) on Zimbabwe, for example, has also provided some persuasive arguments in support of the establishment of an independent civilian oversight authority comprised of individuals from different societal backgrounds such as retired judicial officers and members of the civic society. This is not surprising, however, given what is known and supported by the literature (see, for example, Mugari, 2021), that in the absence of an independent civilian authority, the existing mechanisms (the courts, parliament, the Zimbabwe Human Rights Commission [ZHRC], and CSOs), that are available to attempt to curb police misconduct and abuse of power in Zimbabwe are either inadequate or they have inherent weaknesses.

Similarly in Lesotho, the need for a dedicated independent agency for civilian oversight of the police is demonstrated by the finding of Ramonate (2022), for example, that the country's existing three civilian police oversight agencies—the Police Directorate, the PCA, and the Police Inspectorate—have all been plagued by administrative challenges that have reduced their effectiveness and they have also been victims of legal loopholes that, among other things, enables political interference in the functioning of oversight practices for the Lesotho Mounted Police Service (LMPS) and thus rendering them as "toothless watchdogs." The US Department of State (2022a) has also echoed some of the same concerns pointing to the particular fact that the PCA was ineffective because it was not given any authority to fulfill its mandate, as it could only investigate cases of police misconduct and abuse referred to it by the Police Commissioner or Minister for Police and could act on public complaints only with their approval. The PCA also lacks authority to refer cases directly to the Prosecutor's Office and it does not even publicly publish any reports.

8.3 Key Challenges to Effective Civilian Oversight of the Police

Despite the benefits to be derived by a citizenry in a society where civilian oversight of the police exists, and regardless of the civilian oversight model type of structure adopted, there are some challenges faced by civilian oversight for democratic policing. Drawing from Hope (2019a, 2020) and other resources, we discuss the key ones here. Overcoming any or all of these challenges would go a long way toward improving the effectiveness of the civilian oversight bodies to which they are applicable, and trickle down to the micro level as well.

8.3.1 Insufficient Political and Influential Leadership Support

Where there is insufficient support from the political leadership and other influential local and national leaders, such as those engaged in community affairs and human rights advocacy, civilian oversight of the police will fail as it will lack the required public acceptance and the level of legitimacy needed to function and successfully implement its mandate. In fact, without the necessary political and community leadership support, not only the public but even the police themselves would regard such civilian oversight as something to be disregarded. That, in turn, runs the risk of the civilian oversight body becoming merely symbolic and potentially inactive.

In fact, some civilian oversight bodies have failed, been dissolved, or had to be revamped due to insufficient political and other community leadership support at their inception. For example, this was certainly the case, and as one of the reasons, why the IPID in the Republic of South Africa was created as the successor replacement of the country's Independent Complaints Directorate (ICD). In many instances, such insufficient support tends to stem from the intent by political leaders to render the oversight process less than independent, or the reality as seen by community leaders that the process is indeed not independent. It is a state of affairs reflecting the dichotomy between stakeholders who, on the one hand, support the concept of independent oversight, and, on the other, those who attempt to question its legitimacy and seek to limit its impact (see, for example, Fairley, 2020).

8.3.2 Lack of Disciplining Authority

Almost all civilian oversight of police bodies/agencies still lack the authority to directly discipline police officers and/or modify policing policies. Most of the civilian oversight bodies/agencies can only (1) recommend discipline for the misconduct of individual police officers; (2) recommend changes to policing policies and procedures and suggest improvements in training; (3) arrange for mediation; and (4) assist the police service to develop or operate an early warning system for identifying problem officers (Clarke, 2009; Finn, 2001; Roth, 2015; Stone & Ward, 2000). Each of the types/approaches has strengths and weaknesses or advantages and disadvantages to their use as determined from some reviews and surveys of their application in several jurisdictions and countries (see, for example, De Angelis et al., 2016a, 2016b; Finn, 2001; Hope, 2019a, 2020; Pino, 2009; Prenzler & Ronken, 2001). There is also some emerging research surveys and reviews on the factors that can contribute to the success or failure of each type (see, for example, De Angelis et al., 2016a, 2016b; Hope, 2019a, 2020).

However, from the perspective of this book's author, and as also recognized by Stephens et al. (2018) and Wentkowska (2016), while many of those reviews and surveys are informative, because of the significant variation of oversight from one political jurisdiction or country to another, it may not be useful to make broad generalities. Some analytical views in that regard can be found, for example, in both recent and more settled contributions (see, for instance, Amnesty International, 2015; Byrne & Priestley, 2017; De Angelis et al., 2016a, 2016b; European Partners Against Corruption [EPAC], 2011; Evenson, n.d.; Finn, 2001; Guzmán-Sánchez & Espriú-Guerra, 2014; IACP, 2000; Miller and Merrick, 2002; Sen, 2010; Stageman et al., 2018).

8.3.3 Inadequate Access to Documents and Information

Another challenge centers on the inability of civilian oversight bodies to obtain important documents from the police or to obtain them in a timely fashion, which subsequently inhibits the ability of these bodies to hold police officers accountable for their actions. Such inadequate access to documents—representing a lack of sufficient cooperation from the police—can ultimately render oversight ineffective. Where a police service is not sufficiently cooperative with its oversight body, it can render oversight processes as lengthy exercises and, in some cases, may even lead to the abandonment of such exercises and a lack of completion of oversight functions. That, in turn, can result in public disapproval and mistrust of both the oversight body and the police.

Still, in recent years, and despite some continuing pockets of police resistance, much of the evidence is beginning to demonstrate that police officers are developing a deeper understanding and therefore becoming much more accepting of the role and importance of civilian oversight for police accountability and overall democratic policing, and particularly those officers who perceive greater organizational justice from command officials were significantly more likely to accept and support civilian oversight as legitimate and necessary (see, for example, Crowell, 2016; Hope, 2019a, 2020; Lee et al., 2017; Nix et al., 2018; Seyffert, 2017; Stelkia, 2020; Victoria Police Department [VICPD], n.d.; Wells & Schafer, 2007). This growing acceptance of civilian oversight should have some significant influence on improving police cooperation with the civilian oversight institutions as time moves on.

Nonetheless, in the view of this book's author, all laws establishing civilian oversight bodies should make it mandatory—and through subpoenas if necessary—for the police to cooperate with such bodies including the submission of documents and other information required and requested by such bodies. For the police to do otherwise would suggest that they consider themselves to be above any law, able to act with impunity, and therefore lack any interest in being accountable. No society should tolerate such a state of affairs. It is also this accountability imperative that has been one of the factors that influenced some international and bilateral organizations (such as the UNODC, UNDP, USAID, the EU, and the then UK Department for International Development [DFID] which was replaced in 2020 with the Foreign, Commonwealth & Development Office [FCDO]), for example) to develop and implement technical assistance and other aid packages for the benefit of Global South nations in support of democratic policing through comprehensive security sector reform (SSR) programs. Kenya's police reform program has been a particular beneficiary of this type of assistance.

Democratic policing structures, within SSR programs, are seen as necessary for creating the stability needed to ensure that a developing nation, and especially one emerging from conflict, is afforded the opportunity to build effective policing institutions, within the limits of democratic civilian control, according to the rule of law, and with respect for human rights (see, for example, Ball, 2010; DCAF, 2015b, 2019; Diallo, 2019; Hope, 2016; Shiltson, 2015). This necessity remains a sound rationale despite some recent concerns raised over issues pertaining to sovereignty, external interference, being donor-driven, and even the managerial-technical focus on institution building of the first generation SSR programs (Jackson, 2018).

8.3.4 Limited Budgetary Resources

A final challenge to be observed here, but one that is primarily related to developing countries, is that of limited resources for oversight agencies. Where an oversight body is not well resourced, the lower the probability of its objectives being met and thereby resulting in ineffectiveness and failure (Calderon & Hernandez-Figueroa, 2013). Lack of resources can therefore undermine the thoroughness and timeliness of the execution of the functions of civilian oversight bodies as was found to be the case, for example, in South Africa with its IPID (Bruce, 2020). Civilian oversight for democratic policing can be a very expensive undertaking, particularly in the case of independent agencies that employ professional investigators and conduct their own inquiries separate from internal police processes (Mehta, n.d.). As also observed by Mehta (n.d.), most of the successful examples of police oversight tend to be found in the developed nations where there is usually no sustained resource crunch. However, this is not exclusively so as Beardall (2022), for example, shows.

8.4 Overcoming the Challenges to Civilian Oversight of the Police

Obviously, overcoming the challenges to civilian oversight of the police can drastically improve police accountability. Drawing primarily on the lessons of field experience of this book's author, overcoming most of the challenges can be accomplished in environments and under conditions where the civilian oversight institutions operate as outlined and discussed below.

8.4.1 Nestled in an Appropriate and Transparent Legal Framework

An appropriate and transparent legal framework is necessary to provide for the credibility and legitimacy of the body or bodies that will be charged with the responsibility to oversee police conduct and accountability. It also establishes the statutory basis for the functioning of the oversight body or bodies and the manner in which they are perceived by the public. As observed by King (2015), an oversight body's legitimacy is often dependent on the way that it was created, and that may also affect and/or influence funding and police cooperation.

Moreover, having an appropriate and transparent legal framework provides for a clearly defined and adequate jurisdiction and authority. This is critical since, and as also summarized by the NACOLE (n.d.) and further elaborated on in Vitoroulis et al. (2021, p. 65), "an[y] agency that is not given sufficient authority and jurisdiction to perform its mission simply cannot be effective." The existence of such a framework also removes any potential conflicts or differences of opinion, internally or externally, as to the appropriate role, mandate, and/or functions of the oversight body or bodies.

In addition, an important aspect and benefit of that appropriate and legal framework is the situation of the oversight body or bodies, as the case may be, as an independent entity or entities. That is to say, that they must be stand-alone and not be placed within or under any existing institution such as a government ministry, or any other such equivalent structure. to ensure their impartiality and independence from political pressure and/or the influence of other players such as the police or other special interests. Without full operational and hierarchical independence, an external civilian oversight mechanism would also be vulnerable to the same dangers of corruption and other misconduct that may be inherent in the police service(s) over which oversight is to exercised. Institutional independence will also contribute to performance effectiveness with an emphasis on meeting the mandate fairly as opposed to pleasing one party or the other.

Based on the field experience of this book's author, for African countries, it is recommended that the legal framework must quite clearly set out the categories of public complaints of police misconduct and disciplinary breaches of public trust to

8.4 Overcoming the Challenges to Civilian Oversight of the Police

which said framework applies, as well as the duties and responsibilities of the police in the oversight process. In that regard, it must include, among any others, the following, each of which must also be more specifically defined in that legal framework:

- *Corrupt Practice or Behavior*—Any action or omission, a promise of any action or omission, or any attempt of action or omission, committed by a police officer or a group of police officers, characterized by the misuse of their official position and motivated in significant part with the achievement of personal/private or organizational gain or advantage. This would include, for example, demands for bribes for accessing police services or to avoid a problem with the police.
- *Abuse of Authority*—On-duty police engaging in oppressive conduct towards a member or members of the public, including police brutality, torture or assault of any member or members of the public; any serious injury or death in police custody; and any serious injury or death as a result of police actions.
- *Discreditable Conduct or Police Misconduct*—Any conduct by both on-duty or off-duty police officer(s) that they know, or ought to know, is illegal and would likely bring discredit to themselves or their police service, including rape or any other sexual abuse; and rape or any other sexual abuse of any person in police custody.
- *Accessory to Misconduct*—Police officer(s) being an accessory to any allegation of misconduct against one or more of their fellow officers.
- *Improper Conduct While Off-Duty*—Off-duty police officer(s) conduct that would be considered a breach of discipline had the police officer(s) been on-duty.
- *Use or Care of Firearm(s)*—Police officer(s) discharge of any official firearm, and the failure to use or care for firearm(s) in accordance with standards or requirements established by law or police service regulations or orders.
- *Neglect of Duty*—Police officer(s) failure to promptly or diligently do anything that is in their duty to do, including promptly and diligently obeying a lawful order of a supervisor, without good and sufficient cause, and properly accounting for money or property received.
- *Deceit*—Intentionally making or issuing a false or misleading oral or written statement, or entry in an official document or record, and/or the intent to deceive by altering, destroying, damaging, concealing, erasing, or deleting all or part of an official record.
- *Unauthorized or Improper Disclosure of Information*—Police officer(s) disclosing or attempting to disclose information that has either not been authorized, be done for corrupt reasons, be injurious to police investigations/operations or the administration of justice, or any combination thereof.
- *Misuse or Abuse of Intoxicants*—Police officer(s) appearing unfit for duty due to the effects of intoxicating alcohol and/or any drug.
- *Discourtesy*—Police officer(s), in the performance of police duties, failing to behave with the necessary courtesy to be duly given to a member or members of the public.

- *Damage to Police Property*—Police officer(s) misusing, misplacing, or damaging any police property or property that is in police custody, and/or the failure to report any loss, destruction, or damage to such property.
- *Damage to Property of Others*—Police officer(s) damaging property belonging to a member of the public and/or failing to report such damage, regardless of how it occurred.
- *Monitoring Places of Police Detention*—To determine the conditions of custodial facilities and assess whether detainee human rights are being violated, regular visits (announced or unannounced) by any oversight body or bodies to places of police detention are not to be impeded by the police.
- *Failure to Cooperate*—Police officer(s) failing to cooperate with the oversight body or bodies including failure to produce any document, papers or other thing on the request or order of the oversight body or bodies, or refusal to be examined or to answer questions relating to an inquiry put to them by the oversight body or bodies.
- *Mandatory Referral to the Oversight Body or Bodies*—The requirement that the police administration have a duty to report and/or refer, in a timely manner, any police misconduct and disciplinary breaches of public trust, whether known or not known by the oversight body or bodies, but which fall under the mandate of such oversight body or bodies.
- *Witness Protection*—Witnesses required and/or summoned to participate in any investigation or proceeding of the oversight body or bodies are to be given the same protections and privileges as necessary and within existing law.
- *Informing Parties of Progress and Results of an Investigation*—Parties to any oversight investigation are to be kept abreast of its progress and be advised, as soon as practicably possible, of its outcome at its conclusion.
- *Implementation of Oversight Recommendations*—The manner, method(s), and any procedure(s) for police implementation of the recommendations of the oversight process or reasons for any proposal to depart from, or not to implement, any or some of the recommendations, and what actions can be taken by the oversight body or bodies in the event of dissatisfaction with either implementation progress or any lack of implementation.

8.4.2 Sufficiently Funded

Sufficient funding is essential for operational effectiveness. Having sufficient and secure funding can also free oversight bodies from political manipulation. The already small and mostly non-guaranteed budget is one vehicle by which external actors attempt to undermine oversight efforts (Kim, 2017). Among other things, such funding limitations, in turn, can make it very difficult to recruit and retain the skilled personnel to conduct investigations, for example. Consequently, just as important as having adequate financial resources is the strategic management and allocation of those resources by the oversight institutions.

Also, to be noted here, and for those developing countries where it is sustainable, donor-funded police reform programs ought to support the existing local/national bodies charged with civilian oversight rather than try to establish new structures. This will not only promote the concept of national ownership but also help to build local/national institutional capacity for more effective oversight of the police. As correctly concluded by Aitchison and Blaustein (2013), for example, although external actors may be well placed to support policing for democracy in divided, post-conflict, as well as post-authoritarian contexts, democratically-responsive policing requires greater sensitivity to locally-defined needs, and is undermined when external interventions are driven by the needs, priorities and/or interests of external sponsors. Similar general conclusions have also emerged in Asbjørnsen (2017) and Eckhard (2016), for example.

8.4.3 Fully Supported by the Political Leadership and Other National Governance Structures

If the political leadership and other national governance structures, such as the courts and legislatures, for example, demonstrate no will to support and embrace institutions responsible for the civilian oversight of the police, then such institutions will become moribund and fail since they cannot function without such influential support. There are cases, for example, where influential politicians have either been captured by the police or operate in partnership with the police to engage in corrupt or other felonious activities (see, for example, Hope, 2016; Nagle, 2010). This not only encourages and perpetrates police misconduct but provides cover and impunity for those police so involved. The ultimate effect is to render moot the detection, oversight, and punishment of such conduct.

In fact, in Africa, as demonstrated in Chap. 5, and as also noted by Livingston (2013, p. 14), "the police are not only distrusted but often entirely dismissed from the crime prevention equation," with "high levels of corruption and low levels of accountability of many of Africa's police forces [appearing] to be a major cause of this gap," and "more often than not, there is little political commitment to police oversight or reform. Instead, the police are frequently used to preserve or advance the personal interests of senior officers, officials, or other influential persons."

8.4.4 Bestowed with the Necessary Investigative Powers to Coerce Police Cooperation

Having the full powers and other mechanisms to both investigate and force police cooperation is a particularly necessary requirement here. As Fairley (2020) has noted, a major source of debate is the need for subpoena power to compel both police and civilian witnesses to provide information that is essential and relevant to the investigatory process and in the review and appeals of oversight processes and outcomes. An institution responsible for civilian oversight of the police will be much more effective if it has the ability and authority to subpoena witnesses, documents, and other materials relevant to an investigation (see also Fair and Just Prosecution [FJP], 2021). Conversely, a civilian oversight agency that does not have the authority to compel witness appearances or to gather evidence will have a severely limited ability to make an informed judgment regarding police conduct or misconduct.

8.4.5 Adequately Staffed with the Requisite Personnel and Expertise to Fulfill Their Mandate

In concert with the need for sufficient financial resources is the need for appropriate human resources with the requisite skills to fulfill the mandate of effective civilian oversight of the police. Having qualified staff (such as investigators) with the appropriate skills and training will lend credibility to the conduct of their work and their findings, reports and other outputs stemming therefrom.

In addition, the recruited staff must also be representative of the diversity of the society as a whole as well as that of the police service being overseen. Diversity of staff can garner public trust and provide the necessary public facing view of legitimacy that is an absolute requirement for public acceptance of the outcomes of investigations of police misconduct. In Africa, such diversity must encompass gender, race (where applicable), tribal, language, and regional/geographic differences, for example. Just like we know that diversity in policing can improve police-civilian interactions, the same applies to the staff of police oversight institutions interacting with the civilian victims of police misconduct or their families, for instance.

8.4.6 Operations Conducted Based on a Sound Strategic Plan

Sometimes referred to as a statement of intent, a strategic plan is an organizational management tool that is used to set out strategic objectives (or directions) supported by initiatives and activities and linked to outcomes; outline priorities; focus energy and resources; ensure that employees and other stakeholders are working toward common goals; establish agreement around intended outcomes/results; and assess and adjust the organization's direction in response to a changing environment. It is therefore the process by which an organization determines what it intends to do now, and in the future, and how it will get there in pursuit of its mandate. Understandably, there could be internal or external factors, or some combination thereof, that may impact the successful implementation of the strategic plan.

8.4 Overcoming the Challenges to Civilian Oversight of the Police

However, a well thought out strategic plan, especially where guided with input from stakeholders, offers the best practice approach to potentially successful implementation of a strategic framework for oversight of police misconduct and overall police performance to enhance democratic policing.

In that regard, we can look at the current strategic plans of Africa's two independent civilian oversight of police institutions. In Kenya, the IPOA *Strategic Plan 2019–2024* (68 pages in length) has outlined its Vision as: "A transformative civilian oversight Authority that promotes public trust and confidence in the National Police Service" and a Mission: "To conduct independent and impartial investigations, inspections, audits and monitoring of the National Police Service to enhance professionalism and discipline of the Service" (IPOA, 2019, p. 5). The strategic plan, among other things, also clearly outlines: (1) the benefits of civilian oversight of the police; (2) the challenges IPOA will have to confront in pursuit of those benefits and its overall mandate; (3) the relevance and contributions of the IPOA to the SDGs, including the all-important SDG 16 which was discussed in Chap. 6; (4) the lessons learnt during the implementation of the previous strategic plan that now influences what sub-strategies can or cannot be impactful, for instance; and (5) the strategic objectives or key results areas that will be pursued in implementation, which are: (a) Police accountability; (b) Stakeholder cooperation and complementarity; (c) Research and information management; and (d) Institutional capacity (IPOA, 2019).

In South Africa, the IPID *Strategic Plan 2020–2025*, which is less detailed than the IPOA strategic plan at about one-third the length (24 pages), outlines its Vision as: "An effective independent investigative oversight body that ensures policing that is committed to promoting respect for the rule of law and human dignity" and a Mission: "To conduct independent, impartial and quality investigations of identified criminal offences allegedly committed by members of the South African Police Services (SAPS) and Metro Police Services (MPS), and to make appropriate recommendations in line with the IPID Act, whilst maintaining the highest standard of integrity and excellence" (IPID, 2020, p. 10). In addition, there is an Impact Statement: "Responsive and accountable police service that renders professional service in a human rights environment" (IPID, 2020, p. 17). The Impact Statement is attached to four plan outcomes with associated outcome indicators. The plan outcomes are: (1) Reduced level of police criminality and misconduct; (2) Improved awareness of IPID's services; (3) Effective and efficient administrative support; and (4) Department's legal interests protected (IPID, 2020).

8.4.7 Robust Outreach Exercises Embraced and Implemented

As opposed to being superficial, robust outreach is an important function that not only informs the public and other stakeholders but is critical for building trust with the public. It must be regarded as—and form—a critical part of the strategic plan as discussed above. Indeed, effective outreach is essential to a successful oversight system; otherwise, allegations of misconduct will go unreported and the system will not be used. Civilian oversight bodies must therefore be appropriately visible and accessible to all stakeholders.

Based on the experience of some of Canada's effective civilian oversight bodies, Briggs (2017) has also found outreach to be a significant element for effective civilian oversight of the police. The oversight institutions must take the lead in educating the community about their (the oversight institutions) purpose, mission, goals, and procedures for filing complaints of police misconduct and, as well, assist in promoting efforts to help build trust between the police and the public. This will all shape community confidence that their grievances will be heard and adequately dealt with. Outreach, as a significant element in building trust, is an essential way to improve police legitimacy. As Schaap (2021) has noted, the police need to be seen as legitimate (and hence need to be trusted) not only by citizens but the surrounding agencies and governments as well. Further, and as also argued by Walker (2020) and Witkin (2017), outreach exercises can create a symbiotic relationship between civilian oversight and community policing with the hopeful end result of producing more effective civilian oversight of the police.

In that regard, with respect to Africa, Sigsworth (2019, p. 15) has argued that "direct engagement and collaboration between the public and the police hold significant potential for achieving front-end accountability," and further, "as a key component of democratic policing, public engagement in police accountability [can] provide an accessible way to start this process."

8.5 Improved Police Accountability and Better Security Through Civilian Oversight for Democratic Policing: Final Summary Thoughts

Police oversight institutions are critical components of the accountability framework in modern democracies or countries or political jurisdictions seeking to be democratic and/or wanting to pursue democratic policing, such as many of those in Africa (see, for example, Bruce, 2021; Govender & Pillay, 2022; Hope, 2015). Like all watchdogs that have become more salient in modern governance (see Bovens & Wille, 2021), civilian institutions for oversight of the police play a key role in promoting accountability, transparency, and independence of police work related primarily to misconduct in that work. Independent civilian oversight bodies have the potential to investigate police misconduct much more effectively and without bias, and their findings are often considered more credible by the public (Guittet et al., 2022). Police accountability enhances public trust in the police which, in turn, leads to improved community security. As argued by Africa (2016, p. 1), "civilian democratic oversight and control is a necessary, though not exclusive precondition for accountable and legitimate security. This is the lesson from countries emerging from armed conflict, from authoritarian and undemocratic rule, and even countries that are relatively stable and politically inclusive" and, "where civilian oversight of the security organs of state is absent or weak, there are usually higher levels of impunity, abuse of power and state violence than where there is monitoring, control and oversight of the institutions."

Although there is no best practice(s) type/approach to civilian oversight of the police, and there are some outstanding challenges being faced as discussed above, significant advances have been made across the globe in developing and implementing frameworks for the civilian oversight of democratic policing as also outlined and analyzed in this chapter. In the case of developing countries, much of that progress has occurred through funding from donor-sponsored programs under the umbrella of security sector reform. Consequently, civilian oversight of the police has made major headway in the citizens' desire to bring accountability to policing in their respective political jurisdiction or country. In many instances, this had initially been, or is currently being, spearheaded and influenced by the push from minority or more marginalized ethnic communities that had or have been the most affected by police misconduct and therefore they had been, or are currently, seeking an antidote to the patterns of discrimination and abuse in policing by highlighting police abuses and ultimately promoting meaningful reform (see, for example, Ali & Pirog, 2019; Kwon & Wortley, 2022; Ramsey, 2018; UNHRC, 2022; US Department of State, 2022b; Wilson, 2014; Wilson & Buckler, 2010). Success in this regard is geared towards making police officers responsive to the needs of the citizenry while at the same time improving the efficiency and effectiveness in service delivery (Ofer, 2016; Walsh & Conway, 2011). This augurs well in the shift toward what Friedman (2017) and Ponomarenko and Friedman (2017) refer to as front-end democratic accountability in policing—the transparent rules, guided by public input and are available for all to view, that are in place before police officers act and that therefore regulate police conduct.

As Fairley (2020, p. 50) further observed about the US, but applicable globally, "the recent expansion of civilian oversight, and the fact that many civilian oversight entities have operated for decades, illustrates that civilian oversight has moved into the mainstream as an important component of any police accountability system." Accordingly, civilian oversight can therefore be successful where properly implemented, and once in operation, it can help build community trust in, and public confidence with, law enforcement as long as the public believes that procedural justice is being enhanced as a means to curb police misconduct and hold departments accountable (Fulbright, 2019; Worden et al., 2018). Cooperation and accountability will increase, people will more readily engage in contacting the police with information, and neighborhoods will be made safer and more secure (Hope, 2019a, 2020; Seyffert, 2017). As argued by Stone and Bobb (2002, p. 1), "it is therefore fundamental to democratic societies that police power, including the powers to arrest, to question, and to use lethal and non-lethal force, be closely regulated," and "ultimately be subject to civilian control through democratic institutions. In such societies, a continuing challenge is to create practical mechanisms for ongoing oversight that curb or correct the occasional abuses of police power" (Stone & Bobb, 2002, p. 1). Coming to grips with that challenge remains a fundamental necessity globally given that "the complex and institutionally embedded nature of police power means that external accountability mechanisms that extend beyond legal regulations are required for effective oversight consistent with broader principles of liberal democracy" (Lister & Rowe, 2016, p. 4).

In recent years, much work has begun to take shape in producing more evidence-based research on practices related to civilian oversight of the police. Particularly, the NACOLE and the Policing Project at the New York University School of Law, for example, have been at the forefront of this exercise to enhance fair and professional law enforcement responsive to community needs related to the US. In addition, the Policing Project is aiming to strengthen policing by bringing the ordinary processes of democratic accountability to bear (Policing Project, n.d.). In Africa also, the APCOF has been established as a network that centers its research and advocacy work on promoting police accountability through democratic governance using the mechanism of civilian oversight (APCOF, n.d.). There is also the CHRI which, among other activities, is also engaged in a police reforms program that aims to realize increased demand for rights-based police reform and the strengthening of police accountability in the Commonwealth, including those member states in Africa. The CHRI works with the police, governments, independent institutions, and civil society actors to improve policing, advocating for human-rights based, accountable police practices. Particularly, the CHRI advocates for the establishment of independent bodies to oversee the police, and investigate complaints of police misconduct (CHRI, n.d.). And, in Canada, the CACOLE is a national non-profit organization of individuals and agencies involved in the oversight of police officers in Canada. "CACOLE is dedicated to advancing the concept, principles and application of civilian oversight of law enforcement throughout Canada and abroad" (CACOLE, n.d., p. 1). In addition to CACOLE, there is also the Canadian Association of Police Governance (CAPG) which is similarly a national organization dedicated to excellence in police governance in Canada with the goal to improve the effectiveness of civilian oversight bodies that govern local/municipal police (CAPG, n.d.).

Other research such as that conducted by Rosenthal (2018), Ho et al. (2022), and Cheng and Qu (2022), for example, have been providing evidence on the conditions for successful civilian oversight. The most important of these include agency independence, job security, the need for professional qualified staff, unfettered access to information, the ability to publicly report on the agency's work, representation, empowerment, and a willingness on the part of government officials to tolerate criticism of the police (Rosenthal, 2018; Ho et al., 2022).

Similarly, research with significant cross-country appeal—in further concert with the movement toward civilian oversight as an instrument of police reform for democratic policing— has also been published that outline and incorporate some excellent approaches to performance evaluations of police oversight agencies (see, for example, Ali & Nicholson-Crotty, 2021; Alpert et al., 2016; Faull, 2013; Filstad & Gottschalk, 2011; Karpiak et al., 2022; Prenzler & Lewis, 2005; Walker, 2001). These approaches are intended to provide guidance on methods for evaluating how well or how badly oversight institutions are exercising their functions and to assist in determining whether or not said institutions are making an impact on improving police conduct. This is particularly important given the existence of complaints in some countries and political jurisdictions by members of the public and civil society organizations that the oversight bodies have been merely symbolic rather than operationally functional. As further research efforts continue onward, many (like this book's author who is similarly engaged in some of those efforts) will look forward to the publication of those research products. Undoubtedly, those outputs can only further enhance our knowledge base, add to the stock of the literature, and provide deeper evidence for better policy development and implementation in support of more effective civilian oversight for democratic policing.

For Africa, effective institutions for civilian oversight of the police most certainly need to be established. This is an important tool to try to hold the police to account for their predatory and brutal behavior, and other forms of misconduct, in the context of democratic norms, and will certainly increase public trust in the police and contribute to much more peaceful and stable societies. As noted by Diallo (2019), and as this book has demonstrated, democracy and sustainable development cannot take hold in Africa if security institutions such as the police remain as bad actors outside of the rule of law. Moreover, and as also had been recognized by Francis (2012, p. 20), and is still the case today in Africa, "the diverse contributions of policing to bad governance, violence, civil wars, insecurities, and underdevelopment led to the recognition that policing is in a state of crisis and that both the institution and practice/philosophy needs fundamental reform to make it 'fit for purpose in the twenty-first century'." Police accountability must therefore become a high priority in the good governance and sustainable development quests across the continent.

Such police accountability can be achieved through independent civilian oversight structures as this chapter advocates. The time has long past for such structures to have been put in place given the historically bad behavior of the police with impunity, and the resultant negative consequences on society. Indeed, it remains quite surprising that only Kenya and South Africa currently have such institutions in place. In recognition of that state of affairs and the general concern with police accountability in Africa, an International Conference on Police Accountability in Africa was held in Nairobi, Kenya in July 2019 under the sponsorship of the International Commission of Jurists-Kenyan Section (ICJ-Kenya), the CLEEN Foundation, the Afro-Asian Association for Justice Development (AAAJD), the Institute for Development and Communication-India (IDC-India) and supported by the Open Society Foundation (OSF). The theme was "Achieving Effective, Legitimate and Sustainable Security Sector Reform" (see AAAJD, 2019a). Among other things, the communique of the conference called for and/or noted the following: (1) that institutions providing oversight on police accountability must be established in all African states and exist apart from the police they seek to hold accountable; (2) that all African states make deliberate efforts to adopt mechanisms to limit political interference and control of national police services to provide for a transparent and unbiased process in keeping police institutions accountable; (3) that, to further an agenda of service delivery, it is imperative that all African states evolve from having police institutions that focus on enforcement as result of colonial police infrastructures to become more service-oriented, as well as acknowledge that conversations must move beyond a focus on the challenges of colonialism; (4) that African states must recognize and acknowledge that merely having laws requiring police accountability is not sufficient in ensuring a fair and democratic society, and therefore there should be deliberate efforts to implement the laws through linking them to reform programs, as well as efforts made to draft new laws where needed to further strengthen accountability of the police; (5) that African states should endeavor to develop innovative practices that seek to find ways in which police accountability can be achieved in a manner that is consistent with international best practices while taking note of the different security realities in the region; and (6) that African states should address corruption within their police departments by ensuring that accountable systems are put in place and codes of conduct and ethics for police officers are implemented (AAAJD, 2019b).

In other country specific situations, such as Uganda, for example, after yet another senseless police killing, this time of more than 50 people as a result of their protests against the arrest of an Opposition Leader in November 2020, one analyst and human rights defender pleaded that it was "high time lawmakers in Uganda responded pro-actively and establish once for all, a dedicated independent police oversight system either at the level of a commission or authority that is equipped with the requisite capacity and skills required to investigate complex policing actions and operations" (Ndifuna, 2020, p. 1). Similarly, for Ghana, after the arrest and police killing of a trader in April 2022, the CHRI again called for the government to establish an Independent Police Complaints Commission (IPCC-for Ghana), which Ghana had accepted at the UNHRC since November 2017 (CHRI, 2022; see, also, McDevitt & Bullock, 2021).

For Malawi, the US government, in partnership with the UNDP and the country's Independent Complaints Commission (ICC), has launched an initiative that will enable the Commission to conduct complex investigations aimed at increasing public trust in the Malawi-PS. Through the project, "Strengthening the Independent Complaints Commission," the US government is providing technical and financial support to strengthen the capacity of the ICC as a valuable oversight body in supporting greater levels of professionalism and accountability in the Malawi-PS. The ICC was established in 2020, under Sect. 128 of the 2010 Police Act, to receive and investigate complaints by the public against police officers and the Malawi-PS and ensure the overall accountability of the service (US Embassy in Malawi, 2022). For Zimbabwe, it was strongly argued by Mugari and Olutola (2022) that an independent entity consisting of non-police officers is the most effective mechanism for handling police misconduct and needs to be put in place. However, as this book has also made clear, and Van Der Spuy (2021) has alluded to in the context of South Africa, the establishment of civilian oversight structures is only a necessary first step. It is not sufficient. It must also be accompanied by strategic planning for the actualization of the non-negotiable citizenry demand for legitimate, human rights-compliant, and accountable/effective policing. As was learned from the successful democratic police reform in Georgia, characterized by its emphasis on fighting police corruption and crime (see O'Shea, 2022, 2023), ineffective external oversight removes incentives for the police to moderate their corrupt and brutal behavior.

References

AAAJD. (2019a). Police accountability in Africa Conference. Retrieved from https://aaajd.org/police-accountability-in-africaconference/
AAAJD. (2019b). *Conference communique, International Conference on Police Accountability in Africa*. Retrieved from https://aaajd.org/wp-content/uploads/2019/09/CONFERENCE-COMMUNIQUE-INTERNATIONAL-CONFERENCE-ON-POLICE-ACCOUNTABILITY-IN-AFRICA.pdf
Addo, K. O. (2022). British colonial rule: Its impact on police corruption in Ghana. *International NGO Journal, 17*(2), 12–25. https://doi.org/10.5897/INGOJ2022.0363
Africa, S. (2016). Accountable and legitimate security through civilian democratic oversight and control. [Think Piece No. 1, Learning Lab on SSG in Africa]. Retrieved from https://issat.dcaf.ch/download/108715/1964963/Think%20Piece%20No%201_Civilian%20democratic%20oversight.pdf
Aitchison, A., & Blaustein, J. (2013). Policing for democracy or democratically responsive policing? Examining the limits of externally driven police reform. *European Journal of Criminology, 10*(4), 496–511. https://doi.org/10.1177/2F1477370812470780
Ajilore, O. (2018, June 25). How civilian review boards can further police accountability and improve community relations. [Scholars Strategy Network]. Retrieved from https://scholars.org/print/pdf/node/16105
Alemika, E. E. O. (2011). Policing oversight in Africa: Prospects, opportunities and challenges. In S. Tait, C. Frank, & I. Ndung'u (Eds.), *Workshop report–policing oversight: Advances, challenges and prospects* (pp. 3–8). Institute for Security Studies.
Alemika, E. E. O. (2018). The constraints of rights-based policing in Africa. In E. E. O. Alemika, M. Ruteere, & S. Howell (Eds.), *Policing reform in Africa: Moving towards a rights-based approach in a climate of terrorism, insurgency and serious violent crime* (pp. 14–43). APCOF.
Alemika, E. E. O. (2019, July 3–4). Police accountability in Africa. [Keynote Paper for the Conference on Police Accountability in Africa: Achieving Effective, Legitimate and Sustainable Security Sector Reforms]. Retrieved from https://aaajd.org/wpcontent/uploads/2019/09/International-Conference-on-Police-Accountability-in-Africa-Report_Kenya.pdf
Ali, M. U., & Nicholson-Crotty, S. (2021). Examining the accountability-performance link: The case of citizen oversight of police. *Public Performance & Management Review, 44*(3), 523–559. https://doi.org/10.1080/15309576.2020.1806086
Ali, M. U., & Pirog, M. (2019). Social accountability and institutional change: The case of citizen oversight of police. *Public Administration Review, 79*(3), 411–426. https://doi.org/10.1111/puar.13055
Alpert, G. P., Cawthray, T., Rojek, J., & Ferdik, F. (2016). Citizen oversight in the United States and Canada: Applying outcome measures and evidence-based concepts. In T. Prenzler & G. den Heyer (Eds.), *Civilian oversight of police: Advancing accountability in law enforcement* (pp. 179–204). CRC Press/Taylor and Francis.
Amagnya, M. A. (2023). Police officers' support for corruption: Examining the impact of police culture. *Policing: An International Journal, 46*(1), 84–99. https://doi.org/10.1108/PIJPSM-06-2022-0085
Amnesty International. (2015). *Police oversight*. Amnesty International Dutch Section.
APCOF. (n.d.). Organization strategy. Retrieved from http://apcof.org/about-us/
Asbjørnsen, K. (2017). Succeeding with security sector reform: How important is local ownership. *The SAIS Europe Journal of Global Affairs, 20*(Spring), 75–83.

Attard, B. (2010). Oversight of law enforcement is beneficial and needed—Both inside and out. *Pace Law Review, 30*(5), 1548–1561. http://digitalcommons.pace.edu/plr/vol30/iss5/12

Auerbach, J. N. (2003). Police accountability in Kenya, African. *Human Rights Law Journal, 3*(2), 275–313.

Aydin-Aitchison, A., & Mermutluoğlu, C. (2020). Mapping human rights to democratic policing through the ECHR. *Security and Human Rights, 30*(1–4), 72–99. https://doi.org/10.1163/18750230-03001001

Ball, N. (2010). The evolution of the security sector reform agenda. In M. Sedra (Ed.), *The future of security sector reform* (pp. 29–44). The Centre for International Governance Innovation.

Bangura, I. (2018). Democratically transformed or business as usual: The Sierra Leone police and democratic policing in Sierra Leone, stability. *International Journal of Security & Development, 7*(1), 1–11. https://doi.org/10.5334/sta.601

Bayley, D. H. (2001). *Democratizing the police abroad: What to do and how to do it*. National Institute of Justice, U.S. Department of Justice.

Bayley, D. H. (2006). *Changing the guard: Developing democratic police abroad*. Oxford University Press.

Bayley, D. (2015). Human rights in policing: A global assessment. *Policing and Society, 25*(5), 540–547. https://doi.org/10.1080/10439463.2014.895352

Beardall, T. R. (2022). Police legitimacy regimes and the suppression of citizen oversight in response to police violence. *Criminology, 60*(4), 740–765. https://doi.org/10.1111/1745-9125.12321

Berg, J. (2013). Civilian oversight of police in South Africa: From the ICD to the IPID. *Police Practice and Research, 14*(2), 144–154. https://doi.org/10.1080/15614263.2013.767094

Berg, J. (2021). Policing reform in the context of plural policing: The south African case. *Policing: A Journal of Policy and Practice, 5*(1), 412–424. https://doi.org/10.1093/police/paaa075

Berg, J., & Howell, S. (2016). Civilian oversight of police in Africa: Trends and challenges. In T. Prenzler & G. den Heyer (Eds.), *Civilian oversight of police: Advancing accountability in law enforcement* (pp. 121–138). CRC Press/Taylor and Francis.

Bierschenk, T. (2017). Who are the police in Africa? In J. Beek, M. Göpfert, O. Owen, & J. Steinberg (Eds.), *Police in Africa: The street-level view* (pp. 103–120). Oxford University Press.

Bittner, E. (1980). *The functions of the police in modern society*. Oelgeschlager, Gunn and Hain Publishers.

Bobb, M., & Pearsall, A. (2010). The changing mission of police monitoring. *Community Policing Dispatch, 3*(1), 43.

Boghani, P. (2016, July 13). Is civilian oversight the answer to distrust of police? Frontline. Retrieved from https://www.pbs.org/wgbh/frontline/article/is-civilian-oversight-the-answer-to-distrust-of-police/

Bonner, M. D. (2020). What democratic policing is … and is not. *Policing and Society, 30*(9), 1044–1060. https://doi.org/10.1080/10439463.2019.1649405

Bonner, M. D., Seri, G., Kubal, M. R., & Kempa, M. (Eds.). (2018). *Police abuse in contemporary democracies*. Palgrave Macmillan/Springer Nature.

Bourke, C. (n.d.). Police complaints, civilian oversight, democracy. Retrieved from https://www.yumpu.com/en/document/view/34184047/police-complaints-civilian-oversight-democracy-scadding-court-

Bovens, M., & Wille, A. (2021). Indexing watchdog accountability powers: A framework for assessing the accountability capacity of independent oversight institutions. *Regulation & Governance, 15*(3), 856–876. https://doi.org/10.1111/rego.12316

Briggs, W. (2017). Police oversight: Civilian oversight boards and lessons learned from our neighbors to the north. *Suffolk Transnational Law Review, 40*(1), 139–164.

Bruce, D. (2020). Are South Africa's cops accountable? Results of independent police investigative directorate investigations. [APCOF Research Paper 25]. APCOF.

Bruce, D. (2021). *The African police accountability agenda in the 2020s: Continuity and disruption*. APCOF.

References

Byrne, J., & Priestley, W. (2017). *Police oversight mechanisms in the Council of Europe Member States*. Council of Europe Publishing.

CACOLE. (n.d.). About us. Retrieved from http://www.cacole.ca/index-eng.shtml

Calderon, E. L., & Hernandez-Figueroa, M. (2013). *Citizen oversight committees in law enforcement*. Center for Public Policy, University of California. Retrieved from http://cpp.fullerton.edu/pdf/cpp_policeoversight_report.pdf

Cao, L., Huang, L., & Sun, I. Y. (2014). *Policing in Taiwan: From authoritarianism to democracy*. Routledge.

CAPG. (n.d.). Who we are? Retrieved from http://capg.ca/who-we-are/

Cheng, T., & Qu, J. (2022). Regulatory intermediaries and the challenge of democratic policing. *Criminology & Public Policy, 21*(1), 59–81. https://doi.org/10.1111/1745-9133.12573

Choi, K. J. (2015). *Politics of law enforcement: Policing and police reform in new democracies* (Unpublished PhD dissertation, University of Washington). Seattle.

CHRI. (n.d.). What we do: Police reform. Retrieved from https://www.humanrightsinitiative.org/content/police-reforms

CHRI. (2022, May 17). Independent investigations must be conducted into the killing of Albert Donkor. [Press Release]. Retrieved from https://3news.com/nkoranza-mayhem-parliament-interior-ministry-told-to-urgently-create-police-complaints-commission/

Cintrón Perino, J. R. (2004). Developments in citizen oversight of law enforcement. *The Urban Lawyer, 36*(2), 387–398.

City of Austin, Office of the Police Monitor. (2018). *Police oversight advisory working group recommendations*. Office of the Police Monitor, City of Austin.

Clarke, S. (2009). Arrested oversight: A comparative analysis and case study of how civilian oversight of the police should function and how it fails. *Columbia Journal of Law and Social Problems, 43*(1), 1–49. http://jlsp.law.columbia.edu/wp-content/uploads/sites/8/2017/03/43-Clarke.pdf

CRCC. (2009). *Police investigating police: Final public report*. CRCC.

Crowell, M. (2016). *Police officers' attitudes toward civilian oversight mechanisms in Ontario, Canada*. [PhD thesis, University of Waterloo].

Cruz, J. M. (2015). Police misconduct and political legitimacy in Central America. *Journal of Latin American Studies, 47*(2), 251–283. https://doi.org/10.1017/S0022216X15000085

DCAF. (2015a). The security sector: Roles and responsibilities in security provision, management and oversight. [SSR Backgrounder Series]. DCAF.

DCAF. (2015b). The police: Roles and responsibilities in good security sector governance. [SSR Backgrounder Series]. DCAF.

DCAF. (2019). Police reform: Applying the principles of good security sector governance to policing. [SSR Backgrounder Series]. DCAF.

De Angelis, J., Rosenthal, R., & Buchner, B. (2016a). *Civilian oversight of law enforcement: A review of the strengths and weaknesses of various models*. NACOLE.

De Angelis, J., Rosenthal, R., & Buchner, B. (2016b). *Civilian oversight of law enforcement: Assessing the evidence*. NACOLE.

Decker, S. H., & Shjarback, J. A. (2020). Options for increasing civilian oversight of the police. In C. M. Katz & E. R. Maguire (Eds.), *Transforming the police: Thirteen key reforms* (pp. 113–125). Waveland Press.

den Boer, M., & Pyo, C. Scheltus, C., & Mathai-Luke, R. (2011). *Good policing: Instruments, models and practices*. Singapore: Asia-Europe Foundation and Jakarta, Indonesia: Hanns Seidel Foundation Indonesia. Retrieved from https://www.asef.org/images/docs/Good%20Policing%20-%20Instruments,%20Models%20and%20Practices%20-%20FINAL.pdf

den Heyer, G., & Beckley, A. (2016). Police independent oversight in Australia and New Zealand. In T. Prenzler & G. den Heyer (Eds.), *Civilian oversight of police: Advancing accountability in law enforcement* (pp. 205–225). CRC Press/Taylor and Francis.

Diallo, F. S. (2019). *State policing in sub-Saharan Africa: The weakest link of security sector governance*. L' Harmattan.

Diaz, E. I. (2009). Police oversight. In J. de Rivera (Ed.), *Handbook on building cultures of peace* (pp. 287–301). Peace Psychology Book Series, Springer Nature.

Eckhard, S. (2016). *The challenges and lessons learned in supporting security sector reform*. Friedrich-Ebert-Stiftung.

Ellison, G. (2007). A blueprint for democratic policing anywhere in the world? Police reform, political transition, and conflict resolution in Northern Ireland. *Police Quarterly, 10*(3), 243–269. https://doi.org/10.1177/2F1098611107304735

EPAC. (2011). *Police oversight principles*. Retrieved from https://igp.gouvernement.lu/dam-assets/service/attributions/police-oversight-principles.pdf

Evenson, M. (n.d.). Embracing citizen oversight: A police executive's guide to improving accountability. Retrieved from https://www.coursehero.com/file/44542895/EvensonProjFinal311-1doc/

Fairley, S. R. (2020). Survey says? U.S. cities double down on civilian oversight of police despite challenges and controversy, *Cardozo Law Review de Novo*. Retrieved from http://cardozolawreview.com/wp-content/uploads/2020/01/FAIRLEY.DN_.2019.pdf

Faull, A. (2013). Monitoring the performance of police oversight agencies. [APCOF Policy Paper 8]. Retrieved from http://apcof.org/wp-content/uploads/2016/05/No-8-Monitoring-Performance-of-Police-Oversight-Agencies-Andrew-Faull.pdf

Feys, Y., Verhage, A., & Boels, D. (2018). A state-of-the-art review on police accountability: What do we know from empirical studies? *International Journal of Police Science and Management, 20*(3), 225–239. https://doi.org/10.1177/2F1461355718786297

Fichtelberg, A. (2013). Democratic policing and state capacity in an integrated world. In G. Andreopoulos (Ed.), *Policing across Borders: Law enforcement networks and the challenges of crime control* (pp. 11–26). Springer Science+Business Media.

Filstad, C., & Gottschalk, P. (2011). Performance evaluation of police oversight agencies. *Policing and Society, 21*(1), 96–109. https://doi.org/10.1080/10439463.2010.540653

Finn, P. (2001). *Citizen review of police: Approaches and implementation*. Office of Justice Programs, National Institute of Justice, US Department of Justice.

FJP. (2021). Promoting independent police accountability mechanisms: Key principles for civilian oversight of law enforcement. Retrieved from https://fairandjustprosecution.org/issues/promoting-community-trust-and-police-accountability/

Flores-Macías, G. A., & Zarkin, J. (2021). The militarization of law enforcement: Evidence from Latin America. *Perspectives on Politics, 19*(2), 519–538. https://doi.org/10.1017/S1537592719003906

Francis, D. J. (2012). Introduction: Understanding policing in transition societies in Africa. In D. J. Francis (Ed.), *Policing in Africa* (pp. 3–36). Palgrave Macmillan/Springer Nature.

Friedman, B. (2017). *Unwarranted: Policing without permission*. Farrar, Straus and Giroux.

Friedman, B., & Ponomarenko, M. (2015). Democratic policing. *New York University Law Review, 90*(6), 1827–1907. https://www.nyulawreview.org/issues/volume-90-number-6/

Fulbright, D. W. (2019). The benefit of independent citizen review in police critical incidents. [A Leadership White Paper Submitted in Partial Fulfillment Required for Graduation from the Leadership Command College, Sam Houston State University]. Retrieved from https://shsu-ir.tdl.org/handle/20.500.11875/2643

Goldsmith, A., & Lewis, C. (Eds.). (2000). *Civilian oversight of policing: Governance, democracy and human rights*. Hart Publishing/Bloomsbury.

Goold, B. J. (2016). Policing and human rights. In B. Bradford, B. Jauregui, I. Loader, & J. Steinberg (Eds.), *The SAGE handbook of global policing* (pp. 226–240). Sage.

Govender, D., & Pillay, K. (2022). Policing in South Africa: A critical evaluation. *Insight on Africa, 14*(1), 40–56. https://doi.org/10.1177/2F09750878211048169

Greene, J. R. (2007). Make police oversight independent and transparent. *Criminology and Public Policy, 6*(4), 747–754. https://doi.org/10.1111/j.1745-9133.2007.00477.x

Guittet, E.-P., Vavoula, N., Tsoukala, A., & Baylis, M. (2022). *Democratic oversight of the police*. EU.

References

Guzmán-Sánchez, R., & Espriú-Guerra, A. (2014). External police oversight in Mexico: Experiences, challenges, and lessons learned, stability. *International Journal of Security & Development, 3*(1), 1–15. https://doi.org/10.5334/sta.ek

Haberfeld, M., & Gideon, L. (2008). Introduction: Policing is hard on democracy, or democracy is hard on policing? In M. R. Haberfeld & I. Cerrah (Eds.), *Comparative policing: The struggle for democratization* (pp. 1–12). Sage.

Hall, S. K. (2017). Jamaica moves to regulate the use of force in law enforcement. Council on Hemispheric Affairs. Retrieved from http://www.coha.org/wp-content/uploads/2017/06/Jamaica-Moves-to-Regulate-the-Use-of-Force-in-Law-Enforcement.pdf

Harris, D., & Katusiimeh, M. W. (2019). Public administration and corruption: A comparative case study of the police services in Ghana and Uganda. In A. Graycar (Ed.), *Handbook on corruption, ethics and integrity in public administration* (pp. 255–273). Edward Elgar Publishing Limited.

Harris, F. C. (2013). *Holding police accountability theory to account*. [Unpublished PhD thesis, University of Portsmouth].

Hills, A. (2017). Epilogue. In J. Beek, M. Göpfert, O. Owen, & J. Steinberg (Eds.), *Police in Africa: The street-level view* (pp. 263–268). Oxford University Press.

Ho, L. K.-K., Chan, J. K.-H., Chan, Y.-t., den Heyer, G., Hsu, J.-S., & Hirai, A. (2022). Professionalism versus democracy? Historical and institutional analysis of police oversight mechanisms in three Asian jurisdictions. *Crime, Law and Social Change, 77*(1), 1–25. https://doi.org/10.1007/s10611-021-09981-y

Hope, K. R. (2015). In pursuit of democratic policing: An analytical review and assessment of police reforms in Kenya. *International Journal of Police Science and Management, 17*(2), 91–97. https://doi.org/10.1177/1461355715580915

Hope, K. R. (Ed.). (2016). *Police corruption and police reforms in developing societies*. CRC Press/Taylor and Francis.

Hope, K. R. (2017). *Corruption and governance in Africa: Swaziland [Eswatini], Kenya, Nigeria*. Palgrave Macmillan/Springer Nature.

Hope, K. R. (2018). Institutions and the culture dimension of corruption in Nigeria. *Crime, Law and Social Change, 70*(4), 503–523. https://doi.org/10.1007/s10611-018-9779-6

Hope, K. R. (2019a). Civilian oversight for democratic policing: Concept, models and challenges. In *Research working paper*. Development Practice International.

Hope, K. R. (2019b). The police corruption "crime problem" in Kenya. *Security Journal, 32*(2), 85–101. https://doi.org/10.1057/s41284-018-0149-y

Hope, K. R. (2020). Civilian oversight of the police: The case of Kenya. *The Police Journal: Theory, Practice and Principles, 93*(3), 202–228. https://doi.org/10.1177/0032258X19860727

Hryniewicz, D. (2011). Civilian oversight as a public good: Democratic policing, civilian oversight, and the social. *Contemporary Justice Review, 14*(1), 77–83. https://doi.org/10.1080/10282580.2011.541078

IACP. (2000). *Police accountability and citizen review*. IACP.

INDECOM. (n.d.). Impact of INDECOM: Changing a culture of impunity. Retrieved from https://www.indecom.gov.jm/aboutus/achievements

IPCA-New Zealand. (n.d.). Why police oversight matters. Retrieved from https://most0010142.expert.services/Site/about-us/Why-Police-oversight-matters.aspx

IPID. (2013). *Annual Performance Plan 2013/2014*. Retrieved from http://www.ipid.gov.za/sites/default/files/documents/AAP%202013-14.pdf

IPID. (2020). *Strategic plan 2020–2025*. IPID.

IPOA. (2019). *Strategic plan 2019–2024*. IPOA.

Ivković, S. J., & Borovec, K. (2018). Protecting human rights: A complex story of the democratization of the Croatian police. *International Journal of Comparative and Applied Criminal Justice, 42*(1), 1–31. https://doi.org/10.1080/01924036.2016.1270841

Jackson, P. (2018). Introduction: Second-generation security sector reform. *Journal of Intervention and State-Building, 12*(1), 1–10. https://doi.org/10.1080/17502977.2018.1426384

Jerome, R. (2006). Credibility, impartiality, and independence in citizen oversight. In J. Cintrón Perino (Ed.), *Citizen oversight of law enforcement* (pp. 21–45). American Bar Association.

Jibrin, H., & Yandaki, U. A. (2022). Historical development of police and policing in Africa. In U. Tar & D. M. Dawud (Eds.), *Policing criminality and insurgency in Africa: Perspectives on the changing wave of law enforcement* (pp. 62–78). Lexington Books/Rowman and Littlefield Publishing Group.

Jones, T., & van Steden, R. (2013). Democratic police governance in comparative perspective: Reflections from England & Wales and The Netherlands. *Policing: An International Journal of Police Strategies & Management, 36*(3), 561–576. https://doi.org/10.1108/PIJPSM-07-2012-0059

Kang, W., & Nalla, M. K. (2011). Perceived citizen cooperation, police operational philosophy, and job satisfaction on support for civilian oversight of the police in South Korea. *Asian Criminology, 6*(2), 177–189. https://doi.org/10.1007/s11417-011-9116-9

Karpiak, K. G., Mulla, S., & Pérez, R. L. (2022). The plurality of police oversight: A method for building upon lessons learned for understanding an evolving strategy, *policing: An. International Journal, 45*(4), 648–661. https://doi.org/10.1108/PIJPSM-08-2021-0117

Kessing, P. V. (2018). Police oversight mechanisms. [Note]. Retrieved from https://www.humanrights.dk/sites/humanrights.dk/files/media/dokumenter/udgivelser/hrs/2018/police_complaint_mechanisms_dihr2018.pdf

Kim, A. (2017). Challenges facing new oversight bodies. [CAPI Brief]. Center for the Advancement of Public Integrity, Columbia University. Retrieved from https://www.law.columbia.edu/public-integrity/challenges-facing-new-oversight-bodies

King, K. (2015). Effectively implementing civilian oversight boards to ensure police accountability and strengthen police-community relations. *Hastings Race and Poverty Law Journal, 12*(1), 91–120.

Kunetski, K., & Barkway, K. (2014). Independence in civilian-led investigations of the police. In I. Scott (Ed.), *Issues in civilian oversight of policing in Canada* (pp. 163–184). Carswell/Thompson Reuters.

Kwon, J., & Wortley, S. (2022). Policing the police: Public perceptions of civilian oversight in Canada. *Race and Justice, 12*(4), 644–668. https://doi.org/10.1177/2F2153368720924560

Lee, H. D., Collins, P. A., Hsieh, M.-L., Boateng, F. D., & Brody, D. (2017). Officer attitudes toward citizen review and professional accountability. *International Journal of Police Science & Management, 19*(2), 63–71. https://doi.org/10.1177/2F1461355717695320

Lister, S., & Rowe, M. (2016). Accountability of policing. In S. Lister & M. Rowe (Eds.), *Accountability of policing* (pp. 1–17). Routledge.

Livingston, D. (2004). The unfulfilled promise of citizen review. *Ohio State Journal of Criminal Law, 1*(2), 653–669.

Livingston, S. (2013). Africa's information revolution: Implications for crime, policing, and citizen security. [Research Paper No. 5]. African Center for Strategic Studies.

Manning, P. K. (2010). *Democratic policing in a changing world*. Routledge/Taylor and Francis.

Marenin, O. (2014). Styles of policing and economic development in African states. *Public Administration and Development, 34*(3), 149–161. https://doi.org/10.1002/pad.1683

Mawby, R. I., & Smith, K. (2017). Civilian oversight of the police in England and Wales: The election of police and crime commissioners in 2012 and 2016. *International Journal of Police Science & Management, 19*(1), 23–30. https://doi.org/10.1177/2F1461355716677875

McDevitt, A., & Bullock, J. (2021). *Resisting corruption along drug trafficking routes: An analysis of criminal justice bodies in Latin America and West Africa*. TI.

Mehta, S. (n.d.). Holding police to account for misconduct: Police-specific complaints agencies. Retrieved from http://www.humanrightsinitiative.org/old/programs/aj/police/res_mat/police_specific_complaints_agencies.pdf

Miller, J. (with the assistance of Merrick, C.). (2002, May 5–8). Civilian oversight of policing: Lessons from the literature. [Paper prepared for the Global Meeting on

References

Civilian Oversight of Police]. Retrieved from https://www.vera.org/publications/civilian-oversightof-policing-lessons-from-the-literature

Mugari, I. (2021). Evaluations of selected civilian oversight institutions for police accountability in the Republic of Zimbabwe. *Police Practice and Research, 22*(1), 606–622. https://doi.org/10.1080/15614263.2020.1831921

Mugari, I. (2023). Civilian police oversight: A contemporary review of police oversight mechanisms in Europe, Australia and Africa. *Journal of Applied Security Research, 18*(1), 106–127. https://doi.org/10.1080/19361610.2021.1918524

Mugari, I., & Obioha, E. E. (2022). Curtailing police discretionary powers: Civil action against the police in Zimbabwe. *Cogent Social Sciences, 8*(1), 2075132. https://doi.org/10.1080/23311886.2022.2075132

Mugari, I., & Olutola, A. A. (2022). In search for the best police oversight mechanism for Zimbabwe: The imperative for an independent police complaints board. *Journal of Applied Security Research*. [Advance online publication]. https://doi.org/10.1080/19361610.2022.2105283

Murphy, C., & McKenna, P. F. (n.d.). *Police Investigating Police: A Critical Analysis of the Literature*. Retrieved from https://www.crcc-ccetp.gc.ca/en/police-investigating-police-critical-analysis-literature

NACOLE. (n.d.). Thirteen principles for effective oversight. Retrieved from https://www.nacole.org/principles

NACOLE. (2015, January 9). Building legitimacy and public trust through civilian oversight. [Testimony submitted by the National Association for Civilian Oversight of Law Enforcement to the President's Task Force on 21st Century Policing]. Retrieved from https://d3n8a8pro7vhmx.cloudfront.net/nacole/pages/115/attachments/original/1458135958/NACOLE-Written-Testimony-for-the-Presidents-Task-Force-on-21st-Century-Policing-Final1.pdf?1458135958

Nagle, L. E. (2010). Corruption of politicians, law enforcement, and the judiciary in Mexico and complicity across the border. *Small Wars & Insurgencies, 21*(1), 95–122. https://doi.org/10.1080/09592310903561544

Nalla, M. K. (2016). Police accountability and citizen oversight in emerging democracies in Asia. In T. Prenzler & G. den Heyer (Eds.), *Civilian oversight of police: Advancing accountability in law enforcement* (pp. 139–158). CRC Press/Taylor and Francis.

Nalla, M. K., & Mamayek, C. (2013). Democratic policing, police accountability, and citizen oversight in Asia: An exploratory study. *Police Practice and Research, 14*(2), 117–129. https://doi.org/10.1080/15614263.2013.767091

Ndifuna, M. (2020, December 2). Uganda needs police oversight commission, *Monitor*. Retrieved from https://www.monitor.co.ug/uganda/oped/commentary/uganda-needs-police-oversight-commission-3215988

Newham, G., & Faull, A. (2011). *Protector or predator? Tackling police corruption in South Africa*. Institute for Security Studies.

Nix, J., Wolfe, S. E., & Tregle, B. (2018). Police officers' attitudes toward citizen advisory councils, *policing: An. International Journal, 41*(4), 418–434. https://doi.org/10.1108/PIJPSM-01-2018-0019

Ofer, U. (2016). Getting it right: Building effective civilian review boards to oversee police. *Seton Hall Law Review, 46*(4), 1033–1062. https://scholarship.shu.edu/shlr/vol46/iss4/2

OPCC. (2019). *Annual report 2018/2019*. OPCC.

Ortega, D. E. (2018, March 20). *The challenge of improving police behavior in Latin America*. [Brookings Report]. Retrieved from https://www.brookings.edu/research/the-challenge-of-improving-police-behavior-in-latin-america/

OSCE. (2009). *Guidebook on democratic policing*. OSCE.

O'Shea, L. (2022). Democratic police reform, security sector reform, anti-corruption and spoilers: Lessons from Georgia. *Conflict, Security & Development, 22*(4), 387–409. https://doi.org/10.1080/14678802.2022.2121916

O'Shea, L. (2023). Why democratic police reform mostly fails and sometimes succeeds: Police reform and low state capacity, authoritarianism and neo-patrimonial politics (in the former Soviet Union). *Policing and Society, 33*(3), 245–263. https://doi.org/10.1080/1043946 3.2022.2106983

Pino, N. W. (2009). Developing democratic policing in the Caribbean: The case of Trinidad and Tobago. *Caribbean Journal of Criminology and Public Safety, 14*(1&2), 214–258.

Pino, N. W., & Wiatrowski, M. D. (2006). The principles of democratic policing. In N. W. Pino & M. D. Wiatrowski (Eds.), *Democratic policing in transitional and developing countries* (pp. 69–98). Ashgate/Routledge/Taylor and Francis.

Policing Project. (n.d.). Strengthening policing through democratic governance. Retrieved from https://static1.squarespace.com/static/58a33e881b631bc60d4f8b31/t/59dfa32aa803bb57bb 93316c/1507828522861/Policing+Project+2-pager_8.21.17.pdf

Ponomarenko, M., & Friedman, B. (2017). Democratic accountability and policing. In E. Luna (Ed.), *Reforming criminal justice (Policing)* (Vol. 2, pp. 5–25). The Academy for Justice, Arizona State University.

Porter, L. E. (2013). Beyond "oversight": A problem-oriented approach to police reform. *Police Practice and Research, 14*(2), 169–181. https://doi.org/10.1080/15614263.2013.767096

Prado, M. M., Trebilcock, M., & Hartford, P. (2012). Police reform in violent democracies in Latin America. *Hague Journal on the Rule of Law, 4*(2), 252–285. https://doi.org/10.1017/S1876404512000164

Prasad, D. (2006). Strengthening democratic policing and accountability in the commonwealth Pacific. *Sur - International Journal on Human Rights, 3*(5), 108–131. https://sur.conectas.org/wp-content/uploads/2017/11/sur5-eng-devika-prasad.pdf

Prateeppornnarong, D. (2019). The independent systems for handling police complaints in Thailand: A brief assessment. *Thai Journal of Public Administration, 17*(1), 9–33.

Prateeppornnarong, D., & Young, R. (2019). A critique of the internal complaints system of the Thai police. *Policing and Society, 29*(1), 18–35. https://doi.org/10.1080/10439463.2017.1356298

Prenzler, T. (2011). The evolution of police oversight in Australia. *Policing and Society, 21*(3), 284–303. https://doi.org/10.1080/10439463.2011.570866

Prenzler, T., & Lewis, C. (2005). Performance indicators for police oversight agencies. *Australian Journal of Public Administration, 64*(2), 77–83. https://doi.org/10.1111/j.1467-8500.2005.00443.x

Prenzler, T., & Ronken, C. (2001). Models of police oversight: A critique. *Policing and Society, 11*(2), 151–180. https://doi.org/10.1080/10439463.2001.9964860

President's Task Force on 21st Century Policing. (2015). *Final report of the President's task force on 21st century policing*. Office of Community Oriented Policing Services, US Department of Justice.

Pruitt, W. R. (2010). The progress of democratic policing in post-apartheid South Africa. *African Journal of Criminology and Justice Studies, 4*(1), 116–140.

Ramsey, L. (2018). *Strategies for inclusive and responsive police accountability*. [PhD dissertation, Walden University]. Retrieved from https://scholarworks.waldenu.edu/dissertations/6096/

Ramonate, M. (2022). A situational analysis of civilian police oversight agencies in the ministry of police and public safety, Lesotho. *The Africa Governance Papers, 2*(1), 10–31.

Roach, K. (2014). Models of civilian police review: The objectives and mechanisms of legal and political regulation of the police. *The Criminal Law Quarterly, 61*(1), 29–73.

Rogers, C. (2014). Maintaining democratic policing: The challenge for police leaders. *Public Safety Leadership Research Focus, 2*(2), 1–7.

Roque, P. C. (2021). *Governing in the shadows: Angola's securitized state*. Oxford University Press.

Rosenthal, R. A. (2018). Perspectives of directors of civilian oversight of law enforcement agencies. *Policing: An International Journal, 41*(4), 435–447. https://doi.org/10.1108/PIJPSM-01-2018-0018

Rosenthal, R. A. (2019). Independent critical incident investigation agencies: A unique form of police oversight. *Albany Law Review, 83*(3), 855–930.

Roth, L. (2015). External oversight of police conduct. [Briefing Paper No. 6]. NSW Parliamentary Research Service.

References

Rowe, M. (2020). *Policing the police: Challenges of democracy and accountability*. Policy Press, University of Bristol.

Roziere, B., & Walby, K. (2018). The expansion and normalization of police militarization in Canada. *Critical Criminology, 26*(1), 29–48. https://doi.org/10.1007/s10612-017-9378-3

Sajor, A. (2015). *Ideal police oversight review: The next piece of the community policing puzzle* (Unpublished MA thesis, naval postgraduate school). Monterrey.

Schaap, D. (2021). Police trust-building strategies. A socio-institutional, comparative approach. *Policing and Society, 31*(3), 304–320. https://doi.org/10.1080/10439463.2020.1726345

Scheye, E. (2018). *The effectiveness of police accountability mechanisms: What works and the way ahead*. USAID.

Scott, I., & Lisitsyna, M. (2021). *Who polices the police? The role of independent agencies in criminal investigations of state agents*. Open Society Foundations.

Sen, S. (2010). *Enforcing police accountability through civilian oversight*. Sage Publications.

Seyffert, P. (2017, September 13). Can professional civilian oversight improve community-police relations? *The Police Chief Online*. Retrieved from http://www.policechiefmagazine.org/can-professional-civilian-oversight-improve-community-police-relations/?ref=4d1adf5ce5c011b2e158e9824e61872e

Shiltson, T. (2015). Democratic policing, community policing and the fallacy of conflation in international police development missions. *International Journal of Police Science & Management, 17*(4), 207–215. https://doi.org/10.1177/2F1461355715618331

Sigsworth, R. (2019). Harnessing public engagement for police accountability in Africa. [Africa Report 21, Institute for Security Studies]. Retrieved from https://issafrica.s3.amazonaws.com/site/uploads/ar21-1.pdf

Sklansky, D. A. (2008). *Democracy and the police*. Stanford University Press.

Stageman, D. L., Napolitano, N. M., & Buchner, B. (2018). New approaches to data-driven civilian oversight of law enforcement: An introduction to the second NACOLE/CJPR special issue. *Criminal Justice Policy Review, 29*(2), 111–127. https://doi.org/10.1177/0887403416673415

Stapleton, T. (2011). *African police and soldiers in colonial Zimbabwe, 1923–80*. University of Rochester Press.

Stelkia, K. (2020). An exploratory study on police oversight in British Columbia: The dynamics of accountability for Royal Canadian Mounted Police and municipal police. *SAGE Open, 10*(1), 1–10. https://doi.org/10.1177/2F2158244019899088

Stephens, D. W., Scrivner, E., & Cambareri, J. F. (2018). *Civilian oversight of the police in major cities*. Office of Community Oriented Policing Services, US Department of Justice.

Stone, C., & Bobb, M. (2002, May 5–8). Civilian oversight of the police in democratic societies. [Paper prepared for the Global Meeting on Civilian Oversight of Police, Los Angeles, CA]. Retrieved from https://www.vera.org/publications/civilian-oversight-of-the-police-indemocratic-societies

Stone, C. E., & Ward, H. H. (2000). Democratic policing: A framework for action. *Policing and Society, 10*(1), 11–45. https://doi.org/10.1080/10439463.2000.9964829

Stuurman, Z. (2020). Policing inequality and the inequality of policing: A look at the militarization of policing around the world, focusing on Brazil and South Africa. *South African Journal of International Affairs, 27*(1), 43–66. https://doi.org/10.1080/10220461.2020.1748103

Tabassi, T., & Dey, A. (2016). *Police militarization is global*. Retrieved from https://wri-irg.org/en/story/2016/police-militarisation-global.

Terrill, W., & Ingram, J. R. (2015). Citizen complaints against the police: An eight-city examination. *Police Quarterly, 19*(2), 150–179. https://doi.org/10.1177/2F1098611115613320

Ungar, M. (2011). *Policing democracy: Overcoming obstacles to citizen security in Latin America*. Johns Hopkins University Press.

UNHRC. (2022). *Promotion and protection of the human rights and fundamental freedoms of Africans and of people of African descent against excessive use of force and other human rights violations by law enforcement officers through transformative change for racial justice and equality: Report of the United Nations high commissioner for human rights*. UN.

UNODC. (2011). *Handbook on police accountability, oversight and integrity*. UN.
US Department of State. (2022a). *Lesotho 2021 human rights report*. US Department of State.
US Department of State. (2022b). *Mauritius 2021 human rights report*. US Department of State.
US Embassy in Malawi. (2022, November 2). United States and UNDP launch new partnership to strengthen the Independent Complaints Commission (ICC) in MW. [Press Release]. Retrieved from https://mw.usembassy.gov/united-states-and-undp-launch-newpartnership-to-strengthen-the-independent-complaints-commission-icc-in-malawi/
Van Der Spuy, E. (2021). Vagaries and challenges confronting police accountability in the south African post-colony as revealed by recent commissions of inquiry. *International Journal of Comparative and Applied Criminal Justice, 45*(3), 329–343. https://doi.org/10.1080/01924036.2021.1916971
van Sluis, A., & Devroe, E. (2020). Checks and balances in democratic control of public police: A case study of the Dutch national police after the reform. *Police Practice and Research, 21*(6), 670–686. https://doi.org/10.1080/15614263.2019.1699410
VICPD. (n.d.). *Professional standards section*. Retrieved from https://vicpd.ca/contact-us/compliments-complaints/professional-standards-section/
Vitoroulis, M., McEllhiney, C., & Perez, L. (2021). *Civilian oversight of law enforcement: Report on the state of the field and effective oversight practices*. Office of Community Oriented Policing Services, US Department of Justice.
Walker, M. (2020, November 4). How civilian review of law enforcement can improve police-community relations. [Police 1]. Retrieved from https://www.police1.com/chiefs-sheriffs/articles/how-civilian-review-of-law-enforcement-can-improve-police-communityrelations-CPcxRXZkbnixDknZ/
Walker, S. (2001). *Police accountability: The role of citizen oversight*. Wadsworth/Thomas Learning.
Walker, S., & Archbold, C. A. (2014). *The New World of police accountability*. Sage Publications.
Walsh, D. P. J., & Conway, V. (2011). Police governance and accountability: Overview of current issues. *Crime, Law and Social Change, 55*(2–3), 61–86. https://doi.org/10.1007/s10611-011-9269-6
Wells, W., & Schafer, J. A. (2007). Police skepticism of citizen oversight: Officers' attitudes toward specific functions, processes, and outcomes. *Journal of Crime and Justice, 30*(2), 1–25. https://doi.org/10.1080/0735648X.2007.9721233
Wentkowska, A. (2016). Let us be judged by our actions: Oversight mechanisms of policing in comparative outline. *Polish Review of International and European Law, 5*(2), 45–72. https://doi.org/10.21697/priel.2016.5.2.02
Wiatrowski, M. D., & Goldstone, J. A. (2010). The ballot and the badge: Democratic policing. *Journal of Democracy, 21*(2), 79–92.
Wilson, S. (2014). Civilian review boards. In J. S. Albanese (Ed.), *The Encyclopedia of criminology and criminal justice*. Retrieved from. https://doi.org/10.1002/9781118517383.wbeccj154
Wilson, S., & Buckler, K. (2010). The debate over police reform: Examining minority support for citizen oversight and resistance by police unions. *American Journal of Criminal Justice, 35*(4), 184–197. https://doi.org/10.1007/s12103-010-9079-x
Witkin, N. (2017). The police-community partnership: Civilian oversight as an evaluation tool for community policing. *The Scholar: St. Mary's Law Review on Race and Social Justice, 18*(2), 180–228. https://commons.stmarytx.edu/thescholar/vol18/iss2/2
Worden, R. E., Bonner, H. S., & McLean, S. J. (2018). Procedural justice and citizen review of complaints against the police: Structure, outcomes, and complainants' subjective experiences. *Police Quarterly, 21*(1), 77–108. https://doi.org/10.1177/2F1098611117739812

Index

A

Accountability, 9, 23–24, 100, 102, 134, 147, 155, 168, 170, 173
   diagonal, 147
   government, 8, 15, 132
   horizontal, 147
   police (*see* Police accountability)
   social, 170
   vertical, 147
Addis Ababa Action Agenda (AAAA), 154
Ad-Hoc Security Initiatives (ASIs), 15
Africa Governance Report (AGR), 24
African Capacity Building Foundation (ACBF), 3
African Charter on Democracy, Elections and Governance (ACDEG), 13, 15
African Charter on Human and People's Rights (ACHPR), 13
African Continental Free Trade Area (AfCFTA), 13
African Development Bank (AfDB), vi, 36, 39
African Governance Architecture (AGA), 13, 24
African National Congress (ANC), 46
African Peace and Security Architecture (APSA), 13–14, 24–25
African Peer Review Mechanism (APRM), 2, 23–25
African Standby Force (ASF), 14
African Union (AU), 13–15, 20–22, 24, 25, 35, 164
African Union Convention on Preventing and Combating Corruption (AUCPCC), 13
African Union Development Agency-New Partnership for Africa's Development (AUDA-NEPAD), 2, 24–25
Agenda 2030, 5, 17, 20, 23–25, 132–135, 148, 151–155, 163, 165
Agenda 2063, 20, 23–25, 131, 140–142
Albanese, Jay S., 161
All-Africa Conference of Churches (AACC), 70
Al-Qaeda, 108
Al-Shabaab, 108–113, 116
Americas, 25, 76, 141
Amoako, K.Y., 23
Angola, 60, 70
Anti-corruption, 2, 13, 17, 19, 25–27, 38, 47, 50, 67, 71–73, 76, 89, 93, 111–112, 134, 164, 166, 168–169, 171–173
Anti-Corruption Agencies (ACAs), 25, 73
Anti-Corruption Bureau (ACB), 38
Anti-fraud measures (AFMs), 49
Antigua and Barbuda, 136
Anti-money laundering, 45, 49–50
Anti-Terrorism Police Unit (ATPU), 109, 112
Armenia, 135, 136
Asia, 18, 25, 76, 114, 140, 141, 146, 148, 156, 180, 189
   Central, 65, 137, 139, 140
   Eastern, 65, 108, 138–140
   South Eastern, 140
   Southern, 65, 109, 137–140
   Western, 139
Asia-Pacific, 139, 149, 153
Asset recovery, 25, 73–74, 112

Australia, 135, 136, 138, 139, 180, 183, 186, 189

B
Bahrain, 135, 136
Banks, 42, 44, 45
Belgium, 180, 186
Benin, 90
Bern Data Compact, 152
Bhutan, 135, 136
Biya, Paul, *see* President Paul Biya
Botswana, 3, 26, 28, 40, 72, 73, 90, 93
Bribery, v, 4, 8, 13, 39–43, 46, 48–49, 61, 87, 91–98, 100, 102, 104, 110, 115, 134, 136, 139, 145, 148, 149, 151, 161–173
    electoral, 40–43
Bribes, *see* Corruption, bribes
Burkina Faso, 16, 21, 45, 90, 113

C
Cabo Verde, 28, 39, 40, 70, 73, 90, 92, 134
Cameroon, 18, 40, 90, 173
Canada, 135, 136, 180, 183–186, 189, 190, 204
Canadian Association for Civilian Oversight of Law Enforcement (CACOLE), 179, 204
Capacity, 3, 22, 24, 50, 71, 104, 108, 145–147, 150–152, 154, 199, 201, 206
    building, 23, 140, 150, 152, 171
    development, 145, 150–151, 154
    human resource, 145
    institutional, 145, 147, 199, 201
Cape Town Global Action for Sustainable Development Data (CTGAP), 151–152
Capital flight, 44, 58–59, 154
Capitalism, 27, 45
Captain Ibrahim Traoré, 21
Caribbean, 65, 137–140
Cayman Islands, 180, 183
Central Africa, 141, 142
Chad, 16
Chakwera, Lazarus, *see* President Lazarus Chakwera
Chief Justice Raymond Zondo, 46, 47
Child, 15, 37, 47, 49, 59, 60, 135, 136, 139, 143, 146
    discipline, 143
    education, 59

    health, 59
    labor, 37, 49
    mortality, 59
China, *see* People's Republic of China
Citizen engagement, 147
Civil services, 151
Civil society organizations (CSOs), 149, 151, 155, 192
Civil wars, 138, 205
Climate change, 133, 144, 148
Colonel Mamady Doumbouya, 16
Colonialism, 12, 206
Commonwealth Africa Anti-Corruption Agencies Conference, 71
Commonwealth Anti-Corruption Benchmarks (CACBs), 2, 25
Commonwealth Human Rights Initiative (CHRI), 89, 204, 206
Commonwealth Secretary-General, 71
Condé, Alpha, *see* President Alpha Condé
Conflict, 1–4, 11, 14, 15, 17–19, 24, 26, 28, 101, 112, 113, 133, 144, 147, 152, 153, 156, 180, 188, 195, 199
    armed, 113, 136, 202
    of interest, 4, 101, 188, 189
    prevention, 152
    violent, 14, 18, 113, 144
Continental, 13, 14, 24, 28, 118, 141, 142
Continental Early Warning System (CEWS), 14
Control of corruption (CoC), 62, 65, 69, 70
    See also Corruption, control
Corruption, 4, 8
    bribes, 4, 6, 35, 37, 39–42, 91–93, 96, 99, 107, 109, 110, 115, 118, 167–169, 171, 197
    channels, 4, 6–7, 35–50
    clientelism, 4, 42
    control, 28, 62, 67, 73, 75, 88, 115, 169–171 (*see also* Control of corruption (CoC))
    definition, 4
    embezzlement, 4, 6, 35–38, 61
    facilitation payments, 4, 43
    favoritism, 4, 5, 107
    fraud, 4, 36, 37, 41, 44, 46–49, 106, 109
    illegal commission, 4
    illicit financial flows, 4, 6, 35–37, 43–44, 50, 68, 73, 74, 136, 148, 154, 162
    kickbacks, 4, 6, 35, 37, 39, 43, 45, 93, 167, 169
    money laundering, 4, 6, 8, 35, 37, 43–50, 73, 74, 106, 136, 172
    nepotism, 4, 94, 96, 103, 115

Index

patronage, 4
perceptions, 39, 61, 62, 65, 88–91, 94, 114, 115, 155, 166, 171
pervasive, 3, 35, 48, 57, 87, 88, 107
police (*see* Police corruption)
rampant, 2, 7, 26, 27, 67, 68, 88, 91, 95, 105, 145, 177
state capture, 4, 6, 35, 37, 43, 45–47, 72
theft, 4, 6, 35, 37–38, 48, 61, 87, 99
unlawful gratuity, 4
Corruption Perceptions Index (CPI), 61, 62, 65, 66, 70, 76
Corruption Risk Forecast (CRF), 171
Côte d'Ivoire, 38, 90
Counter-terrorism, 117, 149
Coups, vi, 5–7, 12, 16–18, 20, 21, 25, 26, 138
See also Military coups
COVID-19, v, vi, 67, 69, 148, 153, 172–173
Crime, 2, 3, 5, 25, 27, 35–51
economic, 7, 35–50, 172
financial, 7, 35–50
organized, 3, 5, 27, 44, 50, 59, 107, 108, 136, 149, 162
Currency substitution, 73
Czech Republic, 180

D

Damiba, Paul-Henry, *see* Lieutenant Colonel Paul-Henry Damiba
Data4Now, 151, 152
Debt (public), 23, 63–64, 69–71, 148, 173
Decentralization, 151, 152
Delattre, François, 3
Democracy index, 28
Democratic backsliding, 28
Democratic policing, 89, 177–207
Democratic Republic of the Congo (DRC), 38, 92, 138, 156
Democratization, 18, 188, 189
Denmark, 180, 183
Despots, 155
Diaspora knowledge networks, 150
Dictators, 155
Digitalization, 75
See also E-government
Director of Public Prosecutions (DPP), 99, 100
Domestic resource mobilization (DRM), 153, 154
Doumbouya, Mamady, *see* Colonel Mamady Doumbouya
Dubai Declaration, 152

E

East Africa, 40, 67, 73, 89, 140–142
East African Bribery Index (EABI), 91
Eastern and Southern Africa Anti-Money Laundering Group (ESAAMLG), 50
Economic and Financial Crimes Commission (EFCC), 37
Economic Community of West African States (ECOWAS), 13, 20, 21
Economic development, 2, 7, 27, 36, 44, 47, 48, 57, 58, 60, 64, 67, 68, 133, 148
Economic efficiency, 60
Economic growth, v, 5, 13, 19, 23, 26, 36, 60, 64, 67–68, 71, 75–76, 107, 132, 133, 143, 144, 150, 154
Economist Intelligence Unit (EIU), 28
Ecuador, 135, 136
Education, 36, 39, 50, 59, 60, 62, 64, 87, 132, 133, 136, 141, 143, 148, 154, 170, 172
E-government, 74–76
See also Digitalization
E-government development index (EGDI), 75–76
Egypt, 135, 136
Embezzlement, *see* Corruption, embezzlement
England, 186, 189
Environmental degradation, 152
Environmental goals, 133, 134, 152
Environmental protection, 5
Environmental spillovers, 136
Environmental sustainability, 5
Equatorial Guinea, 18
Eritrea, 70, 134
Eswatini, 90
Ethics and Anti-Corruption Commission (EACC), 92
Ethiopia, 16, 95, 134
Europe, 26, 45, 65, 76, 137, 139, 141, 178
European Commission (EC), 45, 49, 50
European Research Center for Anti-Corruption and State-Building (ERCAS), 166, 169–171
European Union (EU), v, 24, 45, 49, 139, 195
Extra-judicial killings, 15, 97, 100, 191

F

Financing, 3, 25, 43, 45, 49, 58, 71, 74, 136, 147–148, 153–154, 172, 173
Food, 37, 41, 42, 59
crisis, 133
insecurity, 59, 133, 144
security, 148

Foreign aid, 23, 38, 58
Foreign direct investment (FDI), 58, 59, 107, 133
France, 3
Frantz, Doug, 156
Fraud, see Corruption, fraud
Freedom, 110, 111, 142, 149, 165, 169, 171, 192
Freedom House, 171
Freedom of the press, 165, 169, 171

G
G7, 50, 64
G8, 24
Gabon, 42, 90
Gender, 3, 132, 140, 141, 143, 149, 200
　discrimination, 140
　equality, 3, 132, 141, 172
　inequality, 141
　violence, 140, 141
Geneva Center for Security Sector Governance (DCAF), 17
Georgia, 105, 206
Ghana, 40, 67, 75, 90, 92, 134, 166, 189, 206
Girls, 140, 141, 143
Githongo, John, 111
Gordhan, Pravin, 46
Governance, 1–9, 11–15, 17–28, 35, 40, 41, 45, 49, 58, 59, 62, 64, 67–69, 73, 74, 76, 85, 88, 95, 108, 114, 132–136, 145, 150, 152, 154, 155, 165, 166, 168, 171–173, 178, 186, 187, 190, 192, 199, 202, 204, 205
　bad, 1, 6, 11, 22, 35, 67, 205
　democratic, 187, 190, 192, 204
　good, 2, 3, 5, 8, 12, 14, 17, 19–23, 25, 26, 28, 40, 133–136, 145, 150, 154, 155, 172, 205
　poor, 1, 22, 58, 59, 69, 88
Greece, 135, 136
Grenada, 135
Gross domestic product (GDP), 4, 18, 35, 36, 40, 44, 58, 59, 64, 66–71, 75, 144, 147, 148, 153, 154
　growth of, 4, 63, 66–68
　per capita, 19, 59, 63, 66–68, 144
　real, 63, 68
Guinea, 16, 21, 40, 90, 135, 136
Guinea Bissau, 16
Guterres, António, see UN Secretary-General António Guterres

H
Health, v, 36, 39, 50, 59, 60, 62, 63, 75, 86, 132, 133, 141–143, 148, 154, 155, 170, 172, 173
High-Level Political Forums (HLPFs), 134
HIV/AIDS, 60
Homicides, 140, 141
Honduras, 105, 106
Hong Kong, 180, 184–186
Horn of Africa, 144
Human rights, 2, 3, 12–14, 22, 23, 49, 60, 85, 89, 94, 95, 97, 100, 103, 105, 117, 132–136, 140, 142, 143, 147, 149, 155, 156, 183, 188, 191–193, 195, 198, 201, 204, 206
Hungary, 135, 136

I
Ibrahim Index of African Governance (IIAG), 168–169
Inclusive institutions, 8, 131–132, 135–137
Independent Corrupt Practices and other Related Offences Commission (ICPC), 26
Independent Police Investigative Directorate (IPID), 99, 117, 177, 183, 193, 195, 201
Independent Policing Oversight Authority (IPOA), 95–102, 177, 183, 201
India, v, 146, 205
Index of Public Integrity (IPI), 169–171
Inequality, 2, 3, 20, 26, 59, 64, 132, 140, 141, 144, 156
Infant mortality rates, 66, 133
Insecurity, 1, 6, 11, 16–18, 20, 21, 28, 100, 102, 105, 106, 108, 109, 111, 113, 116, 117, 133, 144, 191
Instability, 2, 3, 6, 11, 16–18, 20, 113, 134, 138, 144
　political, 6, 18, 113, 138
Institute for Economics and Peace (IEP), 1, 16, 133, 146
Institution building, 154, 195
Inter-Governmental Action Group against Money Laundering in West Africa (GIABA), 50
International Budget Partnership (IBP), 170
International Center for Transitional Justice (ICTJ), 105
International Monetary Fund (IMF), 24, 25, 68, 133
International Spillover Index (ISI), 136
Ireland, see Republic of Ireland

Index

J
Jamaica, 180, 183, 189, 190
Japan, 64
Jihadists, 113
Judiciary, 15, 40, 45, 91, 167, 169, 170
Justice, 2, 7, 8, 15, 23, 46, 50, 88, 91, 95, 97, 99, 105, 106, 131–137, 139, 142, 145, 148, 150, 152, 154, 156, 180, 183, 190, 191, 194, 197, 203, 205

K
Kenya, 7, 9, 36, 38, 40, 42, 48, 69, 75, 85–118, 173, 177, 180, 183, 189, 201, 205
    Nairobi, 89, 108, 109, 111, 113, 205
Kenya Human Rights Commission (KHRC), 89
Kenya Medical Supplies Authority (KEMSA), 173
Kenya National Commission for Human Rights (KNCHR), 97, 102, 108, 109
Kenyatta, Uhuru, *see* President Uhuru Kenyatta
Khama, Seretse, *see* President Sir Seretse Khama
Kickbacks, *see* Corruption, kickbacks
Kleptocratic behavior, vi, 22, 37
Kleptocrats, v, 50, 74, 155

L
Lake Chad Basin, 144
Latin America, 18, 45, 65, 137–140, 191
Latvia, 135, 136
Leadership, 2–4, 8, 12, 15, 20, 22, 26, 71–73, 116, 148, 151, 154, 155, 161, 162, 165, 171, 172, 189, 193, 199
    administrative, 8, 161, 162, 172
    business, 8, 161, 162, 172
    democratic, 4
    ethical, 3
    good, 154
    influential, 193
    political, 2, 15, 148, 155, 193, 199
    transformational, 155
Lesotho, 90, 93, 99, 100, 192
Lesotho Mounted Police Service (LMPS), 192
Liberia, 39, 40, 90
Lieutenant Colonel Paul-Henry Damiba, 21
Life expectancy, 19, 59, 66, 133, 173
Local governments, 151, 152

M
Madagascar, 36
Mbasogo, Teodoro Obiang Nguema, *see* President Teodoro Obiang Nguema Mbasogo
Malawi, 36–38, 90, 93, 173, 206
Malawi Anti-Corruption Bureau (MACB), 93
Malaysia, 146
Mali, 16, 18, 21, 44, 45, 90, 113, 135, 136
Malta, 135, 136, 180
Maternal deaths, 59
Marginalization, 1, 19
Mauritius, 28, 40, 76, 90, 92, 180
Mbeki, Thabo, *see* President Thabo Mbeki
Middle East and North Africa (MENA), 28, 109, 137, 139
Military coups, 16, 18
    See also Coups
Modernization, 59
Mo Ibrahim Foundation (MIF), 16, 168
Money laundering, *see* Corruption, money laundering
Morocco, 45
Mozambique, 27, 59, 70, 90
Multidimensional Poverty Index (MPI), 62, 63, 65
Museveni, Yoweri, *see* President Yoweri Museveni

N
Namibia, 36, 90, 93, 136
National Anti-Corruption Institutions of West Africa (NACIWA), 26
National Anti-Corruption Strategy (NACS), 27
National Association for Civilian Oversight of Law Enforcement (NACOLE), 179, 190, 196, 204
National Bureau of Statistics (NBS), 40
National Police Service (NPS), 98, 100–104, 107, 111, 115, 117
National Police Service Commission (NPSC), 100, 101, 103–105
National Security Council (NSC), 107
National Statistical Offices (NSOs), 152, 163
Nepotism, *see* Corruption, nepotism
Netherlands, 189
New Partnership for Africa's Development (NEPAD), 2, 22–25
New Zealand, 138, 139, 180, 183, 189, 190
Niger, 16, 90, 113, 150

Nigeria, 12, 22, 36, 39, 42, 64, 67–69, 74, 90, 92, 102, 103, 106, 108, 113, 117, 173
Non-governmental organizations (NGOs), 135, 149, 163, 164
North Africa, 28, 65, 109, 137, 139–142
Norway, 180

O

Obasanjo, Olusegun, *see* President Olusegun Obasanjo
Oceania, 76, 137–139, 141
Open Budget Survey (OBS), 170
Organization for Economic Cooperation and Development (OECD), 24, 36, 112, 135–137, 156
Overseas development assistance (ODA), 38, 58, 153
Oversight, 8–9, 17, 24, 47, 50, 89, 95, 99, 102, 107, 117, 146, 147, 150, 177–207
   civilian, 8–9, 99, 102, 107, 177–207
   parliamentary, 47, 150
   police model types, *see* Police oversight
Owasanoye, Bolaji, *see* Professor Bolaji Owasanoye
Oxfam, 13

P

Pacific, 26, 65, 139, 141, 149, 153
Panel of the Wise (PoW), 15
Paraguay, 150
Paris Agreement, 144
Paris Principles, 140
Partnerships, 22, 48, 117, 172
Peace, 1–3, 5, 6, 8, 11–15, 17, 19–22, 24–28, 41, 43, 85, 107, 112, 113, 116, 118, 131–137, 144, 145, 152, 155, 161
   negative, 20
   positive, 20, 27
Peace and Security Council (PSC), 13–15, 21, 25
Peace Fund (PF), 15
People's Republic of China, v, 180, 184–186
Philippines, 146
Police abuse, 94, 95, 98–100, 106, 190–192, 197, 203
Police accountability, 8–9, 88, 99, 177–183, 186, 188–192, 194–196, 199, 201–206
Police bribery, 87, 91–94, 96, 98, 100, 102, 104, 110, 115

Police brutality, 94, 96, 99, 100, 106, 113, 115, 189, 191, 197
Police code of silence, 108, 188
Police cooperation, 194, 196, 199, 203
Police corruption, 7, 85–118, 177, 189, 207
Police criminality, 94–100, 201
Police governance, 7, 9, 85, 88, 204
Police misconduct, 86, 89, 90, 94, 96, 99, 101, 103, 106, 118, 180–182, 185–187, 189–193, 196–204, 206
Police oversight, 117, 177–207
Police recruitment, 100–103
Police reform, 8, 88, 89, 103, 114–116, 195, 199, 204–206
Police vetting, 103, 106
Policy, v, 1, 2, 6–8, 12–15, 22–25, 45, 48, 50, 57–59, 61, 62, 71, 72, 74, 86, 88, 97, 112, 113, 131–133, 140, 148–151, 156, 171, 172, 190, 205
   analysis, 150, 151
   approaches, 149, 156
   change, 150
   development, 50, 148, 205
   fiscal, 153
   framework(s), 12, 13, 48, 62, 72, 73, 172
   implications, v, 1, 6, 7, 57, 58, 71–76
   options, 2
   solutions, 2, 8, 131, 132
   statements, 113
Political will, 26, 146, 148–149, 154–155
Post-conflict, 3, 14, 152, 199
Poverty, 2, 5, 16, 20, 22, 26, 36, 38, 57, 59, 60, 62–66, 71, 75, 131–133, 141, 143, 144, 154–156, 161, 172, 173
Predatory behavior, 6, 11, 22, 92, 98, 113, 191, 205
President Abdoulaye Wade, 22
President Alpha Condé, 16
President Cyril Ramaphosa, 47, 71
President Denis Sassou, 18
President Jacob Zuma, 46
President Lazarus Chakwera, 93
President Olusegun Obasanjo, 22
President Paul Biya, 18
President Sir Seretse Khama, 72
President Teodoro Obiang Nguema Mbasogo, 18
President Thabo Mbeki, 22
President Uhuru Kenyatta, 111, 115, 116
President William Ruto, 100
President Yoweri Museveni, 18
Pretrial detention, 142–143
Prime Minister Lee Kuan Yew, 72

Index

Principles of Effective Governance for Sustainable Development (PEGSD), 24, 25
Professor Bolaji Owasanoye, 26
Protocol Against Corruption (PAC), 13
Public Expenditure Tracking Surveys (PETS), 37
Public Procurement Anti-Corruption Agency (PPACA), 47

Q
Quantitative Service Delivery Surveys (QSDS), 37

R
Racketeering, 46
Ramaphosa, Cyril, *see* President Cyril Ramaphosa
Ransley, Philip, *see* Retired Justice Philip Ransley
Reporters Without Borders (RWB), 17
Republic of Ireland, 135, 136, 180
Republic of South Africa, 9, 22, 23, 28, 36, 44, 46, 48, 49, 66–69, 71, 75, 76, 90, 99, 102, 107, 114, 117, 146, 177, 180, 183, 189, 193, 195, 201, 205, 206
Republic of the Congo, 18, 67, 70
Retired Justice Philip Ransley, 94, 100
Rule of law, 3, 7, 13–15, 19, 23, 26–28, 45, 85, 88, 102, 132–137, 139, 142, 148, 154, 156, 165, 168, 178, 181, 187, 195, 201, 205
Russia, vi
Ruto, William, *see* President William Ruto
Rwanda, 26, 40, 72, 75, 99, 134

S
Safety, 5, 85, 108, 112, 116, 153, 173, 178, 191, 192
Sahel, 113, 144
Saint Lucia, 134
São Tomé and Príncipe, 70
Sassou, Denis, *see* President Denis Sassou
Scotland, 180, 184, 186
SDG 16 Data Initiative, 151, 152
Security Council, 3, 12, 13, 107, 112, 144
Security, definition of, 5
Security sector, 7, 13, 17, 20, 88, 114, 179, 195, 203, 205
Security sector governance (SSG), 17

Security sector reform (SSR), 17, 195
Senegal, 22, 45, 90, 135, 136
Seychelles, 26, 73, 76
Sierra Leone, 27, 39, 90
Sierra Leone Anti-Corruption Commission (SLACC), 27
Singapore, 72, 135, 136
Somali, 108, 112
Somalia, 95, 109–111, 114
Socio-economic development, 47, 48, 57, 58, 68, 133
South Africa, *see* Republic of South Africa
South African Police Service (SAPS), 117, 201
South Asia, 65, 109, 137, 138
Southern Africa, 21, 50, 140–142
Southern African Development Community (SADC), 13, 21
South Sudan, 45
Spain, 134–136
Sri Lanka, 135, 136
Stability, 1–3, 5–9, 11, 13, 14, 17, 19–21, 23, 25, 27, 28, 41, 71, 85, 107, 154, 161, 195
Standard of living, 63
State capture, *see* Corruption, state capture
State-owned enterprises (SOEs), 46, 47, 71
Street-level bureaucrats, 15, 86
Structural adjustment programs (SAPs), 12
Sudan, 16, 90
Super Cops, 106
Sustainable Development Commission (SDC), 5
Sustainable Development Goals (SDGs), 2, 3, 8, 20, 24, 28, 40, 44, 58, 131–156, 161–173, 201

T
Tax, 4, 36, 37, 39, 42–44, 46, 48, 49, 58, 59, 71, 74, 75, 91, 148, 154
  administration, 75, 154
  avoidance, 43, 44
  base, 154
  burden, 91
  compliance, 154
  collection, 44, 74, 75
  evasion, 37, 43, 44, 46, 48, 49, 59, 74
  fraud, 36
  reforms, 154
  revenues, 4, 36, 58, 71, 75, 148
  value-added, 75
Tanzania, 36, 37, 42, 90
  Dar es Salaam, 108

Terrorism, 3, 5, 14, 16, 43, 49, 50, 74, 96, 108–117, 140, 149
   attacks, 16, 105, 108–111, 114, 116, 117
   fatalities, 109, 110, 114
   financing, 43, 45, 49, 50, 74, 136
   index, 16
   radicalization, 108–109, 112–114
   recruitment, 112, 113
Thailand, 189
Theft, *see* Corruption, theft
The Gambia, 66
Togo, 90
Tourism, 114–115
Trade, v, vi, 13, 23, 36, 43, 44, 136, 169, 170
Trade mis-invoicing, 36, 43–44
Transparency, 23–25, 49, 61, 74, 88, 102, 105, 134, 165, 168–171, 173, 178, 180, 186–190, 202
Transparency and Accountability Initiative (TAI), 147
Traoré, Ibrahim, *see* Captain Ibrahim Traoré
Trinidad and Tobago, 180, 183

U

Uganda, 40, 45, 89, 90, 173, 206
Ukraine, vi
United Kingdom (UK), 166, 180, 184, 186, 189, 195
United Nations (UN), 2, 3, 12, 17, 24, 25, 44, 75, 95, 131, 133, 135, 140, 144, 155, 170
United Nations Children's Fund (UNICEF), 143
United Nations Committee Against Torture (UNCAT), 95, 97
United Nations Committee of Experts (UN-CEPA), 24, 25
United Nations Conference on Trade and Development (UNCTAD), 44, 58, 162
United Nations Convention Against Corruption (UNCAC), 13, 72
United Nations Development Program (UNDP), 62, 164, 173
United Nations Economic and Social Council (UNECOSOC), 24
United Nations Economic Commission for Africa (UNECA), 23, 24, 47, 56
United Nations Human Rights Committee (UN-HRC), 95
United Nations Human Rights Council (UNHRC), 95, 206
United Nations Office on Drugs and Crime (UNODC), 25, 140

United States (US), v, xi, 24, 99, 106, 108, 109, 114, 162, 165, 180, 183–186, 188, 190, 203, 204, 206
United States Agency for International Development (USAID), 24
UN Secretary-General António Guterres, 2
Urbanization, 59, 87

V

Vanuatu, 134
V-Dem Institute, 165–167
Viet Nam, 135, 136
Violence, 2, 5, 14, 15, 19–21, 25–28, 41, 88, 99, 106, 112, 116, 117, 133–136, 138–141, 143, 146, 147, 152, 154, 156, 191, 203, 205
Voluntary National Reviews (VNRs), 134–136, 150
Vote buying, 40–43
   See also Bribery, electoral

W

Wade, Abdoulaye, *see* President Abdoulaye Wade
Wales, 186, 189
West Africa, v, 17, 20, 21, 26, 50, 141, 142
West African Economic and Monetary Union (WAEMU), 70
Western Asia, 139
Women, 15, 19, 22, 96, 135, 136, 139–141
World Bank, 24, 38, 43, 62, 133, 164, 173
World Economic Forum (WEF), 170
World Press Freedom Index (WPFI), 171

Y

Yemen, 137
Yew, Lee Kuan, *see* Prime Minister Lee Kuan Yew

Z

Zambia, 90
Zimbabwe, 40, 45, 67, 69, 70, 74, 90, 173, 192, 206
Zimbabwe Asset Management Company (ZAMCO), 70
Zimbabwe Human Rights Commission (ZHRC), 192
Zondo Commission, 46–47
Zondo, Raymond, *see* Chief Justice Raymond Zondo
Zuma, Jacob, *see* President Jacob Zuma